TRANSFORMING SPIRITUALITY

Integrating Theology and Psychology

F. LeRon Shults
AND
Steven J. Sandage

Baker Academic
Grand Rapids, Michigan

Published by Baker Academic
a division of Baker Publishing Group
P.O. Box 6287, Grand Rapids, MI 49516-6287
www.bakeracademic.com

Printed in the United States of America

Library of Congress Cataloging-in-Publication Data
Shults, F. LeRon.
    Transforming spirituality : integrating theology and psychology / F. LeRon
  Shults and Steven J. Sandage.
       p.   cm.
    Includes bibliographical references and index.
    ISBN 10: 0-8010-2823-X (pbk.)
    ISBN 978-0-8010-2823-6 (pbk.)
    1. Spirituality. 2. Christianity—Psychology. 3. Psychology, Religious.
  4. Psychology and religion. I. Sandage, Steven J. II. Title.
  BT590.S65S58 2006
  261.5′15—dc22   2006004488

The abbreviations *NPNF¹* and *NPNF²* refer to *Nicene and Post-Nicene Fathers*, Series 1, ed. P. Schaff, 14 vols. (1886–90; reprint, T&T Clark/Eerdmans, 1979–); and *Nicene and Post-Nicene Fathers*, Series 2, ed. P. Schaff and H. Wace, 14 vols. (1890–1900; reprint, Hendrickson, 1994).

To Our Mentors
James E. Loder and
Everett L. Worthington Jr.

CONTENTS

TRANSFORMING
SPIRITUALITY

ACKNOWLEDGMENTS

We would like to acknowledge the generosity of the John Templeton Foundation, which provided us with a research grant that helped us carve out more time for relational integration. Special thanks to Paul Wason, director of science and religion programs at JTF, for his advice and support. We also appreciate the enthusiasm of Bob Hosack, our acquisitions editor at Baker Academic, who encouraged us to continue our interdisciplinary efforts after the publication of *The Faces of Forgiveness* (2003). Most of all we are grateful to our wives and children, in relation to whom our own spirituality is continuously transformed.

I (LeRon) am thankful for the many students over the years who provided feedback to formal and informal presentations of the material that now appears in part 1 of the present book. They are too many to list here, but two in particular deserve special mention. Ken Reynhout served as my research assistant for the four years during which I worked out the matrix of theological inquiry that guides my contribution to this book; his calm presence and critical insight have been a constant encouragement to me. Andrea Hollingsworth read the penultimate draft of my parts of this book and generously took the time to ask helpful questions of clarification and to offer extensive comments about the manuscript. This book is dedicated to key mentors in our lives, and readers who have read the work of James E. Loder will recognize his influence on my theological efforts. Those who knew him personally will not be surprised to hear that his way of facing me during my years at Princeton mediated my own experience of the intensity of spiritual transformation.

11

I (Steve) am grateful to the Lilly Endowment and the Fund for Theological Education for supporting our longitudinal research project on spiritual formation at Bethel Seminary. I am thankful for several transformative contexts that have shaped my understanding of relational spirituality. Carla Dahl and my colleagues in the Center for Spiritual and Personal Formation at Bethel have provided a supportive and enriching community for my own personal and scholarly growth. James Maddock and my fellow group members in his clinical consultation group at Meta Resources in St. Paul have helped me view human development and spirituality more ecologically. Tom Hainlen and Carol Morgan and my clinical colleagues at Arden Woods Psychological Services cultivate a warm environment that has greatly facilitated my clinical practice. Todd Hall and my research colleagues at the Institute for Research on Psychology and Spirituality continue to both broaden and deepen my understanding of the integration of science and religion. Ian Williamson has been a formative collaborator in my research and theorizing about spirituality. My research assistants Deanne Truax, Marie Anderson, and Troy Hemme have worked with an enjoyable blend of curiosity and care. My late friend Randall Lehmann Sorenson has had an enormous influence on me personally and professionally, and I miss him greatly. I am pleased to dedicate this book to my mentor Everett L. Worthington Jr., who has generously modeled spiritual maturity in so many relationships.

1

INTRODUCTION

How do people change? This is surely one of the most significant questions in life. Allow the question to become more personal: How can I change in ways that will bring me greater happiness and make my life more meaningful? How can the people I care about know peace and well-being? How can my community become a better place for those coming behind me? As we allow ourselves to dwell on these questions, we might begin to feel the importance of the need to search for pathways toward change. But it is also painfully obvious that change does not always happen in the ways most of us would like. In fact, those people we most desperately want to change often stubbornly refuse to cooperate. That can hold true for the person we see when we look in the mirror. Life, however, brings change whether we like it or not. The human life cycle instigates a variety of changes, both marvelous and tragic. As the Hebrew sage puts it in Ecclesiastes, "There is a time for everything, and a season for every activity under heaven: a time to be born and a time to die" (Eccles. 3:1–2 NIV).

The quest for a deeper understanding of and participation in spiritual transformation strikes us as central to a meaningful journey in life. All of our hopes and fears are wrapped up in our longings for intimacy in our relationships with others and with the ultimate Other we hold to be sacred. When these relationships are profoundly altered such a change qualifies as a *spiritual transformation*. Although spirituality can be a powerful source of transformation, we all probably know people who have participated in spiritual or religious communities for decades with apparently no change at all. The processes of spiritual transformation can be painful, and yet without them life can be reduced to little more than "a time to be born and a time to die."

Our own interest in the topic of transforming spirituality is influenced by our national and global contexts, where the hunger and pursuit of spirituality and the sacred are ubiquitous. The exponential growth of interest in and openness to the practices of spirituality—both old and new—has naturally led to a revival of scholarly dialogue and research on the topics of spirituality and spiritual transformation. Our goal in this book is to contribute to this ongoing conversation by outlining and exploring conceptual models of spirituality that have emerged out of our own seeking and dwelling in interdisciplinary dialogue. We are interested in transforming *spirituality* by shaping the way in which this concept itself is understood and utilized in theological and psychological discourse. We are also interested, however, in facilitating the practices of spirituality that are *transformative* of human life and relationships. By exploring the dynamics of spiritual transformation from within the relation between the disciplines of Christian theology and social science, we hope to contribute to the understanding and practice of transforming spirituality.

Spirituality

The concept of "spirituality" itself is ambiguous and multivalent, which partially explains why well over a hundred definitions of the term have been offered in recent scholarly literature.[1] Each of these definitions is shaped by the context, tradition, and concerns of those who are doing the defining. We want to be explicit about our own social location. As a theologian and a psychologist, we are both concerned about the way in which spirituality is understood and practiced in our own Christian context. We believe that the convergence of interest in

1. Cf. Lucy Bregman, "Defining Spirituality: Multiple Uses and Murky Meanings of an Incredibly Popular Term," *Journal of Pastoral Care and Counseling* 58, no. 3 (2004): 157–68.

this theme in the scholarly disciplines of religion and science,[2] as well as among practitioners of spiritual direction and pastoral counseling, offers a new opportunity for transforming the way we think about and experience spirituality.

The role of spirituality in the Christian tradition and the complex history of its development over the centuries have been well documented in the scholarly literature.[3] In the chapters that follow, we will often take the opportunity to critically engage aspects of, and recover resources from, this rich and diverse tradition. One of the reasons for the surge of interest in spirituality is the growth of ecumenical dialogue. Although Protestant spiritual experience has been shaped by the distinctives of its own various traditions, from Pietism to Pentecostalism, Protestant Christians—both evangelical and mainline—have increasingly been drawn to practices of spirituality that characterize the Roman Catholic and Eastern Orthodox traditions. This is evident, for example, in the growing popularity among Protestants of spiritual retreats and the writings of Catholic contemplative writers such as Thomas Merton, Thomas Keating, and Henri Nouwen. As our late modern culture increasingly attends to the importance of *image* as well as *word* for human experience, the resources of the aesthetic and iconic spirituality of the East also become more and more attractive.

Interest in the renewal of the practices of spirituality has been particularly prevalent in North American evangelicalism. This tradition has often had a deep suspicion of "experience" and "mysticism" and a tendency to focus on the propositional content of doctrine as the key marker for Christian identity. The early work of Richard Foster was influential in bringing some of these resources back into the discussion about the nature of the Christian life.[4] In the last few decades, evangelical theologians and philosophers have increasingly argued

---

2. The issue of spirituality has increasingly come into the forefront of discussions at both the American Academy of Religion (e.g., the "Christian Spirituality" and "Person, Culture, and Religion" groups) and the American Psychological Association, Division 36.

3. Elizabeth A. Dreyer and Mark S. Burrows, eds., *Minding the Spirit: The Study of Christian Spirituality* (Baltimore: Johns Hopkins University Press, 2005); Cheslyn Jones, Geoffrey Wainwright, and Edward Yarnold, *The Study of Spirituality* (New York: Oxford University Press, 1986); Lawrence Cunningham and Keith J. Egan, *Christian Spirituality: Themes from the Tradition* (New York: Paulist, 1996); Gordon Mursell, ed., *The Story of Christian Spirituality: Two Thousand Years from East to West* (Minneapolis: Fortress, 2001); Bradley Hanson, *Modern Christian Spirituality: Methodological and Historical Essays* (Atlanta: Scholars Press, 1990); Philip Sheldrake, *Spirituality and History: Questions of Interpretation and Method*, 2nd ed. (Maryknoll, NY: Orbis, 1998); *Spirituality and Theology: Christian Living and the Doctrine of God* (Maryknoll, NY: Orbis, 1998).

4. Richard J. Foster, *Freedom of Simplicity* (San Francisco: Harper & Row, 1981); *Money, Sex, and Power: The Challenge of the Disciplined Life* (San Francisco: Harper & Row, 1985); *Celebration of Discipline: The Path to Spiritual Growth*, 1st rev. ed. (San Francisco: Harper

that spiritual formation is integral to the Christian life[5] and that the study of spirituality is integral to Christian theology.[6] Part 1 aims to contribute to these ongoing integrative efforts. Some evangelicals have been hesitant to emphasize spiritual transformation for fear that this would challenge our absolute dependence on the grace of God for salvation. In chapters 2–5, LeRon will argue for an understanding of Christian spirituality as a way of living that is absolutely originated, upheld, and oriented by divine grace. The theological presentation of the transforming dynamics of life in the Spirit (*en pneumati*) will be carried out in explicit dialogue with developments in the doctrine of the Holy Spirit as well as insights from contemporary philosophy and science.

In part 2 (chapters 6–9), Steve will explore the dynamics of spirituality with special attention to the transformation in the field of psychology that has occurred in the past two decades. Throughout most of the twentieth century, the dominant literature in North American psychology and psychoanalysis tended to reflect either antagonistic or disinterested orientations toward both religion and spirituality.[7] The antagonistic attitude was reflected in the writings of seminal thinkers such as Sigmund Freud, who argued that religiosity was mostly pathological or immature and certainly inconsistent with mental health. Yet there has always been a remnant of psychologists who have remained more favorable toward the empirical study and health potential of spirituality and religion. William James helped pioneer the modern psychological study of religion and spirituality, and he was quite sympathetic to the possible transformative benefits of religious and spiritual experience on psychological functioning. Carl

---

& Row, 1988); *Streams of Living Water: Celebrating the Great Traditions of the Christian Faith* (New York: HarperSanFrancisco, 1998).

5. E.g., Timothy George and Alister E. McGrath, *For All the Saints: Evangelical Theology and Christian Spirituality*, 1st ed. (Louisville: Westminster John Knox, 2003); Dallas Willard, *The Spirit of the Disciplines: Understanding How God Changes Lives* (San Francisco: HarperCollins, 1988); Ray S. Anderson, *Living the Spiritually Balanced Life* (Grand Rapids: Baker, 1998); Alister E. McGrath, *Spirituality in an Age of Change: Rediscovering the Spirit of the Reformers* (Grand Rapids: Zondervan, 1994); *Beyond the Quiet Time: Practical Evangelical Spirituality* (Grand Rapids: Baker, 1995); *Christian Spirituality: An Introduction* (Malden, MA, and Oxford, England: Blackwell, 1999); Rodney Clapp, *Tortured Wonders: Christian Spirituality for People, Not Angels* (Grand Rapids: Brazos, 2004).

6. E.g., Simon Chan, *Spiritual Theology: A Systematic Study of the Christian Life* (Downers Grove, IL: InterVarsity, 1998); Miroslav Volf and Dorothy C. Bass, eds., *Practicing Theology: Beliefs and Practices in Christian Life* (Grand Rapids: Eerdmans, 2002); Ellen T. Charry, *Inquiring after God: Classic and Contemporary Readings* (Malden, MA, and Oxford, England: Blackwell, 2000); Mark Allen McIntosh, *Mystical Theology: The Integrity of Spirituality and Theology* (Malden, MA: Blackwell, 1998).

7. R. L. Sorenson, *Minding Spirituality* (Hillsdale, NJ: Analytic Press, 2004).

Jung differed from his mentor Freud in suggesting that religion and spirituality can provide archetypal symbols that facilitate the quest for wholeness. Humanistic psychologists (e.g., Abraham Maslow and Gordon Allport) and object relations theorists (e.g., Harry Guntrip, Donald Winnicott, and Ana-Maria Rizzuto) also explored forms of spirituality and religiosity that could be consonant with psychological health and development. It is easy for North American psychologists to underestimate the global range and diversity of social-scientific research on religion and spirituality.[8]

Interest in spirituality and religion in the field of psychology has intensified in the past two decades. The increased quantity, quality, and breadth of psychological research and clinical writing on religion and spirituality since the mid-1980s justify the word "transformation."[9] Debates continue about the best ways to define, differentiate, and measure spirituality and religion. Too often a simplistic contrast of spirituality as interior and religion as institutional has limited capacities for understanding the diverse range of ways people relate to the sacred. The positive psychology movement has also encouraged advances in the scientific study of spirituality and religion as well as many health-related strengths or virtues (e.g., forgiveness, gratitude, wisdom, awe, compassion, and hope). Freud turned out to be largely wrong in his global pathologizing of religion and spirituality. Empirical studies have found many positive relationships between indices of religion and spirituality and measures of mental and even physical health.[10] Certain aspects of spirituality and religion often appear to be consistent with health, whereas other aspects can be unrelated or inconsistent with health. In chapters 6–9, Steve will develop a relational model of spirituality and explore the psychological dimensions of spirituality in relation to health, darkness, and maturity. Developmental and systems theories from the social sciences will be utilized for understanding the epistemological (knowing), ethical (acting), and ontological (being) dynamics within the processes of spiritual formation and transformation.

8. See D. M. Wulff, *Psychology of Religion: Classic and Contemporary*, 2nd ed. (New York: John Wiley & Sons, 1997).

9. P. C. Hill and K. I. Pargament, "Advances in the Conceptualization and Measurement of Religion and Spirituality: Implications for Physical and Mental Health Research," *American Psychologist* 58 (2003): 64–74.

10. W. R. Miller and C. E. Thoresen, "Spirituality, Religion, and Health: An Emerging Research Field," *American Psychologist* 58 (2003): 24–35; T. G. Plante and A. C. Sherman, eds., *Faith and Health: Psychological Perspectives* (New York: Guilford, 2001); R. J. Taylor, L. M. Chatters, and J. Levin, *Religion in the Lives of African Americans: Social, Psychological, and Health Perspectives* (Thousand Oaks, CA: Sage, 2004).

Transformation

Our interest is in spirituality that *transforms*. Not all change qualifies as transformation. Family systems theorists were among the first to clarify a difference between "first-order" and "second-order" change, with the latter qualifying as transformation.[11] First-order change is primarily behavioral and limited to conserving one's current coping repertoire.[12] It typically involves a determined attempt to "do more of the same." Second-order change involves a more complex systemic transformation that changes coping strategies and ways of relating to a system altogether. In the field of learning theory, Jack Mezirow distinguishes between "formative" learning in which new content is placed into conventional socialized schemes and perspectives, and learning in which the meaning-schemes and meaning-perspectives themselves are transformed.[13] Along these lines, when we speak of spiritual "transformation," we do not mean merely gaining more knowledge about spiritual issues, or even adding to our repertoire of practices, but developing qualitatively more complex ways of holding and being held in relation to others and the Other.[14] We will spell out in more detail various models for understanding this transformation later, but it will be helpful to clarify some of these distinctions here at the beginning.

Transformations or second-order changes involve pursuing new goals (e.g., spiritual intimacy with God vs. begrudging obedience) or new pathways toward one's goals (e.g., surrender vs. determination).[15] Numerous psychological mechanisms or pathways of change have been identified, and these are reflected in differing models of psychotherapy. James Prochaska and John Norcross have outlined a transtheoretical model of the change process, suggesting not only that there are multiple mechanisms of personal change but that differing mechanisms prove to be optimal for differing stages of the change process.[16] People often go

11. G. Bateson, *Steps to an Ecology of Mind* (New York: Ballantine, 1972); P. Watzlawick, J. Weakland, and R. Fisch, *Change: Principles of Problem Formation and Problem Resolution* (New York: W. W. Norton, 1984).

12. K. I. Pargament, *The Psychology of Religion and Coping: Theory, Research, and Practice* (New York: Guilford, 1997).

13. Cf. Jack Mezirow, *Transformative Dimensions of Adult Learning* (San Francisco: Jossey-Bass, 1991); *Learning as Transformation* (San Francisco: Jossey-Bass, 2000). Similar distinctions have been made in organizational and leadership theory; cf. Robert Quinn, *Deep Change* (San Francisco: Jossey-Bass, 1996).

14. Cf. F. LeRon Shults, *Reforming Theological Anthropology: After the Philosophical Turn to Relationality* (Grand Rapids: Eerdmans, 2003).

15. Pargament, *Psychology of Religion and Coping*.

16. J. O. Prochaska and J. C. Norcross, "Stages of Change," in *Psychotherapy Relationships That Work: Therapist Contributions and Responsiveness to Patients*, ed. J. C. Norcross (New York: Oxford University Press, 2002), 303–13.

through a process of contemplating a major change, such as giving up smoking, long before acting on it in a transformative way. Many spiritual writers have described an analogous process of "seeds being planted" for subsequent spiritual transformation.

Contemporary theoretical paradigms have broadened to include the study of both sudden and gradual spiritual changes, as well as increasing attention on contextual influences.[17] To date, the body of social-scientific research suggests that religious conversions and spiritual transformations involve profound changes in self-identity and meaning in life, often following periods of significant stress and emotional turbulence. Self-reports of profound spiritual and religious changes are typically associated with positive mental health rather than psychopathology despite the intense stress that is also frequently reported as a precursor.[18] The question of whether transformations and second-order changes are uniformly positive has also been raised. People do report dramatic experiences of negative transformation.[19] Most spiritual traditions, however, also suggest that even positive transformations often involve some stressors, hardships, or negative consequences. Furthermore, specific relational contexts do not always support certain expressions of spiritual transformation, which can contribute to some of the stress or dislocation that can follow spiritual transformation as well as other experiences of change.

Transformative change can also be gradual or sudden. William Miller and Janet C'de Baca interviewed fifty-five "quantum changers," or people who reported experiencing a sudden, dramatic life transformation, which they defined as "a deep shift in core values, feelings, attitudes or actions."[20] Quantum changers described two main types of transformation: insightful and mystical. Insightful transformations tended to have more continuity with a person's prior developmental and cognitive process

17. R. W. Hood Jr., B. Spilka, B. Hunsburger, and R. Gorsuch, *The Psychology of Religion: An Empirical Approach*, 3rd ed. (New York: Guilford, 2003); B. J. Zinnbauer and K. I. Pargament, "Spiritual Conversion: A Study of Religious Change among College Students," *Journal for the Scientific Study of Religion* 37 (1998): 161–80; A. Mohoney and K. Pargament, "Sacred Changes: Spiritual Conversion and Transformation," *Journal of Clinical Psychology* 60 (2004): 481–92.

18. R. F. Paloutzian, J. T. Richardson, and L. R. Rambo, "Religious Conversion and Personality Change," *Journal of Personality* 67 (1999): 1047–79.

19. See also W. R. Miller and J. C'de Baca, *Quantum Change: When Epiphanies and Sudden Insights Transform Ordinary Lives* (New York: Guilford, 2001); W. R. Miller, "The Phenomenon of Quantum Change," *Journal of Clinical Psychology* 60 (2004): 453–60; J. C'de Baca and P. Wilbourne, "Quantum Change: Ten Years Later," *Journal of Clinical Psychology* 60 (2004): 531–41.

20. W. R. Miller and J. C'de Baca, "Quantum Change: Toward a Psychology of Transformation," in *Can Personality Change?*, ed. T. F. Heatherington and J. L. Weinberger (Washington, DC: American Psychological Association, 1994), 253–80, quote from p. 259.

whereas mystical transformations involved a sense of being dramatically acted upon by an outside force. Both types of quantum changers often reported a period of stress or discontent that precipitated their transformation, and about one-third reported praying or being prayed for around the time of their experience. Many quantum changers interpreted their transformative experiences by using spiritual language and categories, and some did not. This highlights the significant point that transformative experiences become *hermeneutical* and lead to interpretations, and not everyone interprets their transformation in spiritual terms.

These hermeneutical observations remind us of the importance of attending to our use of linguistic categories as we attempt to articulate the meaning of spirituality in all its dimensions. In *The Faces of Forgiveness*, we identified three semantic domains within which the concept of "forgiveness" operated.[21] Similar distinctions should be made with reference to the use of the term "transformation" in various fields of discourse. Clarifying the sociolinguistic role of the concept can facilitate its heuristic usefulness in interdisciplinary dialogue. The first and narrowest field of meaning for the concept of transformation we may call *functional.* For example, if a person is struggling with a particular problem, such as alcoholism, and then learns behaviors that inhibit drinking, this could be a functional transformation. The ego functions or coping strategies that upheld one pattern of functioning have been slightly altered to change the behavior. This is an important and necessary part of development, but it is limited to first-order change or the *assimilation* of new information into existing structures of meaning. By itself first-order change does not bring healing and mature integrity to the person, although it may help prevent more-severe problems or even foster the process of further change that can be profoundly transformative.

The term "transformation" also operates within a second and broader semantic field: systems theory discourse. What we will call *systemic* transformation is more explicitly concerned with the healing or reordering of the broader relations within which a person's spirituality is embedded. In this use of the concept, the focus is on the health and wholeness of the human spirit in all its relational contexts, not simply the alteration

21. We observed that in some circles the term is used primarily in a *forensic* sense; forgiveness has to do with agreeing not to seek retribution or payment of a debt. Although this is important, it does not itself bring healing of interpersonal and political relations. The term "forgiveness" is sometimes used to refer to the facilitation of a healing of systemic relations or at least the mental health of the forgiver. This is how "forgiveness" is typically used in the *therapeutic* domain. Finally, in theological discourse, *redemptive* "forgiveness" indicates the manifestation of divine grace, which incorporates but is irreducible to the forensic and therapeutic. Distinguishing these semantic fields helped us attend to the shifts in meaning as terms move across disciplinary boundaries.

of behavior or even the improvement of assimilative capacities. Accommodation is the developmental transformation or "paradigm shift" that occurs when relational structures of meaning change in response to new input. Transformation can be optimally fostered by therapists, spiritual directors, and counselors who can attend to both their own relational dynamics with people they work with and to the broader systems that may facilitate or hinder transformation for that person. This usually includes attention to the functional or behavioral level but also has a wider relational perspective and orientation.

Ecological and systems theorists have also suggested that transformation is an ongoing process in the life cycle as human systems (i.e., persons, families, communities) are continually challenged to adapt to their changing ecological contexts. This requires *ecological balancing*, which James Maddock and Noel Larson define as "a process of transforming the relationships between subsystems in an ecosystem without either losing the interdependence between them or destroying the overall integrity of the ecosystem of which they are a part."[22] This intersystemic model of transformation suggests that individuals and relational systems, such as families, are transformed by balancing the needs to both change and maintain continuity. For example, married or committed couples often face the transforming challenge of mutually adapting to shared life together while also holding on to their own distinct identities as individuals.[23]

Finally, the term "transformation" also operates in the field of *religious* discourse, in which it takes on a unique meaning. Here we are dealing explicitly with the relation of human desire to the sacred, or that which is believed to constitute ultimate meaning. Religions have diverse ways of naming the sacred; the generic terms "divinity" and "God" are the most common in our context. The relation to the sacred is mediated and conditioned by the community but not wholly determined by it. How do we negotiate the boundaries between our selves and the sacral Other? We will explore ways in which persons who have had intense experiences of spiritual transformation that led to increased health and psychological integrity have tended to "sanctify" or "spiritualize" all (or

22. J. W. Maddock and N. R. Larson, *Incestuous Families: An Ecological Approach to Understanding and Treatment* (New York: W. W. Norton, 1995), 25; "The Ecological Approach to Incestuous Families," in *Handbook of Stress, Trauma, and Family*, ed. D. R. Catherall (New York: Bruner-Routledge, 2004): 367–92.

23. Certain phases of the family life cycle can press for transformations (e.g., the introduction of children and parenthood responsibilities), and these transitions are sometimes ritualized or sacralized with spiritual significance. When couples or families cannot make transformations that facilitate adaptive functioning as a system, this increases the possibility that the system will at least temporarily dissolve as a functioning unit (e.g., in some divorces) or remain stuck in styles of functioning that generate symptoms of pathology.

significant parts) of life without separating themselves from the "secular." We will also examine how such persons deal with the relation of the self to the community with a similarly healthy tension—maintaining a dialectic between the self and the community as the source of criteria for determining the meaning of the sacred. When the religious dimension of human life emerges within the therapeutic process, this opens up the possibility of an ultimate transformation, a new ordering of the human spirit in relation to the divine or sacred. This calls for a kind of "sacramental hermeneutics" to describe the meaning-making of persons who have experienced profound types of spiritual transformation.

For Christians, this third semantic field can be spelled out in terms of *redemptive* transformation because the relation to the sacred is interpreted in light of the redemptive work of God in Christ through the Spirit.[24] This ultimate transformation, which is wholly dependent on the grace of God, includes and incorporates the transformation of our behavior and the systems in which we live. We are interested in all three uses of the phrase "spiritual transformation," but we will pay special attention to the interpreted experience of Christians who believe that as we share in the "well-being" (grace) that ultimately comes from God we can be truly transformed toward maturity or *shalom*. Because God's grace heals the way we relate in and to the lived world, however, interdisciplinary efforts at understanding the dynamics of human behavior and participating in their systemic healing are essential to our task.[25]

Relationality and Interdisciplinarity

In our earlier book, *The Faces of Forgiveness*, we described our interdisciplinary approach as one of "relational integration." Too often discussions of integration describe the task as focused purely on integrating abstract bodies of knowledge (i.e., psychology and theology), or concepts within these fields. It is easy, however, to miss the fact that ultimately it is particular persons-in-relation (psychologists and theologians) who are experiencing integration (and disintegration). Our conceptual models have been shaped by our personal engagement in relation with one another and within the relation between psychology and theology. Just as overcoming racial segregation requires real collaboration between

24. For a discussion of the importance of the modifier "redemptive" because of ways in which the term "transformation" has been used in other literature, cf. Dana R. Wright and John D. Kuentzel, eds., *Redemptive Transformation in Practical Theology* (Grand Rapids: Eerdmans, 2004), introduction.

25. Cf. Gerald G. May, *Addiction and Grace: Love and Spirituality in the Healing of Addictions* (San Francisco: HarperSanFrancisco, 1988).

persons, so too overcoming disciplinary segregation can only be successful as we actually transgress the boundaries and learn to become nonanxiously present to each other.

Our interdisciplinary approach to relational integration is also modeled on our understanding of healthy relationships as well differentiated. Individuals with high levels of differentiation of self are able to hold on to their own identities while also connecting closely with others. In contrast, a fused relationship is one in which individual identities and relational boundaries dissolve. Such relationships are vulnerable because the lack of differentiation tends to promote emotional reactivity and discourages the acceptance of differences. The relationship is maintained by extremes of power and control and by one or both parties "selling out" whenever differences emerge.[26] Fused relationships are extremely difficult to transform until (at least) one member is willing to differentiate. In a parallel manner, our attempts at integration are not meant to fuse the disciplines but to maintain the boundaries that differentiate them. The fields of theology and psychology are each constituted by a unique set of research interests and methodologies.

Nevertheless, the identity of each discipline is partially mediated by its differentiation from the other. The disciplines always and already interpenetrate one another, and our goal is to make this explicit—to explicate the reciprocity between the fields and their modeling of spirituality. We each want to acknowledge the limits of our disciplinary expertise without falling prey to *borrowed functioning*, which occurs in an adult relationship when one person gets another to carry out an adult function for them (i.e., borrows this functioning from them). Instead of a psychologist simply trusting the theological opinions of a given theologian (or vice versa), we both want to embrace the responsibility of interdisciplinary integrity in our models. At the same time, this does not mean that discourse cannot begin until both interlocutors understand an equal amount about each discipline; in such a case, one would be dispensable. Our modeling has been shaped by our dialogue together. Each of us acknowledges and remains open to the expertise of the other while also striving to indwell the discipline of the other and even function within it.

The relation between our disciplines is important because they *already* influence each other, whether we like it or not! Humans engaged in the social sciences operate out of a value-laden understanding of order and ultimate meaning in the world that borders on the religious. Theolo-

---

26. For an excellent presentation of the constructs of differentiation of self, fusion, borrowed functioning, and the notion of relational "selling out," see David M. Schnarch, *Passionate Marriage: Keeping Love and Intimacy Alive in Committed Relationships* (New York: Henry Holt, 1997). On power and control, see Maddock and Larson, *Incestuous Families*.

gians articulate doctrine by using categories that are already shaped by particular anthropological categories. Yet even here the relation can become an abstract object of study, as though the researchers were not already tied up within it. We have aimed to articulate our modeling of spiritual transformation *from within* the relationality of the disciplines, recognizing our own personal embeddedness within the dynamic field of relationality that subtends the disciplines. This is why the ordering of the first two parts of the book (theological and psychological) is not determinative for our methodology. For Christian theologians, the formulation of doctrine is dependent on the experience of divine revelation. However, this experience is always interpreted by and for human persons, which is why thematizing the social dynamics of this reception is crucial for theology. Likewise for Christian therapists and counselors, it is valuable to recognize that psychotherapeutic models from the social sciences carry "deep metaphors and implicit principles of obligation"[27] rooted in notions about the purpose or ultimate meaning of life and redemptive transformation toward that end. This is why thematizing the theological categories that shape our interpretations of the sacred is crucial for psychology and the social sciences.

Our interdisciplinary approach also explicitly attempts to take into account the philosophical turn to relationality. Broadly speaking, this refers to the shift from an emphasis on the concept of "substance" to an emphasis on "relation" as a key hermeneutical category.[28] Much of the Western philosophical (and theological) tradition was influenced by Aristotle's privileging of the concept of substance in his *Categories*. Defining the essence of a thing has to do primarily with identifying its genus and species. The category of "relation" was not as significant for Aristotle; we can understand a thing's essence without understanding its relation to other things. The difficulties with ignoring the importance of relationality eventually led Immanuel Kant to reverse Aristotle on this point when he outlined his own list of categories in the *Critique of Pure Reason* (1787). For Kant, the categories of "substance and accident" are subcategories of the broader category "Of Relation." This shift should not be understood as a simple linear evolution toward relationality, for already in ancient philosophy—and more explicitly in patristic Christian theology—the importance of relationality was emphasized among those who were less reliant on Aristotle. This is why we may speak more properly of a theological *re*-turn to relationality, for late modern theology has been increasingly shaped by a retrieval of traditional emphases on

27. D. S. Browning and T. D. Cooper, *Religious Thought and the Modern Psychologies*, 2nd ed. (Minneapolis: Fortress, 2004).

28. For a more detailed history of this shift, cf. Shults, *Reforming Theological Anthropology*, ch. 1.

relational categories. Recovering and refiguring traditional voices that have contributed to this new emphasis on relationality can help us open up space for fresh articulation of the Christian understanding of spiritual transformation (part 1).

The (re)turn to relationality has also impacted the social sciences, and this will shape the articulation of the relational dynamics of spiritual transformation in psychology (part 2). Numerous contemporary theoretical paradigms in the social sciences are also emphasizing relationality and contextualization in contrast to a modernistic focus on the decontextualized individual subject.[29] Social scientists and psychotherapists increasingly construe the self as constituted in and through relationships.[30] For example, a large body of empirical research on the processes and outcomes of psychotherapy supports relational factors (e.g., empathy) as powerful sources of therapeutic change.[31] This suggests that it is important to focus on the relationship between a person's sense of self and the sacred.[32] From a social-scientific perspective, _relational spirituality_ can be defined as "ways of relating to the sacred." There are a multitude of ways of relating to the sacred, ranging from hostile to loving, active to passive.

A more theoretical and practical elaboration of this relational definition will be outlined in the following chapters, but a few points are important to introduce here. First, internal working models of relationships or relational schemas are developed through relational experiences in life. These relational schemas can influence internal representations (or interpretations) of spiritual experience even outside conscious awareness.[33] This is what we would call our "unconscious theology." For example, someone whose primary caregiver early in life was emotionally distant is more likely to initially experience God or

---

29. S. A. Mitchell, _Relationality: From Attachment to Intersubjectivity_ (Hillsdale, NJ: Analytic Press, 2000).

30. S. M. Anderson and S. Chen, "The Relational Self: An Interpersonal Social-Cognitive Theory," _Psychological Review_ 109 (2002): 619–45; M. W. Baldwin and P. Fergusson, "Relational Schemas: The Activation of Interpersonal Knowledge Structures in Social Anxiety," in _International Handbook of Social Anxiety: Concepts, Research, and Interventions Related to Self and Shyness_, ed. W. R. Crozier and L. E. Alden (New York: John Wiley & Sons, 2001), 235–57; Sorenson, _Minding Spirituality_.

31. J. C. Norcross, ed., _Psychotherapy Relationships That Work: Therapist Contributions and Responsiveness to Patients_ (New York: Oxford University Press, 2002).

32. Also see J. W. Jones, _Terror and Transformation: The Ambiguity of Religion in Psychoanalytic Perspective_ (New York: Brunner-Routledge, 2002).

33. M. W. Mangis, "An Alien Horizon: The Psychoanalytic Contribution to a Christian Hermeneutic of Humility and Confidence," _Christian Scholar's Review_ 28 (1999): 411–31; T. W. Hall and S. L. Porter, "Referential Integration: An Emotional Information Processing Perspective on the Process of Integration," _Journal of Psychology and Theology_ 32 (2004): 167–80.

a Higher Power as distant, although this can change over time. Second, relationships are often instrumental in promoting or inhibiting spiritual formation and transformation. Relational attachments with sacred figures, both living and deceased, can influence the processes of spiritual stagnation and change.[34] Third, spirituality involves ways of relating to and within social and relational contexts. Sociologist of religion Robert Wuthnow has described the changing spiritual landscape in North America as a movement from primarily spiritualities of *dwelling* increasingly toward spiritualities of *seeking*.[35] Spiritual dwelling involves attaching to a particular community and tradition, typically provided by a religious group. Spiritual seeking involves a process of open questing and journeying toward new spiritual experiences and understandings both within and beyond the formal boundaries of religious institutions.

We will suggest that the dynamic and dialectical tension between spiritual dwelling and seeking is an essential characteristic of transforming spirituality, which takes shape within the complex relations of our representations of self, others, and God. In the remainder of this introduction, we outline the conceptual models that will guide our interdisciplinary exploration of spiritual transformation.

The Classical "Ways" and the Dynamics of Intensification

One of the most popular models for conceptualizing spiritual transformation in the Christian tradition is often referred to as the "three ways" of purgation, illumination, and union.[36] Although there was divergence in the interpretation and even numbering of these "ways,"[37] by the thirteenth century it was the overarching schema that shaped the Christian understanding of spiritual growth. Aristotelian and Neoplatonic assumptions about the anthropological and cosmological structure of creation shaped theological explanations of the experience of these ways. For example, St. Bonaventure explains that the threefold movement of ascent is based on the threefold "existence of things: in matter, in the mind and in the

34. D. S. Hardy, "A Winnicottian Redescription of Christian Spiritual Direction Relationships: Illustrating the Potential Contribution of Psychology of Religion to Christian Spiritual Practice," *Journal of Psychology and Theology* 28 (2000): 263–75.

35. R. Wuthnow, *After Heaven: Spirituality in America since the 1950s* (Berkeley: University of California Press, 1998).

36. For an introduction to this literature, see Benedict Groeschl, *Spiritual Passages: The Psychology of Spiritual Development* (New York: Crossroad, 1993); and Roger L. Ray, *Christian Wisdom for Today: Three Classic Stages of Spirituality* (St. Louis: Chalice, 1999).

37. E.g., in the early seventh century, John Climacus differentiated thirty "steps" in *The Ladder of Divine Ascent*, trans. C. Luibhuid and N. Russell (New York: Paulist, 1982).

Eternal Art [Logos]."[38] This threefold model had become so dominant by the sixteenth century that leading spiritual writers felt compelled to structure their presentations in accordance with this scheme.[39] It makes sense to attend to the testimony of those in the Christian tradition who focused their whole lives most intensely on the dynamics of spiritual transformation. Our attempts to model the dynamics of transforming spirituality are explicitly oriented toward conserving the intuitions that led to this classical approach, but to articulate this experience in a way that engages the plausibility structures of contemporary anthropology and cosmology.

The "purgative" way is typically related to an experience of "awakening." One awakens into a new awareness that one's way of life is tending toward death. A recognition that particular habits or attachments are hindering true life leads the seeker into a period of openness to being "purged." This is a painful experience, which some mystics and contemplatives have referred to as the "dark night of the soul."[40] Spiritual transformation often aborts early in this process because it is difficult to face the depths of darkness that threaten nonbeing; it is tempting to revert back into the comfortable sleepiness of life before the experience of awakening. It is precisely through the endurance of the darkness as one seeks for the promise of new being, however, that a person is opened up to the experience of the "illuminative" way. Here one experiences a new sense of joy and peace in the presence of God.

This illumination transforms persons as they come to understand, perceive, and interpret themselves and the world in the "light" of the divine presence. This does not mean that the darkness is completely removed and now one simply "sees" everything, for the experience of the brilliance of divine luminescence is still described as an "unknowing."[41] As a person learns to depend on God rather than his or her own capacity to "know," it becomes easier to detach from unhealthy habits and desires. The "unitive" way, which is well attested throughout the centuries in the literature of spirituality, generally refers to a process through which one comes into an experience of relational unity with the divine (or absolute).

38. Bonaventure, *The Soul's Journey into God*, in *Selections*, trans. E. Cousins (New York: Paulist, 1978), 61.

39. E.g., St. Ignatius of Loyola tried to link his "exercises" to the threefold way in the introduction to his *Spiritual Exercises*, although they do not easily fit; Ignatius of Loyola, *Spiritual Exercises and Selected Works*, ed. George E. Ganss (New York: Paulist, 1991), 123–24. However, there are obvious and important exceptions such as St. Teresa of Ávila who differentiated seven levels, or "mansions," in her *Interior Castle*, ed. and trans. E. A. Peers (New York: Doubleday, 1961).

40. E.g., John of the Cross, *The Dark Night of the Soul*, trans. E. A. Peers (Garden City, NY: Image Books, 1959).

41. Cf. *The Cloud of Unknowing*, ed. James Walsh (New York: Paulist, 1981).

The very meaning of "experience" itself is transformed in this "unity" of intimacy with God, which is sometimes described as an "infusion" of the absolutely gracious gift of divine presence.

Every manifestation of the "three ways" model throughout the centuries was shaped by the anthropological and cosmological categories of its own cultural context. How can we conserve the intuitions that led to this model and express them in a way that is compelling and illuminative today? It is important to face squarely the problematic philosophical assumptions that underlie some of the formulations of the classical ways, which include a reliance on Neoplatonic dualism, a focus on the individual, and a linear conception of the ways as discrete "stages." As we will see in chapter 2, these issues are interrelated. The idea of discrete and sequential stages of "ascent" makes sense within the context of a Neoplatonic dualism in which the individual soul moves away from the bodily and toward the mental. The distinction between the "active" life, which is "lower," and the "contemplative" life, which is "higher," is evidence of this assumption.[42] Our goal is to reconstructively articulate a Christian understanding of spiritual transformation in a way that engages the categories of our own contemporary cultural context.

LODER

A helpful starting point is James Loder's depiction of the "transformational logic of the Spirit," which he argues operates within all kinds of human activity, from mathematics to therapy to social change.[43] The first step in this logic is "conflict," in which an apparent rupture emerges in a person's lived world. This leads to what Loder calls an "interlude for scanning," which involves indwelling the situation and playing out possible solutions. The third step is a "constructive act of the imagination," which often involves the integration of seemingly divergent realities into a new context in which the elements are transformed within a more complex integrative frame. This results in a "release" of energy that had been bound in tension, through which the person experiences an opening up of his or her life into or for a broader context. The fifth step is "interpretation," which involves working out the solution, making explicit congruent connections, and pursuing verification in communal correspondence. Over time, a new conflict may emerge and the

---

42. Cf. Sheldrake, *Spirituality and History*, 188–89.

43. James E. Loder, *The Transforming Moment* (Colorado Springs: Helmers & Howard, 1989), 35–64. In his more detailed explication of the dynamics of human development in theological perspective, Loder also used the classical "ways" of spiritual formation to illustrate some of his case studies; James E. Loder, *The Logic of the Spirit: Human Development in Theological Perspective* (San Francisco: Jossey-Bass, 1998), ch. 3. Cf. Loder, "Incisions from a Two-Edged Sword: The Incarnation and the Soul/Spirit Relationship," in *The Treasure of Earthen Vessels: Explorations in Theological Anthropology*, ed. Brian H. Childs and David W. Waanders (Louisville: Westminster John Knox, 1994), 151–73.

logic of transformation begins again. These are not five linear stages of "human development" but the structural dynamics that are operative in the ongoing movement of the human spirit within all of its relational contexts.[44]

Our modeling attempts to incorporate Loder's insights but expands beyond his project in several ways. Our proposals will place the discussion of human spirituality even more radically in Pneumatological perspective, emphasizing more explicitly the significance of Infinity, Trinity, and Futurity in the doctrine of God for our understanding of transformation (part 1), and engage a broader array of insights from research in the social sciences (part 2). In addition, we aim to bring the voices of the classical tradition, including the three ways, more deeply into the very structuring of the model itself. We may begin the conceptual reconstruction by overlaying the three classical ways onto Loder's five steps of transformational logic, which can help us start to think of the ways not merely as stages but as intercalated moments in the ongoing process of transformation. The dynamics of purgation seem naturally correlated to the experiences that Loder described in terms of the conflict and tension that lead to scanning. The dynamics of illumination are more easily connected to what Loder called imaginative insight, the construction of a new way of understanding one's self as spirit in relation to one's neighbors and God. Finally, the unitive dynamics of the classical third way can be described in terms of the release and opening of the human spirit into a new sense of relational unity and intimacy.

Our interest is less in delineating stages than it is in understanding the dynamic movement of the human spirit itself, and so we want to refigure the ways within a description of the patterns of an ongoing process of the qualitative *intensification* of relationality. The concept of "intensification" can help us avoid the linear, individualistic, and dualistic tendencies of some previous formulations of the three ways. The interrelated dynamics of *intensity, intentionality*, and *intimacy* provide an organizing integrative scheme for presenting the process of intensification in spiritual transformation in part 1. Broadly speaking, these may be correlated with the classical ways of purgation, illumination, and union. Rather than relying on the notion of the ascent of the individual soul through linear stages, however, LeRon will emphasize the way in which the dynamics of intensity, intentionality, and intimacy

44. In a book with physicist W. Jim Neidhardt, Loder outlined the "relational logic of the Spirit" in dialogue with neurobiology, anthropology, and other disciplines; James E. Loder and W. Jim Neidhardt, *The Knight's Move: The Relational Logic of the Spirit in Theology and Science* (Colorado Springs: Helmers & Howard, 1992), ch. 12.

are mutually implicated and together shape the narrative structure of human spirituality.

A sufficiently complex form of relational *intensity* is necessary for human life, and consciousness requires some form of *intentionality* in relation to another. Human personhood emerges as this intentional intensity takes form as a longing for *intimacy* in relation to a personal other. An intense tending toward intimacy is itself an intimation of personhood (see chapter 2). Each of these interpenetrating dimensions of personal life is fully operative at every moment in the dynamic process of spiritual transformation. The intensity and intentionality between persons in relation do not cease when intimacy is experienced—they are intensified. Our experience of intensity and intentionality in relation to others is already shaped by our painful memories and hopeful anticipation of intimacy. Intentionality does not aim at the dissolution of all tension (which would be death) but at a way of tending and being tended to that holds us in faithful, loving, and hopeful communion. Intimacy is not simply a final stage of a linear process; in the "consummation" of healthy intimacy, the desire for intentional relational union is not quenched but intensified. Not all kinds of intimacy are healthy; an ideology of intimacy can be as dangerous as an ideology of individualism if it leads to forms of tension that are destructive to ecologies of human development.[45]

We are interested in understanding and facilitating the intensification of *redemptive* intimacy, which emerges in and through the gracious transformation of the tension and intentionality that shape our lives in relation to God and one another. The intensive experience of being tended to by and in the divine Spirit is infinitely overwhelming. We cannot control it with our own intentions. As we will see in part 1, the intimacy that Paul describes as becoming "one spirit" with the Lord (1 Cor. 6:17) involves the transformation of the knowing, acting, and being of the human spirit. This redemption of personal intentionality transforms our interpreted experience of the intensity of creaturely life, so that our intimate tending to others, to ourselves, and to God is increasingly characterized by faithfulness, love, and hope. The redemptive transformation of our longing for intimacy is wholly dependent on divine grace, but this does not mean it is isolated from the real dynamics of our daily behavior as we struggle for healthy systemic relations in our life together.

45. Cf. Patrick R. Keifert, *Welcoming the Stranger: A Public Theology of Worship and Evangelism* (Minneapolis: Fortress, 1992), 170; S. J. Sandage, C. J. Aubrey, and T. K. Ohland, "Wearing the Fabric of Community: A Model for Counselors and Therapists," *Marriage and Family: A Christian Journal* 2 (1999): 381–98.

The Crucible of Spiritual Transformation

One helpful metaphor that overlaps our interdisciplinary concerns is the "crucible" of spiritual transformation. In part 2 Steve will build upon theory and research in the social sciences to articulate a crucible of spiritual transformation. A crucible is a container or melting pot for holding the intense heat and pressure that can transform raw materials and catalytic agents into qualitatively different substances. Couples therapist David Schnarch defines a crucible as a "resilient vessel in which metamorphic processes occur."[46] Several clinical theorists, most notably Schnarch, have applied the crucible metaphor to the dynamics of relational transformation in couples and families by emphasizing the roles of stress and conflict as challenging opportunities for growth.[47] Using the crucible metaphor, the resiliency and nonreactivity of the container is essential to the transformative process. Crucibles or containers with melting points lower than the chemical reaction inside will crack under pressure and fail to hold the potential transformative process.[48]

A crucible has also been defined as a "severe test" or a "trial by fire." Many spiritual traditions have described spiritual transformation as a process involving severe tests, ordeals, and rites of initiation.[49] Often the metaphors of journey or pilgrimage through the desert are combined with crucible-like images of suffering, testing, and death that leads to rebirth. Theologian Gustavo Gutiérrez described the social context of intense poverty and oppression in Latin America as a "crucible" that was forming a new indigenous spirituality of communal solidarity in following Jesus.[50] The Hebrew Bible often uses the imagery of a refiner's fire to describe the experience of being brought into right relation with God (Zech. 13:9; Mal. 3:2–3). Across diverse contexts and traditions, the imagery of heat

46. David M. Schnarch, *Constructing the Sexual Crucible: An Integration of Sexual and Marital Therapy* (New York: W. W. Norton, 1991), xv.

47. D. B. Allender and T. Longman III, *Intimate Allies* (Wheaton: Tyndale House, 1995); V. T. Holeman, "Mutual Forgiveness: A Catalyst for Relationship Transformation in the Moral Crucible of Marriage," *Marriage and Family: A Christian Journal* 2 (1999): 147–58; A. Y. Napier and C. A. Whitaker, *The Family Crucible* (New York: Harper & Row, 1978); David M. Schnarch, *Constructing the Sexual Crucible*; *Passionate Marriage*; *Resurrecting Sex: Resolving Sexual Problems and Rejuvenating Your Relationship* (New York: HarperCollins, 2002).

48. Schnarch, *Constructing the Sexual Crucible*; Holeman, "Mutual Forgiveness."

49. R. L. Moore, *The Archetype of Initiation: Sacred Space, Ritual Process, and Personal Transformation* (Philadelphia: Xlibris, 2001).

50. Gustavo Gutiérrez, *We Drink from Our Own Wells: The Spiritual Journey of a People*, 20th anniversary ed. (Maryknoll, NY: Orbis, 2003), 25.

and fire is also a common symbol of the internal intensification that is an essential part of crucibles of spiritual transformation.[51]

Schnarch developed a crucible model of transformation in couples' relationships by suggesting that intimate relationships involve a systemic balancing of cycles of growth and stability.[52] Relational systems such as marriage maintain states of equilibrium or stability with predictable forms of relating. The relationship may or may not be satisfying or intimate, but a sense of safety and security can come from the stability and consistency of the relational patterns. At a certain destabilizing point that Schnarch refers to as "critical mass," one or both partners become willing to tolerate the anxiety and change that are part of a transforming growth cycle. This can involve "dark nights of the soul" as anxiety intensifies and partners are challenged to stretch toward increased differentiation of self and personal maturity. Marital partners rarely change in a synchronous fashion, meaning that one partner usually embraces the growth cycle before the other, who often initially feels controlled by the changes. In some cases, the pursuit of growth and change in marriage might result in divorce, which is one reason some spouses prefer the safety of the status quo. Individuals will enter the crucible of growth only if they are willing to differentiate from their partner, that is, to develop the ability to hold on to their identity in the presence of the other person.

We adapted Schnarch's crucible model of transformation in couples' relationships to depict our intensification model of spiritual transformation (see fig. 1).[53] In our model, spirituality involves a balancing of seeking and dwelling that roughly parallels the cycles of relational growth and stability in Schnarch's model. The inner circular ring of figure 1 represents the cycle of spiritual dwelling, which involves relating to the sacred in ways that feel familiar, comfortable, and safe.[54] At its best, spiritual dwelling can include connection to a spiritual community and tradition that legitimize certain rituals and spiritual practices and provide a sense of continuity to spiritual experience. But spiritual dwelling can also eventually lead to boredom and disappointment as spiritual practices and experiences become too predictable or lacking in the vitality necessary for certain developmental challenges. Spiritual detachment or denial can result as spiritual dwellers distance from spiritual boredom or deny their disappointment. At this point, a person can move toward spiritual

51. Mircea Eliade, *Patterns in Comparative Religion*, trans. Rosemary Sheed (Lincoln: University of Nebraska Press, 1958).

52. Schnarch, *Passionate Marriage*.

53. Schnarch acknowledges Don and Barbara Fairfield as the original developers of the figure in his book.

54. Our use of the language of spiritual dwelling and seeking builds upon Wuthnow, *After Heaven*.

Figure 1. Balancing Spiritual Seeking and Dwelling

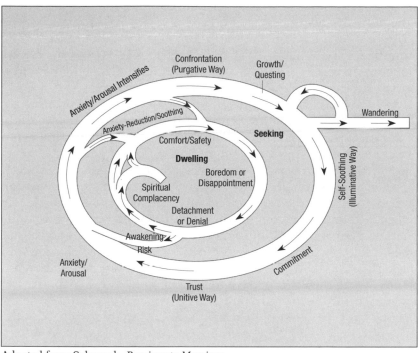

Adapted from Schnarch, *Passionate Marriage*

complacency (at least temporarily) in an attempt to resist change, which can result in a lack of spiritual intimacy. We are not saying that a state of spiritual complacency is necessarily terminal for a person's spirituality, although some people do seem to become cut off or divorced from relating to the sacred. The transforming alternative is that a person can experience a spiritual awakening that involves moving into the risk of intensified anxiety and arousal (depicted on the left side of fig. 1).

The move into the outer circular ring of figure 1 takes a person into the growth cycle of spiritual seeking that is necessary for both systemic and redemptive transformation. This is initially destabilizing and stressful but often focuses attention. Spiritual traditions use various metaphors to describe this experience, including the dark night, the desert, and the wilderness. A person might start authentically asking new spiritual questions, pray or meditate in a new way, or explore a different spiritual practice. It can feel scary to question one's community or tradition, like a loosening of one's moorings. If persons' desire for comfort and safety exceeds their motivation to tolerate the intensified anxiety of seeking, they might opt for a return to familiar forms of spiritual dwelling. But if they choose to tolerate the anxiety and ambiguity of seeking, there can be a move into the forms of spiritual confrontation we are likening to the purgative way. The forms of purgation vary but can include a focusing of attention or commitment, a willingness to simplify priorities and make sacrifices, or an openness to facing painful realities about self and other. The courage, honesty, confrontation, and questing of the purgative way can lead to the new spiritual insights of the illuminative way. These transforming moments of illumination involve new understanding of self and other in relation to the sacred. This can include an initial conversion experience or new levels of spiritual commitment and trust within the ongoing transformational process. Schnarch describes an analogous process for relational partners where one or both go through intensified anxiety and confrontation with their own personal challenges, potentially leading to deepened relational commitment and trust. A key transformational dynamic in both models is the pattern of intensified anxiety and arousal that is eventually soothed by new, growth-generating insights and commitments rather than by a return to safe but stagnant familiarity.

The outer circular ring of the purgative, illuminative, and unitive ways in figure 1 can cycle toward a return to the comfort of spiritual dwelling. This might involve a return to former relationships of spiritual dwelling or the discovery of new communities and can be a wise move after an intense cycle of spiritual growth in the desert. It would be unrealistic and perhaps even grandiose to attempt to remain in a perpetual cycle of spiritual seeking and questing without dwelling. But spiritual dwelling after the growth cycle of seeking is different from that before seeking. Spiritual dwelling after a growth cycle can involve new levels of spiritual maturity with less use of rigid defenses against insecurity, questions, and conflict. Relational attachments become more secure and intentional and less anxiety-driven. Like Schnarch, we suggest that spiritually transformed persons should develop a more differentiated sense of self that allows them to better handle both relational connection and autonomy or community and solitude. As Bonhoeffer put it, the person who cannot be alone should beware of community and the one who cannot be in community should beware of being alone.[55]

Spiritual seeking, however, does not always lead to illumination and enhanced spiritual dwelling. On the right side of figure 1, there is a pathway toward spiritual wandering. Some seekers find themselves on a quest away from their familiar sources of spiritual dwelling, and they simply continue to wander for years or even a lifetime. There can be many

55. Dietrich Bonhoeffer, *Life Together*, trans. J. W. Doberstein (New York: HarperSan-Francisco, 1954), 77.

reasons for this. Some feel deeply disappointed by God or their spiritual communities and do not find a pathway toward repair. Others may find it hard to make commitments to particular relationships, communities, or traditions that offer sources of spiritual dwelling. Individuals can also be unjustly excluded from spiritual community. Some seem to enjoy the freedom of wandering and experience it as a quest whereas others feel trapped in a lonely, painful form of alienated wandering. The pathway back to spiritual dwelling after wandering can require great courage and may involve grieving disappointments and mourning lost ideals as well as a return to the growth cycle of spiritual seeking.

The outer circular ring in figure 1 depicts the transformational dynamics that lead to spiritual union or the unitive way. Mystics and contemplatives have described union as deepened spiritual intimacy. Capacities for love and compassion are intensified. The primary difference that emerges after a person has experienced the illuminative way is the potential for a maturing ability to spiritually self-confront and self-soothe. This is not to imply a lesser role for the Holy Spirit in transformation.[56] Rather, less anxiety is needed for the person to be willing to participate in ongoing spiritual transformation, and there is less resistance to the Spirit-initiated process. At earlier phases of spiritual formation, anxiety often must become extremely intense before a spiritual awakening is even perceived. The natural human preference for stability means that people tend to initially resist change until absolutely necessary, particularly when people feel low levels of self-efficacy for managing change in that domain. One of the powerful benefits of surviving an intense spiritual transformation (or two) is that a person can develop a stronger sense of spiritual efficacy or agency for engaging the risk of further cycles of transformation. *Amen*

The metaphors of crucible and intensification are not intended to deny the heuristic value of other metaphors but to complement them. The image of a journey is perhaps the most popular; the story of a "pilgrim's progress" is easier to tell. As we will see, another important metaphor is that of ascent, a movement of the soul upward away from earthly concerns and toward contemplation of heavenly things and ultimately union with the divine. Rather than "up," Lawrence Cunningham and Keith J. Egan have suggested the metaphor of "widening

Self-Soothing

56. In theological terms, this "self-soothing" is not a Pelagian reliance on one's own power to soothe but a reception of, and participation in, divine grace, by which one is consoled and learns to console others (cf. 2 Cor. 1:3–7). We understand self-soothing, as a relational construct, to mean ways of relating to self that include taking responsibility for effectively soothing anxiety. A capacity for self-soothing reduces the risk for unhealthy dependence upon others.

the circle."[57] Here spiritual growth involves an enlarging of one's area of relational concern, which increasingly engages one in the concrete and communal activity that is being transformed by divine love.

We hope to account for the intuitions of these (and other metaphors) as we stress that spiritual transformation is not simply a "transcendence" of space and time but a transformation of our experience of spatiotemporal conditions that is wholly dependent on divine grace. In accordance with our desire to maintain the integrity of each discipline while acknowledging an appropriately differentiated reciprocal relation between them, we have not suggested a single model that encompasses both fields. LeRon's theological proposals in part 1 will emphasize the language of intensification; Steve's theological proposals in part 2 will rely more heavily on the crucible metaphor. In part 3 we will test the fecundity of our modeling in the context of several practical case studies that aim more explicitly at integration. However, we hope that some of the ways in which our interdisciplinary dialogue has mutually enhanced our distinct approaches to a shared task—searching for new ways of understanding and facilitating spiritual transformation—will already have become clear to the reader as we explore more fully the dynamics of transforming spirituality in theology and psychology.

57. Lawrence Cunningham and Keith J. Egan, *Christian Spirituality: Themes from the Tradition* (New York: Paulist, 1996), 59.

PART 1

Transforming Spirituality in Theology

F. LeRon Shults

2

REFORMING
PNEUMATOLOGY

Christian discourse about redemptive transformation is embedded
within a broader matrix of theological concerns that shape our understanding and practice of spirituality. For example, discussing the concept
of the human "spirit" (*pneuma*) requires us to engage in theological
anthropology, and reflecting on the social dimensions of spiritual transformation leads us to questions about the nature and task of the church
(ecclesiology). Because our understanding of the transformation of the
creaturely *human* spirit will be shaped (whether consciously or not) by
our understanding of the creative *divine* Spirit, one of the most relevant
theological themes for understanding spirituality is Pneumatology—the
doctrine of the Holy Spirit. Given its implicit significance, it is initially
surprising that so many popular Christian treatments of spirituality do
not embed their presentations within an articulation of the doctrine of
the Holy Spirit.[1]

1. E.g., Dallas Willard, *The Divine Conspiracy: Rediscovering Our Hidden Life in God*
(San Francisco: Harper, 1998), dedicates less than two pages to an explicit treatment of
the Holy Spirit. Even in his promisingly titled *The Spirit of the Disciplines* (San Francisco:

As we will see below, spirituality and theology (and so Pneumatology) were intimately connected in much of the Christian tradition but drifted apart during the early modern period. A growing number of scholars are working to heal this divorce between Pneumatology and discourse about spirituality, which hurts the church by cutting it off from theological resources for reflection and practice.[2] As Mark McIntosh insists, we will not be able to heal this fracture simply by adding one more topic (e.g., "spiritual theology") to a theological curriculum; we must reintegrate the profound questioning of the human spirit into the task of theology.[3] I hope to contribute to this ongoing reconstructive process by organizing my presentation of redemptive spiritual transformation around the human desire for truth, goodness, and beauty and by explicitly thematizing the mutual shaping of Pneumatology and spirituality.

The programmatic suggestions for reforming Pneumatology in the following chapters aim to conserve the intuitions of the biblical tradition by liberating them for illuminative dialogue with late modern philosophy and contemporary science. This is part of a broader theological project that I call "reforming theology." On the one hand, *reforming* theology refers to the task faced by every generation of the Christian church: reconstructively articulating the biblical Gospel in a way that engages its contemporary cultural context. Christian theology—like the church itself—should always be open to reformation by the grace of God.[4] My chapters in *The Faces of Forgiveness* were an attempt to contribute to the perennial reformation of the Christian doctrines of salvation (soteriology) and the church (ecclesiology) in dialogue with cultural thought-forms that have been shaped by the philosophical (re)turn to relationality.[5] In *Reforming Theological Anthropology* and *Reforming the Doctrine of God*, I outlined directions for the articulation of these traditional loci in late

HarperCollins, 1988), Willard shows little sensitivity to the significance of Pneumatology for spirituality; "spirit" appears in the index only with reference to the human spirit.

2. Cf. Philip Sheldrake, *Spirituality and Theology: Christian Living and the Doctrine of God* (Maryknoll, NY: Orbis, 1998), 33–64; James J. Buckley and David S. Yeago, *Knowing the Triune God: The Work of the Spirit in the Practices of the Church* (Grand Rapids: Eerdmans, 2001); Miroslav Volf and Dorothy C. Bass, eds., *Practicing Theology: Beliefs and Practices in Christian Life* (Grand Rapids: Eerdmans, 2002).

3. Mark Allen McIntosh, *Mystical Theology: The Integrity of Spirituality and Theology* (Malden, MA: Blackwell, 1998). Simon Chan, *Spiritual Theology: A Systematic Study of the Christian Life* (Downers Grove, IL: InterVarsity, 1998), has argued that although it would be ideal for there to be no separation between "spiritual" and "dogmatic" theology, we should at least be engaged, given the division of the curriculum, in a "spiritual theology" that attends to the experience behind systematic formulations.

4. In the Reformed tradition, this is expressed by the phrase *ecclesia reformata et semper reformanda*.

5. F. LeRon Shults and Steven J. Sandage, *The Faces of Forgiveness: Searching for Wholeness and Salvation* (Grand Rapids: Baker, 2003).

modern culture.[6] In the last section of this chapter, I will spell out the connections among these projects in more detail. The purpose of the three chapters that follow is not to provide a complete presentation of Pneumatological doctrine but to offer a general outline of a theological understanding of the Holy Spirit that can provide the conceptual space for clarifying and facilitating the dynamics of transforming spirituality in contemporary Christian life.

Another aspiration that drives this project is the desire to facilitate the transformation of the human spirit in relation to the redemptive presence of the Holy Spirit. This brings us to the second sense in which we are interested in "reforming theology"—theology that *reforms us*. I hope that readers will find here resources for a *reformative* Pneumatology. As our minds are renewed and our practices redeemed by the gracious transforming presence of the Spirit, the articulation of Christian doctrine can serve the reformation of the church and the world. Attending to Pneumatology is reformative insofar as it leads us into the relational presence of the Spirit, who awakens and arouses us, calling us into intimate fellowship with God in Christ. Longing to understand the Spirit of the biblical God is not a neutral or abstract endeavor, for here we are dealing not simply with one object of study among many but with the all-embracing and all-pervading divine presence that originates, upholds, and orients all creaturely longing. Treatments of spirituality that stay at the level of functional (or even systemic) transformation can easily be isolated from the Gospel, leading merely to a list of rules or steps for change. If an articulation of the dynamics of spirituality is intrinsically connected to an understanding and experience of the Spirit, however, it may more easily become part of a presentation of the good news that we are called to share in divine grace as we participate in the redemptive transformation of the world.

The Reformative Appeal of Pneumatology

We begin by identifying some of the relatively recent historical and theological developments that have contributed to the renewal of interest in the doctrine of the Holy Spirit and in the practice of spirituality. Pneumatology has been an important theme throughout church history, but attention to its reformative appeal is often heightened during times of crisis or revival. For example, reflection on the experience of life in the Spirit took on a special significance for the Cappadocian fathers, the

6. F. LeRon Shults, *Reforming Theological Anthropology: After the Philosophical Turn to Relationality* (Grand Rapids: Eerdmans, 2003); *Reforming the Doctrine of God* (Grand Rapids: Eerdmans, 2005).

leaders of spiritual movements in the Middle Ages, the early Protestant Reformers, and many of the theologians who wrote during the Great Awakenings.[7] In the last few decades, Pneumatology has once again come to the fore as a crucial theme within several influential systematic theological proposals.[8]

One of the most significant factors in the renewal of interest in the doctrine of the Holy Spirit in the twentieth century was the worldwide growth of the Pentecostal and charismatic movements.[9] As Richard Shaull observes, Pentecostals experience the Spirit as the presence in history of the resurrected Jesus; "poor and broken people discover that what they read in the Gospels is happening NOW in their midst."[10] The theological task of articulating the doctrine of the Holy Spirit became more poignant as the experience of the reception of the *charismata* began to transform Christian liturgy and daily life. The distinctive emphasis on the Spirit among Pentecostal theologians is increasingly registering an effect on the broader academic guild. As one example of this trend, we may point to the work of Amos Yong, who argues that Pneumatology can (and should) play a central and regulative role in systematic theology and in the dialogue with world religions.[11] Yong also illustrates the openness of Pentecostal scholars to the late modern recovery of the category of relationality, which can facilitate the interpretation of the biblical witness to the experience of the Spirit.[12]

The appeal of the charismatic experience of the Spirit in the Christian community reaches transversally across cultural contexts and traditions. Partly in response to these developments, we also find a revival of interest in the Spirit among many mainline Reformed and Lutheran theologians. This has often taken shape as an appeal to the Pneumatological insights of

7. For an overview of the history of the doctrine of the Holy Spirit, see Stanley M. Burgess, *The Holy Spirit*, 3 vols. (Peabody, MA: Hendrickson, 1989–1997).

8. Shults, *Reforming the Doctrine of God*, part 2, provides a detailed analysis of several contributors to this revival of interest in Pneumatology, including Barth, Gunton, Jenson, Jüngel, Moltmann, Pannenberg, Rahner, and Zizioulas.

9. Cf. Walter J. Hollenweger, *Pentecostalism: Origins and Developments Worldwide* (Peabody, MA: Hendrickson, 1997).

10. Richard Shaull and Waldo A. Cesar, *Pentecostalism and the Future of the Christian Churches: Promises, Limitations, Challenges* (Grand Rapids: Eerdmans, 2000).

11. Amos Yong, *Beyond the Impasse: Toward a Pneumatological Theology of Religions* (Grand Rapids: Baker; Carlisle, England: Paternoster, 2003). The emergence of Pentecostal academic journals such as *Pneuma* illustrates the growing desire to link theology to the experience of the Spirit.

12. Amos Yong, *Spirit–Word–Community: Theological Hermeneutics in Trinitarian Perspective* (Aldershot, England, and Burlington, VT: Ashgate, 2002), part 1. Cf. Veli-Matti Kärkkäinen and Amos Yong, *Toward a Pneumatological Theology: Pentecostal and Ecumenical Perspectives on Ecclesiology, Soteriology, and Theology of Mission* (Lanham, MD: University Press of America, 2002).

the early Reformers themselves. In the middle of the last century, several Reformed theologians noted the need to recover the relation between the Holy Spirit and the human spirit in a way that does not deny the freedom of the latter, as it often appears in some versions of predesti-nation. For example, Arnold Come argued that the key to the meaning of the whole of Calvin's *Institutes* may be in his treatment of the Holy Spirit in Book III. He observed that "Calvin, unlike his followers, did not place the doctrine of predestination at the front of his system, but buried it in the depths of his doctrine of the Holy Spirit."[13] Around the same time, Lutheran scholars came to a fresh awareness of the importance of the *Spiritus Creator* in the theology of Martin Luther. For example, Regin Prenter began his influential book on this topic with this explicit claim: "The concept of the Holy Spirit completely dominates Luther's theology."[14] This was the beginning of a broader interest among Reformed and Lutheran theologians in the doctrine of the Holy Spirit.[15]

The dialogue among Roman Catholic theologians leading up to and flowing out of Vatican II also contributed to a fresh awareness of the significance of Pneumatology. This is evident, for example, in the theology of Karl Rahner. In his *Spirit in the World*, Rahner attempted to retrieve and refigure Thomas Aquinas's use of the concept of "spirit" in light of a phenomenological analysis of human experience.[16] Building on in-sights from twentieth-century philosophical anthropology, he argued that human beings are spirit insofar as their life in the world is characterized by a striving for the Absolute, which takes shape as an openness to the future. The divine Spirit is present everywhere and always, although the ecclesial experience of this charismatic presence is unique.[17] Atten-tion to the significance and reformative appeal of Pneumatology is also evident in Yves Congar's influential *I Believe in the Holy Spirit*, where he emphasizes the positive impact of the charismatic renewal in the

13. Arnold B. Come, *Human Spirit and Holy Spirit* (Philadelphia: Westminster, 1959), 174–75. Cf. George S. Hendry, *The Holy Spirit in Christian Theology* (Philadelphia: West-minster, 1956).

14. Regin Prenter, *Spiritus Creator*, trans. John M. Jensen (Philadelphia: Muhlenberg, 1953), ix.

15. E.g., Reformed theologian Michael Welker (*God the Spirit* [Minneapolis: Fortress, 1994], 280–83) argues for an understanding of the Spirit as the liberating and self-giving presence of God, and Lutheran theologian Robert Jenson (*Systematic Theology*, 2 vols. [New York: Oxford University Press, 1997–1999], 146) argues that Pentecost is a peer of Easter.

16. Karl Rahner, *Spirit in the World*, trans. William Dych (New York: Herder and Herder, 1968).

17. Karl Rahner, "The Spirit That Is over All Life," in *Theological Investigations* (New York: Herder and Herder, 1971), 7:193–201; "Observations on the Factor of the Charismatic in the Church," in *Theological Investigations* (Baltimore: Helicon, 1961), 12:81–97.

Roman Catholic Church.[18] The broader revival of trinitarian doctrine in Western theology has also naturally generated further reflection on the relation of the Spirit to the Father and the Son, fueling discussions about Pneumatology and its relevance for Christian life.

The intensification of ecumenical dialogue in the twentieth century also contributed to the renewal of theological interest in the Holy Spirit. Encountering the robust Pneumatology of Eastern Orthodoxy has led many Western theologians to a fresh evaluation and appropriation of traditional resources. The Orthodox tradition was deeply shaped by the fourth-century Cappadocian fathers, who went out of their way to stress the importance of the doctrine of the Holy Spirit for Christian life.[19] As Vladimir Lossky observes, the "economy of the Holy Spirit" is as important in Eastern theology as the "economy of the Son." This is part of the rationale for the Orthodox antagonism toward the Western addition of the *filioque* ("and the Son") clause to the Nicene-Constantinopolitan Creed.[20] This tradition speaks of the Holy Spirit as the source of the uncreated grace that is given to creatures in salvation, an uncreated "divine and deifying energy in which we really participate in the nature of the Holy Trinity."[21] The Eastern concept of *theōsis* ("deification") is easily misunderstood if divorced from the broader understanding of the Spirit and the "energies" of God.[22] Ecumenical dialogue on explicitly Pneumatological issues has played a role in encouraging fresh reflection on the relation between the outpouring of the Spirit and the resurrection of the Son.

Reforming Pneumatology is also appealing for the growing number of theological voices calling for a spirituality that *liberates*. Theologians who speak for and work among the poor and oppressed may be more open to calling out for the disturbing, convicting power of the Spirit than those who are happy with the status quo. Leonardo Boff speaks of the Spirit as "the power of the new and of the renewal of all things . . . the liberating principle freeing us from the oppressions of our sinful

18. Yves Congar, *I Believe in the Holy Spirit*, 3 vols. (New York and London: Seabury, 1983), 3:149–72.

19. Cf. Gregory of Nyssa, *On the Holy Spirit* (*NPNF*[2] 5:315–25); Gregory of Nazianzus, fifth theological oration, *On the Holy Spirit* (*NPNF*[2] 7:318–28); and Basil of Caesarea, *On the Holy Spirit* (*NPNF*[2] 8:1–50).

20. The phrase "and the Son" was inserted into the creed in some Western liturgies: we believe in the Spirit, "who proceeds from the Father and the Son [*filioque*]." Many Eastern theologians took this to imply a subordination of the Holy Spirit, leading to a debate that contributed to the split between East and West in AD 1054.

21. Vladimir Lossky, *The Mystical Theology of the Eastern Church* (London: J. Clarke, 1968), 213; cf. 162.

22. For a discussion of this Eastern theme, cf. Duncan Reid, *Energies of the Spirit: Trinitarian Models in Eastern Orthodox and Western Theology* (Atlanta: Scholars Press, 1997).

situation . . . imbuing [the poor] with hope that they can shake off the oppression that they bear . . . and inspiring them to struggle to bring it about."[23] This understanding of the experience of the Spirit encourages us to embrace liberating forms of spirituality that transform not only the inner states of individuals but also our real embodied relations in community. Jon Sobrino argues that Christian spirituality involves confronting our current history as Jesus confronted his—a spirituality of liberation that engages the real world.[24] This concern is not limited to "liberation" theologians. For example, Owen Thomas has argued that spirituality must incorporate practical engagement in the material, social, and political world and not simply be about the "interiority" of the individual soul.[25] In other words, a radically reformative spirituality will be concerned with the redemptive transformation of the totality of our lived existence.

Theological reflection that attends more carefully to the transformation of women's experience has often led to new emphases in the doctrine of the Holy Spirit. For example, Elizabeth Johnson has stressed the liberating dynamic of the Spirit, who frees captives and compassionately calls creatures into life's flourishing.[26] Feminist theology in general is characterized by a retrieval of biblical metaphors that evoke traditionally feminine imagery of connecting, nurturing, embracing, and so forth. Although all feminist theologians recognize the potential of patriarchal church structures for oppression, many struggle to renew the spiritual riches of the church from within, calling all Christians toward a spiritual maturity that balances independence and vulnerability.[27] Theological reflection on the relation of the divine Spirit to the rest of creation has also led to calls for an understanding of spirituality that is linked to human participation in life on the earth. For example, Mark Wallace suggests an "ecological pneumatology" that builds on biblical metaphors like breath, wind, and living water and emphasizes the role of the Spirit

23. Leonardo Boff, *The Trinity: Perfect Communion*, trans. P. Berryman (Maryknoll, NY: Orbis, 2000), 86–87.

24. Jon Sobrino, *Spirituality of Liberation: Toward Political Holiness*, trans. Robert R. Barr (Maryknoll, NY: Orbis, 1988).

25. Owen C. Thomas, "Interiority and Christian Spirituality," *Journal of Religion* 80, no. 1 (2000): 41–60.

26. Elizabeth A. Johnson, *She Who Is: The Mystery of God in Feminist Theological Discourse* (New York: Crossroad, 2002), 124–49. Cf. Catherine Keller, "Pneumatic Nudges," in *The Future of Theology: Essays in Honor of Jürgen Moltmann*, ed. Miroslav Volf, Carmen Krieg, and Thomas Kucharz (Grand Rapids: Eerdmans, 1996), 142–53.

27. E.g., Joann Wolski Conn, "Toward Spiritual Maturity," in *Freeing Theology: The Essentials of Theology in Feminist Perspective*, ed. C. M. LaCugna (San Francisco: HarperCollins, 1993): 235–59.

as the divine healing and life-giving force of creation.[28] The contributions of these and other developments may be critically appropriated for reconstructing Pneumatology (and spirituality), but we must first clarify the challenges and opportunities that face us in this task.

The reformative appeal of Pneumatology crosses all kinds of boundaries, which suggests that the term "spirit" might serve as an integrating motif for interdisciplinary dialogue. Indeed, several scholars working at the intersection of Christian theology and natural science have recently attempted to reconstruct the idea of "spirit" in light of developments in late modern philosophy.[29] This is initially surprising, since by the mid–twentieth century the category of "spirit" had been marginalized from mainstream philosophy and science in English-speaking scholarship.[30] In popular discourse, the idea of "spirit" is sometimes reduced to vague references to that which energizes or emanates from interpersonal activity (e.g., "team spirit"). Although the sentiment "I'm spiritual but not religious" is common in contemporary culture, we would find it odd to hear someone claim, "I am a spirit." Why are so many of us comfortable with the idea of "spirituality" but allergic to the idea of "spirit"? If we hope to rehabilitate this term for use in contemporary theology, we must recognize the conceptual shifts that have altered the semantic field within which it now operates.

Early Modern Concepts of "Spirit"

The concept of "spirit" has a long pedigree in both philosophy and science; its role as a regulative concept can be traced in the work of ancient philosophers and scientists such as Epictetus and Galen and in their counterparts throughout history, such as G. F. W. Hegel and James Clerk Maxwell in the nineteenth century. As the meaning and use of the term have changed over time, however, so has its role in Christian theology. Elsewhere I have traced developments in biblical scholarship, philosophy, and science that have raised questions about the early mod-

28. M. I. Wallace, *Fragments of the Spirit* (New York: Continuum, 1996). Cf. Sigurd Bergmann, *Creation Set Free: The Spirit as Liberator of Nature*, trans. D. Stott (Grand Rapids: Eerdmans, 2005).

29. E.g., W. Mark Richardson et al., eds., *Science and the Spiritual Quest: New Essays by Leading Scientists* (London: Routledge, 2002); Denis Edwards, *The Breath of Life: A Theology of the Creator Spirit* (Maryknoll, NY: Orbis, 2004); Lindon Eaves and Lora Gross, "Exploring the Concept of Spirit as a Model for the God-World Relationship in the Age of Genetics," *Zygon* 27 (1992): 261–85.

30. The situation is different in the discussion in mainland Europe, where the semantic range of the German *Geist* and the French *l'esprit* led to a different set of conceptual issues.

ern understanding of matter, person, and force and their function in contemporary theological discourse.[31] In order to provide some background for the constructive proposals of chapters 3–5, I offer the following brief synopsis of the way in which the early modern theological use of the idea of "spirit"—both human and divine—was complicated by the dominance of three categories that shaped the philosophical and scientific conceptual framework of the seventeenth century: dualism, individualism, and mechanism.

René Descartes's *Principles of Philosophy* (1644) illustrates the hardening of the conceptual division of the world into two types of substance—"extended" things and "thinking" things. This basic ontological dualism naturally led to the placement of the human "spirit" into the latter category and left open the question how an immaterial substance (a soul) could interact with a material substance (a body). The focus on the particular individual implicit in this question was in large part due to the rising popularity of nominalist philosophy. This atomistic privileging of particulars tended to foster anthropological models in which individual souls were the basic unit of analysis; this is evident even in the political philosophy of Hobbes's *Leviathan* (1651). The prevalence of mechanical metaphors for depicting nature also had ramifications for the idea of the human "spirit." Although Isaac Newton himself tried to maintain some sense of a living principle that activates inert matter, the success of his *Principia Mathematica* (1687) quickly led to the displacement of organic and dynamic images for nature by the metaphor of a great machine. The notion that the universe can be explained by the mathematical measurement of extended substances whose future movements are determined by past efficient causes naturally led to the exclusion of questions about the "subjective" experience of spirituality from discussions of the real, "objective" world.

Under the constraints of these categories, the concept of "spirit" appeared irrelevant or nonsensical; it would come to be derisively referred to as the idea of a "ghost in the machine." Inevitably this framework registered its effect on the understanding and practice of Christian spirituality. One of the unfortunate results of a harsh dualism between the substances of the soul and the body was the way in which it contributed to an understanding of spirituality as distinct (or even escape) from embodied existence. This problem continues to be addressed in both popular and academic treatments of contemporary spirituality.[32] The concept of "spirit" was increasingly marginalized

31. For readers who are interested in the details of this history, cf. Shults, *Reforming the Doctrine of God*, part 1.

32. E.g., Rodney Clapp, *Tortured Wonders: Christian Spirituality for People, Not Angels* (Grand Rapids: Brazos, 2004); Robert McAfee Brown, *Spirituality and Liberation: Overcom-*

as the medieval definition of "person" as "an individual substance of a rational nature" (Boethius) was refigured within the atomistic categories of early modern philosophy. The experience of transforming spirituality was difficult to articulate under the constraints of the dominant focus on the individual "faculties" of the intellect and will, which were typically understood to be discrete from, and (ideally) unaffected by, the passions. This fascination with the abstract "powers" of the individual draws attention away from the importance of the contextual and communal relations that mediate spiritual experience, contributing to the individualistic focus so prominent in popular Western literature on spirituality.[33]

The rise of mechanistic conceptions of natural motion, which focused on the efficiency of past causes that determine present and future effects, also had radical implications for understanding human spirituality. How could the dynamic movement of the human spirit have any real effect on the mechanical forces of the material world? There does not seem to be any place for the human spirit to fit into such a linear chain of determined mechanical causes. Some early modern theologians forced their articulation of the dynamics of spiritual change into the same kind of deterministic scheme that explained all other changes, leading to a focus on the ordered movement of individual souls through the "states" of salvation—the so-called *ordo salutis*.[34] Frustration with the apparent failure of this conceptual framework to make sense of the qualitative experience of new life in the Spirit also influenced the rise of pietistic reactions to Protestant Scholasticism.

The harsh dualism between material and immaterial substance, the rise of the individualistic ideal of autonomous subjectivity, and the use of mechanical metaphors for understanding movement in the world also created problems for the formulation of Christian Pneumatology.

---

ing the Great Fallacy (Philadelphia: Westminster, 1988). Brown uses the phrase the "Great Fallacy" to refer to the hardening of various dualisms, such as inner/outer, theory/practice, spiritual/material, etc., which contributed to the isolation of the experience of spirituality from embodied life in community.

33. E.g., Dallas Willard rather uncritically depends on the categories of early modern faculty psychology (and substance metaphysics) as he emphasizes the transformation of the individual's mind and will; cf. *The Divine Conspiracy*, 80–82. He recognizes that spirituality also has a social dimension, but his focus on the habits of the individual heart lead him to claim that "the kingdom of God is not essentially a social or political reality at all" (p. 25). In his *Renovation of the Heart: Putting On the Character of Christ* (Colorado Springs: NavPress, 2002), 15, Willard insists that "social arrangements" are not a "fundamental part" of the means to spiritual transformation, which primarily have to do with the character of the "deepest layers" of the soul.

34. For a reformulation of this soteriological theme as the "salutary ordering" of the community of God, Shults and Sandage, *The Faces of Forgiveness*, ch. 4.

The anthropological enigma of the interaction of an immaterial soul and a material body had its parallel in the doctrine of God; how could an unextended, immaterial divine Spirit have an effect on an extended, material cosmos? This conundrum led some thinkers toward materialism (for Thomas Hobbes everything is material, including the Creator) and others toward idealism (for George Berkeley everything is immaterial, including creation). Accepting the presuppositions of substance metaphysics also seemed to force a decision between one of two logical conclusions: either God and the world are two separate substances (dualism) or they are one substance (monism or pantheism). The former option maintained the transcendence of the Spirit but made it difficult to explain divine immanence. The latter option, on the other hand, upheld the immanence of God in the world but risked the conflation of divine Spirit and human spirit.

The early modern individualistic concept of "person" also affected Pneumatology. Theologians who began with the idea that God is "a" person were tempted to speak of the Spirit merely as the "will" of God (and the Son as the "intellect" of God). This anthropological projection of faculty psychology onto the divine made it more difficult to maintain the early patristic insistence that God is three persons in one essence, and easier to slide into an understanding of the Logos and the Spirit as powers (or faculties) of God as a single subject. The articulation of the doctrine of the Holy Spirit was further complicated by the reliance on the idea of God as first efficient cause of all motion in the created world. These categories eventually led to the metaphor of God as a Watchmaker, designing and winding up the mechanical clockwork of the cosmos. This way of thinking about God tempted many philosophers toward deism (God is Spirit but irrelevant) and eventually contributed to the emergence of modern a-theism (an absolute intelligent causal substance does not exist).

The need to rely on these categories for articulating the concept of "spirit" has been undermined by several developments in late modern philosophy and science. In contemporary natural science, "matter" itself is no longer about "substances" but is understood as inextricably wrapped up dynamically within the concept of "energy" ($E = mc^2$). In contemporary social science, the study of human persons is no longer limited to analysis of autonomous individuals and the function of their faculties but is grounded in a broader understanding of the concrete embodied social relations that mediate personality. The philosophical turn to "Futurity," which may be traced in a variety of philosophical movements (from pragmatism to existentialism) also opens up a new way of thinking about spirit in relation to the human experience of openness to the future, which structures what we call the arrow of time.[35] Natural scientists no longer explain motion primarily in mechanical terms (bodies bumping into each other deterministically) but in terms of fields of force within which new systems of organized complexity emerge. We will return to some of these insights in chapters 3–5 as we explore the conceptual space within which a discussion of the idea of "spirit" may now occur in contemporary culture.

Biblical scholarship has also helped to unleash theological reflection on the concept of "spirit" from the hermeneutical framework of early modern anthropology and cosmology. As we will see, the witness of the biblical tradition to the experience of the Spirit of God does not require us to rely on early modern dualistic, individualistic, or mechanistic categories. In the Hebrew Bible, the divine Spirit is not described as one type of substance, that is, one part of the whole cosmos defined by its difference from matter. The inescapable presence of the Spirit of God qualifies all of creation as the basis and condition for life (cf. Gen. 1:2; Pss. 104:29 30; 139:7). The "personality" of God in the New Testament is not depicted in terms of the autonomous self-sufficiency of a divine individual but in terms of the loving relations among the Father, Son, and Holy Spirit. Finally, the Spirit of the biblical God is not described in mechanical terms as a first efficient cause but as a promising presence that calls creatures into being and toward fellowship in the arriving reign of divine peace.

Allowing the presentation of Pneumatology in our contemporary context to be constrained by early modern categories makes it difficult to make sense of the Christian experience of spiritual transformation. This may partially explain the bifurcation between doctrine and spirituality in streams of the Christian tradition that continue to rely on seventeenth-century theological formulations. The best way to conserve the intuitions of the biblical tradition about the concept of "spirit" is to liberate them for transforming dialogue in our own cultural location. As we participate in this ongoing task, we remain committed to upholding the distinction between finite creaturely spirit and infinite Creator Spirit, to integrating the trinitarian relations within our understanding of the Spirit, and to accounting for the eschatological dimension of redemptive experience—being called toward a share in the eternal life of God.

___

35. Physicists such as John Wheeler have argued that the whole universe participates in each quantum effect in real time, which challenges the coherence of the early modern understanding of the concept of a first cause (supported by classical mechanics); see John Archibald Wheeler, with Kenneth William Ford, *Geons, Black Holes, and Quantum Foam* (New York: W. W. Norton, 1998). For a more detailed treatment of these late modern scientific and philosophical developments, cf. Shults, *Reforming the Doctrine of God*, ch. 3.

Traditional Resources for Reconstruction

An essential aspect of this reconstructive project is the appropriating of resources in the Christian tradition that do not rely primarily on the concepts of "immaterial substance," "single subject," and "first cause" for articulating the doctrine of the Holy Spirit. We are aided in this process by three late modern trajectories in Christian theology: the retrieval of divine Infinity, the revival of trinitarian doctrine, and the renewal of eschatological ontology.[36] My interest here and in the remainder of part 1 is in recovering and refiguring the voices of authors who struggled to integrate their experience of spiritual desire immediately into their writings. If our goal is a *reformative* Pneumatology, it makes sense to attend to the testimony of those who have dedicated their lives to understanding and experiencing spiritual transformation.

Many early Christian theologians struggled against the dominant dualism of Greek philosophy, insisting that the "distinction" between the infinite Creator and finite creatures is not like creaturely distinctions between types of substances, which were defined by their boundaries, that is, their being limited in relation to other substances. As the fourth-century Cappadocian theologian Gregory of Nyssa observed: "If the Divine is perceived as bounded by something, one must by all means consider along with that boundary what is beyond it. . . . God, if he is conceived as bounded, would necessarily be surrounded by something different in nature."[37]

If we try to define the Infinite by marking off its limits from other "things"—even the totality of the finite—then it is limited and so not truly Infinite. God is not finite, but this "definition" must be qualified. God cannot be "de-fined" even by the boundary between Creator and creature, for God is not simply on one side of this "difference" but the absolute ground of the difference itself. In his eighth-century summary exposition of the orthodox faith, John of Damascus insisted that God "does not belong to the class of existing things. . . . [God is] above all existing things, nay even above existence itself."[38] God is not one kind of substance (immaterial) over against other (material) substances. This insight leads to an awareness of a distinctive distinction, an infinite

---

36. I outlined these trajectories briefly in Shults and Sandage, *The Faces of Forgiveness*, ch. 4, and illustrated them in more detail in Shults, *Reforming the Doctrine of God*, part 2.

37. Gregory of Nyssa, *The Life of Moses* (New York: Paulist, 1978), 115–16. The distinction between the divine essence and the divine energies in the East was explicitly developed in order to uphold the criterion of true divine Infinity; human creatures may participate in the energies of God without grasping the divine essence.

38. John of Damascus, *Exposition of the Orthodox Faith* (*NPNF²* 9:4).

qualitative difference between Creator and creature—and so also between Holy Spirit and human spirit.

The importance of divine Infinity continued to be stressed by medieval and Reformation spiritual writers. For example, the twelfth-century German mystic Hildegard of Bingen emphasized (in Book III of her *Scivias*) that human knowing cannot comprehend God in the way it comprehends finite, bounded things. She insisted that neither in the heights of heaven nor in the depths of the abyss may any boundary to the power and glory of God be found. She did not mean that we have no knowledge of God but that we should humbly acknowledge that our finite knowing is inherently limited in relation to the infinite presence of God, who "encircles" and "enkindles" all things.[39] John Calvin also emphasized the inherent limits of human reason and its inability to define the Infinity of God. This is implied by the biblical claim that we "live and move and have our being" in God (Acts 17:28), which is the first verse quoted by Calvin in his 1559 *Institutes*. He alludes to this passage several times in the first four chapters, insisting that we cannot transcend our being, which "is nothing but subsistence" in God (*Institutes* I.1.1). This means we can not conceptually draw a line around the Creator or even mark off the boundary between God and the world—for this boundary constitutes our creatureliness. Instead of starting with the concept of a particular type of substance, this trajectory provides us with a new opportunity to retrieve and refigure an understanding of the divine Spirit that begins (with Calvin and others) with an idea of God as the all-embracing, life-giving presence *in* whom we live and move and have our being.

Resources for reconstructing our understanding of the Holy Spirit may also be found by listening to the voices of robustly trinitarian theologians throughout the Christian tradition. Insofar as mystical theology is developed out of the experience of being transformed by the Spirit of Christ, who reconciles us to the Father, it is not surprising that trinitarian categories would serve a central function in articulating the relation between human spirit and Holy Spirit. Richard of St. Victor stands out among medieval Western theologians for his emphasis on the dynamic relations among the persons of the Trinity. He argued that because God is the ultimate Good and Goodness is inherently oriented toward sharing itself in communion, there must be eternal communion in the life of God. Richard's interest in fostering spiritual transformation is the explicit context for his trinitarian discussion.[40] The importance of the

---

39. Hildegard of Bingen, *Scivias*, ed. and trans. Columba Hart and Jane Bishop (New York: Paulist, 1990), 316–17. The title, which is short for *Scito vias Domini*, means "Know the ways of the Lord."

40. Richard of St. Victor, *The Twelve Patriarchs; The Mystical Ark; Book Three of The Trinity*, trans. and intro. Grover A. Zinn; pref. by Jean Châtillon (New York: Paulist, 1979).

Trinity among spiritual writers is also illustrated in Julian of Norwich, an English theologian writing at the turn of the fifteenth century. In her *Showings* she often refers to the material significance of a trinitarian understanding of God for spiritual experience: "The Trinity filled my heart full of the greatest joy. . . . For the Trinity is God, God is the Trinity. . . . The Trinity is our endless joy and our bliss, by our Lord Jesus Christ and in our Lord Jesus Christ."[41]

Trinitarian dialogue across traditions has resulted in a richer discussion in the literature and practice of spirituality. The idea of *theōsis*, which has often appeared problematic to the West, becomes less worrisome if we think of spirituality not as becoming part of a divine "substance" but as entering into the dynamic life of the trinitarian God. As the fourteenth-century theologian Gregory Palamas made clear, reflection on "deification" is not an abstract academic endeavor but "participating in the inseparable life of the Spirit . . . who by nature deifies from all eternity."[42] The Palamite's use of the metaphor of participation has increasingly shaped discussions of spirituality as the limitations of the Augustinian and Thomistic emphasis on the metaphor of vision have become evident. We can "see" something or someone without true intimacy.[43] Redemptive transformation involves sharing in the life of the trinitarian God. Michael Downey summarizes the growing consensus when he asserts that "all Christian spirituality is Trinitarian—a way of perceiving and being by which we are conformed to the person of Christ, brought into communion with God, other persons, and every living creature by the creative and bonding presence of the Holy Spirit, Love's Gift/ing."[44]

The renewal of eschatological ontology is the third trajectory that can help us articulate a reforming Pneumatology. Here we are dealing with what is sometimes called divine Futurity—the intuition that creaturely being (as becoming) is granted by the gracious presence of the Spirit, who calls the world into existence and toward a share in the eternal life of the infinite trinitarian God. This idea is perhaps the hardest for many Western readers to understand, in part due to the linear conception of

41. Julian of Norwich, *Showings*, ed. E. Colledge and J. Walsh (New York: Paulist, 1978), 181. Her famous refrain that "all will be well and every kind of thing will be well" is interpreted in explicitly trinitarian terms in chapter 31 of the Long Text (p. 229).

42. Gregory Palamas, *The Triads*, ed. and trans. John Meyendorff (New York: Paulist, 1983), 71.

43. "Seeing" the other is important and even transforming, but this metaphor does not go far enough. The language of "participating" suggests a deeper redemptive intimacy that can help protect against settling for visual delight (at best) or spiritual voyeurism (at worst).

44. Michael Downey, *Altogether Gift: A Trinitarian Spirituality* (Maryknoll, NY: Orbis, 2000), 132.

time and causation that has so deeply saturated our consciousness and colonized our interpretation of experience.[45]

For our current purposes, the main point is the way in which so many mystical theologians refuse to think of the temporal experience of desire for God as ending the way a linear cause-and-effect sequence comes to an end. The seventh-century theologian John Climacus argued that if love never fails (1 Cor. 13:8), "then love has no boundary, and both in the present and in the future age we will never cease to progress in it." In his discussion of the final "step" on the ladder of divine ascent, he notes that love "is an abyss of illumination, a fountain of fire, bubbling up to inflame the thirsty soul. It is the condition of angels, and the *progress of eternity*."[46] In his influential *Ladder of Divine Ascent*, the twelfth-century theologian Bernard of Clairvaux observed that the psalmist desires to "always seek" the face of God (Ps. 105:4). Bernard noted that "even when it has found him [God] the soul will not cease to seek him. God is sought not on foot but by desire. And the happy discovery of what is desired does not end desire but extends it. The consummation of joy does not consume desire, does it? . . . There will be no end to desire, and so no end of seeking."[47]

Many Western Christians are not aware of the prevalence of this emphasis on eschatological ontology in the tradition, especially among writers for whom spirituality and theology were essentially integrated. For the seventh-century theologian Maximus Confessor, creaturely participation in God involves our being "delighted and ever insatiably satisfied with the one who is inexhaustible." Because God is "beyond fullness" and "beyond essence," the orientation of human desire for the divine is not satiated like the desire for finite things.[48] Gregory of Nyssa had also made explicit the link between (what we are here calling) Futurity and divine Infinity in the experience of spiritual desire. If God is the Good and Infinite, then it follows that "since this good has no limit, the participant's desire itself necessarily has no stopping place but stretches out with the limitless."[49] For a more recent example, we can also point

45. The most common misunderstanding of the idea of divine Futurity is to take it to mean that God is "in" the future or simply is "the future" defined in contrast to the other modes of time. For a discussion of "absolute" Futurity and its implicit connection to Infinity and Trinity, cf. Shults, *Reforming the Doctrine of God*, chs. 7–10.

46. John Climacus, *The Ladder of Divine Ascent* (New York: Paulist, 1982), 251, 289; emphasis added. John deconstructs his own metaphor of "ladder" and does not see the "steps" as a simply linear process.

47. Bernard of Clairvaux, Sermon 84, in *Selected Works*, trans. G. R. Evans (New York: Paulist, 1987), 274.

48. Maximus Confessor, "The Four Hundred Chapters on Love," in *Selected Writings*, ed. George C. Berthold (New York: Paulist, 1985), 67; cf. 129.

49. Gregory of Nyssa, *The Life of Moses*, 31.

to the work of the eighteenth-century Reformed theologian Jonathan Edwards. In his *Miscellanies* he speaks of an "eternal progress" in the discovery of beauty and suggests that "we shall forever increase in beauty ourselves."[50] The renewal of this emphasis can help us as we seek to articulate an understanding of the temporal experience of creaturely desire as constituted by the promising presence of the Creator Spirit, who graciously opens time into Eternity.

All three of these intuitions about Infinity, Trinity, and Futurity are evident in the works of Pseudo-Dionysius, which have registered a profound impact on both Eastern and Western spiritual writers.[51] He spoke of God as the insurpassible Infinity "beyond being" in and toward which human desire emerges. As the ineffable source of being, God is "the boundary to all things and is the unbounded infinity about them in a fashion which rises above the contradiction between finite and infinite."[52] The *Mystical Theology* concludes with Pseudo-Dionysius's observation that although we make assertions and conceive of things that have limits, God is Infinite—beyond the constraints of Aristotelian predication theory. It is important to observe, however, that this influential text begins with the following words: "Trinity!! Higher than any being, any divinity, any goodness! Guide of Christians in the wisdom of heaven!"[53] Creaturely desire in relation to that which infinitely transcends being takes shape as a longing to share in the Logos's relation to the Father through the Spirit. When Pseudo-Dionysius did use the term "cause" of God, his interest was not in determining the first in a temporal series of efficient causes but in witnessing to the evocative presence that constitutes creaturely desire. "The irrepressible cause of all yearning has command and primacy over them and is the cause beyond them all and indeed is the goal toward which everything everywhere strives upward, each as best it can."[54] In this sense, God is the source of all things precisely as the destiny of all things.

Pseudo-Dionysius's writings are clearly shaped by the underlying assumptions of Neoplatonic cosmology and anthropology. We could (and

---

50. Jonathan Edwards, *The Philosophy of Jonathan Edwards from His Private Notebooks*, ed. Harvey G. Townsend (Westport, CT: Greenwood, 1972), no. 198, p. 195.

51. The background and setting of this author, who wrote in the fifth or sixth century under the pseudonym of Dionysius the Aeropagite, are still unclear. His works, however, shaped the writings of mystics and contemplatives throughout the Middle Ages and those of the Reformers, and they continue to capture the attention of late modern thinkers interested in retrieving the insights of the apophatic tradition.

52. Pseudo-Dionysius, "The Divine Names," in *The Complete Works*, trans. Colm Luibheid and Paul Rorem (New York: Paulist, 1987), 103. God is not susceptible to the measurements of quantity, nor is God limited or bounded by creaturely being; God is "not contained in being, but being is contained in him" (p. 101).

53. Ibid., 135.

54. Ibid., 83.

should) note how all spiritual writers and theologians have attempted to formulate their understanding of the Spirit in light of their own experience, which was mediated through and articulated within their own social locations. Recognizing the courage with which they struggled to present an illuminative and transformative understanding of the Spirit of God in dialogue within their own cultural contexts can inspire us to take up the task bequeathed to every generation: conserving the intuitions of the biblical tradition about Pneumatology and spirituality by liberating them for engagement with contemporary discourse about the human experience of becoming in the world.

Chapters 3–5 will attempt to contribute to this ongoing task of reforming Pneumatology by exploring human knowing, acting, and being "in" the Spirit in light of the recovery of Infinity, Trinity, and Futurity—with explicit attention to late modern developments in biblical scholarship, philosophy, and science. The remainder of this chapter introduces the conceptual framework that will guide our exploration.

Spirituality, Relationality, and the Intensification of Creaturely Life

We suggested in the introduction that the idea of intensification may facilitate the interdisciplinary discussion about the dynamics of transforming spirituality. This section will provide an initial outline of the dynamics of redemptive transformation in light of the semantic shifts in the concept of "spirit" after the (re)turn to relationality. We need a concept of human spirituality that accounts for the communal dynamic of mediated personal experience and that is not isolated from the body or reliant on ancient or early modern anthropology. If we begin with the significance of relationality in human life, we may have better success in articulating an understanding of spirituality that accounts for the emphasis on dynamic becoming in the biblical tradition and connects to contemporary expressions of desire.

A helpful starting point is Kierkegaard's description of the self as spirit: "A human being is spirit. But what is spirit? Spirit is the self. But what is the self? The self is a relation that relates itself to itself or is the relation's relating itself to itself in the relation; the self is not the relation but is the relation's relating itself to itself." This relation must be established by another outside the self, for the relation's relating to itself cannot establish the relation itself, from which it derives. This means that the human self (or spirit) is a "derived, established relation, a relation that relates itself to itself and in relating to itself relates itself to another."[55] Adaptation of Kierkegaard's relational understanding of the human spirit for our context will require some modification. First, as a result of the complex history of the use of the term "self" among competing schools of psychology in the twentieth century (e.g., Freud, Jung, Mead, Erickson), it seems unwise to use it as a synonym for "spirit," as Kierkegaard did. As I set out my model below, I will differentiate between the broader and holistic meaning of "spirit" and the narrower psychological use of the idea of "self" as it emerges in the formation of ego functions.

What are the *relata* in the relation in which and to which the spirit relates itself to itself as it relates itself to an other? Kierkegaard spoke of the human person as a relation or "synthesis" between the physical and the psychical; the spirit (or self) is this relation's relating itself to itself (as a "positive third"). Kierkegaard was interested both in protecting the psychosomatic unity of the person and in affirming the dependence of the finite and temporal creature on the infinite and eternal Creator, who establishes the relation itself. In our contemporary context, we can spell out these *relata* in other ways as well. For example, we may speak of the dialectical relation between the centripetal organizing capacities of a person's ego (the "I") and his or her centrifugal orientation toward the other. The human spirit is this relation's relating itself to itself as it relates itself to others. This dynamic movement that constitutes the human spirit is dialectical in the sense that both the self-organization of the "I" in relation to itself and the orientation of the "I" to others is already and always mediated by the "not I," that is, by the plurality of existentially relevant others in relation to whom the person finds himself or herself. The chapters that follow will spell this out in terms of the dialectical identity, agency, and presence of the human spirit.

Another way to explicate the dynamics of the human spirit is to begin with the relation between remembering the *past* and anticipating the *future* in the constitution of the *present* of self-consciousness. The living present of personal experience requires an extension of awareness that can move back and forth in the relation between memory and expectation. Human personhood involves the imaginative indwelling of a future into which one's past may be incorporated. We may think of the human spirit as this temporal relation's relating itself to itself as it relates to others.

How are we to understand the whence and whither of these relational dynamics; what is their ultimate source and destiny? The remaining

55. Søren Kierkegaard, *The Sickness unto Death* (Princeton, NJ: Princeton University Press, 1980), 13. Cf. Kierkegaard, *The Concept of Anxiety: A Simple Psychologically Orienting Deliberation on the Dogmatic Issue of Hereditary Sin*, ed. and trans. Reidar Thomte and Albert Anderson (Princeton, NJ: Princeton University Press, 1980), 43, 88–89.

chapters of part 1 will outline a reformative Pneumatology that argues for the illuminative power of the Christian understanding of the Spirit of the biblical God as the absolute origin, condition, and goal of the creaturely experience of temporality and the human openness to, and longing for, a lively future. A relational model of "spirit" can help us articulate a theological understanding of human spirituality vis-à-vis the Holy Spirit—the originating, upholding, and orienting presence that establishes the self-in-relation along with all of creation.

The first point to make is that, from a biblical perspective, we should recognize that in the broadest sense spirituality has to do with creaturely *life*. The psalmist recognizes that living things are dependent on the divine Spirit, or *ruakh*, for their very lives (Ps. 104:29–30). The gracious upholding of creaturely existence in relation to the divine Spirit is the condition for life. The biblical idea of creaturely spirit is not unique to humanity; Ecclesiastes 3:18–21 indicates that the Israelites considered even animals to have "spirit." All of creation is dependent on the establishing presence of the Spirit. Genesis 1:2 depicts the creative presence of the Spirit as sweeping over the waters, structuring the forms of creaturely life. In the broadest sense, then, we may think of all creation as constituted by the tending of the divine Spirit.

The process of intensification characterizes all of creation: to be a finite creature is to exist in the tensional field of space-time. There could be no life without tension, but the tensive existence of a system or organism must be balanced between its self-stabilizing tendencies and its openness to energy in relation to other creatures. If the tension is sufficiently complex and appropriately organized, we call a creature "living." The emergence of living organisms is characterized by increasing levels of complexity in the process of differentiation and self-organization. Living creatures may be destroyed by too much tension or insufficient tension, and they strive to maintain a balance as they tenaciously hold on to life. The specification of differentiated parts within an organism can lead to new capacities for the orderly distribution of energy, which in turn can enhance the organism's ability to accommodate and adapt to its environment. This reordering of its tensive relationality may allow the organism to invest its energy in new ways, opening up the possibility for increasingly complex functions. One of the tasks of Christian Pneumatology is to outline the intelligibility of the claim that these dynamics of intensification in creation are originated, upheld, and oriented by the divine Spirit.

In a narrower sense, however, we may speak of *human* spirituality—the dynamic liveliness characteristic of members of the species *Homo sapiens*. The intensity of the human experience of dependence on the Spirit's tending is unique. We do not need to speak of the spirit as one *part* of a human being; we may use the term to refer to the relational dynamics that condition the liveliness of the whole person. In *Reforming Theological Anthropology*, I outlined ways in which the (re)turn to relationality can help us articulate the doctrines of human nature, sin, and image of God in more dynamic terms. Embracing relational conceptions of human life is not a mere reaction to culture but a recovery of a holistic emphasis in biblical anthropology. Biblical authors generally used terms such as "spirit," "mind," "heart," "soul," and so forth, not as abstract, discrete faculties but as registers of the whole person in concrete relation. Even Paul's well-known distinction between living according to the "flesh" and according to the "spirit" in Romans is not an opposition "between the incorporeal or non-material and the corporeal or material, but between two ways of life."[56] The Pauline usage of the term "spirit" (for humans) typically designates the whole person oriented in a particular way (cf. 1 Cor. 5:3; 7:34; 16:18; 2 Cor. 7:1, 13; Col. 2:5; 2 Tim. 4:22). In this sense, "spirit" indicates a qualification of the whole person in all of his or her desiring.

With the emergence of *personality*, human creaturely spirituality takes on a more complex form of self-relationality, which makes the experience of life even more intense. Here we are dealing with the irreducible self-relationality that constitutes our experience as persons oriented to others in time and space. For human creatures, self-awareness emerges out of an interpersonal relational tension, within which we respond intentionally as others tend to us. We become aware that we are defined in tensional relation with others and that we cannot completely control this tension, upon which we are inescapably dependent. Our attending to one another is overshadowed by pretense as we struggle to bring the other into (or keep the other out of) the orbit of our own intentions. We fear this lack of control and desire to find equilibrium, a relational tension between self and other that is peaceful. Personal human life exists in the same tensive field of creaturely finitude upheld by the Spirit, but it experiences this field as a *self*-intensification in relation to other creatures. A person's spirituality is the form of his or her life, whether anemic or energetic, anxious or peaceful, in relation to self, others, and God. Personal spirituality has to do with the way in which our longings—our desire to know, act, and be in relation—take shape in the ongoing formation of our coming-to-be in relation.

The recovery of traditional resources that emphasize Infinity, Trinity, and Futurity helps to provide conceptual space for understanding and articulating the dynamics of the intensification of the human spirit in

56. Walter Principe, "Toward Defining Spirituality," *Sciences religieuses/Studies in Religion* 12, no. 2 (1983): 127–41, at 130.

relation to the Creator Spirit. Paul's adaptation of the idea that "we live and move and have our being" in God (Acts 17:28) suggests an understanding of the divine as an intensively *infinite* presence that graciously sustains creaturely life itself. As the human spirit gropes after God, its finite intentional desire is opened up to a gracious transformation in relation to the Infinite.[57] Divine grace originates and upholds all life in a unifying tension, calling self-conscious creatures toward an intensification that brings new life. Because we are dealing with the Spirit of the *trinitarian* God, disclosed in the life of Jesus Christ, we must also recognize the intrinsically personal relationality that characterizes life in the Spirit. The transformation of the finite through participation in the life of the Trinity is made possible by the *eschatologically* evocative presence of the Spirit, who graciously calls creatures into the "newness of life" (Rom. 6:4). The intense human search for *koinōnia* is constituted by the gracious arrival of its goal—the presence of the eternal Spirit, who opens up time and space for redemptive fellowship in the relationality of divine life.

This way of conceptualizing intensification can also help us begin to overcome some of the problems that arise in Christian doctrine as a result of a hard dichotomy between nature and grace. The gracious transformation that characterizes the Christian experience of redemptive spirituality is a qualitative intensification of the relationality that orders the very nature of the human spirit; this natural relationality, however, is already and always conditioned by the gracious presence of the divine Spirit. Defining nature and grace within the constraints of substance metaphysics too easily leads to the opposing dangers of simplistically dividing or completely fusing them. But we can avoid these extremes by thinking of divine grace as the intensively infinite presence of the trinitarian God, whose eternally shared life is the all-embracing origin, condition, and goal of natural human longing. All things are from, through, and to God (Rom. 11:36) and in this sense "in" the dynamic presence of God. The intensification of natural creaturely life manifested in the complex relationality of human persons, however, is graciously constituted by the invitation to live intentionally in intimate relational union with the trinitarian God. We will spell this out below in terms of knowing, acting, and being in the Spirit.

Rather than tie the Christian articulation of the concept of "human spirit" to the idea of an individual rational substance, we may attempt to refigure our understanding of spirituality in relation to our dynamic

57. David Tracy (*The Analogical Imagination* [New York: Crossroad, 1991], 125) speaks of intensification as a "journey into particularity in all its finitude and all its striving for the infinite."

experience of embodied social life. If human personhood is formed within the centripetal and centrifugal dynamics that shape the relation between the self and the other and we define the human spirit as the relation's relating itself to itself in the relation, then we may think of spirituality as the way in which we live and move (and "breathe") in the world. In other words, spirituality has to do with the liveliness with which the human spirit relates itself to itself in the relation between the remembered past and the anticipated future. We say a person is "high spirited" if he or she is active, full of energy, and bounding into the future. If a person has been knocked down and seems to be unable to find the strength to go on, we say his or her "spirit is broken." In this sense, *personal* "spirituality" has to do with the dynamic movement of one's whole life as a person in relation.[58]

The more popular use of the term "spirituality" typically refers to the *religious* dimension of human life—the way in which a person explicitly thematizes the form of his or her life in relation to the sacred or ultimate reality. Christians thematize this relation in light of the redemptive experience of being graciously called into the form of life manifested in Jesus Christ. *Christian* spirituality therefore has to do with the transformation of the life of human persons through spiritual union with God in Christ. This ongoing intensification of intimacy takes shape as an entry into Jesus' way of *relating* to the One he called Father, wholly relying on the promising presence of the life-giving Spirit as he tended to his neighbors.

Most of my focus throughout part 1 will be on this Christian experience of the intensification of religious spirituality.[59] The purpose of this section has been to provide a broader understanding of the concept of "spirituality" that can account both for our holistic experience of embodied social life and for our longing for a gracious intensification of life "in" the Spirit. This way of modeling spiritual transformation is intended to shift attention away from the question, "What stage am I in (in distinction from you)?" and promote the ongoing query: "How am I tending to my experience of the crucible of intensification (in communion with you)?" Any presentation of a Christian theology of spirituality is embedded within a broader set of theological concerns;

58. Theology and social science may often be interested in the same phenomena—the dynamics of human life—but they attend to them differently. What a theologian means by spirituality is not *identical* to what a psychologist means by self-consciousness. Theological explication is not reducible to the categories of social science, but the latter may be helpful in *identifying* the nature and structure of personal reality. Theology tends to the ways in which such creaturely phenomena are related to the Creator (*sub ratione Dei*).

59. In part 2 Steve will show in more detail how psychology illuminates the ways in which religious spirituality is influenced by embodied and social dimensions of human life.

before exploring the dynamics of becoming wise, just, and free in the Spirit, it will be helpful to make explicit the matrix that is guiding this organization of the themes.

Desiring Truth, Goodness, and Beauty

My task is to present the Gospel of the Spirit of God, who redemptively transforms creaturely life, in a way that is faithful to the intuitions of the biblical tradition and engages contemporary culture. I will explore the dynamics of spiritual intensification by attending to the human desire for truth, goodness, and beauty. Late modern discourse exhibits both a fascination with these desires and a suspicion of early modern attempts to nail down these "transcendental" concepts. Here my interest is not in discussing how we can determine the intelligibility of particular objects, identify which particular actions will mark the good life, or discern which particular experiences evoke the greatest feelings of pleasure. My concern is with the underlying longings to know and be known, to love and be loved, to belong-to and be longed-for, that characterize the structural dynamics of human spirituality.

The interrelated human desires for truth, goodness, and beauty have served as a matrix for thematic organization in several of my other writings. This section summarizes some of the relevant treatments of these issues in other places in order to provide a context for understanding the proposals of the remainder of part 1, which spell out the Pneumatological themes in more detail and link them explicitly to the dynamics of spiritual transformation. It is important to emphasize, however, that this distinction between the longings for the True, the Good, and the Beautiful is simply for the sake of analysis and is not meant to imply that these desires can be compartmentalized. The separation of the search for the True and the search for the Good in early modernity is in part responsible for the bifurcation between theology ("truth") and spirituality ("goodness"). This split had already begun to emerge in the Middle Ages, as evinced in the work of fourteenth-century theologian Jean Gerson, but by the seventeenth century it has become commonplace to assume that only a few are called to the "spiritual" life, which has to do with the "inner" life.[60] My argument for a *reforming* Pneumatology insists that the *conceptual* space in which we search for truth ought not to be abstracted from the *practical* space in which we pursue goodness and the liturgical space in which we adore the beautiful. For this reason, I will often

60. Cf. Michael Downey, *Understanding Christian Spirituality* (New York: Paulist, 1997), 60–62.

point to the interpenetration of these desires, and this integration will be made even more explicit in the case studies of part 3.

It makes sense, however, to distinguish between the desires for truth, goodness, and beauty in order to help us reflect on the general ways in which people search for God. Although each spiritual journey is unique, we may still observe broad tendencies amidst the diversity. The way in which we find ourselves attracted to God will shape our journeys of spiritual transformation. Some of us are prone to search for God by our orientation toward truth; others, toward goodness; still others, toward beauty. I have become increasingly convinced that an integrated spirituality requires pursuing all three, and this is why being in community (with others who desire differently) plays such an important role in the transformation of our longing to know, act, and be in redemptive relation to the Spirit of God. This methodological differentiation will also help us to link Pneumatological themes both to our natural (created) desires as human beings and to the concerns of the three general areas of philosophical inquiry: epistemology, ethics, and metaphysics.[61]

Table 1. A Matrix of Theological Inquiry

Desiring Truth	Desiring Goodness	Desiring Beauty
Human Knowing and Personal Identity	Human Acting and the Doctrine of Sin	Human Being and the Image of God
Epistemic Anxiety	Ethical Anxiety	Ontological Anxiety
Omniscient Faithfulness	Omnipotent Love	Omnipresent Hope

The second row in table 1 represents the reconstructive chapters (8–10) of *Reforming Theological Anthropology*, which dealt with the classical themes of anthropology within this conceptual framework. I explored the challenges and opportunities provided by the philosophical turn to relationality for articulating the traditional loci of personal identity, sin, and image of God within the broader context of a theology of human knowing, acting, and being.

In *The Faces of Forgiveness* I examined ways in which the experience of forgiveness (as sharing in divine grace) is inhibited by our fear, the epistemic, ethical, and ontological anxiety (cf. table 1, third row) which may be overcome through the Christian experience of faith, love, and hope. Chapters 8–10 of *Reforming the Doctrine of God* articulated several traditional attributes of God in light of this matrix of themes, proposing that we speak of the knowing, acting, and being of the biblical God as

---

61. One might expect "aesthetics" here in place of "metaphysics" as the correlate to the desire for beauty. In chapter 5 I explore the link between aesthetics and metaphysics by attending to the human longing for being-in-relation, the desire to belong within a harmonious, peaceful whole, without losing one's particularity.

the origin, condition, and goal of human noetic, moral, and aesthetic desire.

Table 2. Overview of Chapters 3 through 5

Becoming Wise (ch. 3)	Becoming Just (ch. 4)	Becoming Free (ch. 5)
Knowing in the Spirit	Acting in the Spirit	Being in the Spirit
Sharing in the Knowledge of Jesus Christ	Sharing in the Suffering of Jesus Christ	Sharing in the Glory of Jesus Christ
Intensification of Faith	Intensification of Love	Intensification of Hope
Transforming Prayer	Transforming Service	Transforming Hospitality

The remaining chapters of part 1 outline a programmatic proposal for articulating the dynamics of the transformation of the human spirit as becoming wise, just, and free through the intensification of life in the Spirit (cf. table 2). The emphasis on *becoming*, on the process of the converting dynamics of life in the Spirit, pervades the New Testament.[62] If we focus too exclusively on the product of transformation, we miss the dynamic process—the asking and knocking, seeking and finding that *are* transforming life. In addition to the sense in which those who are in the Spirit *have been* saved, the biblical authors also emphasize the *present* experience and ongoing *anticipation* of this gracious experience of becoming in the Spirit. In the letters to the Corinthians, Paul speaks of those who "are being saved" (1 Cor. 1:18; cf. 2:6–7; Acts 2:47). The switch from past to present tense in 1 Corinthians 15:1–2 makes this even more explicit; you "received" the good news but now "you are being saved." In the second letter he explains that believers "are being transformed" (2 Cor. 3:18; cf. 2:15) and that their nature "is being renewed day by day" (4:16–18). The Philippians are urged to press on, straining forward with Paul who is "becoming like" (*symmorphizomenos*) Christ (Phil. 3:10). The Ephesians are encouraged to continue being filled (*plērousthe*) with the Spirit (Eph. 5:18). The Petrine Epistles also emphasize that believers are called to "grow into salvation" (1 Pet. 2:2); readers are urged to "grow in the grace and knowledge" of God (2 Pet. 3:14–18). Spiritual transformation involves growing "up in every way . . . into Christ" (Eph. 4:11–16; cf. Col. 1:28; 4:12; Heb. 5:11–14; James 1:2–4).

The first three subsections of each chapter treat their themes in light of the four desiderata of theological presentation: accounting for the testimony of the biblical witness, critically appropriating the tradition, engaging the relevant philosophical issues, and illuminating human experience. These sources of theology overlap and interpenetrate each

62. Cf. Richard Peace, *Conversion in the New Testament: Paul and the Twelve* (Grand Rapids: Eerdmans, 1999).

other. For example, our location in a particular tradition will shape which philosophical issues we find most significant. Similarly, our reading of Scripture will be influenced by the totality of our life experience. Accounting for the biblical witness to the experience of knowing, acting, and being in the Spirit may be facilitated as we recover resources from other streams of the Christian tradition.

The last four (reconstructive) subsections of these chapters (represented by the four rows of table 2) will also deal with the themes of knowing, acting, and being but with special attention to the transformative dynamics of intensification in the Spirit of Christ. In *The Faces of Forgiveness* I described the dynamics of salvation in terms of finding personal identity in Christ, dying to sin with Christ, and being conformed to the image of Christ. In the following chapters, I will explore what it means to share in the *spirituality* of Jesus. Through the resurrection he became a "life-giving spirit" (1 Cor. 15:45), and so his life is more than a model—Christian spirituality is constituted by *sharing* in this gift of new life that comes through Christ and in the Spirit.

The dynamics of spiritual transformation will be described in terms of a Christian understanding of the intensification of faith, love, and hope—the three that "abide" (1 Cor. 13:13).[63] Finally, each chapter will examine some of the specific implications for practicing wisdom, justice, and freedom. In concrete terms, this means life shaped by transforming prayer, ministry, and hospitality. In this way we share in God's gracious fulfillment of the human longing to know and be known, to love and be loved, to belong-to and be longed-for in peaceful community. Our focus will be less on the *extensive* stages through which the individual soul is led, and more on the *intensive* dynamics by which embodied and socially embedded human spirituality is transformed. The basic question is not "What stage am I in?" but "How am I experiencing the crucible of intensification in relation to you?"

My purpose in this context is not to provide an exhaustive exploration of all of these dynamics or an overview of the history of spirituality. The more modest goal is to show how new insights emerge as we explore the issues of spiritual transformation in light of the human spirit's desire for truth, goodness, and beauty, making explicit connections to other doctrinal themes. In this sense, my part of the project is programmatic, marking off the conceptual space (and time) within which further reflection can occur. Throughout this brief exposition, we will remind ourselves that this conceptual exploration cannot be isolated but emerges out of, and is oriented toward, the practical and liturgical space (and time) of

63. The order in which I treat these three themes follows the more common ordering in the New Testament; cf. Col. 1:4–5; 1 Thess. 1:2–3; 5:8.

Christian existence. These reconstructive efforts may also facilitate an interreligious dialogue that is itself transformative, a truly *reforming* Pneumatology. Our task now is to outline these dynamics in relation to human knowing, acting, and being, illustrating how the intensification of faith, love, and hope in the Spirit of God takes shape as we become wise, just, and free in community.

3

BECOMING
WISE

We turn now to an exploration of the redemptive dynamics of spiritual transformation in relation to the human desire to *know and be known* in faithful intimacy. The Gospel is an invitation into an intensification of this longing through the experience of life in the Spirit of truth as we share in the knowledge of Jesus Christ, who "became for us wisdom from God" (1 Cor. 1:30). Our participation in the eternal intimacy that is the life of the trinitarian God is transformed as we become wise, faithfully tending to our relations to others in community. This transformation is wholly dependent on the gracious gift of the "spirit of wisdom," in and through whom we come to know and be known by God (Eph. 1:17). This chapter portrays Christian spirituality as a life of transforming prayer that participates in the creative wisdom of God.

The human spirit longs to understand its relation to the sacred, to interpret the ultimate meaning of its identity in relation to that which is beyond its comprehension. In part 2 Steve will explore psychological theory and research that has shown the relation of wisdom to spirituality. Wisdom has to do with the desire for truth, but this quest is for more than simply a quantitative increase in objective intellectual content or even increased functional competence in the utilization of knowledge. The longing for wisdom ultimately has to do with the quality of our concrete relations in lived community. If we merely stress the importance of the individual's cognitive assent to propositions, we can easily fall into a limited definition of spiritual maturity that is correlated to how much a person knows "about" God. This can obscure the much more intimate understanding of wisdom in Scripture and the Christian tradition, which emphasizes the intimacy of knowing and being known by God *in* the Spirit.

My goal in this chapter is to outline a theological framework for discussing spirituality in relation to the longing of the human spirit for wisdom. A theological mapping of the conceptual terrain can help us conserve the intuitions of the biblical tradition by liberating them for dialogue within late modern culture. This task can be facilitated by engaging contemporary developments in philosophy and science that offer insights into the dynamics of the knowing of the human spirit and by recovering resources from the spiritual writings of Christian theologians over the centuries. We begin, however, by pointing to the significance of the desire for wisdom in the Hebrew Bible and the New Testament.

The Longing for Wisdom in Scripture

The easiest place to illustrate the Israelites' longing for wisdom is—not surprisingly—the wisdom literature of the Hebrew Bible. The book of Proverbs encourages its reader to attend to divine wisdom: incline your heart toward wisdom, cry out for wisdom, seek and you will find (Prov. 2:2–5). The fulfillment of this desire is dependent on the initiative of divine grace: "For the LORD gives wisdom; from his mouth come knowledge and understanding" (2:6). The invitation to enter into intimate relation with divine wisdom (which is personified as a feminine figure), however, assumes the need for a real response and passionate pursuit by the human spirit. "Get wisdom; get insight. . . . Do not forsake her, and she will keep you; love her, and she will guard you. The beginning of wisdom is this: Get wisdom, and whatever else you get, get insight" (4:5–7; cf. 16:16, 22). Wisdom calls out, "Take my instruction instead of silver, and knowledge rather than choice gold." Solomon urges his readers to pursue wisdom above all else, for "all that you may desire cannot compare with her" (8:10–11).

Why is coming into relation with divine wisdom so desirable? She is depicted as a "master worker" alongside God, delightfully forming and faithfully informing the dynamic structures of the cosmos.

> I was daily his delight,
>> rejoicing before him always,
> rejoicing in his inhabited world
>> and delighting in the human race.
> "And now, my children, listen to me:
>> happy are those who keep my ways.
> Hear instruction and be wise,
>> and do not neglect it." (Prov. 8:30–33)

Wisdom is here linked both to divine creativity and to divine providence. Coming into intimate communion with her—attending to her ways—means joyfully coming into right relation with God.

The other books in the wisdom literature also exhort the Israelites to search for wisdom and depict the intimacy of knowing and being known by God. The psalmist expresses this longing, recognizing that intimate knowledge of God is the true goal of this search: "You desire truth in the inward being; therefore teach me wisdom in my secret heart" (Ps. 51:6). The dialogues between Job and his "friends" are saturated by this desire. "Where shall wisdom be found?" asks Job (28:12). "Where then does wisdom come from? . . . It is hidden from the eyes of all living" (28:20–21). Job recognizes that only "God understands the way to it, and he knows its place" (28:23). Job is also aware, however, that human pursuit of wisdom involves moving into right relation to God. "Truly, the fear of the Lord, that is wisdom; and to depart from evil is understanding" (28:28; cf. 12:12–13). God finally answers Job and his friends in the form of several questions: "Who has put wisdom in the inward parts, or given understanding to the mind? Who has the wisdom to number the clouds?" (38:36–37). Job discovers he is utterly dependent on God for understanding and wisdom. Despite the despair that characterizes much of the book of Ecclesiastes, there is nevertheless a recognition that "wisdom gives life to the one who possesses it" and that "wisdom makes one's face shine" (Eccles. 7:12; 8:1).

The desire for wisdom could also be traced throughout the other genres of the Hebrew Bible.[1] In the second creation story in Genesis, the fruit of the forbidden tree is tempting to Eve precisely because it "was to be desired to make one wise" (Gen. 3:6). One of the major theological points of this story is that true wisdom comes only through intimacy with God and the attempts to secure wisdom outside this fellowship are doomed to failure. The historical books also recognize that human knowledge is dependent on the Spirit of wisdom. Joshua is able to lead

---

1. For an overview, cf. Anthony R. Ceresko, *Introduction to Old Testament Wisdom: A Spirituality for Liberation* (Maryknoll, NY: Orbis, 1999).

the people wisely because he was "full of the spirit of wisdom" (Deut. 34:9). The wisdom evident in Ezra's efforts to organize the people of Israel is "God-given" (Ezra 7:25). The prophets also depend on divine wisdom, as Belshazzar comes to understand through his encounter with Daniel (Dan. 5:11). Isaiah announces that the ultimate leader of the people of God will depend on the Spirit of the Lord, which "shall rest on him, the spirit of wisdom and understanding, the spirit of counsel and might, the spirit of knowledge and the fear of the LORD" (Isa. 11:2). Jeremiah warns those who trust in their own wisdom, insisting that it is the presence of divine wisdom that establishes true order (Jer. 9:23–10:12).

The personification of divine wisdom as a feminine figure also occurs in the apocryphal literature, but here it is more explicitly linked to the idea of Spirit. Wisdom is a "kindly spirit," and because the Spirit of the Lord "has filled the world, and that which holds all things together knows what is said," nothing escapes divine knowledge (Wis. 1:6–7). Divine wisdom is linked not only to God's intimate knowledge of the inmost feelings of the human heart but also to God's upholding and renewing the whole cosmos.

> For wisdom is more mobile than any motion;
>   because of her pureness she pervades and penetrates all things.
> For she is a breath [*ruakh*] of the power of God,
>   and a pure emanation of the glory of the Almighty. . . .
> Although she is but one, she can do all things,
>   and while remaining in herself, she renews all things. (Wis. 7:24–27)

The cosmological scope and eschatological power of the creaturely experience of divine wisdom are maintained in the New Testament but refigured in trinitarian terms in light of the outpouring of the Spirit at Pentecost after the resurrection of Jesus Christ. The apostle Paul worships the "only wise God" (Rom. 16:27), but the mediation of divine wisdom is explicitly understood as "through" Jesus Christ and "in" the Holy Spirit (cf. Rom. 7:6; 8:9–11; 2 Cor. 3:4–6). The christological hymn of Colossians 1:15–20 explicitly applies the Hebraic understanding of divine wisdom to the risen Christ:

> He is the image of the invisible God, the firstborn of all creation; for in him all things in heaven and on earth were created, things visible and invisible, whether thrones or dominions or rulers or powers—all things have been created through him and for him. He himself is before all things, and in him all things hold together. . . . For in him all the fullness of God was pleased to dwell.

Here is the New Testament answer to Job's question: it is in Jesus Christ that the wisdom of God is to be found.[2] The experience that "the truth is in Jesus" (Eph. 4:21) binds believers together as they learn to live wisely in community. At the same time, becoming wise cannot be separated from the Spirit, whose intimate presence is manifested in the human experience of wisdom (1 Cor. 12:8; cf. Luke 1:17; Acts 6:3, 10). The New Testament interprets divine wisdom in relation both to Jesus Christ, who "became for us wisdom from God" (1 Cor. 1:30), and to the Spirit of wisdom, who rested upon him and who is now given to believers: "I pray that the God of our Lord Jesus Christ, the Father of glory, may give you a spirit of wisdom and revelation as you come to know him" (Eph. 1:17).

The biblical longing for wisdom is linked to the desire for truth, but for the Israelites, "truth" (*emet*) is not primarily about abstract assertions but about concrete relations of "faithfulness" (*emunah*). Wise persons are identified not simply by the propositional content of their intellects but by the way in which they bind themselves in fiduciary relations within community. Whether the truth is "in" a person (e.g., Gen. 42:16) is judged by his or her trustworthiness and fidelity. "True" persons are identified by the way they manifest faithfulness, the way in which they identify with others. In the New Testament as well, truth is not merely about assertions but about unveiling (*alētheia*), a dynamic disclosure that invites into relation. We become wise as we come into a transforming relation with divine wisdom, in which we are invited to share in the intimacy of the dynamic knowing and being known that is the life of the infinitely faithful trinitarian God.

The Johannine literature is particularly rich in its expression of the human desire for truth and of its relation to the trinitarian dynamics of intimate divine knowing and being known. John explains in his first epistle that it is through the Spirit, who "*is* the truth" (5:6), and through the Son of God, who "has given us understanding," that we "know him who is true" and "we are *in him* who is true, in his Son Jesus Christ" (5:20). In John's Gospel, Jesus announces that "I am the way, and the truth, and the life" (14:6). Truth (and grace) "came through Jesus Christ" (1:17), and those who accept Jesus' testimony acknowledge that "God *is* true" (3:33) and are promised the "Spirit of truth" (16:13), who will guide them into all truth. Truth is not here primarily about propositions but about the faithful personal presence of divine wisdom that liberates human beings. Jesus tells his disciples that they will know the truth "and

2. Cf. Morna Hooker, "Where Is Wisdom to Be Found? Col. 1:15–20," in *Reading Texts, Seeking Wisdom: Scripture and Theology*, ed. David Ford and Graham Stanton (Grand Rapids: Eerdmans, 2004), 116–28.

the truth will make you free" (8:32). The truth is not simply a message
to which one gives cognitive assent. Those who *"do* what is true" (3:21)
are those who are in the light of the Gospel. When Jesus prays for his
disciples, he longs for them to be sanctified *in* the truth (17:16–19), to
become wise through intimate fellowship with one another and the
Father in the Holy Spirit.

Spirituality and Truth in the Christian Tradition

The biblical emphasis on the connection between the longing for wisdom and the experience of being held in the Spirit of truth became an
important theme in the Christian tradition, especially in the writings of
theologians who struggled to hold together spirituality and theological
reflection. Over the centuries Christian contemplatives have devoted their
lives to attending to their being known by God, and although we must
recognize the need to criticize some of their particular anthropological
and cosmological assumptions, we may still attempt to incorporate their
intuitive insights about God's faithful embrace within our articulation
of the dynamics of spiritual transformation.

One way in which the implicitly spiritual dimension of theology was
emphasized was through a distinction between "knowledge" (*scientia*),
which has to do with the intelligibility of creation, and "wisdom" (*sapientia*), which has to do with a relational and dynamic orientation toward
living in faithful community wholly dependent on God. Augustine's articulation of this distinction in *On the Trinity* became deeply influential
in the Christian West. Commenting on passages such as 1 Corinthians 12
and Colossians 2:1–3, which maintain both a distinction and a connection
between wisdom and knowledge, he argues that the "intellectual cognizance of eternal things belongs to wisdom, but the rational cognizance
of temporal things to knowledge." Wisdom is clearly to be preferred,
but knowledge has value if it orients us toward wisdom; his readers are
encouraged to "stretch through knowledge to wisdom."[3]

In *The Confessions*, Augustine notes that the human mind desires
that nothing should be concealed from it, but also that it keeps itself
concealed from others. In other words, we both desire and fear intimacy
with the truth. Christian joy is oriented toward the hope that we shall
one day "come to rejoice in that sole Truth by which all things are true."[4]
Elsewhere Augustine suggests that the mind is "formed by truth itself"

3. *Tendimus per scientiam ad sapientiam*; Augustine, *On the Trinity* XIII.19, p. 181. Cf.
(*NPNF¹* 12.15).

4. Augustine, *The Confessions*, trans. F. J. Sheed (London and New York: Sheed &
Ward, 1944), 191.

without any mediation,[5] and he argues that eternal Truth kindles the desire of reason, through an "indwelling truth" that is "supremely spiritual."[6] This means that the longing for truth in the human spirit is not accidental but constitutive of rational desire itself, which is essentially oriented by and toward God.

One of the most important resources for linking the biblical understanding of truth to spirituality is the *apophatic* tradition in Christian theology, which has consistently emphasized the inherent limitations of human reasoning and language. Recognizing that the finite human mind is incapable of comprehending (wrapping itself around) the Infinite helps the theologian maintain an appropriate humility in the pursuit of truth. The fact that the divine cannot be grasped by human reason in the same way that finite things are grasped does not mean that the idea of God is incoherent. This is simply an acknowledgment that insofar as human knowing lives and moves and has its being in God (Acts 17:28), it cannot escape from that movement and find some Archimedean point from which to leverage a neutral concept of the divine. Human spirituality is constituted by the presence of divine Truth, which upholds and orients the longing for wisdom. The writings of Pseudo-Dionysius have been particularly influential in this stream of the tradition. He notes that the unnameable divine is "there at the center of everything and everything has it for a destiny. . . . All things long for it." Intelligent creatures "long for it by way of knowledge."[7] Divine wisdom is "the source, the cause, the substance, the perfection, the protector, and the goal of Wisdom itself, of mind, of reasoning and of all sense perception."[8]

The fifteenth-century theologian Nicholas of Cusa emphasized this qualitatively different experience of knowing through "unknowing" in his *On Learned Ignorance*. God is infinitely beyond all that can be named (finite things), and spiritual maturity involves learning to respond appropriately to divine ineffability—acknowledging our limitation as a delightful dependence on being known by and within the inaccessible light of divine Truth. For Nicholas, "God is unknowable either in this world or in the world to come, for in this respect every creature is darkness, which cannot comprehend light. . . . The precise truth shines forth

---

5. Augustine, *Eighty-Three Different Questions*, trans. David L. Mosher (Washington, DC: Catholic University of America Press, 1982), q. 51.4, p. 87.

6. Augustine, *Of True Religion*, trans. J. H. S. Burleigh, intro. Louis O. Mink (Chicago: Regnery, 1959), 69.

7. Pseudo-Dionysius, *The Complete Works*, trans. Colm Luibheid and Paul Rorem (New York: Paulist, 1987), 312; cf. 54. In chapter 8 Steve will bring this tradition into dialogue with contemporary psychology.

8. Ibid., 107.

incomprehensively in the darkness of our ignorance."[9] In *On Seeking God*, he calls presumptuous those who consider themselves wise and trust in their own intelligence. But he praises philosophers who saw that "they could not attain wisdom and eternal intellectual life unless they were given by a gift of grace" and "have become humble, acknowledging themselves to be ignorant, and have ordered their life as those desiring eternal wisdom."[10] For Nicholas, transforming spirituality involves forsaking all other loves for the sake of seeking to apprehend eternal wisdom.

In *On the Vision of God*, Nicholas writes in the style of a prayer directly addressed to God: "[You] are the form of every desirable thing and the truth which is desired in every desiring." He recognizes that God is "unknown" to all creatures so that they may find "in this most sacred ignorance a greater rest, as if in an incalculable and inexhaustible treasure." It is precisely the incomprehensible Infinity of God that constitutes the desiring of the human spirit. Learned ignorance is "the most desirable nourishment for my intellect."

> O Fountain of riches, you will to be grasped and possessed by me and yet to remain incomprehensible and infinite. For you are the treasure of delights of which no one can desire an end. For how could the appetite desire not to exist? For whether the will desires to be or not to be, the appetite itself cannot find rest but is borne to eternity. . . . For intellectual desire is not borne toward that which can be greater or more desirable. But everything this side of infinite can be greater. Therefore, the end of desire is infinite. You, therefore, O God, are infinity itself, which alone I desire in every desiring. . . . For the intelligible which the intellect knows does not satisfy it, nor does the intelligible of which it is totally ignorant, but only the intelligible which the intellect knows to be so intelligible that this intelligible can never be fully known can satisfy the intellect.[11]

The human longing for truth is naturally insatiable; it cannot ultimately be sated by the accumulation of finite objects of knowledge. The true delight of the human spirit is in the ever-intensifying intimacy of knowing and being known, but this requires a relation to that which "can never be fully known." This is not like the ignorance we have about finite things but an intentional delight in the infinitely desirable. Nicholas's prayer is an expression of the desire of the human spirit for knowledge, which he experiences as a passionate being-called into intimate relation with the truly infinite Fountain of Truth.

9. Nicholas of Cusa, *Selected Spiritual Writings*, trans. H. Bond (New York: Paulist, 1997), 126–27.
10. Ibid., 227.
11. Ibid., 265–67.

Though setting aside the Neoplatonic imagery of the gnostic ascent of the individual that characterizes this tradition,[12] we can still affirm the intuition behind it: creaturely spirituality cannot escape its essential dependence upon, and orientation toward, divine wisdom, through which it is called into relation to divine Truth. "Knowing" divine Truth is not, however, simply the opposite of "not-knowing." Nor is the "unknowing" that characterizes the experience of the human spirit in relation to the God of Truth simply the opposite of "knowing." The spiritual writers of the Christian tradition have gone out of their way to emphasize that the "cloud of unknowing" that overshadows the longing for truth does not mean that believers have no knowledge of God. Rather, it is precisely in the recognition of the essential limitation of finite understanding that the human spirit knows God because it is the infinite God who alone is the limit of understanding.[13] This "knowing by unknowing" is beyond the dialectic between "knowing" and "not-knowing" that characterizes the human understanding of finite things. Knowing the truly infinite God is an experience of being known that requires the negation of our own intellectual power to grasp and control objects of knowledge.

This insight is also maintained in most of the medieval tradition of Christian spirituality. St. Bonaventure's *The Soul's Journey into God*[14] illustrates this in the context of linking the human desire for truth and knowledge to the spiritual quest. The prologue places the book in the context of a prayer for peace that surpasses all *understanding* (cf. Phil. 4:7). The final (seventh) chapter also begins with a longing for peace (which makes sense for a Franciscan theologian) but recognizes that this is found only as dependence on intellectual activities is left behind. Passing over into union with God requires a kind of death, a crucifying of the hubris of the intellect, so that our cares, desires, and imaginations can be silenced as we pass into peaceful union with the Father through the Spirit. In this process our affection is "transferred and transformed into God." Bonaventure emphasizes that this "mystical wisdom" is revealed "by the Holy Spirit" in the one whose very marrow is inflamed by the

12. Rahner, among others, has been critical of the role of gnosis in this manner of articulating the three ways. See Karl Rahner, "Reflections on the Problem of the Gradual Ascent to Christian Perfection," in *Theological Investigations* (London: Darton, Longman & Todd, 1964), vol. III, 3–23.

13. This is classically expressed by the unknown author of *The Cloud of Unknowing*; see *The Cloud of Unknowing and Other Works* (New York: Penguin, 1961), 144–46.

14. *Itenerarium mentis ad Deum*. The term *mens* is related to the English concept of mentality. For Bonaventure, however, this was not limited to intellection but engages the whole soul; hence it is often translated *The Soul's Journey into God*. Mystical experience tends to break down the compartmentalization of faculty psychology.

fire of the Holy Spirit.[15] The first six chapters deal with Bonaventure's version of the threefold way, which he sees as corresponding to the existence of things: matter, mind, and Eternal Art. Once again we can see here vestiges of Neoplatonic cosmology and epistemology, but the intuitions are manifest: God is the origin, condition, and goal of the human striving for truth, and the reception of divine wisdom is a deeply intimate experience.

For the most part, the early Protestant Reformers carried on this tradition of linking truth and spirituality through a recognition of the limits of reason as a gracious manifestation of the utter dependence of human knowledge on divine grace, which takes shape as "experimental wisdom" (Luther) and is characterized by "dread and wonder" (Calvin). With the rise of rationalism in the early modern period, however, some theologians were increasingly tempted to focus on the truth of propositions about God. By the end of the nineteenth century, Charles Hodge would define the "science" of theology as the collection and arrangement of the truths contained in the Bible.[16] In this model, the passionate desire of the human spirit for knowing and being known is a "subjective" factor that should be avoided; spirituality is a topic and practice that are discussed and explored after "objective" knowledge about God is secured. It is not surprising that theology (thus defined) and spirituality—i.e., doctrine and practice—so often remain separated in streams of the evangelical tradition that continue to rely on this epistemological dichotomy.

Several late modern theological developments have contributed to the recovery of a more relational understanding of truth and led to a renewed awareness of the essential and appropriate role of the spiritual desire for wisdom in theology. We might illustrate this in a variety of ways, but it is particularly evident in the work of liberation theologian Gustavo Gutiérrez. He bemoans the separation of theology and spirituality, especially in the thirteenth and fourteenth centuries, as the emphasis on *sapientia* was separated from *scientia*. He argues that theology is "of necessity both spirituality and rational knowledge. . . . Both functions must be salvaged . . . from the division and deformations they have suffered throughout history." Building on the emphasis, especially in Ignatian spirituality, that sought for "contemplation in action," Gutiérrez describes theology as "critical reflection on practice."[17] In other essays on the relation between

15. Bonaventure, *The Soul's Journey into God*, in *Selections*, trans. Ewert H. Cousins (New York: Paulist, 1978), 113; cf. 116.

16. Charles Hodge, *Systematic Theology*, 3 vols. (Grand Rapids: Eerdmans, 2001), I:1–3.

17. Gustavo Gutiérrez, *A Theology of Liberation: History, Politics, and Salvation* (Maryknoll, NY: Orbis, 1988), 4–6. Cf. Jon Sobrino, *Spirituality of Liberation: Toward Political Holiness*, trans. Robert R. Barr (Maryknoll, NY: Orbis, 1988), 14–20.

spirituality and truth, he is more explicit. Observing that "truth in the scriptures is a relation not between things and concepts but between promise and fulfillment" helps make sense of Jesus' statements about the call to "do the truth" (John 3:19–21). This means that theology is to take place as a following in the way of Jesus Christ, in and through whom the truth sets free (John 8:32) those whose personal relations are painfully bound.[18] When we understand the spiritual longing to become wise in relation to this conception of truth, its *inherent* role within redemptive transformation begins to come into focus.

Insights from Philosophy and Natural Science

Before exploring the possibilities for sharing in the recovery of these resources, it will be helpful to observe some of the developments in late modern philosophy and science that have also helped open up conceptual space for reforming Pneumatology. The enterprise of philosophy (which is named after the human love [*philia*] of wisdom [*sophia*]) has a long history of struggling to explain human knowledge and how it is related to the divine. As we attempt to understand our own context in order to articulate and facilitate spiritual transformation in relation to the longing for truth, it makes sense to engage current epistemological debates. The natural sciences also study the nature and structure of human knowing. Although we might explore insights from several sciences, we will limit ourselves to some of the general developments in the theory of human knowing that have been impacted by evolutionary theory. After all, such sciences are interested in the emergence of *Homo sapiens*—the hominid species that is differentiated from others by its *sapientia*. Engaging contemporary understandings of human knowing can help us articulate the Christian experience of becoming wise in a way that connects to late modern culture.

Most ancient Greek philosophers believed that human knowing was dependent upon a divine reality. The term "epistemology" itself derives from a distinction between *epistēmē*, which is true knowledge of eternal reality, and *doxa* ("opinion"), which is the shadowy perception of temporal reality. The reliance of human rationality on the divine was built into the dualistic cosmology of Plato, who depicted the god Eros (Love) as guiding the soul away from the changing material world and toward contemplation of the unchanging immaterial realm of divine Forms.[19] Aristotle's *Metaphysics* begins with his well-known assertion

18. Gustavo Gutiérrez, "The Truth Shall Make You Free," in *The Truth Shall Make You Free: Confrontations* (Maryknoll, NY: Orbis, 1990), 97; cf. 35–37.

19. E.g., Socrates' speech in Plato's *Symposium* 201d–212c.

that all persons by nature desire to know, but he soon makes it clear that the movement of rational desire is dependent on an ultimate unmoved mover (God), who moves all things by being desired.[20] Most of the Stoics thought of human minds as having (or being) seeds (*spermatikoi*) of the divine Logos, which is what enabled them to know and think logically. The implicit connection between human knowing and the divine remained intact, for the most part, in Western philosophy up until the early modern period.

Part of the Enlightenment project was to unleash human reason from its reliance on the divine. Optimism about the innate power of the intellect led to a model of rationality that held up as its ideal the "man of reason," who could erect a system of apodictic knowledge about the whole of nature by following rules of logic that build upon self-evident foundations. Anything that was not susceptible to the control of human rationality was removed from "enlightened" discourse and secluded into the arena of "faith." This way of separating faith and reason increasingly led to the dominance of the latter over the former.[21] As the power of the sciences spread, so did the hubris that the human mind could control reality and secure certain foundations for truth. In this model, knowing has to do with objectively assenting to true propositions, which could be separated from subjective feeling and acting.

Resistance to this "modern" epistemological ideal is a significant part of what has come to be called "postmodern" philosophy, which has increasingly emphasized the way in which the particular context of the embodied subject shapes every knowing event. In some cases, this takes an extreme relativistic form in which "epistemology" itself is rejected; since there is no *epistēmē* that provides access to absolute foundations for knowledge, we must be satisfied with *doxa* and the relativized play of hermeneutics. This extreme response to epistemological foundationalism is sometimes called antifoundationalism. Unfortunately, these mutually defined approaches are often held up as the exhaustive options. Both sides of this polemic, however, share a set of assumptions—for example, that either we must have absolute foundations for knowledge or truth is relative. As I have illustrated in *The Postfoundationalist Task of Theology*,[22] a growing number of philosophers are contesting this either/or dichotomy.

---

20. Aristotle, *Metaphysics* I.1, cf. XII.7.

21. This turn is already evident in John Locke's observation in the late seventeenth century that although any divine revelation would by definition be true, "it belongs to Reason to judge of its being a Revelation, and of the signification of the Words, wherein it is delivered." *An Essay concerning Human Understanding*, ed. Peter H. Nidditch (Oxford: Clarendon, 1979), Book IV, ch. 18, p. 685.

22. F. LeRon Shults, *The Postfoundationalist Task of Theology* (Grand Rapids: Eerdmans, 1999).

A postfoundationalist model of rationality challenges the appropriateness of the assumptions that force this choice and attempts to navigate between the extremes, urging a relentless interrogation of the facile foundationalism of modernism while not denying the ideal of objective truth.[23] The main point for our purposes here is that this opens up conceptual space for recovering the humbler epistemology manifest in the theological resources we explored above, which emphasize the dependence of finite knowledge on the truly infinite God who is beyond creaturely being. As Diogenes Allen points out, recognizing that God is not a "member of the universe" and thematizing our own inquiry into God can help us avoid the impasse of foundationalism versus antifoundationalism. Affirming our ongoing dependence on divine self-manifestation means that theology "is not based on the possibility of an incorrigible foundation, nor is it threatened by the absence of such a foundation."[24] This suggests that a reasonable assessment of human reason is that it is essentially dependent, naturally limited by that which is always beyond it.[25]

These developments have led to a renewed interest in the apophatic tradition in contemporary philosophy.[26] This recovery of the traditional emphasis on wisdom is evident, for example, in the work of Paul Ricoeur, who struggled to integrate epistemology and hermeneutics within an understanding of the narrative structuring of human experience and interpretation. He observes that narrative intelligibility, which is displayed in the configurational acts of emplotment, "shows more kinship with practical wisdom or moral judgment than with theoretical reason."[27] This is not a denial of rationality or truth but a recognition that narratives in some sense are constitutive of the identity of persons and communities. We might also point to the contributions of feminist philosophers as well as social scientists who have observed how disembodied ideals of rationality have obscured the importance of contextual-

23. For a discussion of these developments and its impact on theological method, cf. ibid., chs. 2 and 5.

24. Diogenes Allen, "Intellectual Inquiry and Spiritual Formation," in *Inquiring after God: Classic and Contemporary Readings*, ed. Ellen T. Charry (Oxford, England, and Malden, MA: Blackwell, 2000), 27.

25. Alasdair MacIntyre (*Dependent Rational Animals: Why Human Beings Need the Virtues* [New York: Open Court, 2001]), argues that human beings are essentially dependent and that becoming wise requires acknowledging this dependence.

26. Merold Westphal provides a summary of philosophical resources in the continental tradition in *Transcendence and Self-Transcendence: On God and the Soul* (Bloomington: Indiana University Press, 2004), esp. part 2, and explores the impact on theology. Cf. Graham Ward, *Barth, Derrida, and the Language of Theology* (Cambridge and New York: Cambridge University Press, 1995).

27. Paul Ricoeur, *Figuring the Sacred: Religion, Narrative, and Imagination*, trans. David Pellauer (Minneapolis: Fortress, 1995). Cf. Ricoeur, *Oneself as Another*, trans. Kathleen Blamey (Chicago: University of Chicago Press, 1992), 113–68.

ity and embodiment in human knowing.[28] The human longing for truth is not satisfied by abstract, timeless propositions; cognitive assent has its function but is ultimately incorporated within and serves the deeper desire to know and be known in the trustworthy relations of concrete, temporal communion.

Developments in the natural sciences have also contributed to the recognition that knowing is dynamically embedded within particular communal relations. Human thinking cannot be divorced from embodied feeling and acting. Paleobiologist Terrence Deacon argues that rationality (and language itself) emerged alongside the evolution of the brain in hominids; as we learned to use tools and communicate, we became what he calls the "symbolic species."[29] This indicates that knowing and becoming wise (interacting in trustworthy ways in community) are genetically connected for *Homo sapiens*. The sciences of neurobiology also support the contention that human knowledge is essentially embodied, but this does not necessitate a unilateral reductionism of religious experience to the level of neural or chemical explanation. For example, Eugene d'Aquili and Andrew Newberg argue that "a neuropsychological analysis of theology or mysticism" does not alter "their true spiritual and possibly transcendent nature."[30] They suggest that the interdisciplinary dialogue goes both ways; theology (broadly understood) can also explicate the ultimate origin of neurophysiological phenomena. Wisdom has become an important integrating theme in the work of several scholars working at the intersection between theology and contemporary natural science.[31]

A growing number of theologians are positively engaging the sciences of evolutionary biology as they seek to clarify the human experience of becoming in orientation toward the divine. For example, John Haught argues that evolution may be a gift to theology, providing an opportunity to move beyond early modern mechanical conceptions of the relation of God to the world. He suggests that evolution "seems to require a divine

28. Cf. Mary Field Belenky et al., *Women's Ways of Knowing: The Development of Self, Voice, and Mind* (New York: BasicBooks, 1997).

29. Terrence W. Deacon, *The Symbolic Species: The Co-evolution of Language and the Brain* (New York: W. W. Norton, 1997); cf. William Noble and Iain Davidson, *Human Evolution, Language, and Mind: A Psychological and Archaeological Inquiry* (New York: Cambridge University Press, 1996).

30. Eugene d'Aquili and Andrew Newberg, *The Mystical Mind: Probing the Biology of Religious Experience* (Minneapolis: Fortress, 1999), 176. Cf. Antonio Damasio, *Descartes' Error: Emotion, Reason, and the Human Brain* (New York: Avon, 1994), 250; *The Feeling of What Happens: Body and Emotion in the Making of Consciousness* (New York: Harcourt, 1999).

31. See esp. the essays in Warren Brown, ed., *Understanding Wisdom: Sources, Science, and Society* (Radnor, PA: Templeton Foundation, 2000).

source of being that resides not in a timeless present located somewhere 'up above,' but in the future, essentially 'up ahead,' as the goal of a world still in the making."[32] These developments in philosophy and science suggest that a theological articulation of spirituality does not need to remain within the constraints of the problematic early modern concepts of "spirit" that we observed in the previous chapter. This new conceptual space may facilitate a reconstructive presentation of a reformative Pneumatology that engages the human longing to become wise.

Knowing in the Spirit

We turn now to an exploration of the possibilities opened up by these developments for articulating the dynamics of transforming spirituality in terms of *knowing* in the Spirit. "All things" are from, through, and to God (Rom. 11:36), and this includes the human longing to know and be known. To account for this biblical intuition and the testimony of contemplative theologians to the all-embracing intimacy of divine wisdom, we may begin to articulate a reformative Pneumatology with the claim that the divine Spirit is the *origin, condition,* and *goal* of human knowing. All knowledge is "spiritual" in the broad sense outlined in chapter 2; the search for intelligibility emerges out of the complex, dynamic self-relationality that constitutes the human spirit. The personal experience of redemptive spirituality, however, involves an intensification of human creaturely life in the Spirit of wisdom—an intensification that takes shape concretely by sharing in the knowledge of Jesus Christ. Our task is to outline ways in which the late modern recovery of traditional resources can help us articulate an understanding of the human spirit transformed by knowing and being known in the Spirit.

What is the relation between creaturely spirit and Creator Spirit in the dynamic process of redemptive transformation? In the first letter to the Corinthians, Paul argues that the person who is connected to Christ "becomes *one spirit* with [the Lord]" (1 Cor. 6:17) and that "no one can say 'Jesus is Lord' except by [*en*] the Holy Spirit" (12:3b). Paul tells the Romans that it is the Spirit of God in them who "intercedes with sighs too deep for words," since they do not know how to pray as they ought (Rom. 8:26). He also indicates that his self-knowledge, his knowledge

---

32. John F. Haught, *God after Darwin: A Theology of Evolution* (Boulder, CO: Westview, 2000), 84. For other helpful summaries and attempts at integration, cf. Denis Edwards, *The God of Evolution* (New York: Paulist, 1999); Kenneth R. Miller, *Finding Darwin's God: A Scientist's Search for Common Ground between God and Evolution* (San Francisco: HarperCollins, 1999); Jerry D. Korsmeyer, *Evolution and Eden* (New York: Paulist, 1998); Keith B. Miller, ed., *Perspectives on an Evolving Creation* (Grand Rapids: Eerdmans, 2003).

of others, and his knowledge of "the truth in Christ" are all interwoven and confirmed "by [en] the Holy Spirit" (9:1). When the Ephesians are encouraged to "pray in the Spirit at all times," this does not exclude their need to "keep alert" and "persevere" (Eph. 6:18). Jude's exhortation to pray *in* the Spirit is similarly connected to the need for the beloved to "build yourselves up" (Jude 1:20). Jesus encourages the disciples not to worry about knowing what to say, for it is not they who speak but the Spirit who speaks through them (Mark 13:11). What happens to the identity of the knowing human spirit if it becomes "one" with the infinite divine Spirit? Is it the human spirit who is speaking, praying, and knowing, or has an "other" (divine) identity taken over in these activities?

How are we to make sense of the idea that the longing of the human spirit to know and be known in faithful intimacy occurs "in" the Spirit? The concept of *dialectical identity* can help us articulate this relational unity in a way that avoids the dangers of two extreme positions—thinking of the human spirit as either absorbed by or alienated from the Holy Spirit. I have described the idea of dialectical identity in more detail elsewhere, and so a brief summary will suffice.[33] One of the clearest expressions of dialectical identity is Paul's claim that "it is no longer I who live, but it is Christ who lives in me. And the life I now live in the flesh I live by faith in the Son of God, who loved me and gave himself for me" (Gal. 2:20). This dialectical "I, yet not I" forms Paul's identity. This intrinsically relational understanding of the identity of the human spirit opens up conceptual space for articulating a reformative Pneumatology that accounts for the ambiguous human longing for wisdom.

The first step is to recognize that all personal knowing is dialectical, mediated through relations with others who are "not I." Even knowing one's self is mediated through knowing and being known by the other. My identity is mediated to "me" by others who are "not me." The boundaries of my identity are discovered as "I" am confronted by existentially relevant others who limit me. The "I" is formed in relation to these others. In this sense the formation of human identity is "dialectical"—it is constituted by the relationality between self and non-self. Human persons are identified by and identify others; this mutual identification is the interpersonal field within which identity is formed. Freud's idea of the superego pointed to the way in which the early formative identification of

33. For an outline of these dynamics in the context of other doctrinal themes, cf. F. LeRon Shults and Steven J. Sandage, *The Faces of Forgiveness: Searching for Wholeness and Salvation* (Grand Rapids: Baker, 2003), ch. 5; F. LeRon Shults, *Reforming Theological Anthropology: After the Philosophical Turn to Relationality* (Grand Rapids: Eerdmans, 2003), chs. 4 and 8; *Reforming the Doctrine of God* (Grand Rapids: Eerdmans, 2005), ch. 8. Chapters 4 and 5 of the current project will expand this discussion to incorporate the ideas of dialectical agency and dialectical presence.

significant others continues to form the identity of a person throughout life. Finding one's personal identity occurs within a tensive struggle to protect one's "self" from being crushed or abandoned by others. We long to know and be known, to be mutually self-identified without becoming co-opted or codependent. Personal knowing is a dialectical process that emerges within, and is mediated through, communal relations.

A reformative Pneumatology that recovers the insights of the tradition with reference to Infinity, Trinity, and Futurity can help us make sense of the formation of this dialectical identity in relation to the longing for intimacy with(in) the Spirit of wisdom. Unlike the finite others who identify us and threaten our identity, the infinite divine Spirit is essentially inexhaustible, an absolute fullness that cannot be grasped by human knowing precisely because it constitutes creaturely noetic desire as its conditioning goal. The Spirit's faithful evocative presence is closer to us than we are to ourselves, opening us up to knowledge of self and other. The Creator Spirit is not simply defined over against the creaturely spirit but is the absolute origin of its dynamic lively search for identity. The gracious arrival of the truly infinite Spirit neither absorbs nor abandons the human spirit, for this intimate divine presence upholds and orients the relationality that constitutes creaturely knowing itself. In the dynamics of redemptive transformation, the human spirit comes to recognize that its identity is mediated by the all-pervading and all-embracing presence of the Spirit of the trinitarian God, who calls creatures toward participation in eternal life.

If Christian spirituality involves knowing in the Spirit of the biblical God, then we must link divine Infinity to a robust understanding of the Trinity. The biblical understanding of the longing for wisdom is inherently reformative because that which originates, upholds, and orients our knowing is the infinitely intense intimate knowing and being-known that is the life of the trinitarian person. Some members of the church in Ephesus were identifying themselves and others by focusing on the differences between the circumcised and the uncircumcised, but they were urged to find their identity in Christ through fellowship with one another. This is possible because in Christ both groups have access, in the one Spirit, to the Father (Eph. 2:18). As we find our identity mediated by the presence of the eternal Spirit, our way of knowing and being-known is transformed; our desire for wisdom takes shape as an identification with the reconciling faithfulness of God in the world. As we will see below, this means that the Christian experience of becoming wise involves participating in Jesus Christ's trusting of the Father in the Spirit.

The desire that characterizes the redemptive transformation of human knowing in the Spirit does not hope for an "end" in the same way that we seek closure in our longing to understand a finite object of knowledge. This is because the creaturely desire for an intimate relation to divine wisdom is wholly conditioned by the gracious arrival of its goal. The presence of the Spirit opens up the temporal experience of creaturely becoming, which cannot escape its absolute dependence on the power that establishes it. The eschatological opening up of creaturely temporality is experienced by human persons as absolute Futurity—as the constitutive arrival of Eternity that evokes noetic desire and conditions its pursuit of truth by upholding the modes of time. Creaturely knowing is oriented toward the future as it remembers the past, and this asymmetric structure of the human longing to know and be known is graciously constituted by the evocative presence of the Spirit of wisdom. Eternal life *is* knowing the one true God (John 17:3). Entering into the trinitarian fellowship of knowing and being-known frees us from epistemic anxiety about securing our identity. The experience of Christian redemption is knowing transformed—coming to be as we find our "selves" in the Spirit, hid with Christ in God (Col. 3:1–3).

Sharing in the Knowledge of Jesus Christ

In Matthew 11:27 Jesus says that "no one knows the Son except the Father, and no one knows the Father except the Son." In 1 Corinthians 2:11 Paul argues that "no one comprehends what is truly God's except the Spirit of God." This suggests that creatures are able to "know" God only by participating in this knowing and being-known that is the trinitarian life. Christians experience redemptive transformation as they come to share in Jesus' way of faithfully identifying, and being identified by, the Father in reliance on the Spirit of wisdom. The identity of Jesus of Nazareth was also dialectical; his knowledge of himself and his neighbors was ultimately mediated by his knowledge of the One he intimately called "Abba" (Mark 14:36). Jesus also experienced *becoming wise*; he "increased in wisdom" vis-à-vis God and his neighbors (Luke 2:52). For Jesus, no other future could threaten the promise of God's faithful creative upholding of the world by the life-giving power of the Spirit.

What does it mean for us to *share* in this knowledge? If knowledge has to do with assenting to propositions, then it would mean that we learn some of the truths that Jesus also knew. Christian spirituality surely includes this but is by no means limited to it. The believer is called into Jesus' way of knowing and being-known in intimate fellowship. It is precisely through and in the Spirit "bearing witness with our spirit" that we become children of God and are enabled to cry with Jesus, "Abba! Father!" (Rom. 8:15–16). God has sent the Spirit of his Son into our hearts, crying, "Abba! Father!" (Gal. 4:6). In Luke 4 Jesus interpreted his own experience of becoming wise in light of the Isaianic prophecies of the coming servant, "The spirit of the Lord shall rest upon him, the spirit of *wisdom* and understanding" (Isa. 11:2). As we share in the knowledge of Jesus, we experience the faithfulness of the divine Spirit as an intimate presence that holds us, loves us, and draws us into the knowledge of the Father.

The idea of *sharing* in Jesus' knowledge (as well as in his suffering and glory; cf. chapters 4 and 5) must be understood in the broader context of the biblical claim that believers "may become participants [*koinōnoi*] of the divine nature" (2 Pet. 1:4). Western theologians have often resisted the Eastern emphasis on the idea of divinization, or *theōsis*, worrying that it blurs the distinction between Creator and creature. We should be careful, however, not to overlook the implicitly Christological and Pneumatological mediation of this "sharing" in the nature of God. If the divine nature *is* this knowing and being-known of the trinitarian persons, manifested in Jesus' intimacy with the Father through the Spirit of wisdom, then divinization is best understood as "christification."[34] For Athanasius, the incarnation and the creature's orientation toward sharing in the divine nature cannot be separated: "For He was made man that we might be made God."[35] As Maximus Confessor insists, deification does not mean that the finite becomes infinite or participates in the essence of God, for "God infinitely transcends all things which participate or are participated."[36] Nevertheless, "God wills always and in all things to accomplish the mystery of his embodiment [incarnation],"[37] which means that God's relation to the finite world is always and already mediated through the Word that became flesh in Jesus of Nazareth.

The transforming spirituality that the East calls divinization is also mediated through the Spirit, who is perichoretically united to the eternal Son and the Father in the mutuality of their intimate knowledge. Maximus also insists that creatures participate in the relation of the Word to the Father through sharing in the gracious gifts of the Holy Spirit.[38] Later Gregory Palamas would similarly emphasize that deifica-

34. Panayiotis Nellas (*Deification in Christ* [Crestwood, NY: St. Vladimir's Seminary Press, 1997]) argues that this has been the dominant emphasis in Eastern theology.

35. Athanasius, *On the Incarnation of the Word* (NPNF[2] 4:65).

36. Maximus Confessor, *Chapters of Knowledge*, in *Selected Writings*, ed. George C. Berthold (New York: Paulist, 1985), 137.

37. Maximus Confessor, *Ambiguum 7*, in *On the Cosmic Mystery of Jesus Christ: Selected Writings from St. Maximus the Confessor*, ed. Paul M. Blowers and Robert Louis Wilken (Crestwood, NY: St. Vladimir's Seminary Press, 2003), 60.

38. Maximus Confessor, *The Church's Mystagogy*, in *Selected Writings*, ed. George C. Berthold (New York: Paulist, 1985), 207.

tion occurs "in Christ" and among those who "partake of the Spirit."[39] This emphasis was already present in the fourth-century Cappadocian theologian St. Basil, who also argued that it is only fellowship with and in the Spirit that leads to "abiding in God, the being made like to God, and highest of all, the being made God."[40] This sharing is not something that ends with the final absorption of creation into the divine essence; all of creation *is* coming-to-be opened up to participation in the eternal life of the Trinity. The grace of God grants creatures their own knowing, as they are held in being by the Spirit of wisdom, who invites them into the relational intimacy of the Son and the Father.

The Christian experience of transforming spirituality involves sharing in Jesus' knowledge of the Father in the Spirit, being brought into fellowship (*koinōnia*) with the only wise God. Jesus did not use his wisdom to control and manipulate others, as did the religious and political leaders of his day. Relying on his being-known by the Father, he bound himself in relation to those in need of healing intimacy. He lifted up his disciples in prayer to the Father: "As you, Father, are in me and I am in you, may they also be in us, so that the world may believe that you have sent me" (John 17:21). What does it mean to "believe"? Earlier in Jesus' ministry, some who "believed" (*episteusan*) in him because of the signs he did (2:23) longed to bind him to their own understanding of the Messiah's rule. Jesus did not bind himself to them, however, but refused to "entrust" (*episteuen*) himself to them (2:24). If we speak of "believing" in this robust relational sense, then it has to do with the way we bind and are bound in relation to each other. Jesus calls his disciples into sharing in his *way of being bound* in faithfulness to God and neighbor. Jesus and the Father are "one," and he invites his followers into this intimate union, praying "that they may be one, as we are one" (17:22).

Jesus' intimacy with the Father was mediated by his reception of, and faithful dependence upon, the Spirit of wisdom. Notice that Jesus does not lose his particularity through this dependence; on the contrary, it is precisely through this reliance that he finds his identity in relation to the Father, who identifies him as the Son of God through the resurrection (Rom. 1:4). Jesus' way of life represents the appropriate human response to the faithful divine Spirit, who invites the human spirit into a new experience of trusting intentionality, a way of finding oneself bound to the Father. The same "Spirit of truth" will also abide with and in the disciples (John 14:15–17), which will be manifested in their own intimate fellowship. The interplay of knowing and being-known is

39. Gregory Palamas, *The Triads*, ed. and trans. John Meyendorff (New York: Paulist, 1983), 57–69, 88–92.
40. Basil of Caesarea, *On the Holy Spirit* (*NPNF*[2] 8:16).

explicit: "Righteous Father, the world does not know you, but I know you; and these know that you have sent me. I made your name known to them, and I will make it known, so that the love with which you have loved me may be in them, and I in them" (John 17:25–26).

Jesus' intimate knowledge of the Father and his reliance on the Spirit of wisdom were also manifested in his passion, crucifixion, and resurrection. It is often observed that Jesus did not answer Pilate when he asked his famous question, "What is truth?" (John 18:38). We may think of the entire passion, however, as Jesus' answer. The right human relation to the one true God is that of trusting in the life-giving power of the Spirit of the Father, even in the face of hostile enemies. It was "through the eternal Spirit" that Jesus offered his whole life to God (Heb. 9:14). His life of faithfulness took the form of humbling himself in relation to the Father, becoming "obedient to the point of death—even death on a cross" (Phil. 2:8). Jesus entrusted himself to the One who judges justly; this was his whole way of life, which sets an example for us (1 Pet. 2:21–23). The resurrection of Jesus discloses the eschatological intention of human creation; he is the *eschatos* Adam (1 Cor. 15:45). As the "first-born from the dead," he has "first place in everything," but through him the Father has enabled us to "share in the inheritance" of the kingdom (Col. 1:11–20). As we share in Jesus' way of knowing and being-known by the Father, we become wise—learning to trust the Spirit as we bind ourselves faithfully to our neighbors.

The Intensification of Faith

Personal attachments emerge within an interpersonal field of mutual binding and being-bound in relation. In this general sense, the human spirit is formed in the context of "faith"—in the tensive struggle to bind oneself in trustworthy relations. This is what Erik Erikson referred to as the "basic trust" that is a condition for the emergence of healthy identity in children.[41] Relationships continue to shape our identity throughout life, and the longing for intimacy that drives human knowing is transformed precisely in and through these relations.[42] Even scientific inquiry is shaped by "methodological faith," the implicit commitments shared by a community of scholars that hold together

41. Erik Erikson, *Identity and the Life Cycle* (New York: W. W. Norton, 1980), 57–67. Cf. Steve's discussion of John Bowlby's concept of "secure attachment" in chapter 6.
42. Cf. Ruthellen Josselson, "Relationship as a Path to Integrity, Wisdom, and Meaning," in *The Psychology of Mature Spirituality: Integrity, Wisdom, Transcendence*, ed. Polly Young-Eisendrath and Melvin E. Miller (London and Philadelphia: Routledge, 2001), 87–102.

and guide research projects.[43] Christian faith is an experience of the gracious transformation of this natural longing for truth, an intensification of the desire for intimacy in relation to the Spirit of wisdom, who holds all things together and invites us into the mutual knowing of the Son and the Father.

This dynamic process of becoming wise *is* transforming spirituality. The Colossians are "filled with the knowledge of God's will in all spiritual wisdom and understanding" as they "*grow* in the knowledge of God" (Col. 1:9–10). Having been clothed with a new self, "which *is being renewed* in knowledge according to the image of its creator" (3:10), they are urged to live together, teaching and admonishing one another "in all wisdom" as the word of Christ "dwells" in them richly (3:16). We must be careful not to focus so intently on our adherence to the articles of faith (*fides quae creditur*) that we miss the importance of the way in which we are bound in faith (*fides qua creditur*) to God as we are called to adhere to the eschatological presence of the Spirit of Christ. The transformation of human faith requires more than the communication of propositional content from an infinite Mind to a finite mind. It involves coming to have the "mind of Christ" (1 Cor. 2:16), which means an ongoing renewal of our way of *minding* our relations to God and others (cf. Rom. 12:2; Phil. 2:1–13).

Kierkegaard defines faith by contrasting it with sin, both of which have to do with the relational constitution of the human spirit (which he sometimes equates with "the self"). Faith is the state of the self when despair is completely rooted out: "In relating itself to itself and in willing to be itself, the self rests transparently in the power that established it."[44] In other words, in and through faith the human spirit comes to find its identity in its intimate relation to the divine Spirit, who holds it together. Kierkegaard challenges the idea that faith is an easy first step, the starting point at which just about everybody in Christendom begins. On the contrary, coming to faith involves a passionate "fear and trembling." In his reflection on the story of Abraham, he concludes that "there perhaps are many in every generation who do not come to faith, but no one goes further."[45]

Coming to faith is not simply a starting point that the Christian refers to in the past but a way of living that is graciously oriented toward participating in divine faithfulness. In this model, doubt is not necessarily

43. For a discussion of the methodological faith that is implicit in all inquiry, cf. Shults, *Reforming Theological Anthropology*, ch. 2.

44. Søren Kierkegaard, *The Sickness unto Death* (Princeton, NJ: Princeton University Press, 1980), 14; cf. 77, 131.

45. Søren Kierkegaard, *Fear and Trembling*, ed. and trans. Howard V. and Edna H. Hong (Princeton, NJ: Princeton University Press, 1983), 122.

opposed to faith but may very well be the sign of an emerging tension that can lead to a deeper experience of knowing and being-known in relation to God. The previous chapter described the dynamic relation between the centripetal organizing and centrifugal orienting tendencies of the ego vis-à-vis existentially relevant others. The human spirit is this relation's relating itself to itself in the relation. The dependence of the ego on the other leads to anxiety; either the ego tries to bind the other to itself or it hides from the other to avoid being bound. This anxious longing to trust and be trusted by an other is inherently temporal. Awareness of a personal "present" requires the memory of past mutual identification and the imaginative extension of one's identity into an anticipated future. I long for a future in which I am bound in faithful communion, yet I worry about the trustworthiness of others because of past infidelities. The redemptive intensification of faith transforms the human spirit so that it comes to find its identity—its relating itself to itself in the relation—mediated by the gracious arrival of the intimate faithfulness that is the knowing and being-known of the infinite trinitarian God.

We can spell out the redemptive dynamics of becoming wise in terms of the intensification model outlined in the introduction and chapter 2. First, the human spirit must be purged of its reliance on its own capacity to bind others to itself, its attachment to particular ways of manipulating those in relation to whom its identity is mediated. This process is *intense*. As St. John of the Cross observed, the experience of being purged by the divine light is called a "dark night" because "this Divine wisdom is not only night and darkness for the soul, but is likewise affliction and torment."[46] St. Teresa of Ávila points out that we must deal with the "venomous reptiles" in the outer mansions of our spiritual life; only through the intensity of facing these beasts can we escape from their binding power and move into the more intimate chambers of the "Interior Castle."[47] Facing our epistemic anxiety is a necessary condition for redemptive transformation. We long for intimacy in trusting relations, but we cannot hold our selves and others together with our own noetic power.

The finite human spirit is terrified of true intimacy, afraid to trust its fragile identity to another. Our identity is constantly threatened by others, and this makes us tense. Overshadowing this desire is the awareness of the ultimate threat to our identity—death itself. Repressing this fear does not secure our identity; it only camouflages the existential anxiety with the functional busyness of the ego. Ironically, it is precisely this

46. John of the Cross, *Dark Night of the Soul*, ed. and trans. E. A. Peers (Garden City, NY: Image Books, 1959), 100.

47. Teresa of Ávila, *Interior Castle*, ed. and trans. E. A. Peers (New York: Doubleday, 1961).

capacity to hide behind the façade of our ego structures that inhibits the very intimacy that we so desperately desire. The ego struggles to protect the self from the invasion or evasion of the other. When the intensification has to do not merely with the functional capacities of the ego but with the ultimate threat to its very existence, the need for *redemptive* transformation comes to the fore. The tension that is at stake in religious faith is the ultimate tension between life and death. The ultimate threat to human identity is death, the final enemy of the desire to know and be known. As the human spirit attends to this tension and gives up its own tendency to hold off death on its own, it is opened up to receive its identity through an intimate dependence on the infinite faithfulness of the Holy Spirit.

The intensity of the Spirit's convicting negation of our reliance on the ego to hold on to and protect our identity is truly gracious. This illuminative experience expands our intentionality, our way of interpreting the world. Resting in the infinite faithfulness of the divine Spirit, we are opened up into new life—receiving our identity as we are bound together with Christ in relation to God. This gracious constitution of the self liberates us from the tension of an ego-centric life. The human spirit comes to rest in the infinite Power that holds it together and calls it into a share in the intimacy of divine life. This spiritual union with God involves sharing in the knowledge of Jesus Christ, who laid down his life in order to take it up again in utter dependence on the Father (John 10:17–18). The same Spirit that raised Christ from the dead dwells in us (Rom. 8:11) so that we may now become wise as we learn to lay down our ego functions as the ground of our identity, taking them up again only as we live in faithfulness to the Son of God (Gal. 2:20). The intensification of faith—our being bound in and to the absolute mutual fidelity that is the divine life—enables us to lose our lives in order to find them truly in the Spirit (Matt. 10:39; 16:25).

Transforming Prayer

One way to spell out these dynamics is to thematize the formative power of Christian prayer. Broadly understood, prayer is an expression of the Christian's experience of knowing and being-known by God. The form of our praying manifests our understanding of, and our way of trusting in, divine faithfulness.[48] In other words, the identity of the Christian is

---

48. This connection is expressed in the traditional dictum *lex orandi, lex credendi*—prayer and belief are mutually implicated. Cf. Geoffrey Wainwright, *Doxology: The Praise of God in Worship, Doctrine, and Life: A Systematic Theology* (New York: Oxford University Press, 1980), 218–83.

formed by and forms the practice of prayer. How are we to think about (and practice) prayer in light of the reformative Pneumatology we have been exploring? Our goal is an understanding (and experience) of prayer that transforms *us*. It is crucial to acknowledge first that both wisdom and prayer are interpreted (or held on to) differently as one experiences the intensification of intimacy in the Spirit. Thinking about the practice of prayer in connection with the formation of Christian identity and the dynamics of intensification can help us understand why the focus of prayer is so different among believers.[49]

Petitionary prayer is both biblically sanctioned and existentially important, especially during times of intense anxiety when our comfortable "dwelling" has been upset and we find ourselves propelled into a time of "seeking." But as long as our seeking is primarily about securing particular creaturely attachments (or avoiding others) as the basis of our identity, the deeper work of spiritual transformation cannot occur. If our default form of prayer is always petitionary, this may signify that our intentions are narcissistic or ego-centered ("I want a . . . ," or "make . . . go away"). It is natural to ask for help in acquiring a particular object we desire or to ask for relief from a perceived source of tension, but moving beyond childish forms of intimacy with God will require a willingness to endure the crucible of intensification. In popular Christian discourse, we often speak of the "prayer of salvation"—people's explicit confession of their inability to save themselves and a declaration of their trust in Christ as Savior. This form of prayer—asking for help—can and should remain throughout the life of a Christian. As we learn to dwell in the infinitely faithful tending presence of the Spirit, however, the mode of our seeking will itself be transformed.

Through the ongoing experience of illumination, prayer often begins to take a more contemplative form; the focus is less on our anxiety about particular attachments and more on the enjoyment of knowing and being-known. This process of intensification does not take us out of space and time but redeems our interpretation of them, expanding our intentionality so that we are able to act faithfully in relation to others as we invite them to trust in the divine Spirit. Our lives become a "prayer of salvation." This way of identifying one's self with the reconciling faithfulness of God alters how we might answer this common evangelical question: "How many people have you led to the Lord this week?" This is normally intended as an inquiry concerning the number of persons who were led to repeat a particular formulaic prayer. But if we think of prayer as participation in the faithfulness of God, a redemptive

49. Cf. Benedict J. Groeschel, *Spiritual Passages: The Psychology of Spiritual Development* (New York: Crossroad, 1984).

experience of intentionality transformed in the enlightening presence of divine life, then we might answer the question very differently. Leading a person to the Lord means inviting a person into a new way of intending and being-tended-to in his or her relation to God through Christ in the Spirit. In this model, we could hope to respond to the query by answering, "I have led every person I met this week to the Lord, not only those who briefly broke into the perimeter of my life but also my family and my fellow Christians."

Christian prayer—like Christian faith—is not just about the contents of one's intellect, but the way in which one intends the presence of divine faithfulness in relation to others, participating in the transforming grace of the Spirit of wisdom, who binds us to God and to one another as we share in the knowledge of Jesus Christ. This way of linking prayer to the concrete, holistic experience of practicing fidelity in relation to others has become a significant theme in contemporary literature on spirituality. Richard Foster, for example, encourages us to engage in "radical" prayer, which transforms us as we move into the world like the classical prophets, calling others into intimacy with God.[50] Thomas Keating emphasizes the importance of "centering" prayer, but he is careful to point out that this way of praying does not simply turn the self inward—it orients the "intentions" of the self in new ways in relation to God and others.[51] The way in which we pray signifies our faith(fulness) as Christians. If we think about "prayer life" as limited to one compartmentalized part of the day (or week), then this might be taken to imply that we should judge our faith by the intensity of an inner feeling during this period. If we understand the intensification of faith as sharing in the intentionality of divine faithfulness, however, then prayer becomes a way of life. We identify ourselves (as believers) by the way we prayerfully tend to our neighbors, welcoming them into the light of divine grace.

As our "union" with(in) the intimate mutual knowing that is the life of the trinitarian God is intensified, we are opened up to an experience of prayer as an "infused contemplation." This is often characterized by a loss of defenses and quiet ecstasy. As we are transformed by these experiences of intimacy, we are able to "pray without ceasing" (1 Thess. 5:17), for our life itself becomes a participation in the faithfulness of God as we faithfully tend to others. This is what Brother Lawrence called practicing the presence of God.[52] This practice transforms our lives,

50. Richard J. Foster, *Prayer: Finding the Heart's True Home* (San Francisco: Harper-SanFrancisco, 1992), 243–56.

51. Thomas Keating, *Intimacy with God* (New York: Crossroad, 1994), 55–71.

52. Brother Lawrence of the Resurrection, *The Practice of the Presence of God*, trans. John J. Delaney (Garden City, NY: Image Books, 1977). Cf. Richard N. Longenecker, *Into God's Presence: Prayer in the New Testament* (Grand Rapids: Eerdmans, 2001).

empowering us to become a faithful presence to others. Anxiety about death is overcome as we depend on the life-giving divine Spirit, who draws us into the eternal life of trinitarian knowing and being-known, binding us together with Christ in relation to God (cf. John 17:3; Col. 3:1–3). In and through faith, we are called to a life of prayerful tending to the presence of the Spirit of wisdom, responding and inviting others to respond to the invitation to intimacy with God.

This understanding of the human longing for wisdom as infinitely upheld by the divine Spirit does not threaten the integrity of scientific inquiry, nor is it threatened by it. Reforming Pneumatology attends to the ultimate origin, condition, and goal of the dynamics that characterize the human search for truth in all its modes (including science and philosophy). Becoming wise cannot be divorced, however, from becoming just and free in the Christian experience of the redemptive transformation of spirituality. Part 3 will thematize the importance of linking our longing for truth to our desire for goodness and beauty, in the context of three concrete case studies. But first we need to outline the dynamics of transforming spirituality as sharing in the redemptive grace of God in terms of acting in the Spirit (chapter 4) and being in the Spirit (chapter 5).

4

BECOMING
JUST

The search for trustworthy relations in faithful community cannot be separated from our longing *to love and be loved* as we live the good life together. In other words, the redemptive transformation of human spirituality takes shape not only through knowing but also through *acting* in the Spirit. The agency of the human spirit naturally uses its finite power to secure the objects of its desire, attempting to hold on to that which it loves or perceives to be good. Under these conditions, it seems inevitable that community life will be characterized by the struggle for power over "goods." The transformation of human agency requires dependence on the infinitely gracious power of the Spirit of God, whose presence welcomes us into participation in the absolute Goodness of divine life. The Israelites placed their hope in the promising presence of the "spirit of justice" (cf. Isa. 28:6), who shapes the life of the community, healing its unjust relations and orienting it toward peace. Christians interpret this hope in light of the New Testament claim that through the Spirit of Christ believers may "*become* the righteousness [or justice] of God" (2 Cor. 5:21).

My goal here is to outline the redemptive experience of spirituality in relation to the dynamics of becoming just "in" the Spirit, who transforms human agency so that it may share in the self-giving "suffering" love of Jesus Christ that manifests the arriving reign of divine peace. The literature on spirituality in recent years has increasingly emphasized the intrinsic link between spirituality and the issues of morality, virtue, and the pursuit of the good life.[1] In part 2 Steve will engage some of the significant psychological studies that show the relation between the virtues and human health and wholeness. In this chapter I will point to the growing number of theological voices that are insisting that spirituality should not—and ultimately cannot—be separated from *justice*.[2] I might have titled this chapter "Becoming Good," but this phrase is too easily reducible to individualistic terms, to an inner feeling of well-being. This anemic, self-centered spirituality does not provide what we most deeply desire. The longing to love and be loved in peaceful fellowship can only be satisfied as our agency is transformed by the Spirit, who forms us into a just community that manifests true love as Christ did: by laying down our lives for one another (1 John 3:16). Transforming spirituality is not merely about changing particular functional behaviors or developing an inner feeling that one is "right" because of an external decree—it is about *becoming just* through spiritual union with God in Christ.

The Longing for Justice in Scripture

In the biblical witness, the desire for personal righteousness—being considered "good"—is not divorced from the broader longing for *justice* in community. A brief excursus on the translation of a key biblical term may help explain why this connection is often missed in the English-speaking world. In the Sermon on the Mount, Jesus is explicit about the

1. For an overview, see Richard M. Gula, *The Good Life: Where Morality and Spirituality Converge* (New York: Paulist, 1999); and Mark O'Keefe, *Becoming Good, Becoming Holy: On the Relationship of Christian Ethics and Spirituality* (New York: Paulist, 1995).
2. For examples, cf. Matthew L. Lamb, "Christian Spirituality and Social Justice," *Horizons* 10 (1983): 32–49; William R. Callahan, "Spirituality and Justice: An Evolving Vision of the Great Commandment," in *Contemporary Spirituality: Responding to the Divine Initiative*, ed. Francis A. Eigo (Villanova: Villanova University Press, 1983), 137–61; Alice de V. Perry and John S. Rolland, "Spirituality Expressed in Community Action and Social Justice: A Therapeutic Means to Liberation and Hope," in *Spiritual Resources in Family Therapy* (New York: Guilford, 1999); Rosemary Haughton, "The Spirituality of Social Justice," in *To Do Justice and Right upon the Earth*, ed. Mary E. Stamps (Collegeville, MN: Liturgical Press, 1993), 1–15; Ada María Isasi-Díaz, "To Be Fully Alive Is to Work for the Common Good: Spirituality, Justice, and Solidarity Are Combined in This Struggle," *Church and Society* 89 (1998): 11–18; Kevin W. Irwin, "Liturgy, Justice, and Spirituality," *Liturgical Ministry* 7 (1998): 162–74.

proper object of human desire: "strive first for the kingdom of God and his *righteousness*" (Matt. 6:33). The Greek word that is translated by the NRSV and most English versions as "righteousness" is *dikaiosunē*. In Spanish this word is usually rendered *justicia*, and in French, *justice*. In both of these languages, translators typically do not separate divine justice from the divine reign (as most English versions do) but make them parallel concepts. For example, one popular French translation renders the text, "Cherchez premièrement *le royaume et la justice* de Dieu."[3] This approach lines up with the Latin Vulgate, which also linked these concepts: we are primarily to seek God's *regnum et iustitiam*. In Luther's translation of Matthew 6:33, the term *dikaiosunē* is rendered *Gerechtigkeit*, which has a connotation closer to "justice" than the individualistic meaning that has come to accompany the English term "righteousness." Whereas the latter easily lends itself to an individualistic (and inner-oriented) view of salvation, the connotation of "justice" reminds us that the agency of God that grants us life in the Spirit also orients us outward to our neighbors.[4]

A similar phenomenon is evident in the translation of the Hebrew word *tsedeq*, which is typically rendered with terms that connote "justice"—except in English. Scholars are increasingly challenging this prevailing tendency, arguing that "justice" better captures the communal aspect of this term in the political and religious life of Israel and the early church.[5] A willingness to acknowledge the link between spirituality and justice is (not surprisingly) more evident among theologians and biblical scholars working with or for the oppressed.[6] Of course, we are not forced to choose: *either* individualistic righteousness *or* social justice. The two are intrinsically related in the longing for a right relation to God and one's neighbors. In his polemic against those in the community of Israel who

3. *La Sainte Bible* (Deerfield, FL: Vida, 1991).

4. We might speculate that a preference for the former soteriological approach in English theological discourse was bolstered by the 1611 version of the Bible authorized by King James. Both the individualistic anthropology of early modern philosophy and the anxiety of seventeenth-century monarchs about prophetic demands for justice might help to explain the translators' preference for "righteousness," which can promote a piety that is focused on the inner self.

5. Cf. Steven M. Voth, "Justice and/or Righteousness: A Contextualized Analysis of *sedeq* in the KJV (English) and RVR (Spanish)," in *The Challenge of Bible Translation*, ed. Glen G. Scorgie, Mark L. Strauss, and Steven M. Voth (Grand Rapids: Zondervan, 2003), 321–45; Jason J. Ripley, "Covenantal Concepts of Justice and Righteousness, and Catholic-Protestant Reconciliation: Theological Implications and Explorations," *Journal of Ecumenical Studies* 38, no. 1 (Winter 2001): 95–108.

6. E.g., Humberto Alfaro, "Faith and Justice: The Spirituality of the Hebrew Scriptures," in *The Agitated Mind of God*, ed. Dale T. Irvin and Akintunde E. Akinade (Maryknoll, NY: Orbis, 1996), 103–14. This is also evident in the work of many liberation and feminist theologians, as we will see below.

claim to be in right relation to God but are acting unjustly by oppressing others, the prophet Amos insists that an individual's fulfillment of sacrificial regulations cannot mediate the good life.

> I hate, I despise your festivals,
>   and I take no delight in your solemn assemblies.
> Even though you offer me your burnt offerings and grain offerings,
>   I will not accept them;
> and the offerings of well-being of your fatted animals
>   I will not look upon.
> Take away from me the noise of your songs;
>   I will not listen to the melody of your harps.
> But *let justice roll down like waters*,
>   and *righteousness like an ever-flowing stream*. (Amos 5:21–24)

God calls the community into a transformed restructuring of their life together, which requires justice and righteousness.[7] Amos urges the rich—those "cows of Bashan" (4:1), whose relation to the goods of the world is inhibiting a just society—to pursue the truly good life that requires self-giving love for the other.

The prophetic call to redemptive spirituality was tied to the longing for justice. As we have seen, the Hebraic understanding of "spirit" (*ruakh*) has to do with life, with the breath that "motivates" human agency. Micah summarizes what God requires of the Israelite who seeks the good life: "He has told you, O mortal, what is good; and what does the LORD require of you but to do *justice*, and to love kindness, and to walk humbly with your God?" (Mic. 6:8). Isaiah prophesies that God does not want sacrifices; those who stretch out their hands and make many prayers will not find God. They are urged to cease their oppressive behavior and instead: "*seek justice*, rescue the oppressed, defend the orphan, plead for the widow" (Isa. 1:17). The peaceful reign of God will be manifested through the outpouring of a Spirit from on high; "Then justice will dwell in the wilderness, and righteousness abide in the fruitful field" (Isa. 32:15–16).

In his rebuke of Jehoiakim, the prophet Jeremiah makes clear that an intimate relation with God—a "right" relation to divine agency—takes shape in concrete love for the other:

> Are you a king
>   because you compete in cedar?

7. Note the pairing of the terms *mishpat* (here: "justice") and *tsedeq* (here: "righteousness") in the last two lines. These concepts overlap, but generally speaking, the first has to do with forensic issues that are treated in a court of law whereas the latter is a broader (and higher) standard that is recognized among the members of the community.

> Did not your father eat and drink
>   and *do justice and righteousness?*
> Then it was well with him.
> He judged the cause of the *poor and needy;*
>   then it was well.
> *Is not this to know me?*
>   says the LORD. (Jer. 22:15–16)

The Hebrew Bible testifies to the Israelites' longing for the good life in a diversity of ways and throughout a variety of genres.[8] Already in the call of Abraham, and on through the story of the exodus, it is a longing for justice, for peaceful community, that leads the people of Israel forward. Being in right relation to God has an irreducibly social dimension, and this permeates Israel's experience and understanding of good and evil.[9] The ambiguity of the role of the Torah in the development of Hebrew moral and social regulations has been well documented.[10] It seems clear, however, that the "law" came to function in a way that mediated Yahweh's governance of the ethical life of the community. It was a guide to the truly good life, even if this was not measured in the commodities that earthly rulers tend to value. For the psalmist, the law mediated the justifying presence of Yahweh: "Happy are those who keep his decrees, who seek him with their whole heart" (Ps. 119:2). Seeking the good life into which the law leads is associated with seeking God. "See, I have longed for your precepts; in your righteousness give me life" (119:40). Throughout the Psalms, God's decrees (or statutes, commandments, words, etc.) evoke happiness and delight, for they call the Israelites into the just community they desire.[11]

Becoming just has to do with the transformation of the way in which we use our power in relation to finite others. The provision of the law orients the community toward a particular ideal: there will "be no one in need among you" (Deut. 15:4). In the New Testament, this ideal shapes the community that receives the Spirit of Christ; "there was not a needy person among them" (Acts 4:34). The provision of the trinitarian God creates the conditions for the renewal of community in the Spirit of love and justice.

8. Cf. R. Norman Whybray, *The Good Life in the Old Testament* (London: T&T Clark, 2002). For an overview, cf. Barbara Ellen Bowe, *Biblical Foundations of Spirituality: Touching a Finger to the Flame* (Lanham, MD: Rowman & Littlefield, 2003).

9. Walter Brueggemann, "Theodicy in a Social Dimension," *Journal for the Study of the Old Testament* 33 (1985): 3–25.

10. E.g., cf. Daniel Friedmann, *To Kill and Take Possession: Law, Morality, and Society in Biblical Stories* (Peabody, MA: Hendrickson, 2002).

11. Cf. Paul Joyce, "The Kingdom of God and the Psalms," in *The Kingdom of God and Human Society*, ed. R. Barbour (Edinburgh: T&T Clark, 1993), 42–59.

An emphasis on the biblical longing for justice calls us to rethink our response to the "problem of evil." Jesus' call to seek justice is not characterized by a theoretical defense or justification of the status quo, as in early modern and so many contemporary forms of theodicy, but by an active participation in the transforming agency of divine love that forms righteous persons in just communities. When we look at Jesus' ministry, the problem is not simply the evils of physical suffering and social oppression but also the "goods" of this life that have seduced the healthy into thinking they do not need a doctor and the rich into believing that they do not need a deliverer. In response to the finite evils of sickness and oppression, Jesus heals and sets free, but entering into the kingdom of God (the reign of divine justice) is more difficult for those who are defining their lives by their own attempts to maintain control over finite goods (cf. Luke 6:2–26; 18:18–25). Those who have been seduced by the deceitfulness of wealth, who use their physical or political power to secure their own goods at the expense of others, are called to repent from what keeps them from sharing in the reign of divine justice—the "problem of good."

Because spiritual transformation is a dynamic process, it is important to emphasize that Christian life involves *becoming* just. The New Testament speaks of our salvation—our being brought into health (*salus*)—in past, present, and future terms. Redemptive transformation is experienced as a remembering and anticipating that shape our coming-to-be in the present. Believers are urged to press on toward the goal, to *become* like Christ in his death (Phil. 3:7–16). They are called toward the perfection of the righteousness that is taking form in them (2 Cor. 13:5–9; Heb. 6:1–2). The Corinthians are already "believers," and yet Paul calls them into a more intimate experience of being reconciled with God so that in Christ they "might become the righteousness [*dikaiosunē*] of God" (2 Cor. 5:21), participating in the ministry of reconciliation that creates the good life. This experience is both "already" and "not yet"—we are justified, are becoming justified, and will be justified. God's justifying agency embraces and redeems all the temporal modes of redemptive experience, transforming human spirituality by calling it to participate in the absolute Goodness of the mutual love of the triune life.

Spirituality and Goodness in the Christian Tradition

This biblical longing has been a dominant theme in the Christian tradition, particularly among those whose theological reflection was implicitly connected to facilitating spiritual transformation. The desire for goodness brings up the question of the way in which humans may be related to God, who alone is Good—as Jesus points out in his response to the rich young man (Mark 10:18). Finding the good life we seek, therefore, involves coming into relation with God, which occurs through the gracious agency of the divine Spirit, who draws us into the loving relation between the Father and the Son. As early Christian theologians sought to articulate their understanding of God, they were also faced with the task of showing how the human spirit may be transformed in intimate relation to the divine Spirit who orients and motivates concrete acts of self-giving love in community.

The mystical tradition offers us significant resources for linking spirituality and a theological understanding of God as "the Good." In the prologue of *The Life of Moses*, Gregory of Nyssa asserts, "The Divine One is himself the Good (in the primary and proper sense of the word), whose very nature is goodness."[12] For Nyssa, the truly infinite Good should not be conceived as one good thing among many, nor as the "best" thing around, and not even simply as "good" defined as that which is over against "evil." He acknowledges that it is appropriate to think of evil as that which is other than the Good, and to think of God as the Good by nature. But those who define the Good as essentially bounded by evil make God dependent upon, and limited by, evil. Their argument leads to the conclusion, argues Nyssa, that God "is enclosed by evil. . . . Therefore, no consideration will be given to anything enclosing infinite nature. It is not in the nature of what is unenclosed to be grasped. But every desire for the Good which is attracted to that ascent constantly expands as one progresses in pressing on to the Good."[13] Like so many patristic theologians, Nyssa is influenced here by a Neoplatonic understanding of the relation between the divine and the Good. His explication of the human relation to God as a constantly expanding ascent is shaped, however, by the Christian doctrine of the infinite trinitarian Creator, which leads him to spell out this intensification in explicit relation to the Logos and the Spirit.

Augustine too was concerned with explaining the longing of the human soul for God, whom he described as "the highest good, than which there is no higher." He argued that the human soul (or spirit) is "from" God and yet at the same time longs always for the unchangeable Good.[14] Like Plotinus and many of the Stoics, Augustine believed that the human soul was in some sense already "good" and naturally longed for the Good. As a Christian theologian, however, he was faced with the problem of explaining how the human soul could participate

12. Gregory of Nyssa, *The Life of Moses* (New York: Paulist, 1978), 31.

13. Ibid., 116.

14. Augustine, *Concerning the Nature of Good, against the Manichaeans* (*NPNF¹* 4:351).

in the Good (or, conversely, how God could in some sense be "in" the human soul) without positing the divinity of the soul. Phillip Cary has argued that this is the conundrum that led to Augustine's "invention" of the idea of the "inner self," which has so deeply impacted Western philosophy and theology.[15]

Like Augustine, Thomas Aquinas speaks of God as the "supreme good" (*Summa theologiae* Ia, q. 6, art. 2). His depiction of the human soul's orientation toward the Good is primarily outlined, however, in terms of the "virtues" of the individual (cf. *Summa theologiae* IIa), reflecting his dependence on the Aristotelian tradition of eudaemonistic ethics. Both of these theologians maintained the biblical insistence that human goodness is absolutely dependent on divine grace, and both recognized the implicitly communal nature of the good life. As we have seen, however, some streams of the Western tradition came to focus primarily on the inner goodness of the individual in their depictions of the "spiritual" life.

Pseudo-Dionysius had also affirmed the way in which the sacred writers "preeminently" set apart the name "Good" for the "supra-divine God." The gracious presence of the Good "extends goodness into all things" in such a way that it evokes in creatures their desire for the Good. Intelligent creatures "abide in the goodness of God and draw from it the foundation of what they are, their coherence, their vigilance, their home. Their longing for the Good makes them what they are and confers on them their well-being."[16] The idea that human goodness is a participation in divine goodness was often expressed by mystical writers throughout the centuries.

Julian of Norwich's (1342–c. 1423) *Showings* illustrates the way in which the ideas of Infinity, Trinity, and Futurity shape this spiritual relation. She observes that it is God's "endless goodness" that protects and draws us into relation, evoking a "grace-given desire for our salvation" (LT [long text] 49). Reflecting on her thirteenth revelation, Julian introduces a refrain that will appear throughout the rest of her book: "All will be well, and every kind of thing will be well." In chapter 31, she observes that the Lord comforted her with the words "I may make all things well, and I can make all things well, and I shall make all things well, and I will make all things well; and you will see yourself that every kind of thing will be well." As she makes clear, this divine love that brings well-being (goodness) should be explicated in trinitarian terms.[17]

15. Phillip Cary, *Augustine's Invention of the Inner Self: The Legacy of a Christian Platonist* (New York: Oxford University Press, 2000), 140.

16. Pseudo-Dionysius, *The Complete Works*, trans. Colm Luibheid and Paul Rorem (New York: Paulist, 1987), 71–72.

17. Julian of Norwich, *Showings*, ed. E. Colledge and J. Walsh (New York: Paulist, 1978), 229: "When he says 'I may,' I understand this to apply to the Father; and when he

Another common characteristic of the mystical tradition has been a recognition that spiritual transformation in relation to God as the absolute Good requires detachment from earthly goods. Although this sometimes took excessively ascetic forms, the emphasis on detachment was aimed at accounting for the biblical claim that entering the good life in just community requires a radical sharing with those in need. One of the best-known examples is St. Francis of Assisi, who was born into a wealthy family but experienced a spiritual transformation that led him to strip himself (literally) of worldly attachments and begin a new life of service to the poor and sick. The "little brothers" who followed him over the next few years (and centuries) chose poverty for the sake of the Gospel. Francis urged his followers not to rely on worldly goods but to "pursue what they must desire above all things: to have the Spirit of the Lord and his holy manner of working."[18] His vision of spirituality involved imitating the practice of Jesus Christ—actively laying down one's life for the sake of participating in the reign of divine justice.

After joining the Franciscan order, St. Bonaventure outlined his understanding of Francis's spirituality in explicitly theological terms in *The Soul's Journey into God*. The journey begins with reflection on the order and value of sensible things, which must be left behind as the soul ascends to the higher realm of insensible things. Bonaventure explicitly connects the idea of divine goodness to a trinitarian understanding of God. The Good is inherently "self-diffusive," communicating to the other. If the supreme Good eternally communicates itself, "then you can see that through the highest communicability of the good, there must be a Trinity of the Father and the Son and the Holy Spirit. From supreme goodness, it is necessary that there be in the Persons . . . supreme mutual intimacy."[19] This insight opens up conceptual space for understanding human spirituality as a response to the divine invitation to share in this intimacy of loving and being loved, which transforms us as we show love in concrete ways to our neighbors (and enemies).

The early Reformers also emphasized the way the spirituality of Christian love takes shape in community and transforms political life.

---

says 'I can,' I understand it for the Son; and when he says 'I will,' I understand it for the Holy Spirit; and when he says 'I shall,' I understand it for the unity of the blessed Trinity, three persons and one truth; and when he says 'You will see yourself,' I understand it for the union of all men who will be saved in the blessed Trinity."

18. Francis of Assisi, *Francis and Clare: The Complete Works* (New York: Paulist, 1982), 144.

19. Bonaventure, *The Soul's Journey into God*, in *Selections*, trans. Ewert H. Cousins (New York: Paulist, 1978), 104; cf. 61.

The interplay of religious and social reform in Germany in the wake of Luther's protestations is well known. Calvin's attempts to facilitate a just society in Geneva were inseparable from his desire to orient persons in love toward the infinite source of goodness—God in Christ through the Spirit. In a prefatory address to the king of France, Calvin explains that his *Institutes* was written to help those "who are touched with any zeal for religion" so that they "might be shaped to true godliness."[20] Love and justice are intimately related. Calvin interprets Paul's summary of the whole law in the command "Love your neighbor as yourself" (Gal. 5:14) to mean that "the law only enjoins us to observe right and equity toward men, that thereby we may become practiced in witnessing to a pious fear of him, if we have any of it in us" (*Institutes* II.8.53).[21] The fourth book of the *Institutes* is Calvin's explication of the way in which God "invites" and "holds" us in the "society of Christ," justly ordering the community in love.

The Protestant Scholastic debates over the "order of salvation," which focused on the causes that moved a person from one state to another, contributed to an understanding of spirituality that sometimes appeared overly individualistic and mechanical. Even many of the Pietists and Puritans who reacted against these tendencies continued to think of "goodness" first in terms of the inner state of the individual, which then could (and should) have external effects. As we have seen, however, the biblical understanding of the longing for goodness cannot be separated from the salutary ordering of the community. The last few decades have seen a recovery of the link between justice and spirituality, especially among feminist and liberation theologians.[22] Gustavo Gutiérrez argues that spirituality involves "taking over the historical practice of Jesus," which means making the world of the poor our own as we live out our relationship with God together.[23] Be-

---

20. John Calvin, *Institutes of the Christian Tradition*, ed. John T. McNeill, trans. Ford Lewis Battles (Philadelphia: Westminster, 1960), 9.

21. "Everything undertaken apart from love and all disputes that go beyond it, we regard as incontrovertibly unjust and impious" (*Institutes* IV.20.21). Cf. Carol Johnston, "Essential Connections: Spirituality and Justice in a Reformed Perspective," *Church and Society* 83 (1992): 33–41.

22. Cf., e.g., Jon Sobrino, *Spirituality of Liberation: Toward Political Holiness*, trans. Robert R. Barr (Maryknoll, NY: Orbis, 1988), 189; Sarah Coakley, *Powers and Submissions: Spirituality, Philosophy, and Gender* (Oxford, England: Blackwell, 2002); John W. De Gruchy, *Liberating Reformed Theology: A South African Contribution to an Ecumenical Debate* (Grand Rapids: Eerdmans; Cape Town: David Philip, 1991); Johanna W. H. Van Wijk-Bos, *Reformed and Feminist: A Challenge to the Church* (Louisville: Westminster John Knox, 1991); Allan Aubrey Boesak and Leonard Sweetman, *Black and Reformed: Apartheid, Liberation, and the Calvinist Tradition* (Maryknoll, NY: Orbis, 1984); Leslie Orr Macdonald, "A Spirituality for Justice: The Enemy of Apathy," *Feminist Theology* 23 (2000): 13–21.

23. Gustavo Gutiérrez, *We Drink from Our Own Wells: The Spiritual Journey of a People*, 20th anniversary ed. (Maryknoll, NY: Orbis, 2003), 31.

fore exploring the dynamics of acting in the Spirit and the intensification of love by sharing in the suffering of Jesus Christ, let us identify some developments in philosophy and science that may help us articulate an understanding of spirituality as becoming just.

Insights from Philosophy and Natural Science

As we observed in chapter 2, the dualistic, individualistic, and mechanistic categories that shaped the concept of "spirit" in early modern thought have increasingly been challenged in late modern philosophy and science. This opens up conceptual space for a fresh articulation of the Christian understanding of the relation between spirituality, goodness, and justice. Broadly speaking, ethics is the philosophical area of discourse that is primarily concerned with human acting and the longing for the good life. Insofar as the transformation of the human spirit takes shape within this longing, a reforming Pneumatology should take into account contemporary insights into these dynamics. Part 2 will outline some significant research in the *social* sciences on the importance of virtue in understanding human spirituality, and so we will limit our attention here primarily to some of the *natural* sciences in which the other-regarding agency of human persons has become an object of analysis.

Most ancient Greek philosophers agreed that there is an intrinsic link between the divine and the human desire for the good life; the latter is dependent upon the former. This had direct ramifications for their understanding of ethics, virtue, and justice. In Plato's *Republic*, Socrates is asked to explain the relations among the divine, the Good, and human justice. He suggests a structural similarity between a just person and a just city; both are formed by a proper organization of their constituent parts in a way that orients them toward well-being. Both of these are made possible by the "form of the Good."[24] Aristotle also discusses political justice but focuses more heavily on the virtue (*aretē*) and moral states of the particular individual. The human pursuit of justice is natural in the sense that the proper end or function of the individual is "happiness," or living well (*eudaimonia*), and this naturally takes shape in political form, since "man is the political animal."[25] Aristotle explicitly links his views of ethics to his (theological) metaphysics: an individual's movement toward justice and happiness is ultimately dependent on the first unmoved mover, that is, God.

24. Plato, *Republic*, Book IV.
25. Cf. Aristotle, *Nichomachean Ethics*; *Politics*, 1253a3.

The assumption that human agency in general—and ethical or just behavior in particular—is dependent somehow on the divine was challenged during the Enlightenment.[26] In an attempt to escape the putatively blind faith that drove the interminable religious wars of the early modern period, reason was elevated above revelation and became the arbiter of what is "just." We can understand the philosophical suspicion that many political leaders were using religious metanarratives to defend their own social aims. The attempts to establish a rational theory for a just society was taken up by various thinkers from Rousseau to Marx, but after the world wars of the twentieth century, most philosophers relinquished optimism about the prospects of a society based solely on human reason. Some forms of postmodern philosophy call for the deconstruction of any and all universalizing ethical metanarratives, citing the contextual embeddedness of such theories and their tendency toward totalitarianism. Radically relativistic versions of this approach are caught in the irony of attacking any attempt to hold up the values of one community over another, even as they affirm the value of their own relativistic model—leading us to wonder about the basis for this self-exemption. These ongoing debates demonstrate that the irrepressible human longing for life in relation to the Good (even if there is disagreement about what that life is and how to secure it) is not so easy to dismiss from philosophical discourse.

In some more reconstructive forms of late modern ethical theory, we find insights that can help heal some of the damage caused by the early modern separation between the longing for truth and the longing for goodness (and beauty). One of the best-known philosophers who has responded to the privileging of epistemology (and metaphysics) over ethics is Emmanuel Levinas. He has argued for the priority of the primordial ethical relation of face-to-face encounter, for the "ethical relationship which subtends discourse is not a species of consciousness whose ray emanates from the I; it puts the I in question. This putting in question emanates from the other."[27] Many Enlightenment thinkers considered the presence of a divine Other as a threat to the freedom and power of human reason and agency. For Levinas, however,

---

26. For a historical introduction to this philosophical shift, cf. Charles Taylor, *Sources of the Self: The Making of the Modern Identity* (Cambridge: Harvard University Press, 1989); and Alasdair MacIntyre, *After Virtue*, 2nd ed. (Notre Dame, IN: University of Notre Dame Press, 1984).

27. Emmanuel Levinas, *Totality and Infinity: An Essay on Exteriority*, trans. Alphonso Lingis (Pittsburgh: Duquesne University Press, 1969), 195. "The face opens the primordial discourse whose first word is obligation, which no 'interiority' permits avoiding. . . . Preexisting the disclosure of being in general taken as basis of knowledge and as meaning of being is the relation with the existent that expresses himself; preexisting the plane of ontology is the ethical plane" (p. 201).

the "absolutely other—the Other—does not limit the freedom of the same; calling it to responsibility, it founds it and justifies it. . . . This is the situation we call welcome of the face."[28] Levinas's philosophical emphasis on the role of the primordial ethical relation for human agency (and subjectivity) opens conceptual space for describing the human longing for goodness as constituted by the presence of an infinite Other who invites the creaturely spirit to participate in intimate loving fellowship.

Research on the dynamics of other-regarding agency in human behavior has become an important aspect of the growing interdisciplinary dialogue between science and theology. It is generally agreed that humans act in ways that *appear* altruistic—regarding the other (Latin, *alter*) over the self—but some evolutionary theorists argue that such behavior is reducible to the laws of natural selection at the genetic level or that socially altruistic acts can ultimately be explained in terms of biological functions.[29] This reductionistic interpretation is increasingly challenged not only for its philosophical naïveté[30] but also for its inability to account for the broader scientific data. For example, Elliott Sober and David Wilson have attempted to show how genuinely altruistic behavior is an important feature of human nature, a feature that cannot be explained without reference to the social dynamics that give rise to selflessness.[31] As Jerome Kagan points out, the study of morality engages phenomena that cannot be described in merely biological terms; the unique human awareness of self and other, together with the use of the conceptual categories of "good" and "bad," appeared with the emergence of *Homo sapiens*, but this does not mean that the *intentions* of human agents may be explained in purely functional or behavioral terms.[32]

A growing number of scholars are pursuing the relation between scientific research on altruism and the human religious experience of "unlimited love," which is common to many traditions. The issue of the role of this experience in other-regarding agency is being examined from a variety of disciplinary perspectives, including neurobiology, psychology,

28. Ibid., 197.

29. Cf. Richard Dawkins, *The Selfish Gene* (New York: Oxford University Press, 1989); Edward O. Wilson, *Sociobiology: The New Synthesis*, 25th anniversary ed. (Cambridge: Harvard University Press, 2000).

30. Cf. Alister McGrath, *Dawkins' God: Genes, Memes, and the Meaning of Life* (Oxford, England: Blackwell, 2004).

31. E. Sober and D. Wilson, *Unto Others: The Evolution and Psychology of Unselfish Behavior* (Cambridge: Harvard University Press, 1998).

32. Jerome Kagan, "Morality, Altruism, and Love," in *Altruism and Altruistic Love: Science, Philosophy, and Religion in Dialogue*, ed. Stephen Post et al. (New York: Oxford University Press, 2002), 40–50.

sociology, and theology.[33] In *Unlimited Love: Altruism, Compassion, and Service*, Stephen Post provides a summary of this interdisciplinary project and explores some of the implications for Christian theology and ethics. Building on the work of Sorokin, he suggests empirical questions that can help us study the intensity, extensivity, duration, purity, and adequacy of human love. For our present purposes, however, the more important point is Post's recognition of the implications of this research for our understanding of spirituality and its relation to divine love. He begins by taking seriously the testimony of altruists over the centuries to their experience of a constant and unchanging source of love in the universe. For Christians, true love occurs through communion with God—who is love. This implies that true spirituality is characterized by "the manifestation of abiding love for others, which fully determines the meaning and the goodness of our lives."[34]

The point of this interdisciplinary dialogue is not to prove the existence of a divine Spirit of love; the deconstructive hermeneutics of suspicion will not be satisfied by the testimonies of the Good Samaritans among us. However, the scientific exploration of this other-regarding agency raises questions about the ultimate origin, condition, and goal of human altruism, for here we are dealing with an expression of love that breaks out of the functional competence that guides our concern for passing on our genes. Similarly, the ethical turn in philosophical discourse can remind us as Christians that knowing and acting are mutually implicated in spiritual transformation. Along with the recovery of biblical and traditional emphases on the longing for justice in relation to the gracious and evocative presence of the absolute Good, these developments open up conceptual space for the articulation of a truly *reformative* Pneumatology.

Acting in the Spirit

In the remainder of this chapter we will explore the dynamics of transforming spirituality as an intensification of loving agency in the Spirit, which takes shape in Christian community as a diaconal sharing in the suffering of Jesus Christ. The intensely relational longing to love and be loved that characterizes the intentional agency of human persons is already and always upheld (along with all creaturely life) by

33. For example, cf. Stephen G. Post et al., eds., *Research on Altruism and Love: An Annotated Bibliography of Major Studies in Psychology, Sociology, Evolutionary Biology, and Theology* (Philadelphia: Templeton Foundation, 2003).

34. Stephen G. Post, *Unlimited Love: Altruism, Compassion, and Service* (Philadelphia: Templeton Foundation, 2003), 135.

the divine Spirit. In the New Testament the manifestation of divine love is explicitly tied to the presence of the Spirit in human life. In Romans 5:5 Paul says that "God's love has been poured into our hearts through the Holy Spirit that has been given to us." The Spirit that God gives is a Spirit of "power and love" (2 Tim. 1:7; cf. Col. 1:8). One way to outline the intelligibility of this redemptive experience in late modern culture is to explicate the claim that the Spirit of the biblical God is the origin, condition, and goal of human acting.

First, let us point briefly to the significance of the New Testament call to a new way of living that shares in the justifying agency of the Spirit of love. John encourages his readers to "love, not in word or speech, but in truth and *action*" (1 John 3:18). As we saw above, Jesus summarized the ethical demand that confronts human acting in terms of the call to love God and one's neighbors (and even one's enemies). The book of Acts tells the story of the transformed agency of the apostolic community, which received new power and new life through the Spirit. Paul interpreted this agency in terms of living "in," "by," or "according to" the Spirit. If human agents depend on the flesh or on the law to secure the good life, they will inevitably fail (Rom. 5:12–14). Paul argues that "those who live according to the flesh set their minds on the things of the flesh, but those who live according to the Spirit set their minds on the things of the Spirit." The former way of acting brings death, but the latter brings life and peace. "But you are not in the flesh; you are *in the Spirit*, since the Spirit of God dwells in you. . . . But if Christ is in you, though the body is dead because of sin, the Spirit is life because of righteousness [*dikaiosunē*]" (Rom. 8:5–10; cf. Gal. 5:16). The opposition between acting in the flesh and acting in the Spirit does not have to do with two substances that make up a human person but with two different ways in which the whole person may orient his or her embodied and socially implicated longing to love and be loved—either depending on the finite power of the ego or on the infinite gracious agency of the Spirit to bring about the good life.

But how are we to make sense of the idea of acting "in" the Spirit? The previous chapter introduced the dynamics of the dialectical identity of the human spirit. Here we may make a similar reconstructive move by suggesting the concept of dialectical *agency*. Here "agency" is not meant to refer to a mechanical force or even the power of the faculty of the "will." Although we may distinguish between them for the sake of analysis, human agency and human identity cannot ultimately be separated, for these are simply two ways of explicating the dynamic coming-to-be that human persons *are*.

Several passages in the New Testament suggest the idea of a human agency that is both "I" and "not I." On the one hand, it is the believer who acts, but on the other hand, it is the Spirit who acts "in" or "through" the believer. For example, Jesus encourages his disciples with these words: "When they bring you to trial and hand you over, do not worry beforehand about what *you are to say*; but say whatever is given you at that time, for it is *not you* who speak, but the Holy Spirit" (Mark 13:11). The power of God motivates and strengthens the believer "through" the Spirit (Eph. 3:16). Prophetic agency is depicted in a similar way: "no prophecy ever came by human will, but men and women moved by the Holy Spirit spoke from God" (2 Pet. 1:21).

The way in which salvation is "worked out" is dialectical. This is expressed in Paul's exhortation to the Philippians to "work out your own salvation with fear and trembling; for it is God who is at work in you, enabling you both to will and to work for his good pleasure" (Phil. 2:12–13). Paul can "do all things" but only "through" the One who strengthens him (4:13). The Holy Spirit "activates" and "manifests" divine love for the common good of the community, and yet it is really human agents who are exercising these "gifts" (1 Cor. 12:1–11; cf. 2:4). The divine initiative is manifested in reconciliation of the world to God "in Christ," and yet we are called to share in this "ministry of reconciliation" (2 Cor. 5:18–20).

The transformed agency of the human spirit in the Christian experience of redemption is dependent on the initiative of divine grace, and yet this does not exclude the real speaking, working, or ministering of human persons. How can we think about the relation between the agency of the human spirit and the Holy Spirit so as to make sense of their *unity* but not obliterate the *distinction* between creature and Creator? It is important to recognize first that *all* personal agency is already dialectical. As the agency of a small child develops, an "ethical self" is formed and mediated through the child's relation to others (e.g., parents and peers), who act intentionally toward the child. The criteria for the evaluation of a "good" life are shaped by the primary *care*-givers, who are also typically the primary *law*-givers. The agency of the child is both gift and task. Ego functions are forged within the child's relations to others, but precisely because this relation to others involves an invitation to reciprocal intentionality. An agency that is overly reliant on finite others may become absorbed into codependence, whereas overly anxious attempts to protect the agency of the finite self over against the other can lead to alienation. Neither of these fulfills the deep longing of human agents for loving and being loved in intimate community.

How, then, can we articulate Christian spirituality as "acting in the Spirit" in a way that avoids these problems? The recovery of the insights of Infinity, Trinity, and Futurity can once again help us in this endeavor. The agency of the Creator Spirit is truly infinite, encompassing and empowering all creaturely agency. This means that human agency is already and always upheld by the gracious reality of God, for "*in* him we *live and move* and have our being" (Acts 17:28). The believer's acting "in the Spirit" should be understood neither as being taken over by an immense potency that completely crushes finite agency nor as magically gaining access to a great force that simply extends the power of the human agent. From a psychological point of view, the former would be a kind of codependence writ large, and the latter a kind of religiously authorized narcissism. But if we remember we are dealing with (or, better, being dealt with by) the *truly infinite* divine Spirit, we can imagine the agency of the human spirit as operating dialectically "in" this Other. The reconciling agency of the Spirit neither crushes nor abandons, but constitutes creaturely agency as it calls us into the omnipotent love of divine life.

Divine agency is not defined over against finite objects of desire, for God *is* love (1 John 4:8). This claim is spelled out theologically in terms of the doctrine of the Trinity. God's life is the mutual love of the trinitarian persons. This eternal loving and being loved is the goal of human moral desire; it is the evocative agency of the Creator that graciously constitutes the conditions for creaturely participation in the good life of the Trinity. Only a trinitarian grammar can make sense of the Christian experience of spirituality. Our sharing in the reconciling activity of God is mediated by the trinitarian relations; it is through Christ that we have access "in one Spirit to the Father" (Eph. 2:18). The agency of one who lives "in" the Spirit is buoyed by the infinite love of divine life. Our destiny is provided by "God the Father," and we are "sanctified by the Spirit to be obedient to Jesus Christ" (1 Pet. 1:2). As we will see in the next section, human participation in divine love takes shape as a sharing in the suffering of Jesus Christ, who shows us what love is: "We know love by this, that he laid down his life for us—and we ought to lay down our lives for one another" (1 John 3:16).

We experience our agency "in" the Spirit as an orientation toward the future, which originates in the divine promise that calls us to share in eternal life. Our attempts to use our own finite power to control the future, to secure our own life against the threat of death, are pervaded by anxiety about our relation to the Good. Recognizing our own powerlessness opens us up to a transforming intimacy with God, upon whose grace our creaturely agency is wholly dependent. Gratefully accepting our agency as the gift and call of divine grace liberates us into a new way of interpreting our temporal experience—as constituted by the arrival of the eternal God of love, whose infinite power conditions and redeems temporality itself. The divine Spirit does not move through time as creatures do, but constitutes the temporal conditions for creaturely becoming. We experience the Spirit of the infinite trinitarian God as the presence of absolute Futurity, which opens up the modes of time, making finite agency possible as it evokes the longing to love and be loved. We no longer need to be anxious about our agency insofar as it shares in the reconciling agency of God in Christ, for the origin (and goal) of this life-giving agency in the Spirit is beyond the power of death.

It is crucial that we recognize the intrinsic role of communal life in the practice of Christian spirituality. In his first epistle, John insists that "eternal life" already abides in (among) those who love. "We know that we have passed from death to life because we love one another. Whoever does not love abides in death. All who hate a brother or sister are murderers, and you know that murderers do not have eternal life abiding in them" (1 John 3:14–15). The "fruit of the Spirit" are manifestations of this transforming agency in community: "love, joy, peace, patience, kindness, generosity, faithfulness, gentleness, and self-control" all occur in relation to the other. To "live by the Spirit," Paul insists, means that we "have crucified the flesh" and no longer compete with and envy one another (Gal. 5:22–24). Acting in the Spirit takes shape in the redemption of human relations, sanctifying the people of God so that they manifest divine love as a community of justice participating in the arriving reign of divine peace (cf. Rom. 15:15–16; 2 Thess. 2:13). The Christian community becomes "the righteousness [*justice*] of God" (2 Cor. 5:21) as it participates in the reconciling agency of the divine Spirit and is conformed to Christ's way of acting in the world.

Sharing in the Suffering of Jesus Christ

In chapter 3 we spelled out the Petrine idea of becoming "participants of the divine nature" (2 Pet. 1:4) in terms of the call to fellowship in Jesus Christ's intimate *knowledge* of the Father in the Spirit. The readers of 1 Peter are also urged to "rejoice insofar as you are sharing [*koinōneite*] Christ's *sufferings*" because whoever has suffered in the flesh (in the way Christ did) "has finished with sin" (1 Pet. 4:1, 13). To be a disciple of Jesus—and so to act in the Spirit as he did—is to suffer for the Gospel and for the kingdom of God. Timothy is encouraged to "share in suffering like a good soldier of Christ Jesus" (2 Tim. 2:3) and to join "in suffering for the gospel, relying on the power of God, who saved us and called us with a holy calling" (1:8–9). The afflictions of the Thessalonians are "intended to make you worthy of the kingdom of God, for which you are also suffering" (2 Thess. 1:5). Throughout the New Testament, the experience of loving and being loved by God takes shape as a way of acting that participates in the suffering of Christ, laying down our lives for one another.

Paul makes it clear that sharing in the glory of Jesus Christ (which we will explore in more detail in chapter 5) is intrinsically linked to fellowship in his sufferings. To the Philippians he writes, "I want to know Christ and the power of his resurrection and the sharing [*koinōnian*] of his sufferings by becoming like him in his death, if somehow I may attain the resurrection from the dead" (Phil. 3:10–11). The connection is also made explicit in his letter to the Romans: the Spirit of God bears witness "with our spirit that we are children of God, and if children, then heirs, heirs of God and joint heirs with Christ—if, in fact, we *suffer* with him [*sympaschomen*] so that we may also be *glorified* with him" (Rom. 8:16–17). Paul explains to the Corinthians that Christ suffered (and was raised) for the sake of others (2 Cor. 5:15). This means that fellowship in Christ's suffering is also a sharing in one another's suffering. All the members of the one body of Christ are called to "suffer together" (*sympaschei*) with the one who suffers (1 Cor. 12:26). As "the God of all consolation . . . consoles us in all our affliction," we are able "to console those who are in any affliction with the consolation with which we ourselves are consoled by God." The affliction experienced by Paul is for the "consolation and salvation" of the Corinthians. Insofar as they are patiently enduring the "same sufferings," his hope for them is unshaken. He assures them that "as you *share in our sufferings*, so also you *share in our consolation*" (2 Cor. 1:3–7).

Jesus' suffering does not mean that believers are now *excluded* from suffering. On the contrary, they are called into a new way of suffering for (and consoling) others. We are *included* in the suffering of Jesus, for this is precisely the way in which we share in the active ministry of the Spirit in the world. "For to this you have been called, because Christ also suffered for you, leaving you an example, so that you should follow in his steps." First Peter takes over the imagery of the suffering servant (cf. Isa. 53) and applies it to Jesus: "When he was abused, he did not return abuse; when he suffered, he did not threaten; but he entrusted himself to the one who judges justly. He himself bore our sins in his body on the cross, so that, free from sins, we might live for righteousness; by his wounds you have been healed" (1 Pet. 2:21–24).

Too often this passage (and others like it) has been used to quiet the voices of those who are abused and oppressed, which is precisely the opposite intention expressed in Jesus' own ministry. Jesus' suffering for and service to others was an active movement into their painful experience, manifesting the liberating love of the Spirit.

> The Spirit of the Lord is upon me,
>   because he has anointed me
>   to bring good news to the poor.
> He has sent me to proclaim release to the captives
>   and recovery of sight to the blind,
>   to let the oppressed go free,
> to proclaim the year of the Lord's favor. (Luke 4:18–19)

Luke's use of this quotation from Isaiah 61 at the inauguration of Jesus' public activity suggests that he understood his whole ministry—his agency in the Spirit—as the transformation of human life through participating in the arrival of divine justice and love.

How are we to understand the role of suffering in the process of spiritual transformation without condoning (or fostering) abuse? First, it is important to realize that the term *paschō* (and its stems and derivatives) had a broader meaning in the Greek language than the English idea of "suffering." Originally it simply referred to the experience of being affected by something beyond one's control, whether good or bad. For example, the NRSV translates the term *epathete* simply as "experience" in Galatians 3:4. We are called to share in Jesus' whole way of experiencing ("suffering") life in relation to God and neighbors. This way of life, which involves actively showing love and manifesting the liberating justice of God, is often met with violence from those whose interests are vested in the power structures of the status quo—leading to "suffering" in the narrower (negative) sense.

Thinking of Jesus' suffering more broadly, as a way of living that consoles others, entrusting one's whole life to the Father in the Spirit, helps us to understand how we can share in it—by acting in the Spirit so that our lives are conformed to the narrative shape of Christ's life. We should interpret Jesus' suffering—or "passion"—not only in terms of the few days leading up to his crucifixion but as the shape of his whole life and ministry, which culminated in those events. Jesus' agency involved a loving acceptance of the other that bore the burdens of injustice and invited his neighbors into a new experience of God—who alone is good (Mark 10:18). His passion was to "let the oppressed go free" (Luke 4:18), and this conflicted with the passion of the religious and political leaders of ancient Palestine. Because his agency was wholly dependent on his relation to the Good, he was able to exhaust himself, to offer all of his power for the sake of manifesting divine love, relying on the life-giving power of the Spirit even with his last breath on the cross.[35]

---

35. According to the book of Hebrews, even Jesus had to learn "obedience through suffering," for he "offered up prayers and supplications, with loud cries and tears, to

Jesus explained that "the Son can do nothing on his own, but only what he sees the Father doing; for whatever the Father does, the Son does likewise. . . . I can do nothing on my own. As I hear, I judge; and my judgment is just, because I seek to do not my own will but the will of him who sent me" (John 5:19, 30). Jesus does only what he sees the Father doing, that is, reaching out to free the oppressed, and so his passion takes the form of suffering at the hands of the powerful. In his last meeting with the disciples, Jesus makes it clear that he is calling them to the same kind of dialectical agency. His commandment is "that you *love* one another as I have loved you." What form does this love take? "No one has greater love than this, to *lay down one's life* for one's friends." Jesus now calls them friends, for he has made the Father known to them so that they can know what the Father is doing and "bear fruit that will last" (John 15:12–17).

Jesus' suffering—his experience of loving God and neighbors—demonstrates a way of acting in the Spirit that participates in the Father's love for the world. The cross represents the intensification of a real dynamic that had characterized his whole life, a way of responding in love to events beyond his control. Christian spirituality takes shape as we share in Christ's suffering, but this is no apathetic tolerance of the abuse of finite power. On the contrary, it is a way of experiencing life that passionately participates in the healing of agents so that they can become just and loving. This transforming process makes agents whole as they came to be wholly dependent on divine grace and are empowered to act as Jesus did. Love is not simply feeling sympathy for those in distress; it involves laying down our lives for others. Although this may eventually mean losing our lives at the hands of violent others, it most certainly means acting in the world in practical ways that bring consolation. "How does God's love abide in anyone who has the world's goods and sees a brother or sister in need and yet refuses help?" (1 John 3:16–17). Loving and being loved by God is not merely an abstract inner feeling but a holistic experience of fellowship that intensifies as we actively participate in Jesus' relation to the Good, which frees us from reliance on the "world's goods."

The "passion" of Christian life is intensely active, participating in the victory of divine love over the power of evil and injustice. This broader understanding of "passion" is evident in the work of Dietrich Bonhoeffer, who argued that Christian ethics *is* formation and "formation comes only by being drawn into the form of Jesus Christ."[36] He insisted that

---

the one who was able to save him from death, and he was heard because of his reverent submission" (Heb. 5:7–8).

36. Dietrich Bonhoeffer, *Ethics* (New York: Simon & Schuster, 1995), 80, 85.

the basis of Christian obedience (which I am calling dialectical agency in the Spirit) is "the *passion* of Christ." Reminding us that Jesus calls those who follow him to "*share his passion*," Bonhoeffer asks, "How can we convince the world by our preaching of the passion when we shrink from that passion in our own lives?" Christian ethics involves a passionate acting in the Spirit of love and justice.

> On the cross Jesus fulfilled the law he himself established and thus graciously keeps his disciples in the *fellowship* of his suffering. The cross is the only power in the world which proves that *suffering love* can avenge and vanquish evil. But it was just this *participation* in the cross which the disciples were granted when Jesus called them to him. They are called blessed [in the Sermon on the Mount] because of their visible *participation* in his cross.[37]

Christian agency takes the form of Christ in the world, sharing in his passionate love for others in dependence on the Spirit of justice. As disciples of Jesus, we are empowered by the Spirit to bear the burdens of the other, sharing in the gracious formation of a just community that manifests the self-giving love of God.

The Intensification of Love

The justice (or law) of God is fulfilled by love, as both Jesus and Paul insist (Matt. 22:36–40; cf. Mark 12:28–34; Rom. 13:8–10; Gal. 5:14; cf. James 2:8). Becoming just therefore involves becoming an agent who manifests love. Finite agents do not have the power to fulfill this law of love, and so becoming just ultimately depends on the grace of God, who calls us to share in divine love by following in the way of Christ in the power of the Spirit. Our moral desire is only conformed to Jesus' way of relating to the Good as we "die to sin" and are "crucified" to the world, no longer relying on our own power to secure the objects of our desire but actively resting in the omnipotent consoling agency of absolute Love. There are no shortcuts to developing a virtuous disposition; it requires the painful process of introspection and working out one's redemptive agency in community. This too occurs by the gracious agency of the

37. Dietrich Bonhoeffer, *The Cost of Discipleship*, rev. and unabridged ed. (New York: Macmillan, 1959), 161; emphasis added. Cf. Bonhoeffer, *No Rusty Swords: Letters, Lectures, and Notes, 1928–1936*, ed. Edwin H. Robertson, trans. Edwin H. Robertson and John Bowden (New York: Harper & Row, 1965); *Letters and Papers from Prison*, rev. ed. (New York: Macmillan, 1967); Geffrey B. Kelly, "Prayer and Action for Justice: Bonhoeffer's Spirituality," in *Cambridge Companion to Dietrich Bonhoeffer*, ed. John W. De Gruchy (New York and Cambridge: Cambridge University Press, 1999), 246–68.

Holy Spirit as Christ is formed in us (cf. Gal. 4:19). As the relation to the Good intensifies, the intentionality of believers is transformed by sharing in the intimate love of the trinitarian life, manifested in the world as self-giving reconciliation.

We can begin to spell out the dynamics of redemptive transformation in relation to human acting by pointing again to the classical "ways." We are awakened by the convicting presence of the Spirit to our own impotence as we struggle to secure the good life through our own agency. As we face the tension of our own (sinful) agency and admit our inability to control the objects of our love, the Spirit gracefully purges us of our attachment to finite desires. This purgation opens up to us a new way of interpreting our own agency in relation to God. Intentionality itself is transformed as our desire is oriented wholly toward and within the infinite Good. This holistic illumination of the relationality in which we find ourselves empowers us to become active participants in the manifestation of the redemptive light of divine love in the world. Although attention may be paid primarily to rules and regulations early in the formation process, redemptive transformation ultimately breaks out of this way of quantifying goodness. Becoming just is not simply conformity to a static external norm; it is a qualitative coming-into-union with the loving agency of the trinitarian God.

This redemptive process is the gracious transformation of the natural (creaturely) longing to love and be loved. A small child awakens to the incapacity of his own agency to secure the objects of his desire. Healthy development involves learning to accept one's interdependency in relation to others, being purged of total self-reliance, being illumined into ever-broadening interpretive horizons as one searches for the experience of peaceful agency wrapped up in an intimate loving union with an other. The divine Spirit is already and always active in the epigenetic development of human agency as the source of all creaturely life and as the evocative presence that upholds and qualifies personal experience in its complex self-relationality. The emergence of the relational structure of ego-functions provides space and time for the person to move from self-oriented agency to other-regarding agency and ultimately into an agency that is increasingly oriented by its relation to the divine Spirit. As "acting in the Spirit" becomes internalized, one is less worried about impressing God and more interested in participating with God in the manifestation of self-giving love.

As we experience the crucible of spiritual transformation we are called to attend to the way in which we are seduced and repulsed by finite goods and evils. The redemptive activity of the Spirit, who is closer to us than we are to ourselves, frees us from the painful tension of this pulling and pushing, calling us out of our self-reliance and into the truly infinite love of God. Formed for the sake of self-protection, our egoistic love is not powerful enough either to bring us into right relations with others or to keep them from crushing or abandoning us. Strengthening the ego fortifies the walls that keep us from intimacy, but weakening the ego leaves it vulnerable to the abusive other. This tension is inevitable as long as dialectical agency is mediated by a finite other. The gift of new life in the Spirit transforms the human spirit by expanding personal intentionality through intimacy with the truly infinite trinitarian God. We become just as we find our agency mediated by the reconciling power of divine love. As we are embraced within the infinite intimacy that is the life of God, we are able to embrace others in vulnerable self-giving love.

We can illustrate this in the life of the apostle Paul. As he found his own agency linked to the resurrected One, who is victor over sin and death, he was able to interpret his own suffering in a radically new way. Paul indicates that his suffering is "not worth comparing" (Rom. 8:18) with the glory being revealed. In 2 Corinthians 4:17 he argues that "this slight momentary affliction is preparing us for an eternal weight of glory beyond all measure." No pain that threatens nor any worldly pleasure that lures disrupts Paul's contentment (Phil. 4:11) because his contentment is grounded in an experience of a dynamic agency that cannot be extensively measured or compared to worldly goods or evils. Entering into this new way of intending, of actively interpreting and engaging one's experience in the cosmos, is an intensive process. Redemptive transformation occurs as we struggle or "grope" after God (Acts 17:27). "Finding" God, however, is first of all a being-found that evokes gratitude for the grace that gives us "life and breath and all things" (17:25). Paul argues elsewhere that our "reasonable worship" is the offering of our whole embodied agency to God, which takes shape as a "genuine" love that "holds fast" to the Good (cf. Rom. 12:1, 9).

Redemptive transformation liberates the human spirit from depending on its own ability to control the goods of the world that it has come to love. As Simone Weil suggests, we are called "to detach our desire from all good things and to wait. Experience proves that this waiting is satisfied. It is then we touch the absolute good."[38] For Weil, God (and so the Good) is beyond worldly necessity, which often bears down on us in painful, distressing ways. "The distance between the necessary and the good is the selfsame distance as that between the creature and the creator." Interpreting the Good in this way allows her to see the apparent absence of God (when the necessity of the world crushes) as "the most

---

38. Simone Weil, *Gravity and Grace*, trans. Arthur Wills (New York: Putnam, 1952), 58.

marvelous testimony of perfect love."[39] "For those who love, separation, although painful, is a good, because it is love. Even the distress of the abandoned Christ is a good. There cannot be a greater good for us on earth than to *share* in it."[40] Weil is even able to interpret extreme affliction—simultaneous physical, psychological, and social distress—as the point of intersection between creation and the Creator.[41]

This way of interpreting suffering may initially appear masochistic, and we should readily acknowledge that New Testament language about suffering with Christ has indeed sometimes been used in sadistic ways to condone oppression and quiet the abused. It is crucial, therefore, that we recognize that such an interpretation of *suffering* becomes redemptive only as a person's *agency* is transformed over time through the intensification of their experience of *being* in the Spirit as they share in the *glory* of Christ (cf. chapter 5). For our purposes here, it suffices to point out that even in the relationship between human lovers, we have ample testimony to the experience of the strengthening of love that comes only through intense times of struggle. The joy of finding one's intentionality transformed in a deeper experience of loving and being-loved leads the lover to interpret the temporary distancing from the beloved as itself gracious, in the sense that it intensifies the promise of well-being. Paul finds his suffering "with Christ"—his experience of distress, famine, and peril for the sake of manifesting the love of the Gospel to others—as "not worth comparing" to the coming glory, for "neither death, nor life, . . . nor anything in all creation, will be able to separate us from the *love* of God in Christ Jesus our Lord" (Rom. 8:17–18, 35–39).

Learning to tend to the intensity of suffering in this way requires the gracious transformation of personal agency, an intensification of the human spirit's way of relating itself to itself. Human personal agency is shaped by the ongoing relation between the centripetal organizing functions of the ego and the centrifugal orientation of the self to the other. I have suggested that we think of the human spirit as this relation's relating itself to itself as it relates to an other, that is, as it "suffers" (experiences) an other. This experience is intrinsically temporal, for personal

39. Ibid., 158–59.

40. Simone Weil, *Waiting for God*, trans. Joseph Marie Perrin (New York: Perennial, 2001), 75; emphasis added.

41. In such experiences, "the infinite distance separating God from the creature is entirely concentrated into one point to pierce the soul in its center. . . . He whose soul remains ever turned toward God though the nail pierces it finds himself nailed to the very center of the universe. . . . This point of intersection is the point of intersection of the arms of the Cross" (ibid., 81). For another moving example of the way mystical experience transforms one's interpretation of suffering cf. Meister Eckhart, "Sermon 2," in *Meister Eckhart: The Essential Sermons, Commentaries, Treatises and Defense*; trans. E. Colledge and B. McGinn (New York: Paulist, 1981), 177–81.

agency requires an imaginative projection of one's intentionality into the future—remembering the experience of lack in relation to an object of desire and orienting one's power to secure it. The finite human spirit cannot secure the future, and so its anxiety about the distance between itself and perceived objects of good intensifies. As it "loses" its tendency to depend on finite goods to secure the good life, the human spirit "finds" true life—an agency that shares in the eternal fellowship of divine love (cf. Matt. 10:39; Luke 17:33; John 12:25). This redemptive intensification of creaturely love transforms the agency of the human spirit as it comes to relate itself to itself in the temporal relation in utter dependence upon the gracious arrival of the justifying love of God. Because its relation to the Good is infinitely secured in the Spirit of love, this redeemed agency can lay down its life in the service of others.

Transforming Service

The intensification of love in Christian agency is formed by and within the practices of ministry. Too often we think of spirituality and ministry as two different aspects of the Christian life, the former dealing with our interior life and the latter as an expression of our external engagement in the world. In this model, "political spirituality" sounds like an oxymoron.[42] But the life of service is not extrinsic to Christian spirituality. To be a follower of Christ is to be called to act in the Spirit of love. We become just and live in love only as we lay down our lives for one another (1 John 3:16). This appears to be an ineffective power, an impotent agency, but this way of ministering serves the reign and justice of God, transforming space and time through redemptive community. Matthew interprets Jesus' ministry as a fulfillment of the promised, suffering servant of God: "Here is my *servant*, whom I have chosen. . . . I will put my *Spirit* upon him, and he will proclaim *justice* to the Gentiles" (Matt. 12:18; cf. Isa. 42:1). It was precisely as Jesus' agency was empowered by the Spirit that his own way of serving transformed the relational structures that inhibited justice and love in human community.

It is important not to pass too quickly over the use of the term "servant," for here we have a key concept for the Christian understanding and practice of spirituality as "becoming just." Jesus is referred to as the "servant" of God several times in Peter's early sermons in the book of Acts (3:13, 26; 4:27, 30). This is in keeping with Jesus' understanding of his own ministry: "For the Son of Man came not to be served but to serve

---

42. Owen Thomas, "Political Spirituality: Oxymoron or Redundancy?" *Journal of Religion and Society* 3 (2001): 1–12; "Interiority and Christian Spirituality," *Journal of Religion* 80 (2000): 41–60.

[*diakonēsai*], and to give his life a ransom for many" (Mark 10:45). Jesus' ministry in the Spirit was *diaconal*, serving others in love. "I am among you as one who serves" (Luke 22:27). After washing the disciples' feet and once again emphasizing his own role as a servant, Jesus tells them, "For I have set you an example, that you also should do as I have done to you" (John 13:15). Jesus insists that "whoever wants to be first must be last of all and servant of all" (Mark 9:35; cf. 10:43). Paul often later refers to himself as the servant of Christ or the Gospel (e.g., Rom. 1:1; Gal. 1:10; Eph. 3:7; Col. 1:23; Titus 1:1), and this practice is also followed by other biblical authors (James 1:1; 2 Pet. 1:1; Jude 1; Rev. 1:1).

Practicing justice as we share in the suffering of Jesus Christ and act in the Spirit of love will take shape differently in various contexts, but it should always take the form of self-giving *service*. This is the "family resemblance" that marks off Christian spirituality. To be a Christian is to be "in" ministry—to be ministering to (serving) others, which is how the Spirit of love is manifested in the community for the "common good" (1 Cor. 12:7). The gifts of the Spirit differ according to the grace given by God (Rom. 12:6–8), but the unity of the body in one Spirit is held together through this divine gifting, which equips "the saints for the work of ministry [*diakonias*], for building up the body of Christ" (Eph. 4:12). Paul argues that God "has made us competent to be ministers [*diakonous*] of a new covenant, not of letter but of spirit; for the letter kills, but the Spirit gives life" (2 Cor. 3:6). This applies whether one is an "elder," "bishop," or "deacon" (cf. 1 Tim. 3). The contractual organization of church polity is subordinate to (and serves) the work of the Spirit in the upbuilding of a community of service. "Like good stewards of the manifold grace of God, serve [or 'minister to,' *diakonountes*] one another with whatever gift each of you has received" (1 Pet. 4:10). We may be tempted to think of ministry only as the end result of spiritual formation, but diaconal praxis is an essential dynamic within the crucible of transformation.

Christian service (ministry) takes the shape of cruciform suffering. In his own struggle for justice, Martin Luther King Jr. insisted that it was Jesus of Nazareth who inspired African Americans to "protest with the creative weapon of love." Like Ghandi, King believed that "suffering is infinitely more powerful than the law of the jungle for converting the opponent and opening his ears which are otherwise shut to the voice of reason."[43] Transforming ministry does not always occur in the broader political arena—it may involve quietly bearing the burdens of others,

43. Martin Luther King Jr., *A Testament of Hope: The Essential Writings and Speeches of Martin Luther King, Jr.*, ed. James Melvin Washington (San Francisco: HarperSanFrancisco, 1991), 16–18.

as in the "little way" of St. Thérèse of Lisieux. Because Thérèse found herself in the "arms of love," she was empowered to suffer with and for Christ as she served others. Her ministry was not only physically caring for others who were suffering but serving them with a smile that intimated that her agency was not her own. This freed her from the need to defend herself or draw attention to her good works.[44] Sharing in the ministry of Jesus by caring for the immediate bodily needs of the other can be a deeply intimate experience, as illustrated by Jesus' washing the disciples' feet and by the woman who washed Jesus' feet with her tears (John 13:1–20; Luke 7:36–50).

Our understanding of spirituality as "becoming just" is intimately tied to the doctrine of justification, which is central to Christian thought and practice. However, we can understand divine justification not simply as a legal declaration that occurs above our heads (*Quae supra nos, nihil ad nos*) but as a transforming agency that permeates our communal relations and makes us just, bringing us into right relation with the Good. In his letter to the Romans, Paul emphasized the judicial aspect of God's gracious agency—which makes sense in light of his audience's interest in Roman jurisprudence. Both in this letter and elsewhere, however, he also stressed the way in which we actually become righteous and holy through divine grace (e.g., Rom. 8–15; 2 Cor. 3:9; 5:21; Gal. 3:11; Phil. 1:11; cf. Eph. 4:24; 2 Tim. 2:22). Becoming just is wholly dependent on the gracious agency of the Spirit, who makes room for creaturely agency to share in the intimate loving and being loved that is the life of the trinitarian God. As we receive our agency from God, we are freed to tend to our selves and to others without destructive or debilitating anxiety. Our lives become a salubrious orientation toward the Good, as we actively participate in the eschatological arrival of eternal Love.

This chapter has argued for a model of (and for) transforming spirituality that attends to the dynamics of *becoming just*—acting in the Spirit as we share in the redemptive suffering of Jesus Christ. Our goal has been to explore possibilities for the articulation of a reformative Pneumatology that conserves the intuitions of the biblical tradition by engaging contemporary philosophy and science. We have attempted to bring the concerns about moral desire and other-regarding agency into dialogue with an understanding of spirituality shaped by the ministry of Jesus Christ. Although we have focused here, for the sake of analysis, on the longing for goodness, it cannot

44. Cf. Thérèse de Lisieux, *The Little Way of Saint Thérèse of Lisieux*, ed. John Nelson (Liguori, MO: Liguori, 1997); *The Autobiography of Therese of Lisieux*, ed. Robert Backhouse (London: Hodder & Stoughton, 1994); Vernon Johnson, *Spiritual Childhood: The Spirituality of St. Therese of Lisieux*, 3rd ed. (San Francisco: Ignatius, 2001).

ultimately be separated from the human desire for truth and beauty. In the context of the case studies of part 3, I will attempt to show the coinherence of the desires more explicitly, as well as their connection to the crucible model that Steve will develop in part 2. First, however, I need to outline the relation between Christian spirituality and the human longing for freedom.

5

BECOMING FREE

The dynamics of transforming spirituality may also be described in relation to the desire to *belong-to and be longed-for* in harmonious and pleasurable fellowship. It is within this interpersonal field of longing for the beauty of intimate communion that a person's feeling of and for the freedom of being-in-relation emerges. Many contemporary discussions of human "freedom" continue to operate within a framing of the question that begins with the idea of the power of the "will." Much of the medieval and early modern debate about whether the human soul "has" free will occurred within the confines of the "faculty psychology" that shaped the anthropological understanding of those periods.[1]

1. For a discussion of the biblical, philosophical, and scientific challenges to faculty psychology, cf. F. LeRon Shults, *Reforming Theological Anthropology: After the Philosophical Turn to Relationality* (Grand Rapids: Eerdmans, 2003), ch. 8. For a more detailed explication of a metaphysical (and aesthetic) understanding of human freedom, cf. Shults, *Reforming the Doctrine of God* (Grand Rapids: Eerdmans, 2005), ch. 10.

How can we articulate a Christian understanding of the relation between freedom and human spirituality in our late modern culture? As we begin this process, it is important to recognize that Scripture does not use the category of "free will." It is the whole person who is "made free" (John 8:32) by the Son. Freedom is present "where the Spirit of the Lord is" (2 Cor. 3:17), for it is the Spirit of life who frees persons in community from sin and death (Rom. 8:2). It is "for freedom [that] Christ has set us free," and this being-called into freedom (Gal. 5:1, 13) is not about the individual's "will" but about the real coming-to-be of human persons through fellowship in the Spirit.

The issue of human freedom should not and ultimately cannot be separated from epistemological and ethical concerns, but including (and even beginning) with an ontological analysis of the concept may help us move beyond some of the impasses that have plagued philosophy and theology.[2] This chapter will explore the dynamics of spiritual transformation in light of an understanding of human freedom as the *real* and actual coming to-*be* of rational agents. The holistic feeling (*aesthesis*) of immediacy that characterizes the experience of the human spirit as it longs for freedom in relation is oriented in hope, called into existence by the gracious presence of divine Beauty. This aesthetic "determination" that evokes in creatures a longing for divine grace does not compete with human freedom but calls it into being.

We will outline the redemptive experience of becoming free as a dynamic reception of the newness of life, as a creaturely "being in the Spirit" that shares in the glory of Jesus Christ. Redemptive transformation involves an intensification of hope that takes shape in community as we participate in the infinite hospitality of divine grace. To provide the context for this reconstructive presentation of the experience of spiritual freedom, we will briefly explore scientific discoveries that contribute to a model of human persons that we might call "emergent holism." We will also discuss the insights of philosophical developments in metaphysics and aesthetics that facilitate the recovery of traditional theological resources that have emphasized the relation between God and beauty. The first step, however, is to point to the radically ontological understanding of freedom and its redemptive transformation in the Hebrew Bible and the New Testament.

2. By challenging the hegemony of the concept of "free will" in philosophical and theological treatments of human freedom, I am not ignoring or denying the phenomena of personal intentionality, deliberation, and choice. I am suggesting that we should no longer feel constrained to interpret these phenomena using the same terminology that came to dominate so much of theological anthropology in Western Christianity after Augustine's reification of ancient Greek notions of the "faculties" of the soul.

The Longing for Freedom in Scripture

The Israelites' desire for wisdom and justice in relation to Yahweh was wrapped up within their longing for freedom, which was expressed in their hope in the divine promise to provide space and time in which the community could experience spiritual well-being. The creative divine presence orients the people of God toward psychological and political freedom, which is a condition for beautiful life together, for a "place" in which peaceful fellowship could flourish. This longing is evident throughout the defining story of the exodus from Egypt and the journey toward the promised land. The Lord heard the "groaning of the Israelites" (Exod. 6:5), and the mission of deliverance given to Moses is based on the divine faithfulness to the covenant that originated in the call of Abraham.

> Say therefore to the Israelites, 'I am the LORD, and I will *free* you from the burdens of the Egyptians and deliver you from slavery to them. I will redeem you with an outstretched arm and with mighty acts of judgment. I will take you as my people, and I will be your God. You shall know that I am the LORD your God, who has *freed* you from the burdens of the Egyptians.' (Exod. 6:6–7)

God sets free not only *from* bondage but also *for* hopeful existence in community. This is manifested in the declaration of the year of Jubilee (e.g., Lev. 25:54); whether or not it was actually practiced, this liberating intention indicates a concern for the human longing for freedom.

The Hebrew poets also expressed this longing for free being-in-relation. This desire is related to the experience of the *presence* of God, often expressed in terms of the divine *face*, which is the most pleasing experience imaginable, promising and evoking hope in new peaceful being.[3] The idiom of the "shining divine countenance" expresses the deepest desire of the wise and just person for the freedom of being-in-relation to God, which liberates the human spirit for gracious relations in community: "Let your face shine upon your servant; save me in your steadfast love" (Ps. 31:16); "let your face shine, that we may be saved" (Ps. 80:3; cf. 67:1–2). The divine presence (face) is constitutive for the being and life of creatures. "When you hide your face, they [living creatures] are dismayed; when you take away their breath, they die and return to their dust" (Ps. 104:29). The psalmist, however, seeks a more intensely

---

3. Both the Hebrew word *panim* and the Greek word *prosōpon* may be translated either "presence" or "face." Cf. Shults, *Reforming the Doctrine of God*, ch. 10; F. LeRon Shults and Steven J. Sandage, *The Faces of Forgiveness: Searching for Wholeness and Salvation* (Grand Rapids: Baker, 2003), ch. 4.

intimate relation to the inescapable divine presence: "My soul thirsts for God, for the living God. When shall I come and behold the face of God?" (Ps. 42:2).

The lack of freedom in relation to God is experienced as a "hiding" of the divine face:[4] "You hid your face; I was dismayed" (Ps. 30:7b); "'Come,' my heart says, 'seek his face!' Your face, LORD, do I seek. Do not hide your face from me" (Ps. 27:8–9a). A sense of secure attachment to the presence of God is essential to feeling free. If the divine face is hidden, sickness or death are at hand. This is the ultimate experience of lack of freedom in relation to divine being. "Do not hide your face from me, or I shall be like those who go down to the Pit" (Ps. 143:7b; cf. 132:10). The fear and desire embedded in the relation to the ambiguous divine countenance are explicitly tied to the longing for freedom.

> Do not hide your face from your servant,
>   for I am in distress—make haste to answer me.
> Draw near to me, redeem me,
>   set me free because of my enemies. (Ps 69:17–18)

This longing for freedom is not expressed in terms of an insistence on the abstract right of the individual to actualize the volitional powers of his or her "will" but in terms of a desire for concrete relations in community that do not crush the whole person.

The agony and ecstasy of this desire is radically ontological, surrounding and permeating the totality of human relational life. Job's feeling of being crushed ontologically is expressed in his wish that he had died at birth and entered the realm of the dead, for there at least "the weary are at rest" and "the slaves are free from their masters" (Job 3:17, 19). The longing for freedom and the gratitude for the divine promise cannot be separated from the basic desires for survival and peaceful existence: "Happy are those whose help is the God of Jacob, whose *hope* is in the LORD their God, . . . who executes justice for the oppressed; who gives food to the hungry" (Ps. 146:5, 7; cf. 102:20; 144:7).

The classical prophets call the people of God into a form of communal praxis that sets free those who have borne the weight of political domination. Jeremiah speaks out against the nation of Judah for its failure to liberate those in the community whose being-in-relation has been crushed by oppression. Their ancestors had ignored the command to set free the slaves every seventh year. "You yourselves recently repented and did what was right in my sight by proclaiming liberty to one another,

---

4. Cf. Samuel Balentine, *The Hidden God: The Hiding of the Face of God in the Old Testament* (New York: Oxford University Press, 1993); Richard Elliott Friedman, *The Hidden Face of God* (San Francisco: HarperCollins, 1995).

and you made a covenant before me in the house that is called by my name; but then you turned around and profaned my name when each of you took back your male and female slaves, whom you had set free according to their desire, and you brought them again into subjection to be your slaves" (Jer. 34:15–16).

The occasional *fasting* of individuals whose lives are typically characterized by filling themselves while others go hungry, is not enough to bring them into right relation with God.

> Is not this the *fast* that I choose:
>   to loose the bonds of injustice,
>   to undo the thongs of the yoke,
> to let the oppressed go free,
>   and to break every yoke?
> Is it not to share your bread with the hungry,
>   and bring the homeless poor into your house;
> when you see the naked, to cover them,
>   and not to hide yourself from your own kin? (Isa. 58:6–7)

The Isaianic vision of the restoration of the land calls the people of Israel toward a hospitable form of life—a holistic way of fasting (controlling their appetites) that sets others free and takes shape as the provision of space and time for the well-being of the other.

The New Testament also depicts the human longing for freedom in relation but proclaims that this desire for liberated being is fulfilled through life in the Spirit of freedom, who orients us into the way of new being manifested in Jesus Christ. Peter's proclamation at Pentecost announces that ultimate freedom—freedom from death—has been displayed in the resurrection of Jesus Christ (Acts 2:24). True freedom is not the uninhibited capacity to exercise one's "will" but an experience of being liberated from the painful relations of sin and into the peaceful relations of fellowship with God and neighbor (cf. 1 Pet. 2:24; Rev. 1:5). Jesus tells the Jews who believe in him, "If you continue in my word, you are truly my disciples; and you will know the truth, and the truth will *make you free*" (John 8:31b–32). Some resist this idea, thinking that they are already free because they are descendants of Abraham, who "have never been slaves to anyone." Jesus responds that he is calling them into a qualitatively different relation within the household of God: "If the Son makes you free, you will be *free indeed*" (John 8:31–36).

For the apostle Paul, the longing for freedom has to do not with the faculty of "free will" but with the whole person's being-made-free in relation to God. The "law of the Spirit of life in Christ Jesus" has set his readers "free from the law of sin and of death" (Rom. 8:2). All of creation longs to be *set free* from its bondage to decay, but this desire takes a uniquely intense form in human persons (Rom. 8:19–23). To the Corinthians he writes that the letter of the law kills but "the Spirit gives *life*." The "ministry of death" that came through Moses had such a glory that the people could not look at Moses' face unveiled; "how much more will the ministry of the Spirit come in glory?" (2 Cor. 3:6–8). "Now the Lord is the Spirit, and *where the Spirit of the Lord is, there is freedom*"—this freedom liberates us into a way of facing and being faced that transforms our spirits; "seeing the glory of the Lord as though reflected in a mirror, [we] are being transformed into the same image from one degree of glory to another; for this comes from the Lord, the Spirit" (2 Cor. 3:17–18).

Paul elsewhere explicitly ties this longing for freedom not only to the Spirit but also to the life-giving work of Christ: "For freedom Christ has set us free. Stand firm, therefore, and do not submit again to a yoke of slavery" (Gal. 5:1). Paul also makes it clear that this longing for freedom in relation to God has radical ramifications for the way in which the community lives together in concrete relations of belonging. The Corinthian church was struggling with a deeply existential question—to whom did they belong? Paul encourages them to realize that their being is eternally secure, "for all things are yours, whether Paul or Apollos or Cephas or the world or life or death or the present or the future—all *belong* to you, and you *belong* to Christ, and Christ *belongs* to God" (1 Cor. 3:21b–23).

The human desire to belong-to and be longed-for in harmonious community is fulfilled through hopeful relation to the Spirit of freedom. Redemptive transformation frees the human spirit from the anxiety that pervades all attempts to secure one's own metaphysical status by opposing and manipulating one's neighbors. As Paul expresses it elsewhere: "For you were called to freedom, brothers and sisters; only do not use your freedom as an opportunity for self-indulgence, but through love become slaves to one another. For the whole law is summed up in a single commandment, 'You shall love your neighbor as yourself'" (Gal. 5:13–14). Transforming spirituality involves an experience of the intensification of freedom in relation to others—a liberating experience of being upheld graciously in the Spirit, who draws us into the beautiful life of God.

Spirituality and Beauty in the Christian Tradition

Among the early church fathers, the biblical expression of this desire of the human spirit for freedom in relation to God was often correlated theologically with the concepts of "hope," "facing," and "beauty." This emphasis can be illustrated in the work of Gregory of Nyssa, especially in his treatment of spiritual desire in *The Life of Moses*. When Gregory comes to Moses' desire to "see" God on the mountain, he reflects on this experience: "Such an experience seems to me to belong to the soul which loves what is beautiful. *Hope* always draws the soul from the *beauty* which is seen to what is beyond, always kindles the *desire* for the hidden through what is constantly perceived." He interprets Moses' bold request as an expression of a longing "to enjoy the Beauty not in mirrors or reflections, but *face to face*."[5]

The desire for this intimate relation to the divine presence is not the kind of desire that aims for final satiation. It is a longing not for the "end" of one's joyful experience of divine Beauty but a quickening of it—an intensification of the relation to the infinite presence of the Aesthetic that evokes and upholds the desire itself. This is another way of expressing the idea of divine Futurity. The temporal experience of personal becoming, which is conditioned by its longing to participate in aesthetically pleasing patterns of being-in-relation, has its origin in its orientation by and to the eschatological presence of the eternal Beauty of the trinitarian God.

One of the most influential sources for theological reflection on the relation between beauty and God was Pseudo-Dionysius. In his treatment of the divine names, he suggests that the human experience of beauty helps us articulate our experience of the ultimately unnameable. He notes that this is why the sacred writers "name it beautiful since it is the all-beautiful and the beautiful beyond all." The ineffable divine is the "superabundant source" of the beauty of every beautiful thing. Arguing that divine Beauty "unites all things," Pseudo-Dionysius depicts it as "the great creating cause which bestirs the world and holds all things in existence by the longing inside them to have beauty. And there it is ahead of all as Goal, as the Beloved, as the Cause toward which all things move, since it is the longing for beauty which actually brings them into *being*." Therefore he says that "Beauty 'bids' all things to itself (whence it is called 'beauty') and gathers everything into itself."[6] Dionysius's play on words—the beautiful (*kallos*) is that which bids or "calls" (*kaleō*)—was borrowed or adapted from Plato's understanding of beauty (e.g., *Cratylus* 416a–d).

Augustine had also refigured the Neoplatonic insight that ultimate Beauty and the divine must be thought together, and this motif was taken up later by medieval Scholastic theologians such as Thomas Aquinas

5. Gregory of Nyssa, *The Life of Moses* (New York: Paulist, 1978), 114; emphases added.

6. Pseudo-Dionysius, *The Complete Works*, trans. Colm Luibheid and Paul Rorem (New York: Paulist, 1987), 76–77; emphasis added.

and Duns Scotus in their treatments of the human desire for God. Like many of his philosophical contemporaries, Augustine defined beauty in terms of the arrangement of things, the proportion and ordering of parts as in the harmony of music or the spatial plan of a city.[7] He makes apologetic use of this point in *Of True Religion*. We find pleasure in beautiful things because their parts are conjoined in a harmonious whole; but no material thing—however beautiful—can ultimately express perfect unity (given the intervals of space and time). It is through the operation of the mind in the intelligible world, therefore, that true beauty is sought, and the Christian religion teaches that the mind was created to contemplate supreme Beauty, which can only be found in God through divine illumination.[8]

In Augustine's *Confessions*, he describes religious desire as oriented toward divine Beauty. In prayer he calls out to God, "O Loveliness that dost not deceive, Loveliness happy and abiding" (II.1), and refers to God as the "Beauty of all things beautiful" (III.6).[9] He insists that we not predicate "beauty" of God in a way that would separate the divine substance from the accidental property of being beautiful. The latter would suggest that "You were a substance in which inhered Your own greatness of beauty," but in fact "Your greatness and Your beauty are Yourself" (IV.16). Augustine reflects on what it is that he loves when he loves God. It is not the beauty or pleasure of any finite created thing, not, for example, the "limbs that carnal love embraces." Yet his spiritual desire for God is "in a sense" a love of a pleasurable "embrace," for he longs for an experience of loving God in which "I lie in the embrace which satiety never comes to sunder. This is that I love, when I love my God" (X.6).

The relation between creaturely pleasure in beautiful things and spiritual union with God was prominent in the work of St. Bonaventure, who also argued that we can be drawn to God through an appreciation for, and pleasure in, created beauty. He described in this way St. Francis's way of living in relation to creation although he was absorbed in desire for God:

> In beautiful things
> he saw Beauty itself
> and through his *vestiges* imprinted on creation
> *he followed his Beloved* everywhere,

---

7. Augustine, *City of God*, XXII.19; cf. XI.18, XVII.14.

8. Augustine, *Of True Religion*, trans. J. H. S. Burleigh, intro. Louis O. Mink (Chicago: Regnery, 1959), 56–59.

9. Augustine, *The Confessions*, trans. F. J. Sheed (London and New York: Sheed & Ward, 1944).

> making from all things a ladder
> by which he could climb up
> and embrace him *who is utterly desirable*.[10]

For Bonaventure, this way of living was possible because all of creation was a manifestation of the Logos as "Eternal Art."[11] The human experience of grasping after pleasurable objects in the world may be transformed as one comes to feel the infinitely pleasurable presence of God through them. This intense experience of ultimate pleasure evokes true freedom—freedom from unhealthy worldly attachments and freedom for hopeful and harmonious belonging in relation to the Creator and all of creation.

This way of understanding the relation between aesthetic desire and God is also illustrated in Teresa of Ávila, for whom it is the beauty and majesty of God that lures the contemplative through the rooms of the interior castle, away from the hideous brokenness of sin.[12] Similarly, St. John of the Cross's *Dark Night of the Soul* points at the need for human desire to be purged of its attachment to created pleasures so that it can become free as it is oriented toward, and infused by, the uncontrollable Beauty of the divine presence. The testimony of these and other theologians in the mystical tradition is not that we should ignore the ugliness or beauty of the created world but that an awareness of our inability to find ultimate pleasure by controlling finite objects can prepare us for a transformation of desire itself as we are drawn in to intimate relation with the intensively infinite origin, condition, and goal of our *aesthesis*—our feeling for life.

The Eastern theological tradition also has a long history of emphasizing the significance of aesthetic desire for spiritual transformation. For Maximus the Confessor, the beautiful things of this world are incapable of satisfying human desire, but through them we may be graciously oriented toward a genuine harmony with God, who is the ground and *logoi* and goal of beautiful things.[13] Gregory Palamas applies this more explicitly to spiritual formation when he says that the saints who are filled by the grace of the Word are "made beautiful by the creative and

---

10. Bonaventure, *The Life of St. Francis*, in *Selections*, trans. E. Cousins (New York: Paulist, 1978), 263; emphases in original translation.

11. Bonaventure, *The Soul's Journey into God*, ibid., 61, 74.

12. Teresa of Ávila, *Interior Castle*, ed. and trans. E. A. Peers (New York: Doubleday, 1961).

13. Maximus Confessor, *Ambiguum 7*, in *On the Cosmic Mystery of Jesus Christ: Selected Writings from St. Maximus the Confessor*, trans. Paul M. Blowers and Robert Louis Wilken (Crestwood, NY: St. Vladimir's Seminary Press, 2003), 183.

primordial Beauty, and illumined by the radiance of God."[14] David Hart has argued that in the "advent of beauty," theology is able to hear "the declaration of God's goodness and glory, and to see, in the attractiveness of the beautiful, that creation is invited to partake of that goodness and glory." For Hart, "God's pleasure—the beauty creation possesses in his regard—underlies the distinct being of creation, and so beauty is the first and truest word concerning all that appears within being; beauty is the showing of what is. . . . Beauty evokes desire."[15]

The resources of Eastern Orthodox reflection on the theological significance of beauty may be particularly helpful for those of us whose Western traditions were forged in the context of *icon*oclasm, which continues to register its effect on the way we repress our longings for pleasure. While many early Protestant theologians consistently maintained the traditional emphasis on the relation between God and beauty, the destruction of images in previously Roman Catholic churches was a manifestation of a different attitude toward the aesthetic in the formation of the human spirit. As mechanical metaphors came to dominate seventeenth-century philosophy and science, spiritual development was increasingly described in terms of the efficient causes that moved an individual from one state to another (the so-called *ordo salutis*). Experiences of the pleasurable enjoyment of beauty were not essential (and might even be detrimental) to spirituality.

By the eighteenth century, however, theologians such as Jonathan Edwards had already come to realize the inadequacy of this approach, which tended to obscure the qualitative feeling of desire that characterizes spirituality. Dynamic and relational categories were central to Edwards's philosophical theology, and he depicted the relation of creatures to God in terms of dispositions toward supreme Beauty. The doctrine of the Trinity was explicitly articulated in aesthetic terms for Edwards; he described the relationality of the persons of the Trinity as "the supreme Harmony of all."[16] Edwards not only privileged the Beautiful over the other transcendental concepts but also explicitly depicted spiritual formation in aesthetic terms.[17] These and other resources in the tradition are increasingly appropriated in the current literature and

14. Gregory Palamas, *The Triads*, ed. and trans. John Meyendorff (New York: Paulist, 1983), 33.

15. David Hart, *The Beauty of the Infinite: The Aesthetics of Christian Truth* (Grand Rapids: Eerdmans, 2003), 17–19. The importance of beauty in this tradition is also evident from the significant use of icons in Eastern Orthodox liturgy and prayer.

16. Cf. Jonathan Edwards, *Selections: Scientific and Philosophical Writings*, ed. Wallace Earl Anderson (New Haven: Yale University Press, 1980), 182.

17. Cf. ch. 2, n. 49, above. For analysis, cf. Robert W. Jenson, *America's Theologian: A Recommendation of Jonathan Edwards* (New York: Oxford University Press, 1988); Amy Plantinga Pauw, *"The Supreme Harmony of All": The Trinitarian Theology of Jonathan Ed-*

practice of Western spirituality as the importance of images, music, poetry, and other expressions of the aesthetic come to the fore in late modern discourse.[18]

Insights from Philosophy and Natural Science

In addition to attending to these biblical and traditional resources, our articulation of the dynamics of "becoming free" in spiritual transformation may also benefit from an awareness of developments in philosophy and natural science. The arenas of philosophy that are most directly relevant to these issues are metaphysics and aesthetics, and as we will see the implicit relation between being and beauty has come to the fore in recent philosophical discourse. With reference to the natural sciences, we will briefly examine theories on the emergence of self-organizing complexity (and beauty) in natural systems. These interdisciplinary developments raise new questions about the importance of the aesthetic in the human experience of being and becoming. A theological explication of the dynamics of becoming free in the Spirit of Christ should engage and account for contemporary understandings of human freedom as inherently linked to openness, creativity, and the feeling of being-in-relation.

Both metaphysics and aesthetics (like epistemology and ethics) were inherently connected to the idea of the divine in most ancient Greek philosophy. For Plato, the longing for beauty guides the soul toward contemplation of the eternal forms.[19] Aristotle solidified the definition of beauty in terms of order and arrangement, together with its connection to the experience of that which is pleasing.[20] As we saw above, many early Christian theologians adapted these philosophical insights. Because of its dominance, this constellation of themes in the Western aesthetics has been called the "Great Theory" of beauty.[21] This theory declined during the Enlightenment as the experience of beauty was increasingly placed in the realm of the "subjective," as opposed to the "objective" world that is measured by neutral observers through classical mechanics. The lesser role played by beauty in the empirical philosophy of Locke and Hume

---

wards (Grand Rapids: Eerdmans, 2002); Sang Hyun Lee, *The Philosophical Theology of Jonathan Edwards*, expanded ed. (Princeton, NJ: Princeton University Press, 2000).

18. See, e.g., Elizabeth A. Dreyer and Mark S. Burrows, *Minding the Spirit: The Study of Christian Spirituality* (Baltimore: Johns Hopkins University Press, 2005).

19. E.g., Plato, *Symposium* 210b; *Republic* 476, 479; *Phaedo* 78d; *Phaedrus* 250b.

20. E.g., Aristotle, *Rhetoric* 1371b; *Poetics* 1450b35.

21. W. Tatarkiewicz, "The Great Theory of Beauty and Its Decline," *Journal of Aesthetics and Art Criticism* 31 (1972): 165–80.

contributed to the isolation of aesthetics from metaphysics (as well as epistemology and ethics). Kant provided three separate "critiques"—dividing and analyzing pure reason, practical reason, and judgment; his treatment of the Beautiful (and the sublime) is for the most part limited to his analysis of the sphere of aesthetic judgment.

Many late modern philosophers have struggled to overcome this bifurcation between the aesthetic and the metaphysical. Although this is connected to the epistemological healing of the fracture between "subject" and "object" as well as the renewal of the significance of ethical agency in debates over "reality," our interest here is in the revival of the philosophical insight that beauty and being cannot be so easily separated. George Steiner reminds us of the irreducible metaphysics of "presence" that cannot be deconstructed any more than it can be controlled. Metaphysics cannot leave out the aesthetic (or poetic) because it is an essential dimension of the experience of being human. "The encounter with the aesthetic is, together with certain modes of religious and of metaphysical experience, the most 'ingressive,' transformative summons available to human experiencing."[22] Edward Farley argues for a transmutation of the "Great Theory" that maintains its intrinsic linking of beauty and being but also recognizes the postmodern critique of its Neoplatonic and early modern formulations. Building on some of the insights of process philosophy, he argues that beauty is a movement that both "resolves chaos to order and yet introduces novelty into that very act of resolution." As the synthesis and intensity of experience, beauty is "the primordial and universal creativity" of the processes of the world. It is the creative "advance into novelty." This leads Farley to claim that "being—that is, creativity—is beautiful."[23]

Another philosophical shift that has opened up space for linking metaphysics and aesthetic desire is the retrieval and refiguring of Plato's cryptic comment in Book VI of the *Republic* that the Good is superior to or "beyond" being. In *God as Otherwise Than Being*, Calvin Schrag summarizes the problems associated with placing both God (as the Good) and creaturely goods under the category of "being." This approach—sometimes called "onto-theology"—easily leads to a metaphysic in which God is one "being" among many. Schrag suggests that we use the semantics of "the Gift" to indicate that God is not simply "a" being but the infinite presence that makes possible the human longing for the Good (and the Beautiful). God is "beyond being" yet experienced by human persons as a "futurity" that is "always a coming-to-presence," as

22. George Steiner, *Real Presences* (Chicago: University of Chicago Press, 1989), 143.
23. Edward Farley, *Faith and Beauty: A Theological Aesthetic* (Aldershot, England: Ashgate, 2001), 25.

the "gift" of "unconditioned alterity" that calls "to the inhabitants of a conditioned economy," awakening awareness of a different economy with "intimations of eternity within the folds of time."[24] This metaphysical semantics allows us to imagine God as the source of aesthetic desire and not simply the most pleasurable object among those for which we long. These philosophical insights can be appropriated by Christian theology as we seek to articulate an understanding of the presence of the divine Spirit as the origin, condition, and goal of the human longing for the beauty of being-free in intimate communion.

Natural scientists have also increasingly come to acknowledge that interest in the beautiful is an irreducible dimension of human inquiry into nature. Astronomers often express their feeling of awe and wonder at the order of the universe, and most theoretical mathematicians admit that the beauty of an abstract equation is part of what compels their belief that it must also render intelligible some concrete phenomenon in the cosmos. Furthermore, most contemporary scientific reflection operates out of a sense of the dynamic interconnection of all things. As we saw in chapter 2, mechanistic models of science, which privileged past-oriented efficient causality and led to deterministic theories, have been challenged by more dynamic understandings of the spatiotemporal cosmos. This has contributed to the recognition that the aesthetic desire of human experience is intrinsic rather than foreign to the processes of nature. This opens up space for an ontological understanding of "freedom" as a quality that characterizes all living organisms, although the experience of interconnection for human persons is uniquely intense in its openness to the future.

Various approaches to the study of emergent patterns of self-organizing (autopoietic) systems are now often placed under the general heading of the sciences of "complexity." There is no clear line of demarcation, but typically these sciences attend to macrolevel dynamic systems such as sand piles, turbulent fluids, the economy, or the human brain.[25] Here we are implicitly dealing with the question of the "freedom" of autopoietic systems, that is, their openness and ability to respond to their environments. As Holmes Rolston notes, the autonomy, or freedom, of complex living things involves a blending of determinism and destiny. "Freedom is never freedom from an environment. . . . Freedom is within an en-

24. Calvin O. Schrag, *God as Otherwise Than Being: Toward a Semantics of the Gift* (Evanston, IL: Northwestern University Press, 2002), 135, 142.

25. Cf. Per Bak, *How Nature Works: The Science of Self-Organized Criticality* (New York: Copernicus, 1996); Ilya Prigogine and Isabella Stengers, *Order out of Chaos* (New York: Bantam, 1984); Robert John Russell, Nancey Murphy, and Arthur R. Peacock, eds., *Chaos and Complexity: Scientific Perspectives on Divine Action*, 2nd ed. (Berkeley: Center for Theology and the Natural Sciences, 1997).

vironment."[26] Organisms do not make themselves out of nothing but are emergent complex patterns of relationality. John Campbell suggests that (nonhuman) complex systems somehow also respond to the future emerging whole: "When matter is appropriately organized, it becomes sensitive to causes arising from the future instead of just the past."[27] This seems strange to those of us accustomed to linear classical concepts of time, but contemporary physics and biology compel us to alter our understanding of time in order to make sense of natural processes.

With the intensely organized self-relationality of the human spirit comes an experience of "freedom" in relation to the environment that is at once more agonistic and ecstatic than other creaturely organisms. The self-related complexity of human personhood leads to an intense awareness of and anxiety about the future of one's free being-in-relation. The intensity of the experience of the human person is unique but may also be understood as a *natural* part of the coming-to-be of creation upheld by the gracious presence of the Spirit. The way in which "becoming actual" gives rise to beauty and complexity has led Frederick Ferré to speak of the "kalogenic" nature of the universe. He notes that this leaves open the question of an "ontological grounding" of this becoming, that is, the question of God.[28] Our Western culture is characterized by both a tendency toward the commercial manipulation of the human longing for beauty (a commodification of pleasure) and a general suspicion of attempts to exert control over aesthetic expression. The renewed emphasis on the significance of beauty in late modern discourse does not prove the existence of an all-embracing Being that evokes this longing for free being-in-relation. It does, however, invite theological exploration and explication of the absolute source of the actualization of human becoming.

Being in the Spirit

As we aim to contribute to the ongoing task of reforming Pneumatology, we may draw from all of these sources in order to explicate the

26. Holmes Rolston III, "Kenosis and Nature," in *The Work of Love: Creation as Kenosis*, ed. J. C. Polkinghorne (Grand Rapids: Eerdmans, 2001), 62. In *Genes, Genesis, and God* (New York: Cambridge University Press, 1999), 364, Rolston metaphorically depicts God as "a sort of biogravity that lures life upward . . . [introducing] new possibility spaces all along the way."

27. John H. Campbell, "An Organizational Interpretation of Evolution," in *Evolution at a Crossroads: The New Biology and the New Philosophy of Science*, ed. David J. Depew and Bruce H. Weber (Cambridge: MIT Press, 1985), 154.

28. F. Ferré, *Being and Value: Toward a Constructive Postmodern Metaphysics* (Albany: State University of New York Press, 1996), 340, 367.

Christian claim that the Spirit of the biblical God is the origin, condition, and goal of human *being*. We may start (like Calvin) with Paul's insistence that we live and move and have our being *in* God (Acts 17:28). In line with the biblical understanding that all creaturely life is upheld by and in the Spirit, Calvin argues that this "subsistence" in God is "our very being" (*Institutes* I.1.1). The dynamic character of creaturely being—as becoming—is further emphasized by Paul in Romans 11:36, where he argues that "all things" are *from*, *through*, and *to* God. As we have seen, the intimate relation of believers to God is often depicted by the New Testament writers as a life of knowing and acting "in" the Spirit. The becoming that *is* creaturely being is always and already a gift of the life-giving Spirit, which human persons experience as a gracious call to well-being. The remainder of this chapter will outline an understanding of transforming spirituality as the intensification of hopeful being in the Spirit, which takes shape in Christian community as a hospitable sharing in the glory of Jesus Christ.

First let us outline the biblical semantics of the mutual "indwelling" of human spirit and Holy Spirit and explore how this redemptive experience of being in the Spirit fulfills the creaturely longing for freedom in the intimate presence of an other. Paul writes to the Romans, "you are in the Spirit, since the Spirit of God dwells in you" (Rom. 8:9). He encourages the Corinthians, "you are God's temple and . . . God's Spirit dwells in you" (1 Cor. 3:16; cf. 2 Tim. 1:14). On the one hand, believers are to live "in" the Spirit, but on the other hand, they are also "filled with" the Spirit.[29] In Luke's Gospel, John the Baptist (Luke 1:15), his parents, Elizabeth and Zechariah (1:41, 67), and Jesus (4:14) are all "filled with the Holy Spirit." In Acts 2:4 "all of them" were filled with the Spirit, a theme that runs throughout the book (e.g., 4:31; 5:3; 7:55; 13:52). According to John, the Spirit is "given" in a way that leads to a mutual indwelling in which we abide in God and God abides in us (1 John 4:13).

How can the infinite Creator Spirit "fill" finite human beings without obliterating them? How can a personal creature be "in" the Spirit without losing his or her particularity? We begin by linking the redemptive dynamics of being in the Spirit to the human experience of what I will call *dialectical presence*. Just as identity and agency are dialectically formed in relation, so also is the way in which persons are "present" to one another.[30] The self that "I" present to others has been formed (and

---

29. The latter idea is also present in the Hebrew Bible; a skilled worker is said to be "filled . . . with divine spirit" (Exod. 31:3), and the prophet Micah is "filled" with the Spirit of the Lord (Mic. 3:8).

30. Personal identity, agency, and presence are inseparable, but we may distinguish them conceptually as three ways of explicating the emergent coming-to-be of whole persons in relation.

is being formed) by the way in which others ("not I") have presented themselves to me. The faces of significant others have mediated my facing of myself as well as my images of the divine Face.[31] The search for well-being—which *is* personal existence—emerges "in" the presence of the other (and the Other). The relational dynamics of being-present to self, others, and God are all intertwined in the coming-to-be that *is* the human spirit.

This dialectical being-present in dependent relation to the other shapes the creaturely longing to become free, to belong-to and be longed-for in intimate communion. My sense of being-present to my self is already given in the presence of the other, and so I cannot be the ultimate ground of my own being. Ontological anxiety arises when I realize that I do not have sufficient being to secure the presence of others or my self, much less to maintain a gravitational hold on the infinite reality of God. If the other abandons me or turns his or her face away, then I feel the pain of metaphysical isolation. If the other uses his or her presence to crush me or face me down, I feel the pain of metaphysical incarceration. This dialectical tension leaves me vulnerable as I struggle to feel free in the presence of the other.

What if we explicitly attend to the divine Spirit as the presence that mediates our experience of coming-to-be in relation? It initially seems that the "presence" of an absolute Other would exclude the possibility of free being-in-relation. The recovery of traditional intuitions about Infinity, Trinity, and Futurity can help us here. First, we must remember that the Spirit is not "in" creatures the same way that one finite object fills another. If two finite objects mutually fill each other, then either one is destroyed or takes the place of the other, or there is a mixture that results in a third type of thing. The "outpouring" and "indwelling" of the truly *infinite* Spirit in relation to creatures neither replaces nor absorbs the finite human spirit, for the very coming-into-being that is the particularity of human persons is from, through, and to God. The divine Spirit is not one being among many, not even the "greatest" conceivable being, but the all-embracing presence in which we already "live and move and have *our* being" (Acts 17:28). As the goal of the creaturely longing for freedom, the all-pervading presence of the Creator Spirit constitutes the very conditions for the emergence of aesthetic desire.

The Christian experience of this transformative presence is explicitly trinitarian. The Spirit is present to creatures not as an immense substance but as the welcoming communion that is the life of the *trinitarian* God. The redemptive experience of "being" in the Spirit is an entering into

31. Cf. Ana-Maria Rizzuto, *The Birth of the Living God: A Psychoanalytic Study* (Chicago: University of Chicago Press, 1979).

the perichoretic relationality that constitutes the eternal joy of the fellowship of the Son and the Father. The New Testament call to live "in" the Spirit and be "filled" with the Spirit is intrinsically oriented toward reconciliation with the Father through the Son. The Ephesians are reminded that it is through Christ that we "have access in one Spirit to the Father" (Eph. 2:18). Being "filled with the Spirit" ought to lead them to give "thanks to God the Father at all times and for everything in the name of our Lord Jesus Christ" (5:18–20). In his letter to the Romans, Paul makes explicit the trinitarian structure of the mutual indwelling that characterizes creaturely being in the Spirit: "the Spirit of him who raised Jesus from the dead dwells in you, . . . [the Father] will give life to your mortal bodies also through his Spirit that dwells in you" (Rom. 8:11). The one who "serves Christ" participates in the kingdom of God (the Father), which is "righteousness and peace and joy in the Holy Spirit" (14:17–18). Being present "in" the Spirit of the trinitarian God opens us up in hope as we are drawn into the eternal intimacy of divine life.

The recovery of the emphasis on divine *Futurity* also helps us make sense of the biblical experience of being-called into relation with God by and in the Spirit. The origin and condition of human becoming in freedom is the gracious opening of time in and to the presence of Eternity, which is the infinite life of the trinitarian God. Our being-held in temporal existence by God frees us to know and be known, to love and be loved in community. Eternity is the absolute freedom of the divine persons in and with and for each other. Our ontological desire, which is a real creaturely relation to the reality of God, is constituted by the eschatological presence of Eternity. Creaturely coming-to-be is redeemed as we joyfully accept the gracious gift of our finitude in freedom. Life "in" the Spirit—our spirituality—is becoming free through the intensification of our being vis-à-vis absolute Beauty. As we hope *in* the biblical God, we find the source of our joyful being in our relation to a gracious Presence that frees us from our exhausting pursuit of finite pleasure and into a way of being-for-others that welcomes them into the infinite hospitality of divine life.

The mutual indwelling of the believing community in the presence of the divine Spirit can also be spelled out in relation to the biblical theme of "glory." For example, in 2 Corinthians 3:8 Paul describes the ministry of the Spirit as coming "in glory," and 1 Peter 4:14 speaks of the "Spirit of glory." This is linked to the Hebrew experience of the presence of God, which was often referred to as the "glory of the Lord" that "filled" the temple (e.g., Ezek. 43:5). This way of understanding the divine presence may initially seem unhelpful for dialogue in our late modern context. It seems less foreign, however, when we recognize that the root of the Hebrew word that is translated glory (*kabod*) has to do with heaviness, allowing us to think metaphorically of the "weight" of a reality. The infinite weight of the glory of God is experienced as a terrible and delightful Beauty that evokes both fear and hope in this mysterious divine presence. In the New Testament, the "riches of the glory" of God are made known to believers as they share in this mystery, "which is Christ in you, the hope of glory" (Col. 1:27). Through Christ they come to "belong" in a new experience of freedom in relation to the glorious presence of God.

Sharing in the Glory of Jesus Christ

The New Testament depicts the transforming dynamics of the Christian experience of sharing "in the divine nature" (2 Pet. 1:4) as participation not only in the knowledge and suffering but also in the *glory* of Jesus Christ. In the first Petrine epistle, the author refers to himself as "one who *shares* in the glory to be revealed" (1 Pet. 5:1). In Romans, Paul explicitly links the theme of glory both to hope and to the presence of eternal life: the "hope of *sharing* the glory of God" (Rom. 5:2) secures our being "through the Holy Spirit who has been given to us" (5:5) and is leading us "to eternal life through Jesus Christ our Lord" (5:21). The good news is "the gospel of the glory of Christ, who is the image of God" (2 Cor. 4:4). God "has shone in our hearts to give the light of the knowledge of the glory of God in the *face* of Jesus Christ" (4:6). God calls us *"into* his own kingdom and glory" (1 Thess. 2:12). In the epistle to the Hebrews, the Son is described as the "reflection of God's glory" (Heb. 1:3), who is "now crowned with glory" (2:9); through him God will bring "many children to glory" (2:10).

Under the hegemony of the early modern categories of substance metaphysics, the biblical idea of sharing in divine glory seems like an inappropriate fusing of Creator and creature. The relational categories of the late modern trajectories in the doctrine of God, however, may help us articulate a doctrine of the divine Spirit that recovers some key insights of the biblical tradition and makes sense of the human longing for a beautiful life.[32] First, it is important to remember that the glory of God is truly *infinite*—eternally superabundant—and so can be "shared" with creatures without being limited or diminished. The intensively infinite life of God is present to creatures as the "weight of glory" that is "beyond all measure" (2 Cor. 4:17). The "riches in glory in Christ Jesus" (Phil. 4:19) satisfy *every* need because these "riches of his glory" are

---

32. For a more detailed discussion, cf. Shults, *Reforming the Doctrine of God*, ch. 10.

mediated by the indwelling presence of the infinite divine Spirit, who strengthens their "inner being" (Eph. 3:16–17).

The idea of sharing in the glory of Jesus Christ also makes more sense when we remember that, in the New Testament, divine glory is manifested as a mutual glorification among the *trinitarian* persons. The narrative of the Gospel of John depicts this perichoretic glorifying into which believers are invited. Although Jesus' glory is revealed in various signs (John 2:11), he does not seek his own glory but receives it from the Father (8:50, 54). The glorification is mutual: "The Son of Man has been glorified, and God has been glorified in him" (13:31–32). Jesus tells the disciples that the Spirit of truth will glorify him by taking and declaring to them "what is mine," that is, "all that the Father has" (16:13–15). As the Paraclete (14:16) promised to the disciples, the Holy Spirit will draw them into the glorious relational unity of the Son and the Father. "The glory that you [the Father] have given me I have given them, so that they may be one, as we are one" (17:22). Divine glory is not a substance into which creatures are fused, but the indwelling (or perichoretic) personal relations of the shared life of the Trinity, into which creatures are invited to find a place of eternal belonging.

Finally, the Christian does not simply "have" or become the glory of God; rather, his or her whole being is oriented toward the arriving divine reign. "We wait for the blessed hope and the manifestation of the glory of our great God" (Titus 2:13). Believers are urged to trust God, who is able to make them "stand without blemish in the *presence* of his glory with rejoicing" (Jude 1:24). This presence is experienced by creatures as the coming of divine Futurity, as an orientation toward the arriving reign of eternal peace. Believers are called *into* [*eis*] God's "eternal glory in Christ" (1 Pet. 5:10). Already here and now believers share in the divine glory through life in the Spirit of Christ. This sharing is not complete or finished, however, for believers are encouraged to "rejoice in so far as you share Christ's sufferings, that you may also rejoice and be glad when his glory is revealed" (1 Pet. 4:13 RSV). The Gospel is the good news about life in the Spirit of Christ, a new life that provides ultimate ontological peace because nothing, not even death, can separate us from the freedom of divine love (Rom. 8:38–39).

How did Jesus' way of being glorify God? By manifesting the welcoming presence of divine grace. Jesus did not rely on his own metaphysical weight (glory) but on the life-giving Spirit as he delighted in the presence (face) of the Father. He was present to those crushed by the ugliness of human society, exhausting his own being for them in order to invite them into hopeful communion. Jesus called his neighbors toward a new way of being free in joyful relation to divine grace. His spirituality was not abstracted from the aesthetic pleasures of life but represented a different way of attending to his own embodied needs and the needs of others. In Luke 12:25–28 Jesus describes this life of dependence on the Father, who knows the needs of all creatures. Worrying will not add "a single hour to your span of life," so why should we allow anxiety about our needs to weigh us down?

In this context, Jesus points to the simple splendor of the lilies of the fields, which surpass "Solomon in all his glory," and calls his hearers into a reliance on God's promise to "clothe" them. Here "clothing" surely refers to literal physical attire, but it may also suggest an experience of being covered in the peace that comes from being upheld in the presence of the One who secures all being. The rich store up treasures in barns, thinking they can secure a pleasurable future, but their *gravitas* is impotent to hold off the weight of death. The peace that Jesus promises (John 14:27) is not like the peace the world gives, which is secured only by one's finite power to hold on to or hold off finite others. The truly peaceful life for which we long is being-held "in" the presence of the infinite Beauty and eternal joy of the trinitarian God. This redemptive transformation takes shape as we are emplotted into Jesus' glorious way of being in the Spirit—living in dependence on the presence of the Father. As Paul tells the Corinthians, "All of us . . . are being transformed into the same image from one degree of glory to another; for this is from the Lord, the Spirit" (2 Cor. 3:18). The intensity of being in the Spirit transforms our experience of the weight of glory as we peacefully receive our coming-to-be in freedom, resting in the eternal buoyancy of divine life.

Sharing in the glory of Jesus Christ means participating in his way of being in the world in relation to the Father through the Spirit. This is intrinsic to the spirituality of Christian life—this way of being *is* our freedom in Christ, which liberates us to become a hopeful presence to our neighbors. We must be careful not to separate our being spiritual—or spiritual being—from the real relations that constitute our lives as we come-to-be "in" the Spirit of glory. We are tempted to think of persons as *being* spiritual (or not), and then to ask whether they are *acting* in ways that use their metaphysical weight to provide space and time for those who are struggling to find community. However, the reformative Pneumatology we have been outlining can help us understand that our way of being-present to others in space and time *is* our spirituality.

I have suggested that we may describe the human spirit in terms of the temporal experience of personal consciousness that relates itself both to a remembered past and an anticipated future. The human spirit is this relation's relating itself to itself in the relation as it relates itself to others. This relationality is established by the creative presence of the eternal Spirit, who holds all things together and calls them toward renewal. The human spirit's experience of temporality is shaped by a desire to hold and be held in freedom. We long for our being-in-relation to be wrapped up in a harmonious future that draws us into the fullness of life. Our discussion now turns to the task of spelling out the dynamics of this redemptive transformation in terms of the intensification of hopeful being in the Spirit.

The Intensification of Hope

The desire of the human spirit for redemptive intimacy also takes the form of hope. Of the three that "abide" (1 Cor. 13:13), hope is often less emphasized in Christian teaching than faith and love. In English, the term often connotes an anemic wishing—a mental anticipation of an imagined future that is unsure or even dubious. If we recognize that hoping is essential to all personal becoming, however, we may begin to articulate a more robust metaphysical understanding of hope. As we have seen, being a person involves anticipating the future. In this sense, hoping is an intrinsic dimension of personal experience. Hope is not simply an activity of the intellect or will but the whole person's being-oriented toward the future.

Human freedom is the coming-to-be of persons in hope, which is characterized by a desire to belong-to and be longed-for in harmonious community. We hope to be upheld within a beautiful whole without being drowned out by the weight (glory) of the being of the other(s) in relation to whom we are coming-to-be. In chapter 7 Steve will review some of the empirical research suggesting that hope is the virtue most strongly correlated with a psychological sense of well-being. Before spelling out the dynamics of the doxological intensification of hope in the experience of redemption, it is important to underline the ontological significance of hope in Scripture.

The Hebrew understanding and experience of hope in God is radically ontological and life-giving. "Whoever is joined with all the living has hope," insists the author of Ecclesiastes (Eccles. 9:4–5). The link between hope and life is emphasized in the book of Job: "For what is the hope of the godless when God cuts them off, when God takes away their lives?" (Job 27:8).[33] Those who find their hope in God (Ps. 33:22) and from God (Ps. 62:5) are receiving salvation and life.[34] For the psalmist, God alone is the source of hopeful being (Ps. 62:5) and the all-encompassing

33. Cf. Job 8:13, "Such are the paths of all who forget God; the hope of the godless shall perish."
34. "Truly the eye of the LORD is on those who fear him, on those who hope in his steadfast love" (Ps. 33:18); "Let your steadfast love, O LORD, be upon us, even as we hope in you" (Ps. 33:22).

presence toward which all creaturely hope is truly oriented (Ps. 65:5). In the book of Proverbs, hope is particularly connected to the human experience of longing for lively being in the future: "Surely there is a future, and your hope will not be cut off" (Prov. 23:18). The soul's search for intimate knowledge of God is expressed in similar terms: "If you find it, you will find a future, and your hope will not be cut off" (24:14).

The redemptive presence of the Spirit of God is also linked to the human experience of hope in the New Testament. It is the "God of hope" who fills believers "with all joy and peace in believing, so that you may abound in hope by the power of the Holy Spirit" (Rom. 15:13). Finding our being in the Spirit involves entering into the abundantly joyful and peaceful hope that constitutes our salvation. We are saved in, by, and through hope. Paul tells the Romans that it is "*in* hope we were saved" (Rom. 8:24). The Ephesians are encouraged to attend to the "hope *to which* [God] has called you, . . . the riches of his glorious inheritance among the saints" (Eph. 1:18).[35] This hope is not an enervated wishfulness, but a living and powerful way of being in the world. The Father of our Lord Jesus Christ "has given us a new birth *into* a living hope through the resurrection of Jesus Christ from the dead" (1 Pet. 1:3). The law did not bring about a right relation to the presence of God, but in Christ we have "the introduction of a better hope, *through* which we approach God" (Heb. 7:19). The author of Hebrews further encouraged believers "to seize the hope set before us. We have this hope, a sure and steadfast anchor of the soul, a hope that *enters* the inner shrine behind the curtain, where Jesus, a forerunner on our behalf, has entered" (6:18–20). Hope "anchors" our lives by calling us to follow the way of Jesus into the intimacy of the divine presence.

The dynamics of becoming free in hope may also be described in relation to the classical "ways," refigured in terms of the intercalated concepts of intensity, intentionality, and intimacy. As with the redemptive transformation of faith and love, we are dealing here with a gracious intensification of personal human life. Human personhood is "awakened" as one finds oneself being confronted by the presence of others, being called into a future of mutual facing. This experience is characterized by both anxiety and hope, for the longing to belong in harmonious fellowship with others is shadowed by the fear of being abandoned or crushed by the presence of others. The intensity of our experience of being-present with others leads us to thematize our lack of freedom, the absence of peaceful being-in-relation. Our natural tendency is to protect

35. Cf. Eph. 2:12, "Remember that you were at that time without Christ, being aliens from the commonwealth of Israel, and strangers to the covenants of promise, having no hope and without God in the world."

the presence of the self by relying on the organizing capacity of the ego. The unbearable lightness of its finite being, however, is not sufficiently weighty (glorious) to secure the free being of the self in relation to one's neighbors, much less in relation to the infinite presence of God.

The convicting presence of the Holy Spirit graciously invites the human spirit into the way of purgation, which involves "dying" to its reliance on its own presence or the presence of finite others to secure life. This experience of the "dark night" is intensely painful, so much so that many turn away from the call toward intimate union with(in) the divine presence, preferring the an-aesthetic pleasures of a shallow life. As persons confess their self-reliance and the ugliness of their use of metaphysical weight in relation to others, they may be drawn into the illuminative way. Here they gain a new understanding of their being in dependence upon the intimate divine presence, "the light of the knowledge of the glory of God in the face of Jesus Christ" (2 Cor. 4:6). This intensively infinite light is healing and refreshing, granting a newness of being and a peace that is beyond the seductive or repulsive power of any finite reality. The illuminating presence of the Spirit liberates us into a new understanding of, and dependence upon, an infinitely glorious presence that calls us to share in the Beauty of divine life.

Through the redemptive experience of hopeful life "in" the Spirit, the weight of Eternity comes to be interpreted as the opening up of an infinitely beautiful future. The intentionality of the human spirit is broadened and deepened, attending to the intimate divine presence as it freely invites others to share in the renewal of life in hope. Kierkegaard pointed out that the Christian experience of redemption involves a recognition that Eternity takes "upon itself the form of the future, the possible [and] with the help of hope it brings up temporality's child [the human being]."[36] For living persons, the absolute disjunction between the eternal and temporal becoming is the future, "where the *eternal* relates itself as the *future* to the *person in a process of becoming*. . . . This is why Christianity has proclaimed the eternal as the future, because it was proclaimed to existing persons."[37] Through the intense purging of its intentional dependence on (or hope in) finite being, the human spirit is opened up for the true freedom that is provided by the gracious presence of God, who calls us to share in the perichoretic intimacy of the Son and the Father in the Spirit.

The intensity of the experience of the intimate divine presence transforms our intentionality. The purgative experience leads to a "poverty" of

36. Søren Kierkegaard, *Works of Love*, ed. and trans. Howard V. and Edna H. Hong (Princeton, NJ: Princeton University Press, 1995), 252.

37. Cf. Søren Kierkegaard, *Concluding Unscientific Postscript*, ed. and trans. Howard V. and Edna H. Hong (Princeton, NJ: Princeton University Press, 1992), 1:306–7.

being, the emptying of our metaphysical dependence on our own finite power to secure our presence in space and time. As Thomas Merton observes, we are led by grace through this poverty into an "abyss of freedom" that opens out "within our own midst" and draws "us utterly out of our own selfhood and into its own immensity of liberty and joy. . . . You have only just begun to exist. . . . You have sunk to the center of your own poverty, and there you have felt the doors fly open into infinite freedom, into a wealth which is perfect because none of it is yours and yet it all belongs to you. And now you are free to go in and out of infinity."[38] In his discussion of "Life in Christ," Merton suggests that through the "inspiring" presence of the Spirit, the believer becomes a "new being" no longer pushed and pulled by the vicissitudes of pleasure and pain. "Why should joy excite me or sorrow cast me down, achievement delight me or failure depress me, life attract or death repel me," asks Merton, "if I live only in the Life that is within me by God's gift?"[39]

Divine grace welcomes the human spirit into the truly free intimacy of being-in-relation that is the eternal life of God. Freedom in Christ conquers death because love "transcends death and carries [the believer] over into eternal life with the Risen Christ."[40] The gracious inviting presence of the life-giving Spirit transforms the human spirit by intensifying its *union* with God in Christ. The gravitational allure and threat of worldly pleasure and pain is no longer determinative for one's coming-to-be free. This peaceful experience brings a freedom that is beyond the push and pull of finite being yet wholly embedded within it. We are able to give up our *being* for others because our life is in the Spirit, "hidden with Christ in God" (Col. 3:3), which is the only place in which we can really *be* free, delighting in the infinitely shared pleasure of the beautiful life of God. This hopeful being in the Spirit orients our intentionality toward others as we invite them into the joy of harmonious communion.

Transforming Hospitality

As we become free in the Spirit, our being-in-relation is transformed by grace into a redemptive space that provides time for others to be welcomed into the hospitable presence of the God of hope. Several authors in the last few decades have recovered the significance of the theme of hospitality for spirituality. Henri Nouwen insisted that hospitality is a

38. Thomas Merton, *New Seeds of Contemplation* (Norfolk, CT: New Directions, 1972), 227–28; emphasis added.

39. Ibid., 160.

40. Thomas Merton, *Love and Living* (San Diego, CA: Harcourt Brace Jovanovich, 1985), 103.

central insight of the Christian tradition because it has to do with "the call of God which forms the people of God, creating a shared hope in community."[41] He argued that one of the main movements of spiritual life is "from hostility to hospitality." The latter involves "the creation of a free and friendly space where we can reach out to strangers and invite them to become our friends."[42] We tend to be pre-occupied with ourselves, and we feel overwhelmed when others threaten to occupy our space and time. Christian spirituality is a way of practicing hospitality that transforms our being in the world as we welcome others into our experience of the place of redemption.

Philip Sheldrake has observed the importance of sacred *place* for the experience of spirituality. The testimony of the mystics to their experience of transcendence suggests that they come to interpret their being-present to God as occurring (in one sense) in "no place" and yet (in another sense) as within a kind of "universal place."[43] This is related to aesthetic desire, for the artistic impulse, broadly understood, is a struggle with liminality, with the between-places through which we explore space and time. Whether in the form of music, literature, painting, or some other medium, art invites us into a new place, a new relation to that which is re-presented to us. We are fascinated by and yet afraid of these places because we cannot control them, and so we may be tempted to an-aesthetize our environments in order to numb our fear.[44] We may try to control the uncontrollable through a repression of this desire in an extreme asceticism. As we have seen, the ascetic urge has its place as a necessary component of the purgative way. Unhealthy attachment to particular things becomes idolatrous, blocking intimacy with the absolute Beauty of divine life, which can never be reduced to finite imagery. We should remember, however, that asceticism ought to be oriented toward an intensification, not an annihilation, of our joy in the Aesthetic.

The experience of hospitality for which the human spirit longs requires not only place but also personal *presence*. I have described the human spirit in terms of the relation between the centripetal organizing presence of an ego and the centrifugal orientation toward the presence of others in personal consciousness. The human spirit is this relation's relating itself to itself in the relation as it relates itself to others. This is why spiritual

41. Henri J. M. Nouwen, *The Wounded Healer: Ministry in Contemporary Society* (Garden City, NY: Doubleday, 1972), 93–94.

42. Henri J. M. Nouwen, *Reaching Out: The Three Movements of the Spiritual Life* (Garden City, NY: Doubleday, 1975), 79.

43. Philip Sheldrake, *Spaces for the Sacred: Place, Memory, and Identity* (Baltimore: Johns Hopkins University Press, 2001), 129.

44. Cf. Shults, *Reforming Theological Anthropology*, 69–70. Steve examines the concept of liminality from a psychological perspective in ch. 8 (below).

transformation involves an intensification of our intentionality in relation to the presences (faces) of those persons who have mediated our
desire to belong-to and be longed-for in a hospitable place. The human
spirit finds itself in this vis-à-vis of personal interdependence.

Theologically, however, we must also speak of the absolute dependence
of creaturely spirituality upon the life-giving presence of the Creator
Spirit. We long for a delightful presence that will never go away, for a
hopeful relation to an Other whose being-there will always be welcoming
us, holding us in being by calling us to freedom. A reformative presentation of Pneumatology should articulate the good news of our experience
of the biblical God, whose "presence" graciously provides a "place" for
our transformation. This *place* of redemption is life with Christ in the
eschatological *presence* of the eternal Spirit, who calls us to attend to
the shining countenance of the Father, whose infinite hospitality heals
and transforms our relation to finite others.

Only by sharing in the hospitality of divine grace can the human spirit
become habituated to a way of life that graciously welcomes the other,
providing space and time for redemptive transformation. Recognizing
how difficult it is to overcome the habits of an inhospitable heart, David
Ford suggests that the biblical imagery of feasting at the eschatological
banquet of God can provide us with a vision for inhabiting a space with
others now in a way that brings healing and joy.[45] As we participate in
the divine welcoming it is crucial to remember that we are all *becoming*
free—some members of the human community, especially those who
have been crushed or abandoned, may need a provision of space and
time that excludes the presence of an abuser.[46] It is also important to
recognize that the way in which one interprets the role of the host in this
provision of space, and the appropriateness of his or her vulnerability,
may vary as one goes through the ongoing process of intensification.
The fullness of Christian hope, however, suggests that the intention of
any exclusion should be oriented toward an eschatological inclusion, in
which divine grace will transform all creaturely being (1 Cor. 15:28).

Our longing for a beautiful life is connected to our anxiety about
being. This aesthetic desire is constituted and upheld by the promising
presence of the Spirit of God. This infinitely gracious presence originates
human becoming by calling it into being. The reign of divine justice

45. David Ford, *The Shape of Living: Spiritual Directions for Everyday Life* (Grand Rapids:
Baker, 1998); *Self and Salvation: Being Transformed* (Cambridge and New York: Cambridge
University Press, 1999).

46. As Hans Boersma points out, hospitality is not simply letting the other do whatever
he or she wants; cf. "Liturgical Hospitality: Theological Reflections on Sharing in Grace,"
Journal for Christian Theological Research 8 (2003): 67–77. Cf. Boersma, *Violence, Hospitality,
and the Cross: Reappropriating the Atonement Tradition* (Grand Rapids: Baker, 2004).

was announced and manifested in the ministry of Jesus of Nazareth as he welcomed others into his way of facing and being faced by the Father in the Spirit. Sharing in the redemption of space and time takes concrete form as we (like Christ) mediate the face (presence) of God to others. Our freedom is infinitely secured by the gracious embrace of divine glory, empowering us to bear the weighty burdens of others as we share together in the eternally hospitable life of the trinitarian God. Freed from ontological anxiety, we are liberated into a pleasurable fellowship of being-there for and with the other. As the body of Christ, we are called to a way of being that invites the other into the presence of the Spirit, who bears us up into the peaceful *koinōnia* of eternal life. Christian spirituality is a participation in the transforming hospitality of God, who grants us abundant being in a living hope so that we may share in the glory of Jesus Christ by welcoming others into a future of joy and peace.

Believers are called to present their whole way of being in the world as a "living" offering to God, which is their "reasonable worship" (Rom. 12:1). This means that our "liturgy" should embrace the totality of our lives in relation to God and one another. The ongoing intensification of being-formed in the Spirit is the doxology of Christian life. Christian spirituality is a liturgical being in the Spirit that shapes one's whole life in community. As we are liberated into participation in the freedom of divine life, we may truly belong to one another. In hope we follow the way of Christ, the *leitourgos* who leads us into worship in the presence of God (Heb. 8:2). Through life in the Spirit we come into the experience of true freedom, which is the metaphysical receiving of one's self in thanksgiving and giving of one's self in joy. We are becoming free as we invite our neighbors (including our enemies) into the hope of glory that redeems our space and time together.

This chapter has argued that Christian spirituality may also be understood as *being* in the Spirit, as sharing in the glory of Jesus Christ, which transforms the way in which we belong to and long for one another. I have tried to make explicit the way in which such a reforming Pneumatology aims to conserve the intuitions of the biblical tradition as it engages contemporary philosophy and science. In part 3 Steve and I will attempt to integrate our modeling of transforming spirituality, including a more explicit linking of the desires for truth, goodness, and beauty in the context of three concrete cases. First, however, Steve explores this interdisciplinary space in light of developments in the psychological study of spiritual transformation.

PART 2

Transforming Spirituality in Psychology

Steven J. Sandage

6

SPIRITUALITY AND HUMAN DEVELOPMENT

God has a shit list! And *I've* been on that shit list for forty years!" growled Pete, a shaggy, gray-haired Caucasian man to whom I was extending my hand in greeting in the activity room of a county-funded geriatric facility in Chicago. I was a twenty-four-year-old seminary student trying to complete a final internship (unpaid I might add), and I was knocked on my heels by Pete's unique introduction of himself. Obviously, he already knew my role—the volunteer chaplain. I remember experiencing a wave of speechless anxiety as I immediately realized my pastoral-care training had not included any guidelines for Pete's particular spiritual orientation and theology. I was tempted to move on in search of a friendlier elder to greet, but as I looked down, I saw Pete was a double leg amputee, and I decided to sit down at his card table and hear his story.

Pete had lost both legs in Vietnam, and his life had never been the same. He returned from the war to a young wife who could not cope with his angry depression and a country that did not want to be reminded of the reason for Pete's losses. Now at the age of fifty-one, Pete was actually younger than he looked, and despite his recent homelessness, he was less than grateful to be in this dingy, run-down facility mostly populated by much older people with dementia or severe mental illness. As we talked, he became less bombastic but continued to pepper me with theological questions he drew from his Lutheran upbringing. He was not disinterested in God and the sacred. Rather, he seemed to have a grudge against God, a kind of spiritual ax to grind. Or as his opening statement put it, he seemed to feel that God was working out a grudge against him. He later admitted that he had been very committed to his faith and had prayed throughout his tour of Vietnam until the traumatic day his platoon was attacked, friends were killed, and he was injured. "I lost my faith in a *kind* God over there. And he has been bearing down on me ever since," Pete explained. I actually found myself enjoying Pete the more we talked. If he had initially hoped to get my attention, he certainly succeeded.

Pete had a relationship with God, but his brand of relational spirituality is not the kind typically featured in the plethora of self-help books, seminars, and afternoon talk shows. His own spirituality and religious framework seem to have been attacked or *desecrated* by the traumatic experience of combat and the secondary trauma of social and relational contexts that he felt had failed to support him.[1] The narrative of his spiritual journey was a "contamination story," or a tragic plotline that moves from a good beginning to a contaminating bad event that ruins the rest of the person's life.[2] In psychoanalytic terms, Pete's spirituality was dominated by persecutory anxiety and the horrible sense of being God's "abject," a bad object rejected and punitively thrown away from the good.[3] Perhaps he experienced himself as a social abject, or one that society was trying to throw away and get rid of. Curiously, I found Pete to be much warmer and more accessible once I survived his provocative introduction. These observations and interpretive possibilities move in the direction of the psychology of religion and spirituality. Theology can help us understand spiritual experience, transformation, and questions

1. On trauma and spiritual desecration, see C. Doehming, *Internal Desecration: Traumatization and Representations of God* (Lanham, MD: University Press of America, 1993); K. I. Pargament et al., "Sacrilege: A Study of Sacred Loss and Desecration and Their Implications for Health and Well Being," *Journal for the Scientific Study of Religion* 44 (2005): 59–78.

2. On contamination stories, see D. P. McAdams and P. J. Bowman, "Narrating Life's Turning Points: Redemption and Contamination," in *Turns in the Road: Narrative Studies of Lives in Transition*, ed. D. P. McAdams, R. Josselson, and A. Lieblich (Washington, DC: American Psychological Association, 2001), 3–34.

3. J. Kristeva, *Powers of Horror: An Essay on Abjection*, trans. L. S. Roudiez (New York: Columbia University Press, 1982).

such as whether God really does have a "shit list." Psychology and other social sciences can be useful for developing models of spirituality that have empirical validity with respect to the experiential and relational dynamics of the lived world.

This chapter will outline the developmental contours of a model of relational spirituality. It will suggest that human development moves forward through a dialectical process of *attachment* and *differentiation*.[4] This developmental process offers some intriguing analogies to the larger social process of spiritual transformation in the United States that we mentioned in chapter 1, which sociologist Robert Wuthnow describes as the move from primarily spiritualities of *dwelling* to spiritualities of *seeking*.[5] Wuthnow highlights the post-1950s disembedding of spirituality from the traditional habitat of religious community. Increasing numbers of people in the United States are defining themselves as "spiritual" but "not religious," but this takes us into an important starting point—the murky terrain of defining spirituality and religion.

Defining Spirituality and Religion

There are important distinctions made between religion and spirituality in social-scientific and psychotherapy literature. Psychologist Peter Hill and his colleagues have provided an excellent review of these distinctions. The word "religion" comes from the Latin root *religio*, which connotes "a bond between humanity and some greater-than-human power."[6] Psychology of religion scholar David Wulff has traced the history of the meaning of "religion" and argues that it has historically implied both a personal, dynamic quality of religious experience and the social or institutional dimensions of religion.[7] Religion is best understood as a multidimensional construct that can include an ultimate concern, social and communal identity, ritual and symbolic mediators of sacred space and experience, sacred forms of text and media, and moral and spiritual practices.

The word "spirituality" comes from the Latin root *spiritus*, which means "breath" or "life."[8] This meaning is reflected in the many historical asso-

4. I will largely focus on adult development with some references to earlier developmental dynamics.

5. R. Wuthnow, *After Heaven: Spirituality in America since the 1950s* (Berkeley: University of California Press, 1998), 3–4.

6. P. C. Hill et al., "Conceptualizing Religion and Spirituality: Points of Commonality, Points of Departure," *Journal for the Theory of Social Behaviour* 30 (2000): 51–77.

7. D. M. Wulff, *Psychology of Religion: Classic and Contemporary*, 2nd ed. (New York: John Wiley & Sons, 1997), 3–4.

8. Hill et al., "Conceptualizing Religion and Spirituality," 57.

ciations between spirituality and meditative breathing. A diverse array of definitions of spirituality have been offered by social scientists with little consensus. But like religion, spirituality involves multiple dimensions, including the social, cultural, cognitive, affective, behavioral, neurobiological, and existential. Many people interpret their spiritual experience through a worldview lens informed by their religious communities and traditions. Increasing numbers of individuals in Western societies, however, do not view their spirituality as embedded with religion, and others are spiritually and religiously eclectic.[9] One study which sampled adults in the United States from a wide range of social groupings found that 74 percent of participants defined themselves as "spiritual and religious," 19 percent as "spiritual but not religious," 4 percent as "religious but not spiritual," and 3 percent as "neither spiritual or religious."[10] Obviously, people relate to the relationship between spirituality and religion in differing ways in their personal location of the sacred.

The Sacred

Hill and his colleagues have proposed social-scientific definitions of spirituality and religion as both relate to *a search for the sacred*. More specifically, they suggest that spirituality and religion both involve "feelings, thoughts, experiences, and behaviors that arise from a search for the sacred."[11] They use the term "sacred" to refer not just to personal values (e.g., health or success) but to "a person, object, principle, or concept that transcends the self."[12] The sacred can include "a divine being, divine object, Ultimate Reality, or Ultimate Truth" that is "set apart" as holy and beyond the ordinary.[13] Sacred objects associated with divinity or transcendence can include material objects (rocks, crucifix), time and space (temples, the Sabbath), events and transitions (wedding, death), people (saints, leaders), roles (parent, spouse), and psychological or social attributes (self, national identity).[14] Social-scientific methods cannot determine the ontological origin of the sacred (e.g., in God or the human mind) but can help us understand how people perceive the sacred or sacralize their lives and contexts.

9. W. C. Roof, *Spiritual Marketplace: Baby Boomers and the Remaking of American Religion* (Princeton, NJ: Princeton University Press, 1999).
10. B. J. Zinnbauer et al., "Religion and Spirituality: Unfuzzying the Fuzzy," *Journal for the Scientific Study of Religion* 36 (1997): 549–64.
11. Hill et al., "Conceptualizing Religion and Spirituality," 66.
12. Ibid., 64.
13. Ibid., 66.
14. K. I. Pargament and A. Mahoney, "Sacred Matters: Sanctification as a Vital Topic for the Psychology of Religion," *International Journal for the Psychology of Religion* 15 (2005): 179–98.

By "search," Hill and his colleagues mean "attempts to identify, articulate, maintain, or transform" what is considered sacred.[15] Religion differs from spirituality in their definition in that (a) religion involves means and methods of the search for the sacred that are validated and supported by an identifiable group of people and (b) religion, unlike spirituality, can also involve the search for nonsacred goals (e.g., identity, belongingness, health). This definition's emphasis on the two dimensions of searching and the sacred is grounded in a view of humans as "proactive, goal-directed beings searching for whatever they hold to be of value in life."[16]

Humans invest significant time, energy, and resources into the discovery, conservation, and transformation of the sacred. For many, approaching the "numinous," or sacred parts of life, can elicit strong affective reactions (e.g., love, awe, fear), and attacks on the sacred (desecration) can generate severe reactions. Sacred objects have been intentionally destroyed by oppressive groups, such as the Nazis, in an effort to obliterate sacred sources of human vitality.[17] Desecration carries the potential for generating trauma and suffering. Those who perceived the September 11 terrorist attacks as highly desecrating tended also to report higher levels of anxiety and depression, but spiritual losses were also positively associated with personal and spiritual growth.[18]

The differing ways in which people perceive sacredness or psychologically sanctify their lives can be empirically associated with other health-related factors.[19] For example, one study found that college students who perceived their bodies to be more sacred tended also to place a higher priority on exercise and healthy eating. To perceive something sacred is to consider it ultimate, powerful, and worthy of honor. Mircea Eliade described the sacred as "saturated with being," whereas the profane belongs to the purely natural or the realm of the "pseudoreal."[20] The sacred and the profane form a dialectic in that whatever is not sacred is profane or ordinary. The sacred/profane dialectic implies "a *choice*, a clear-cut separation of this thing which manifests the sacred from everything else around it."[21] Each person, then, finds a way of relating to this

15. Hill et al., "Conceptualizing Religion and Spirituality," 66.

16. Pargament and Mahoney, "Sacred Matters," 181.

17. R. LaMothe, "Sacred Objects as Vital Objects: Transitional Objects Reconsidered," *Journal of Psychology and Theology* 26 (1998): 159–67.

18. Pargament and Mahoney, "Sacred Matters."

19. A. Mahoney, "The Sanctification of the Body and Behavioral Health Patterns of College Students," *International Journal for the Psychology of Religion* 15 (2005): 221–38.

20. Mircea Eliade, *The Sacred and the Profane: The Nature of Religion* (San Diego: Harcourt, 1957), 12–13.

21. Mircea Eliade, *Patterns in Comparative Religion*, trans. Rosemary Sheed (Lincoln: University of Nebraska Press, 1958), 13.

dialectical relationship between the sacred and the profane. Spiritual transformations involve profound changes in how a person relates to the sacred and the profane. Chapter 7 will summarize scientific research on spirituality and health and highlight some of the health-related perils and potentials of differing ways of relating to the sacred and the profane. But first I want to identify some of the key psychological and relational dynamics that shape spiritual development.

Sacred Contexts of Development

Spirituality unfolds in relation to the contexts of human development. The ways in which people relate to the sacred are influenced by the multilevel developmental dynamics and challenges that emerge throughout the life span. By "multilevel," I mean that human development can be understood as involving bidirectional relationships between biological, psychological, social, and cultural levels of organization. I would not reduce spirituality or the sacred to any of these levels, but I also would not suggest that human experiences of spirituality completely bypass these levels of organization. From a social-scientific perspective, it is helpful to consider how Pete's spiritual orientation might be shaped, changed, or reconfirmed by various dimensions of his biology, his personality, his past and present developmental challenges, his social and relational experiences, and the larger cultural contexts of his life journey. My primary discipline—psychology—is particularly helpful for identifying individual differences that can help explain why persons such as Pete feel they are being attacked by God whereas others with seemingly similar levels of life stress and tragedy can feel deeply loved or protected by God and supported by their spirituality.

Individual Differences in Spirituality

That geriatric facility in Chicago harbored deplorable conditions, worse than the many prisons I have worked in. But it also provided a context that offered me many powerful experiences of individual differences in how older adults relate to the sacred. The discipline of personality psychology offers methods for understanding differences between individuals—the ways our unique personalities form our beliefs, experiences, and interpretations. The field of human development investigates the unfolding process of human experience over the life span with attention to patterns of continuity and change. The interaction of personality and developmental process serves to form individual differences in spirituality. A brief description of two other residents from the geriatric facility can illustrate significant individual differences in the form and process of spirituality.

Doris was an eighty-two-year old Caucasian woman who might simply be described as Pete's spiritual and psychological opposite. Whereas Pete's wounded-warrior spirituality seemed dominated by struggle, conflict, hostility, and a sense of persecution, Doris struck me as carrying on a sweet romance with God despite the solitude imposed by her total lack of surviving family. Jungians would probably say Doris had a well-developed *lover* archetype. I would typically find her sitting quietly near a window and knitting or looking into the distance with a smile on her face. She would always greet me warmly, and when I asked how she was doing, she would look me right in the eyes and say something like, "Oh, I'm just sitting here talking with Jesus. You know, he is *so* good to me. I'm just thinking about his love and kindness. And he loves you, too." This last part would usually come with her leaning forward slightly and gesturing gently toward me with her finger.

My subsequent clinical training has taught me to be wary of over-spiritualizing or using spiritual language as a defense against painful realities in life. Doris was an extremely optimistic person, one of those whom William James described as "healthy-minded" in their religious focus on the "sunny side" of life and their seeming obliviousness to the contradictions or tragedies of life.[22] In contrast, Pete fit James's description of the "sick soul" who is deeply sensitive to the effects of evil and suffering in the world. James suggested that sick souls could discover a deeper spiritual orientation than the healthy-minded, but it would have to come through a redemptive spirituality of transformation.

Doris's orientation to reality might be questioned by the fact that nearly every time I talked with her at length, she would eventually tell me how "handsome" I was, which at the time happened to be my only source of romance as a celibate single in a mostly male seminary. Maybe my memory is biased by her affirmations, and maybe her spirituality did involve some flight from the ugly, chaotic, lonely context in which she was spending her final days. But these many years later, I still find myself fondly jealous for her healthy-minded, romantic spirituality. I also wonder about the developmental advantages for an older adult such as Doris in having the strength of a warm, generous personality and spirituality that is so effective in recruiting people to offer interest and support. Her winsomeness and positive attitude were adaptive

22. W. James, *Varieties of Religious Experience: A Study in Human Nature* (New York: Modern Library, 1929), 76–111.

strengths to help limit the onset of further loss for a woman who had no family members "obligated" to care for her. It might be ethically unfair, but Doris was more reinforcing to be with than some other residents who were consistently negative or bitter. More "difficult" residents such as Pete were vulnerable to serious neglect. Some who struggled with depression or orneriness compensated with humor, colorful storytelling, or other relational strengths to buffer the interpersonal impact of their struggles.

Sally was an African American woman I met at the same facility who fit the latter category—spiritually struggling, even despairing, but also able to earn the respect and interest of staff through the strength of her character. She was seventy-eight years old and legally blind when her two adult sons dropped her off at the facility, literally without telling her in advance. I met her on her third day at the facility, and she had still not heard from her sons. About a week later, I walked into her room one evening just before sundown. She was sitting quietly in her bed, and we talked for a few moments about her adjustment to her new residence and her sadness at the abandonment she felt. Once again I found myself in over my head with someone facing a horrible tragedy. I had no idea how someone *could* cope with this kind of situation, which was an impotent feeling for me as a young chaplain. As this realization of my own incompetence was settling in, Sally responded to my momentary silence by starting to pray the name of Jesus, as if our conversation was over and she was going to engage her *real* Helper. By "pray the name of Jesus," I mean she began a slow rhythm of groaning the name of Jesus over and over again. I had never heard anything like it before, but I would now describe it as a kind of self-soothing, trusting lament that came from deep soulfulness. She seemed to be suffering *with* Jesus, the way a woman might breathe deeply to calm herself during the tiring pain of early labor. When I later explored African American spirituals, I began to understand the cultural traditions behind this way of relating to God with authenticity and the courage to cry out.[23] As I listened to her rhythmic lament that night, I settled into my student status and a chair next to the bed of this gray-haired teacher. Over the next thirty minutes, the only word spoken was Sally's prayer as the room turned completely dark, she drifted off to sleep, and I was calmed through this completely new spiritual experience.

23. See James H. Cone, *The Spirituals and the Blues: An Interpretation* (Maryknoll, NY: Orbis, 1991); Arthur C. Jones, *Wade in the Water: The Wisdom of the Spirituals* (Maryknoll, NY: Orbis, 1993); Dan Allender, "The Hidden Hope in Lament," *Mars Hill Review* 1 (1994): 25–37.

Relational Spirituality

I have described three different older adults with three different forms of relational spirituality. In the introduction, I suggested that a social-scientific framework can be helpful for understanding relational spirituality as "ways of relating to the sacred." People sacralize or make sacred certain times, spaces, and objects as holy or spiritually meaningful. The sacred can include divine beings (e.g., God or gods) but can also include spiritual leaders, rituals, practices, stories, texts, and other objects of worship or devotion. To make sacred is to set apart something as special, uniquely transcendent, and not ordinary or profane.

The last point alludes to the fact that individuals and groups do not define, locate, and relate simply to the sacred but also to the profane. To make one day or one text sacred makes others potentially just that—"other" or profane. So, actually, sacred and profane form a ubiquitous dialectic in human experience. It is useful to think of them separately but also as reciprocally defined. Individuals and groups have ways of relating to the sacred and ways of relating to the profane.

The definition of spirituality offered by Hill and colleagues ("feelings, thoughts, experiences, and behaviors that arise from a search for the sacred") is helpful but seems to fit best with cognitive-behavioral models in psychology.[24] Since LeRon and I prefer relational models and categories, we find it helpful to consider spirituality as involving various ways of relating to the sacred. William James defined spirituality as the "feelings, acts, and experiences of individual men in their solitude, so far as they apprehend themselves to stand in relation to whatever they may consider divine."[25] The second part of that definition ("to stand in relation") speaks to the relational dynamics of spirituality. The relational unit of analysis provides a helpful complement to an understanding of spiritual feelings, acts, thoughts, and experiences. Following James, spirituality involves how we each *relate* to the developmental and existential challenges of making meaning in the midst of the ambiguity of life.[26]

A relational view of spirituality also facilitates understanding the profound reciprocal influence of spirituality and interpersonal rela-

24. Hill et al., "Conceptualizing Religion and Spirituality," 66.

25. James, *Varieties of Religious Experience*, 42.

26. C. M. Dahl, "A Phenomenological Exploration of the Definition and Expression of Spirituality within Families" (Ph.D. diss., University of Minnesota, 1994); J. W. Fowler, *Stages of Faith: The Psychology of Human Development and the Quest for Meaning* (New York: HarperSanFrancisco, 1981); Robert Kegan, "There the Dance Is: Religious Dimensions of Developmental Theory," in *Toward Moral and Religious Maturity*, ed. J. W. Fowler and A. Vergote (Morristown, NJ: Silver Burdette, 1980), 403–40.

tionships. The various ways people relate to the sacred can impact the ways they relate to others, for better and for worse.[27] Interpersonal relationships also help shape relational representations of the sacred.[28] Relationships with other people who serve as spiritual mentors, models, authority figures, companions, guides, or narrative imagoes can be highly influential on psychosocial development and spiritual formation.[29]

A less obvious advantage of a relational approach is that it can help overcome a common tendency to view spirituality in exclusively positive or idealistic ways. The historical disparagement of spirituality and religion in social-scientific literature has been countered in recent years by a frequent recasting of spirituality as healthy and positive. Certainly, empirical research often supports the transformation toward more positive views of religion and spirituality. It is rare, however, to see less prosocial or overtly antisocial "alternative" spiritualities, such as Satanism, considered in depth. Some might object that Satanism is not really a form of spirituality, but it can be understood as a way of relating to that which is perceived as sacred. A relational view opens conceptual space for considering a wide variety of spiritual orientations without necessarily validating those orientations as healthy or morally good.

A relational approach to spirituality serves to integrate emerging understandings of personhood in both theological anthropology and contemporary psychological science. For example, neuroscientist Warren Brown has suggested that the personal capacity for "relatedness" to self, others, and God most closely fits the descriptions of human "soulfulness."[30] A relational model of personhood can help overcome a strict dualism that fails to account for the important relationships between spirituality, immune functioning, and health as well as the complex social dynamics that influence those factors.

27. For a review of empirical research on religion and spirituality in relation to marriage and family dynamics, see A. Mahoney et al., "Religion in the Home in the 1980s and 1990s," *Journal of Family Psychology* 15 (2001): 559–96. For examples of the destructive influence of abuse on spirituality, see C. Doehring, *Internal Desecration*; and T. G. Plante, *Bless Me Father For I Have Sinned: Perspectives on Sexual Abuse Committed by Catholic Priests* (New York: Praeger, 1999).

28. R. L. Sorenson, *Minding Spirituality* (Hillsdale, NJ: Analytic Press, 2004).

29. D. P. McAdams, *Stories We Live By: Personal Myths and the Making of the Self* (New York: Guilford, 1993).

30. W. S. Brown, "Psychoneuroimmunology and Western Religious Traditions," in *The Link between Religion and Health*, ed. H. G. Koenig and H. J. Cohen (New York: Oxford University Press, 2002), 262–74, quote from p. 271. Also see W. S. Brown, N. Murphy, and H. N. Malony, eds., *Whatever Happened to the Soul? Scientific and Theological Portraits of Human Nature* (Minneapolis: Fortress, 1998).

Relational Mediation

Relational mediation is central to human development. A person's relationship to the sacred is mediated through various cultural and contextual resources, including rituals, symbols, narratives, music, and spiritual practices.[31] Certain spaces, places, or geographical features can be set apart as sacred or influence ways of relating to the sacred.[32] Many cultural groups have a sacred relationship with the landscape of either their present context or their remembered homeland. Across many expressions of mystical spirituality, transformation seems to empower the imagination to make use of contextual resources for generating spiritual experience.[33]

Cultural and religiously based orienting systems can also contextually mediate spirituality by helping define and interpret experiences of the sacred.[34] Spiritual transformation always occurs within a social context or a set of contexts. Historical, cultural, and political contexts shape social processes and interpretations of spiritual transformation and therapeutic healing, but spirituality can also be a catalyst for transforming social contexts. A relational approach to spirituality can foster attention to the potential bidirectional influence of social and relational mediators of spiritual transformation.

Relational Transformation

A relational framework can also shape our definition of spiritual transformation. I am defining spiritual transformation as *a process of profound, qualitative change in the self in relationship to the sacred*.[35] Several researchers have made connections between relational influences and spiritual transformation. For example, Lewis Rambo suggested that relationships are part of the "matrix of transformation," and he concluded that relationships were "very important to the conversion process" for over 90 percent of the participants in his interview study.[36] In Rambo's model, relationships can be both catalytic and confirmatory in the conversion

31. J. L. Griffith and M. E. Griffith, *Encountering the Sacred in Psychotherapy* (New York: Guilford, 2002); L. Rambo, *Understanding Religious Conversion* (New Haven: Yale University Press, 1993); Wuthnow, *After Heaven*.

32. B. C. Lane, *Landscapes of the Sacred: Geography and Narrative in American Spirituality*, expanded ed. (Baltimore: Johns Hopkins University Press, 2001).

33. Jess Byron Hollenback, *Mysticism: Experience, Response, and Empowerment* (University Park: Pennsylvania State University Press, 1996).

34. A. Mahoney and K. I. Pargament, "Sacred Changes: Spiritual Conversion and Transformation," *Journal of Clinical Psychology* 60 (2004): 481–92.

35. For a similar definition, see ibid.

36. Rambo, *Understanding Religious Conversion*, 107.

process, although he also called for a more systematic examination of relationship dynamics.

Other researchers have also found relationships to influence movement toward religious conversion and transformation. Ullman and Jacobs both implicated relational needs as influential in their interview studies of religious converts.[37] In both studies, family or other relational deficits among converts frequently co-occurred with a strong identification with particular religious leaders and groups. In their study of "quantum changers," Miller and C'de Baca also found that family and relational conflicts often preceded spiritual transformations.[38]

Lee Kirkpatrick has applied the relational paradigm of attachment theory to the quantitative study of religious conversion.[39] His research offers some preliminary support for a compensation hypothesis, suggesting that individuals with an insecure attachment style (particularly avoidant styles) are more likely to report dramatic religious conversions than individuals with a secure attachment style. According to attachment theory and research, insecurely attached individuals have higher levels of relational anxiety than securely attached individuals because of different internal working models of relationships, formed in relationships with caregivers and other attachment figures. This higher level of relational anxiety could create a felt need for more-intense spiritual or religious experiences to compensate for relational insecurity and disappointment.

Relationships may also change as sequelae of spiritual transformation. Most of the major world religious and spiritual traditions suggest that authentic spiritual transformation should result in relational virtues (e.g., compassion, love, forgiveness, gratitude, loyalty, honor, justice). The specific catalogs of relational virtues differ according to spiritual tradition, but authentic transformation should be demonstrated in relational change and virtue. Miller and C'de Baca found that those who reported profound change often indicated positive transformations in relationships and values in relationships.[40] William James recounted the relationally transformed worldview of a recently

37. C. Ullman, *The Transformed Self: The Psychology of Religious Conversion* (New York: Plenum, 1989); J. L. Jacobs, *Divine Disenchantment: Deconverting from New Religions* (Bloomington: Indiana University Press, 1989).

38. W. R. Miller and J. C'de Baca, "Quantum Change: Toward a Psychology of Transformation," in *Can Personality Change?*, ed. T. F. Heatherington and J. L. Weinberger (Washington, DC: American Psychological Association, 1994), 253–80; *Quantum Change: When Epiphanies and Sudden Insights Transform Ordinary Lives* (New York: Guilford, 2001).

39. Lee A. Kirkpatrick, *Attachment, Evolution, and the Psychology of Religion* (New York: Guilford, 2005).

40. Miller and C'de Baca, "Quantum Change: Toward a Psychology of Transformation," and *Quantum Change: When Epiphanies and Sudden Insights Transform Ordinary Lives*.

converted farmer who said, "My horses and hogs and even everybody seemed changed."[41]

Relationships shape a context or ecology in which spiritual trans formation can occur. Robert Kegan suggested that transformation is nested within a social context that provides a "holding environment" or a "culture of embeddedness."[42] These cultures of embeddedness can support transformation qualitatively by providing a caring context, encouraging differentiation and maintaining some continuity during the stress of change. Individuals who experience spiritual transformation, however, do not always describe their specific local contexts as caring or supportive of differentiation. We need a better understanding of ways in which different individuals and groups experience contexts as supportive, as well as unsupportive, of transformation.

The contextualization of spiritual-transformation will also require research that examines potential racial, gender, and class differences. Whereas there is some evidence that women and men might experience differing relational changes following spiritual transformations, racial, cultural, and class differences in spiritual transformation remain relatively unexamined in empirical research.[43] Feminist and liberation thinkers have challenged contemporary theologians and social scientists to engage and integrate the themes of contextuality, relationality, justice, and spirituality. For example, the purgative process, which can lead to spiritual transformation, might often confront men with the limits of narcissism and the need for humility whereas women might often be confronted by the limits of relational dependence and the need for positive self-identity.[44]

Relational Alterity

"Alterity" refers to otherness and the internal configuration of self and other. A relational view of spirituality can also help us acknowledge the reality that we are all challenged to develop ways of relating to the spirituality of others who are different from us. These ways of relating are wide-ranging and can include ignoring, deprecating, idealizing, attacking, acknowledging, fearing, supporting, hating, envying, worshiping,

---

41. James, *Varieties of Religious Experience*, 200.

42. Robert Kegan, *The Evolving Self: Problem and Process in Human Development* (Cambridge: Harvard University Press, 1982).

43. On possible gender effects, see Miller and C'de Baca, *Quantum Change: When Epiphanies and Sudden Insights Transform Ordinary Lives*; B. J. Zinnbauer and K. I. Pargament, "Spiritual Conversion: A Study of Religious Change among College Students," *Journal for the Scientific Study of Religion* 37 (1998): 161–80.

44. Mahoney and Pargament, "Sacred Changes"; Mark Allen McIntosh, *Mystical Theology: The Integrity of Spirituality and Theology* (Malden, MA: Blackwell, 1998).

controlling, trumping, subsuming, swallowing, imitating, respecting, considering, learning, and differentiating. Spiritual differences with others can feel great or small, but human spiritual diversity offers no shortage of challenges in relational alterity. Perhaps the core challenge of spiritual maturity is one of integrity and differentiation, which involves holding on to one's own spirituality while also relating respectfully to others and their spiritualities.[45]

Bringing order, organization, and coherence to the definitions and locations of the sacred is a way individuals and groups make meaning out of the ambiguity of life. This is a central purpose of ritual, or repeated, coordinated, and meaningful, ways of relating to the sacred. Pete's shocking spirituality of construing himself as an abject enemy on "God's shit list" obliterates the boundary between sacred and profane, forcing together images and language that are commonly held separate. This seemed to metaphorically reflect the curse of his Vietnam experience, where the boundaries between sacred and profane were traumatically obliterated without repair. Doris and Sally found differing ways to continue to relate to the sacred with intimate trust in the midst of an amazingly stressful context, one I initially experienced as horribly profane.

People do not simply make something or someone in their lives sacred in a fixed, unchanging way. Rather, I am suggesting that we develop multiple ways of relating to the sacred (and the profane) that evolve or change over time. These ways of relating to the sacred can be positive in the sense of affirming, grateful, loving, trusting, devotional, or worshipful. But it is also possible to use many other, less positive relational descriptors, such as mistrustful, hostile, avoidant, demanding, neglectful, or blasphemous. Many individuals, probably most, seem to relate to the sacred with some level of ambivalence or a mix of trust and mistrust, approach and avoidance.

Although social-scientific models of spirituality are not theologically neutral, their role is not to verify or disconfirm the reality of the sacred in an ontological sense. The social sciences cannot tell us how we ultimately *should* locate or name the sacred. Those are roles for the disciplines of theology and philosophy. Rather, social sciences can help us understand the variety of ways people *do* make meaning in relation to the sacred, as well as the associated empirical correlations and consequences.

45. David M. Schnarch (*Passionate Marriage: Keeping Love and Intimacy Alive in Committed Relationships* [New York: Henry Holt, 1997]) makes the connection between integrity and differentiation of self.

Human Development and Personhood

This relational-spirituality model suggests that the ways people relate to the sacred unfold and evolve in the various contexts of human development. There are many theories of development and personality that can be employed in understanding the relationships between psychological dimensions of personhood and spirituality. Dan McAdams's three-level model of personality provides a helpful organizational framework for considering individual differences.[46] Table 3 provides a summary of McAdams's model and proposes a list of corresponding constructs from psychological literature on religion and spirituality that can be useful for research or assessment.

Level 1 of Personality

Level 1 includes personality traits or dispositions that tend to characterize individuals across time and varying situations. For example, among adults the "Big Five" traits of openness to experience, conscientiousness, extraversion, agreeableness, and neuroticism show high cross-situational consistency and stability over time. The Big Five also demonstrate strong cross-cultural validity. Other personality traits, such as narcissism and shame-proneness, also differentiate individuals and can be linked to psychopathology.

Research in the growing field of positive psychology has led to measures of certain "virtue" traits or dispositions, such as gratitude, hope, and forgiveness. Personality traits differentiate individuals from one another and can help shape the kinds of spirituality a particular individual will find reinforcing or ego-syntonic. An individual quite low in extraversion might be naturally drawn to contemplative prayer, devotional reading, or practicing solitude but less comfortable with small groups that pull for personal disclosure. Those high in neuroticism might find it challenging to enter into singing praise songs. Spiritual formation often requires engaging the comfortable "road less traveled" of our personalities, but it can be helpful to be self-aware of our propensities.

Table 3. Levels of Personality and Corresponding Spiritual and Religious Constructs

Level of Personality	Religious/Spiritual Constructs	References
Level 1 Dispositional Traits (e.g., openness, conscientiousness, gratitude, neuroticism, narcissism, shame)	Religious Temperament God Images Spiritual Transcendence	James (1902) Rizzuto (1979) Piedmont (1999)

46. D. P. McAdams, "What Do We Know When We Know a Person?" *Journal of Personality* 63 (1995): 365–96.

Level of Personality	Religious/Spiritual Constructs	References
Level 2 Personal Concerns (e.g., motives, strivings, coping styles, defense mechanisms, developmental concerns, attachment styles, beliefs, values)	Religious Coping Spiritual Strivings Faith Development Intrinsic/Extrinsic Quest Attachment to God Belief Systems Religious Values	Pargament (1997) Emmons (1999) Fowler (1981) Gorsuch and McPherson (1989) Batson and Schoenrade (1991) Rowatt and Kirkpatrick (2002) Meissner (1996) Worthington (1988)
Level 3 Narrative Identity (e.g., themes, plots, turning points, peak experiences, characters/images)	Religious Images Narrative Themes Religious Styles	McAdams (1993) Ganzevoort (2002) Streib (2001)

Based on McAdams's three-level model of personality (1995).

Psychologists have developed several constructs that apply to Level 1 of personality.[47] For example, William James's previously mentioned distinction between the "healthy-minded" and "sick soul" religious temperaments referred to traitlike dispositions of personality.[48] In contemporary personality assessment, James's categories would likely load on traits of optimism and neuroticism.

The psychoanalytic body of research on God images or psychological representations of God is also relevant to Level 1 of personality. In Ana-Maria Rizzuto's influential work *The Birth of the Living God*, she distinguished between God concepts and God images.[49] God concepts are intellectual or cognitive definitions of God. God images are more intuitive, internal working models of what a person imagines God to be like on the basis of "a set of remembered and interpreted associations and experiences."[50] God images draw upon affectively loaded relational experiences and attachment processes with parents and caregivers. For example, people who experience their parents or primary caregivers as cold and distant could tend to project those relational characteristics onto God, at least at an implicit or nonconscious level of knowing.[51] Those who experienced parents or caregivers as warmly available may tend to hold similar God images. God images are not

47. See, for example, James, *Varieties of Religious Experience*; Ana-Maria Rizzuto, *The Birth of the Living God: A Psychoanalytic Study* (Chicago: University of Chicago Press, 1979); R. L. Piedmont, "Does Spirituality Represent the Sixth Factor of Personality? Spiritual Transcendence and the Five-Factor Model," *Journal of Personality* 67 (1999): 985–1013.

48. James, *Varieties of Religious Experience*, 112–39.

49. Rizzuto, *Birth of the Living God*.

50. R. T. Lawrence, "Measuring the Image of God: The God Image Inventory and the God Image Scales," *Journal of Psychology and Theology* 25 (1997): 214–26.

51. Lawrence, "Measuring the Image of God"; Peter C. Hill and Todd W. Hall, "Relational Schemas in Processing One's Image of God and Self," *Journal of Psychology and Christianity* 21 (2002): 365–73.

completely determinative of spiritual experience or unchangeable, but they are likely to be highly influential on spirituality for those holding theistic worldviews. Assessment of Level 1 constructs can begin to get at what Nancy Duvall has called our "unconscious theology," or what could also be described as implicit spirituality based on relational experience.[52]

Level 2 of Personality

Level 2 of personality in McAdams's model is a level he calls "personal concerns." This level includes dimensions of personality that describe what individuals want during particular periods of life or in specific areas of life, as well as the methods they use to pursue their wants. For example, a reading of Pete's personality traits might tell us that he is low in agreeableness, high in neuroticism, and moderate in his openness to experience. We would need to move to other Level 2 personality descriptors to get a more specific picture of how Pete manages his life and the goals he is striving to achieve. Level 2 includes constructs for assessing specific motivations, goals or strivings, coping styles, defense mechanisms, developmental concerns, attachment styles, beliefs, and values. Developmental and motivational dynamics provide a contextualized understanding of individuals in the temporal unfolding of their lives. Level 2 dimensions of personality are more likely to evidence substantial change over time than Level 1 dimensions, particularly in adulthood.

Most of the research in the psychology of religion and spirituality has focused on Level 2 constructs in areas such as religious coping, religious motivation, faith development, styles of spiritual attachment, spiritual goals or strivings, and religious belief systems and values.[53] For example,

52. Nancy Duvall, "Unconscious Theology and Spirituality" (presentation, the Institute of Spiritual Formation, Biola University, La Miranda, CA, October 17, 2000). Also see T. W. Hall and S. L. Porter, "Referential Integration: An Emotional Information Processing Perspective on the Process of Integration," *Journal of Psychology and Theology* 32 (2004): 167–80.

53. See, for example, K. I. Pargament, *The Psychology of Religion and Coping: Theory, Research, Practice* (New York: Guilford, 1997); R. A. Emmons, *The Psychology of Ultimate Concerns: Motivation and Spirituality in Personality* (New York: Guilford, 1997); Fowler, *Stages of Faith*; R. L. Gorsuch and S. E. McPherson, "The Intrinsic/Extrinsic Measurement: I/E-Revised and Single-Item Scales," *Journal for the Scientific Study of Religion* 28 (1989): 348–54; C. D. Batson and P. A. Schoenrade, "Measuring Religion as Quest: II. Reliability Concerns," *Journal for the Scientific Study of Religion* 30 (1991): 430–47; W. C. Rowatt and Lee A. Kirkpatrick, "Dimensions of Attachment to God and Their Relation to Affect, Religiosity, and Personality Constructs," *Journal for the Scientific Study of Religion* 41 (2002): 637–51; W. W. Meissner, "The Pathology of Beliefs and the Beliefs of Pathology," in Edward P. Schafranske, ed., *Religion and the Clinical Practice of Psychology* (Washington, DC: American Psychological Association, 1996), 241–68; E. L. Worthington, "Understand-

Kenneth Pargament's program of research has generated measures of styles of religious coping. One of the best psychological indices of a person's spiritual and religious orientation is how that person relates to the sacred through styles of coping with stressful circumstances. Numerous researchers in the psychology of religion have also investigated and debated the motivational, health, and maturity correlates of intrinsic, extrinsic, and quest styles of religiosity. Intrinsic religiosity involves an internalized commitment or approach to one's religion as an end in itself. Those high in extrinsic religiosity tend to view their religion as a means to other ends, such as social connection. Extrinsic religiosity can represent lower internalization or levels of faith development, but as a measure, it can also tap into a highly social orientation to religion. Quest religiosity has been defined and measured in different ways but generally involves an openness to changing one's religious beliefs or the valuing of religious doubts. Robert Emmons has studied the ways people sanctify their goals or strivings and the related implications for well-being. Assessment of Level 2 constructs can be useful for understanding how a person is engaging his or her spirituality in the midst of life's goals and concerns. I will utilize many of these Level 2 constructs throughout the following chapter.

Level 3 of Personality

Level 3 of personality in McAdams's model is that of narrative identity, which is one of his unique contributions to the field of personality. McAdams suggests that the development of a person's identity can be likened to the construction of a life story. As McAdams puts it, "identity is the storied self."[54] Identity gives unity and purpose to life, and McAdams suggests that many contemporary democratic societies promote the ideas that (a) adults should know who they are and (b) adult identity must be discovered or created and cannot be simply handed to someone from authority figures or institutions.

Certainly, cultural and developmental differences mean that some people are more individualistic than others in their life story construction. Groups high in vertical collectivism often give a prominent role

---

ing the Values of Religious Clients: A Model and Its Application to Counseling," *Journal of Counseling Psychology* 35 (1988): 166–74. Although this provides a substantive body of research, the emphasis on Level 2 constructs in the psychology of religion over the past fifty years also reflects the "cognitive developmental logic" that Heinz Streib has critiqued as contributing to the relative neglect of relational dimensions of religion and spirituality (H. Streib, "Faith Development Theory Revisited: The Religious Styles Perspective," *International Journal for the Psychology of Religion* 11 [2001]: 143–58).

54. McAdams, "What Do We Know When We Know a Person?" 385.

to authority figures in defining reality, and social identity often takes precedence over individual identity in such groups. But McAdams's narrative theory of identity is still relevant for two reasons. First, the historical forces of globalization and urbanization mean that many people around the world, but particularly in contexts like the United States, are confronted with an increasing array of human diversity in ways of making meaning. This means that life story construction is likely to be an increasingly challenging and important task for large segments of the human population across cultural differences. Second, personal life experience and spiritual narratives are woven together in an intertextual fashion in many spiritual and religious traditions. Biographies and autobiographies of spiritual experience and transformation, such as Augustine's *Confessions*, provide narrative material for integrating the human life journey with spiritual transcendence and meaning. In the Christian tradition, narrative is one way of doing theology.[55] Groups vary in the democracy of their narrative hermeneutic, with conservative groups typically allowing less individual interpretive authority than do liberal groups.[56] But most spiritual and religious communities encourage some use of narrative as a tool for understanding one's identity.

Life stories "thicken" our description of a person's spiritual formation journey. They tell us the particularities, the bends and turns in a person's life. Pivotal characters, settings, and events can be given rich description. Stories appeal to the narrative mode of cognition, which can be contrasted with the logical or analytic mode of cognition. Stories are easily remembered and move people emotionally by inviting the temporary transfer of listeners out of their own lives and into the story itself. This is the spiritual power of testimony, which is so central in some traditions. The Jewish and Christian Scriptures offer rich narratives with diverse characters and plots that serve to theologically locate God amidst the earthy spirituality of life.

Surprisingly, limited psychological research in the psychology of religion and spirituality has been aimed at Level 3.[57] If we broaden this dimension to include hermeneutical perspectives on interpreting spiritual and religious experience, some efforts have been made to investigate dif-

---

55. J. McClendon, *Biography as Theology: How Life Stories Can Remake Today's Theology* (Philadelphia: Trinity Press International, 1990).

56. R. W. Hood, P. C. Hill, and W. P. Williamson, *The Psychology of Religious Fundamentalism* (New York: Guilford, 2005).

57. See McAdams, *Stories We Live By*; R. R. Ganzevoort, "Common Themes and Structures in Male Victims' Stories of Religion and Sexual Abuse," *Mental Health, Religion and Culture* 5 (2002): 313–25. Streib, "Faith Development Theory Revisited," 143–58. Also see Streib, *Hermeneutics of Metaphor, Symbol, and Narrative in Faith Development Theory* (Frankfurt, Germany: Lang, 1991).

fering hermeneutics that individuals and groups apply to the sacred. For example, Heinz Streib has developed a narrative and relational model of religious development, suggesting that "the self-Other interaction has a narrative character dealing with narratively structured themata."[58] By "themata," Streib means relational experiences, even traumatic ones, that form into life themes and interact with developmental schemata (Level 2 constructs). In this way, Streib is indirectly calling for an integration of Levels 1–3 of personality in the area of religious development. Spiritual assessment that ignores any of these levels of personality may result in a truncated picture of human development.

Relational Contexts of Development

Spiritual formation and psychological development unfold not only inside individuals but also in the relationship between individuals and their systemic contexts. The developmental and personality dynamics of individuals interact throughout the life span in relation to systems or contexts at multiple levels to influence meanings and practices of spirituality. Relational systems and contexts offer what Robert Kegan calls "cultures of embeddedness," building on Donald Winnicott's relational notion of holding environments.[59] These systemic cultures of embeddedness can provide a supportive relational context out of which spiritual formation and transformation can emerge. This holding and shaping function has been likened to developmental scaffolding. Systems or context can also oppressively impede the processes of spiritual formation and transformation or even shape the pathology of spiritual malformation.

Some psychological models of development neglect consideration of the relational and cultural contexts that influence development. Sociological or systems-based models of development sometimes carry the opposite limitation of ignoring the intraindividual dimensions of personhood in favor of social, familial, and cultural levels of analysis. The trend in contemporary theories of human development is toward bioecological awareness and a stress on person-context relations.[60] It is valuable to seek to understand persons, contexts, and the changing relations between persons and their contexts. Contexts not only surround

58. Streib, "Faith Development Theory Revisited," 148.

59. Kegan, *Evolving Self*, 115–32.

60. R. M. Lerner, *Concepts and Theories of Human Development*, 3rd ed. (Mahwah, NJ: Lawrence Erlbaum, 2002), 44–45; J. O. Bolswick, P. E. King, and K. S. Reimer, *The Reciprocating Self: Human Development in Theological Perspective* (Downer's Grove, IL: InterVarsity, 2005).

or "nest" individuals, families, and communities; they "weave together" these various threads of influence to form the fabric of human development in community.[61]

To use an analogy, if I want to understand the process of fishing for a specific team of fishers, I will need to understand the structure and functions of their boat and know about the water and weather conditions that provide the fluid context the team is fishing in. I will also need to understand how the various fish function in their ecology. But that is not enough because I will need to examine how the team *relationally* manages the dynamic process of the boat interacting in *relationship with* the water and other ecological elements. Spiritual formation and transformation involve an analogous set of complexities: (a) dynamic (or changing) individuals and communities relating to (b) multiple dynamic contexts in (c) dynamic ways of relating.

The fishing analogy can be used to consider storms in the context that surrounds the fishers, their boat, and their ecology. Contextual factors do not always support human development or indigenous spirituality. For example, theologian George Tinker reminds us that the chronic "storms" of white racism and oppression have meant that many American Indians are surrounded by an imposed cultural context with which they do not identify.[62] So, I am arguing that it is imperative to understand the cultural and relational contexts of human development and spirituality while recognizing the power and control dynamics that generate and maintain injustice and oppression for some groups.

Developmental Systems and Contexts

Donald Ford and Richard Lerner proposed developmental systems theory as a way of overcoming the nature/nurture split in theories of development and to encourage the ecological study of persons-in-context at multiple levels of organization.[63] A complete summary of their complex theory is beyond the scope of this chapter. Three points about this theory, however, are useful for consideration here. First, developmental systems theory suggests that development involves bidirectional influences between individuals and linkages with their multiple contexts. Contexts shape individuals, but individuals also shape their contexts. In fact, health-conducive development involves the capacity for children,

61. Steven J. Sandage and I. Williamson, "Forgiveness in Cultural Context," in E. L. Worthington Jr., ed., *Handbook of Forgiveness* (New York: Routledge, 2005), 41–56.

62. G. E. Tinker, *Spirit and Resistance: Political Theology and American Indian Liberation* (Minneapolis: Fortress, 2004).

63. D. H. Ford and R. M. Lerner, *Developmental Systems Theory: An Integrative Approach* (Newbury Park, CA: Sage, 1992); Lerner, *Concepts and Theories*.

adolescents, or adults to enact age-appropriate agency or the self-regu-
lation to help select and shape their own contexts of development.[64] I
will argue that one of the primary changes in the process of spiritual
formation and transformation involves changes in how persons *relate*
to their various social contexts.

Second, development is open-ended and involves *relative plasticity*,
with an individual's genetic endowment interacting with the conditions
of that individual's environment. Genetic potentials do not determine developmental pathways but interact with the constraining and facilitating
conditions of both biology and environmental contexts. Some evidence
is emerging that genetic factors may influence individual's religious and
spiritual practices, but this does not mean that genes determine religion
and spirituality.[65]

Third, all levels of organization involved in human development are
embedded in history. Historical contexts and changes in these contexts
over time serve to frame development. An obvious example is the changing life expectancy during the twentieth century from forty-nine to sev-
enty-four years. This increased life expectancy creates more time for
continued spiritual formation and transformation, with spirituality and
aging becoming a vibrant area of social-scientific research. This also
creates more time for an elder's spirituality to be stretched by various
forms of loss and decline in functioning.

Fourth, the relational goodness-of-fit between individuals and the
demands and opportunities of their contexts is an important influence
on human development. Developmentalists have suggested that a poor
fit between a child (or adult) and his or her environmental contexts is
predictive of developmental problems unless there is adequate relational
responsiveness from the environment or the child.

Cultures of Embeddedness

As mentioned above, Kegan uses the term "cultures of embeddedness" to describe the psychosocial and cultural environments in which
individuals develop.[66] Drawing on Winnicott's notion of infants' "holding
environments" or the facilitating relational milieu provided by caregivers
that surrounds infant development, Kegan suggests that we experience
a succession of holding environments of varying quality and posture
not just during infancy but throughout the life span. Winnicott's widely

64. Lerner, *Concepts and Theories*.
65. D. H. Hamer, *The God Gene: How Faith Is Hardwired into Our Genes* (New York:
Archer, 2005).
66. Robert Kegan, *Evolving Self*, 115–32; and *In over Our Heads: The Mental Demands
of Modern Life* (Cambridge: Harvard University Press, 1994).

cited statement "There is never just an infant" highlights the essential relational role of caregivers in the development of children.

For Kegan, cultures of embeddedness combine cultural (e.g., narratives) and biological (e.g., food) resources to influence development. Consistent with developmental systems theory, Kegan also argues that individuals benefit from cultures of embeddedness that change or evolve in concert with those individuals' development.

The Winnicottian language of "holding environment" misses another important nuance in Kegan's person-in-context model of development. Kegan suggests that cultures of embeddedness provide three primary functions in facilitating human developing: (a) holding on (confirmation), (b) letting go (contradiction), and (c) remaining in place (continuity).[67] Individuals, particularly young children, need supportive holding in a secure attachment with consistent, available caregivers. Throughout the life span, positive connections to supportive relationships and sources of community are a significant predictor of health and well-being.[68] This is different from a restrictive holding that suffocates and never lets go. Human development requires cultures of embeddedness, including parents, friends, and spiritual leaders, that know when to wisely let go and allow individuation and independence.

Metaphors of Relational Process in Development

Cynthia Neal Kimball employs the Vygotskian metaphor of "scaffolding" to describe the relational supports that can nurture child development and be withdrawn at the optimal time to promote transformation into competent agency.[69] Neal Kimball builds her Christian model of development on Lev Vygotsky's notion of the "zone of proximal development," the region of competence between what a child can do on his or her own and what the same child can do with the assistance of a supportive teacher. From Vygotsky's perspective, human development is transformed through joint activities of social interaction that become internalized to promote higher mental functions. Development involves apprenticeships with parents, mentors, teachers, and advanced peers

67. See also E. Liebert, *Changing Life Patterns: Adult Development in Spiritual Direction*, expanded ed. (St. Louis: Chalice, 2000).

68. S. Cohen, "Social Relationships and Health," *American Psychologist* 59 (2004): 676–84.

69. C. N. Kimball, "Family Brokenness: A Developmental Approach," in *Care for the Soul: Exploring the Intersection of Psychology and Theology*, ed. M. R. McMinn and T. R. Phillips (Downers Grove, IL: InterVarsity, 2001), 346–62; also see C. J. Neal, "A Parental Style for Nurturing Christian Wisdom," in *Limning the Psyche: Explorations in Christian Psychology*, ed. R. C. Roberts and M. R. Talbot (Grand Rapids: Eerdmans, 1997), 165–85.

who relationally form in children the capacity to use cultural tools to facilitate their own continued development.

Both Neal Kimball and Kegan also use the aesthetic metaphor of "dance" to more fluidly describe the evolving, dynamic relationship that develops between parents and children, communities and individuals. Perhaps it's ironic that dance is central to the spirituality of some communities while strictly prohibited by others. I find dance to be a very helpful metaphor for the relational processes of human development and spiritual formation because it implies the challenge of moving in rhythm with someone else who is also moving while introducing new moves with appropriate timing.[70] I can also imagine dance instructors who remain perpetually directive, thereby squelching the unique rhythm or creativity of their instructee, as well as instructors who become so absorbed in their own solo performance that they are oblivious to the movement of the other.

These numerous developmental theories across diverse schools of thought (psychoanalytic, constructive-developmental, family systems, ecological, or contextual) all suggest that human development involves internalizing the processes of relationship or ways of relating. Several important implications for spiritual formation and transformation are generated from this relational framework on development:

1. *Spiritual formation is passed on relationally*. Families and communities pass on formation as ways of relating to the sacred. Piaget observed, "The child spontaneously attributes to his parents the perfections and abilities which he will later transfer to God if his religious education gives him the possibility."[71] The vast psychoanalytic literature on relationally developed representations of God concurs with Piaget that early relational figures offer a powerful influence on God images and understandings of the divine.[72] The Commission on Children at Risk concluded that "early nurturing relationships influence early spiritual development—call it the spiritualization of attachment."[73] Trustworthy and secure relationships with caregivers can facilitate internal representations of a

70. Dance and choreography are also aesthetic metaphors employed by B. P. Keeney, *Aesthetics of Change* (New York: Guilford, 1983).

71. J. Piaget, *The Child's Conception of the World* (London: Routledge and Kegan Paul, 1951), 354.

72. See, e.g., Rizzuto, *Birth of the Living God*; M. H. Spero, *Religious Objects as Psychological Structures: A Critical Integration of Object Relations Theory, Psychotherapy, and Judaism* (Chicago: University of Chicago Press, 1992).

73. Commission on Children at Risk, *Hardwired to Connect: The New Scientific Case for Authoritative Communities* (New York: Institute of American Values, 2003), 27.

trustworthy and secure spiritual realm. Even in neglect or control, families and communities are communicating ways of relating to sacredness. Parents or spiritual leaders who adopt a domineering style of directive instruction with little emotional attunement or developmental sensitivity will foster the internalization of that particular way of relating to self and other. Passive or role-reversing ways of parental relating will likely encourage dysfunctional or malformed ways of relating to the sacred. As suggested earlier, relational experiences, both positive and negative, interact with intrapsychic structures to form the templates of our "unconscious theology."

2. *Spiritual formation is facilitated through quality apprenticeship relationships with mentors, teachers, and spiritual guides.* These student-teacher relationships can and do involve varying levels of formality but seem an essential dimension of spiritual formation and transformation across spiritual traditions and cultures. In the Christian tradition, discipleship can convey this idea of a formative relationship between a teacher and follower. The formal discipline of spiritual direction is probably the clearest Christian example. Sharon Parks's research on the faith development transitions of young adults reported that "the mentoring environment" was a critical factor that influenced continued growth or stagnation.[74] In his program of research on Christians training as professional psychologists, Randell Sorenson found that graduate students' capacities to integrate their faith with their vocation seemed to be more relationally "caught than taught."[75] That is, students seemed to learn about integrating spirituality and vocation through relating to the personhood of their instructors even if *what* they learned was disappointing or unhelpful. Sorenson and his colleagues concluded that students reported they were helped the most by faculty and other mentors who were transparent about their ongoing process of being-in-relationship with God, whether that relationship was joyful or difficult. It would be a mistake to consider the self-other relational matrix of spiritual formation as the individual and God only. Rather, the relational capacities of parents, leaders, and mentors constitute a vital part of the relational matrix of formation.

3. *Spiritual formation requires relationships with attachment figures and communities that can both hold on and let go.* As Kegan sug-

74. S. D. Parks, *The Critical Years: Young Adults and the Search for Meaning, Faith, and Commitment* (San Francisco: HarperCollins, 1991).

75. R. L. Sorenson, K. R. Derflinger, R. K. Bufford, and M. R. McMinn, "National Collaborative Research on How Students Learn Integration: Final Report," *Journal of Psychology and Christianity* 23 (2004): 355–76.

gests, human development and spiritual formation involve the dialectic process of both attaching and separating throughout the life span.[76] Parents, spiritual guides, or communities that "overhold" and fail to allow exploring or separation will eventually block growth, individuation, and the spiritual seeking necessary for maturity. Winnicott identified "transitional space" as the arena for developing religion, creativity, and play because this is where the self emerges out of embeddedness in the self-other matrix.[77] Letting go to offer freedom for exploration and internalization will be particularly hard for parents or leaders who (a) have a strong need to be idealized rather than questioned or (b) have trouble managing their own anxiety about the potential perils of questioning and exploring. Using ecological language of "guest-host," Kegan points out that the evolutionary motion of development inevitably leads to guests testing their hosts' capacities for opposition and otherness.[78] Development involves a process of "throwing away" that in which we have been embedded before, and then finding (it is hoped) a more mature way to reconnect.[79] Children push off from their parents in their anxiety about exploring the world. Adolescents often question their authority figures with an aggressiveness that reveals their anxiety about independence. Adult development also includes the "stranger anxiety" of leaving the familiar faces of community to explore new spiritual terrain, possibly becoming a stranger to closest friends and family.

4. *Spiritual transformation is often generated through relationships with persons and communities that wisely and intentionally face contradiction and foster change.* Change involves tolerating the anxieties of ambiguity, confusion, transition, and disequilibrium. In James Loder's existential model, transformation in human development arises from facing the negation of the void.[80] In chapter 1 LeRon and I suggested intensified anxiety and dark nights of purgation are part of the crucible process of spiritual transformation. When families, communities, and other cultures of embeddedness chronically attempt to protect or rescue their members from contradiction or struggle, they ecologically impede potential growth and transformation. "Sitting with Job" can involve the anxiety of being present to those who are suffering or struggling

76. Kegan, "There the Dance Is"; *Evolving Self*, 109.

77. D. W. Winnicott, *Playing and Reality* (London, England: Tavistock, 1971).

78. Kegan, *Evolving Self*, 127.

79. Ibid., 131.

80. James E. Loder, *The Transforming Moment* (Colorado Springs: Helmers & Howard, 1989), 80–85.

through spiritual darkness and confusion, a context that can make it tempting to inject simplistic "recipe theologies" to reduce one's own anxiety.[81] An opposite ecological mistake can be to unwisely instigate or force contradiction and change prematurely before people have developed "eyes to see and ears to hear." This means that relationships, families, and communities that foster spiritual transformation will need to tolerate and value within-group diversity without high degrees of spiritual and emotional reactivity.

5. *Spiritual formation and transformation are given rootedness by families, communities, and other social networks that generatively remain in place.* Kegan describes "remaining in place" as the third development-enhancing function of cultures of embeddedness after holding on and letting go.[82] Human development requires episodes of relational separation, leaving, and independence from one's familiar context and community. In some cases, this involves temporarily pushing against or pushing away from the cultural communities in which one is embedded. When those communities or relational figures become reactive or punitive, developmental progress can be defeated or at least more difficult. The other potential problem is that both human development and spiritual formation can be enhanced by opportunities to recover or return to our roots in new ways. People "leave home" and leave the relationships in which they have been held in a myriad of ways. To be able to "return home" by recovering and reappropriating in new ways the best parts of one's relationships and communal traditions is a formative gift that Sorenson associates with the virtue of gratitude.[83] Those who have felt embarrassment or other strong emotions in response to remembering a part of their spiritual background know how difficult a task this can be. And as Kegan suggested, to be warmly recognized and received by familiar faces upon return without being forced to pretend there has been no change can be an even greater gift.[84] When families and communities are not able to allow space for questioning, leaving, and differentiating, there is a risk that those who do so will experience little choice but to repudiate their roots and make profane that which was formerly sacred. Spiritual leaders and communities might be most generative, that is, most positively influential on future generations, when they are able to balance the capacity to

81. The term "recipe theology" comes from L. Crabb, *The Silence of Adam* (Grand Rapids: Zondervan, 1995).
82. Kegan, *Evolving Self*, 129–32.
83. Sorenson, *Minding Spirituality*.
84. Kegan, "There the Dance Is."

maintain their own solid identities and values while also remaining receptively open to reconnection with those who have moved on to other loyalties.

Attachment and Differentiation

After highlighting the relational and contextual dimensions of spirituality I now want to focus on the constructs of developmental attachment and differentiation. Attachment and differentiation are two of the most prominent themes in theories of human development, although most theories have tended to emphasize one or the other rather than a dialectic of the two. Kegan comes close with his life span dialectic of independence and inclusion, or integration and differentiation, with each theme alternating priority across developmental periods.[85] I appreciate the thrust of Kegan's dialectical model and find it particularly helpful for application to spiritual formation but will nuance or embellish his definitions of these themes.

Attachment theory is the first psychoanalytic and relational theory of development to generate a large body of empirical literature, perhaps in part because John Bowlby also grounded the theory in evolutionary psychology.[86] Whereas attachment is a well-defined construct within a relatively cohesive school of thought, differentiation is a more heterogeneous construct that can have a variety of meanings, including independence, separation, individuation, and the capacity to balance autonomy and connection in close relationships. I prefer the latter neo-Bowenian understanding of differentiation (or "differentiation of self") as the capacity to balance both autonomy and connection in close relationships, which highlights the mature ability to "hold onto one's self" in the presence of others without defensive reactivity.[87] This is particularly challenging in the anxiety-provoking contexts of interpersonal conflict and interpersonal intimacy and requires a capacity to self-soothe anxiety and self-validate. Narrower understandings of differentiation as simply separating, individuating, or acting independently miss the complex ma-

85. Kegan, *Evolving Self*; also see a classic work by D. Bakan, *The Duality of Human Existence: Isolation and Communion in Western Man* (Boston: Beacon, 1966).

86. For an introductory overview of attachment theory, see J. Bowlby, *Attachment and Loss*, vol. 1, *Attachment*, rev. ed. (New York: Basic Books, 1999); R. Karen, *Becoming Attached* (New York: Oxford University Press, 1994); T. Clinton and G. Sibey, *Attachments: Why You Love, Feel, and Act the Way You Do* (Brentwood, TN: Integrity, 2002).

87. David M. Schnarch, *Constructing the Sexual Crucible: An Integration of Sexual and Marital Therapy* (New York: W. W. Norton, 1991); *Passionate Marriage*; *Resurrecting Sex: Resolving Sexual Problems and Rejuvenating Your Relationship* (New York: HarperCollins, 2002).

turity of this adult capacity to integrate self-validation and attunement to others. This is a limitation of Kegan's use of "differentiation," which he articulated before more recent theoretical and empirical advances. I view the movements of separation and individuation as developmental tasks that recur periodically throughout the life span at culturally shaped intervals, whereas differentiation of self refers to this more complete relational capacity that is necessary for adult intimacy. Like attachment, differentiation of self can begin to develop early with an infant's capacity for self-soothing and the mutual regulation of relationships with caregivers and potentially evolves throughout the life span.

Attachment is a construct that is also often misunderstood with emphases on only the connection, support, or holding functions. Actually, Bowlby described the attachment system between an infant and a caregiver as maintaining proximity for security but also providing a secure base for exploring new territory. Securely attached infants have an internal working model of relationship with their caregiver that generates confidence to explore their environment without becoming preoccupied by debilitating separation anxiety. In contrast, insecurely attached infants do not feel confident of caregiver protection and availability, and this impedes the emotional freedom necessary to explore.

Two general styles of insecure attachment (avoidant and ambivalent) have been identified in infants, children, and adults. Avoidantly attached children and adults tend to show little outward emotional distress but are internally anxious about their relations with caregivers and romantic partners. They tend to minimize their requests for help or connection and, in some cases, externalize their frustration in ways that push others away or simply maintain distance. A subgroup of avoidant children and adults seem to be more fearful than callous or aggressive in emotional tone. Ambivalently attached children and adults tend to show considerable outward emotional distress and can be dramatic, clingy, and frustrated with caregivers and romantic partners. They make frequent attempts at eliciting attention and help, and they often complain of wanting more closeness with others. Attachment security tends to be relatively consistent well into adulthood unless there is a significant relational transformation in a person's life, and so attachment patterns of connecting and exploring are issues across the life span.

Attachment and differentiation of self are both more robust as self constructs than is implied by a simplistic opposition, but there is a relative difference in emphasis that makes them useful in a dialectic model of development. Interestingly, attachment theory has had its strongest impact in research on the developmental periods of infancy and childhood, where a secure attachment style is predictive of emotional well-being, resilience, and self-esteem. Differentiation of self has arguably had its strongest impact in the developmental period of adulthood and models of couples' intimacy and sexuality. I want to briefly consider research on both attachment and differentiation in relation to religion and spirituality and then connect these developmental constructs to our crucible model from chapter 1.

Attachment, Religion, and Spirituality

Empirical studies testing attachment theory are increasing in the psychology of religion and spirituality.[88] Kirkpatrick suggested that many elements of attachment theory make it a promising fit for rapprochement with religious beliefs and behavior, particularly with relational monotheistic religions such as Christianity. For example, attachment theory emphases on the presence of warm, loving, and trusting relationships with attachment figures can be likened to similar relational construals of God. In fact, psychologists studying religious conversions have often reported descriptions that can be likened to "falling in love" with God.[89] God is often described in religious literature, hymns, and personal testimonies as like an exalted attachment figure whose omnipresence offers the ultimate spiritual proximity.

The attachment system safe-haven functions of protection and security are also analogous to prominent spiritual and religious themes of seeking protective shelter and deliverance from enemies. Kirkpatrick points out the parallels between many attachment-seeking behaviors of young children, such as crying or raising arms to be picked up, and similar religious or spiritual behaviors exhibited by adults. He also describes prayer as an analog to the social referencing of young children who intermittently check in with attachment figures to reconfirm their protection and presence.

The correspondence hypothesis in the psychology of religious attachment posits that adults' internal working models of human relational attachment, particularly romantic attachment, may correspond or parallel with their models of attachment with God. Secure attachment with God involves the sense of God as loving, responsive, and present. Avoidant attachment with God involves construals of God as distant and inaccessible. Ambivalent attachment with God involves conflictual images of God as inconsistently available and responsive.

88. For a review of empirical research on attachment theory and religion, see Lee A. Kirkpatrick, *Attachment*.

89. Lee A. Kirkpatrick, "Attachment and Religious Representations and Behavior," in *Handbook of Attachment: Theory, Research, and Clinical Applications*, ed. P. R. Shaver and J. Cassidy (New York: Guilford, 1999), 803–22.

There is some empirical evidence that securely attached adults score higher in religious commitment and are more likely to report being "evangelical Christians" than are avoidant or ambivalent adults.[90] Secure attachment was also predictive of faith maturity in a sample of evangelical Protestant seminary students.[91] The evangelical and Christian emphasis on a loving personal relationship with God seems consonant with a secure attachment. Curiously, there is also some empirical evidence that avoidantly attached adults are more likely to describe themselves as agnostics or atheists and also to report sudden religious conversions during adulthood than the other two groups. The tendency to avoid relational closeness and commitment might be transferred onto the sacred for some, creating the necessity for a sudden conversion after a critical spiritual mass is reached.[92] Ambivalently attached adults are more likely to report glossolalia, or speaking in tongues, which is a relatively dramatic spiritual practice.

A unique study of attachment styles, stress, and forms of prayer among college students found that avoidant individuals engaged in less meditative and conversational prayer, particularly during stress, than nonavoidant individuals.[93] This fits attachment theory if prayer is understood as a spiritual behavior of seeking relational closeness and communication with God. Anxious individuals (as is the case with the abandonment anxiety of the ambivalent style) engaged in more petitionary, help-seeking prayer than nonanxious individuals. This is consistent with an anxious-dependent spiritual posture.

Two longitudinal studies using this attachment model found adult women with negative internal models of self (ambivalent and fearful/avoidant) were more likely to report significant increases in several religious and spiritual measures over time than those with positive models of self.[94] Kirkpatrick interprets these findings as suggesting that traditional religious theologies of humans as unworthy of God's unconditional

90. Ibid.

91. J. R. TenElshof and J. L. Furrow, "The Role of Secure Attachment in Predicting Spiritual Maturity of Students at a Conservative Seminary," *Journal of Psychology and Theology* 28 (2000): 99–108.

92. On the role of critical mass in marital transformation see Schnarch, *Passionate Marriage*.

93. Kevin R. Byrd and AnnDrea Boe, "The Correspondence between Attachment Dimensions and Prayer in College Students," *International Journal for the Psychology of Religion* 11 (2001): 9–24.

94. Lee A. Kirkpatrick, "A Longitudinal Study of Changes in Religious Belief and Behavior as a Function of Individual Differences in Adult Attachment Style," *Journal for the Scientific Study of Religion* 36 (1997): 207–17; "God as a Substitute Attachment Figure: A Longitudinal Study of Adult Attachment Style and Religious Change in College Students," *Personality and Social Psychology Bulletin* 24 (1998): 961–73.

love might be an optimal compensatory fit for adults who feel negative about self and desire closeness with an attachment figure who cannot be driven away. To date there is more empirical support for the protective, safe-haven function of religion and spirituality than the secure-base function. This might be a limitation of research strategies and attempts to measure attachment connections to spiritual and religious exploration. Another possibility is that differentiation is a construct that will more strongly predict spiritual and religious exploration and more mature transformations in future research.

Differentiation of Self, Religion, and Spirituality

In stark contrast to attachment constructs, the differentiation-of-self construct has been largely overlooked in the empirical psychology of religion and spirituality. Rabbi Edwin Friedman applied differentiation of self and a Bowenian theoretical framework to the religious systems of congregations and synagogues.[95] He described ways both family systems and religious systems can hinder differentiation and thereby lower emotional and relational well-being. Friedman even suggests that poorly differentiated individuals and systems can be more susceptible to anxiety contagion and various health problems whereas well-differentiated systems can foster spiritual well-being.

One attempt to study empirical connections between differentiation and religiosity is C. David Batson's quest construct. Batson suggested that those high in quest religiosity tend to engage in more complex thinking about existential dilemmas, religious doubts, and issues of social justice than low questers. Research on the quest construct using Batson's scale and others has generated ambiguous and conflicting results. It appears there are differing types of spiritual and religious questing. Some questers are more intensely doubt-oriented whereas other questers are better described as open to change. In short, an anxiety-driven need to doubt that becomes chronic might reflect spiritual attachment anxiety and limited differentiation. As we suggested in chapter 1, mature differentiation of self should promote the ability to both face and soothe anxieties, including those involving spiritual and religious doubts, as well as the confidence to make spiritual commitments. An openness to new spiritual discoveries and tolerating the anxiety of necessary change represent a point of theoretical convergence for the constructs of secure attachment, differentiation of self, and mature questing.

95. E. Friedman, *Generation to Generation: Family Process in Church and Synagogue* (New York: Guilford, 1985). See also J. Balswick and J. Balswick, *The Family: A Christian Perspective on the Contemporary Home*, 2nd ed. (Grand Rapids: Baker, 1999); Balswick et al., *The Reciprocating Self*; and Kegan, "There the Dance Is."

Dwelling and Seeking

Attachment and differentiation serve as useful psychological constructs for understanding Robert Wuthnow's sociological categories of spiritual dwelling and seeking. Wuthnow has proposed the thesis that the landscape of spirituality in America has been profoundly transformed since the 1950s.[96] The essence of this cultural transformation is a shift from spiritualities of *dwelling* to spiritualities of *seeking*. In short, Wuthnow argues "that a traditional spirituality of inhabiting sacred places has given way to a new spirituality of seeking—that people have been losing faith in a metaphysic that can make them feel at home in the universe and that they increasingly negotiate among competing glimpses of the sacred, seeking partial knowledge and practical wisdom."[97] Spiritual dwelling is oriented toward habitation in the known territories of sacred space whose boundaries are sharply outlined by religious traditions and reinforced by priestly leaders. Spiritual dwelling provides attachment security, rootedness, stability, clarity of meaning, and a shared sense of community. Spiritual seeking is oriented toward the freedom of exploring new uncharted territory described or dreamed by prophets, mystics, and healers. Spiritual seeking is represented by the more fluid themes of the journey, pilgrimage, and quest. Spiritual dwelling offers security whereas spiritual seeking offers freedom from constraint.

Wuthnow relates this cultural transformation in spirituality to (a) the changing cultural diversity and religious pluralism of American society and (b) the large-scale cultural expectation or demand that religion be spiritually practical and consumer-friendly. A spirituality of seeking is, in part, "a movement away from a denial of doubt."[98] Religious traditions that rigidly insist on conformity, homogeneity, and unquestioning allegiance as part of spiritual dwelling have been working against a strong cultural tide. In some postmodern circles, mistrust toward authority figures has produced even stronger resistance to dwelling within traditional religious communities. Moreover, leaders of most religious institutions in America since World War II have tried, at some level, to help make spirituality popular and culturally accessible through various media and technological advances. This has probably facilitated the relocation of spirituality far beyond the walls of sacred dwellings.

These spiritual trends contain complex sociological, psychological, and theological issues. As a sociologist, Wuthnow suggests that there are important strengths and limitations to the spiritual orientations of both

96. Wuthnow, *After Heaven*, 1–18.
97. Ibid., 3.
98. Ibid., 8.

dwelling and seeking, and he proposes a practice-oriented spirituality that attempts to integrate the best of both. In the crucible model of chapter 1 LeRon and I suggested that seeking and dwelling form a necessary spiritual dialectic, and this roughly parallels the attachment-and-differentiation developmental dialectic suggested above. At its best, spiritual dwelling provides a secure attachment to a loving Deity, a supportive communal home, and an anchor in a meaningful tradition. Periodically, developmental transitions and transformative opportunities converge to promote leaving familiar dwellings and seeking to explore new spiritual terrain. This could literally involve the geographical change of leaving home as a missionary, a prodigal, or some other type of spiritual sojourner. Or it could mean spiritual seeking or questing that is more purely internal, perhaps without actually leaving one's dwelling place. This might entail spiritual wondering, questioning, doubting, rethinking, or groping through a dark night of suffering. Dwelling and redwelling in healthy spiritual holding environments offer the sense of community and rootedness that can enhance or even promote well-being. The courage to tolerate the ambiguity, responsibility, and differentiation of spiritual seeking is necessary to move spiritual formation and transformation toward maturity.

Related versions of this dwelling/seeking dialectic are emerging in several interdisciplinary frameworks. Psychoanalyst Stephen Mitchell described the twin longings for safety and adventure that converge in both spirituality and romantic passion.[99] Psychologist of religion Kenneth Pargament suggested two basic types of spiritual and religious coping with stressful threats to significance: conservation and transformation. Conservation includes initial attempts to protect, salvage, retain, or hold on to familiar spiritual significance. Transformation of spiritual significance includes attempts to grow or change either one's valued ends or the pathways to these ends. Intrinsic religiosity is oriented toward internal commitment, attachment, and dwelling. Quest religiosity is oriented toward seeking and doubting. In chapter 7 I will summarize some of the emerging scientific research on spirituality and health and consider the implications of various forms of dwelling and seeking for well-being.

99. Stephen A. Mitchell, *Can Love Last? The Fate of Romance over Time* (New York: W. W. Norton, 2002).

7

SPIRITUALITY
AND HEALTH

The human spiritual pursuit of health weaves a diverse tapestry. The stressors of life require coping strategies, and spirituality and religion offer people a myriad of potential ways for dealing with challenges to health and well-being.

Like many, my own spiritual journey includes a variety of ways of relating to both the sacred and my own health. As a child, I grew up watching Oral Roberts, the television preacher and healer. His program usually included dramatic spiritual healing for people with physical ailments through the laying on of hands. And the show always concluded with the same optimistic song, "Something good is going to happen to you, happen to you, this very day." I am surprised to feel a little rise in hopefulness even now as I remember this familiar lyric.

In late adolescence, I started searching spiritually during an intense family crisis. My search led me back into the lively spirituality of Christian Charismatic and Pentecostal circles, only this time the experiences came in person rather than from watching television. The services and tent meetings I attended were exciting, far different than the more formal and predictable church services I had grown up with. The music was vibrant and informal, with choruses repeated for emotional impact. People raised their hands in the air, danced, spoke in tongues, and sometimes fell to the floor. Evangelists preached about the transforming power of the Holy Spirit to heal sickness, bring financial prosperity, and even raise the dead. God was described as always present, and with the presence of God all things were possible. In some meetings, healers cast demons out from people writhing on the ground or barking like a dog on their hands and knees. This type of spirituality was always interesting and never boring.

Two things happened during this leg of my spiritual journey that eventually sent me searching again. First, a charismatic friend managed to shame me for needing contact lenses when God was willing to heal anyone with enough faith. I threw away my contacts and went forward for healing at the next service. You guessed it—I was not healed. And I knew I had mustered as much sincere faith as I could. The resulting dissonance catalyzed spiritual and theological seeking. Second, I chose psychology as a major in college, naively assuming it might be helpful for my growing interest in ministry. Psychology has proven very helpful to my spiritual formation, but I was initially unprepared for the epistemological conflicts this would spark. I started to grapple with questions about the sources of dramatic spiritual experiences, such as when they were "authentically" spiritual and when they might be a manifestation of psychological dynamics. I also grew more attuned to the confusing reality that people who reported profound spiritual experiences for years could sometimes also exhibit very poor emotional and relational health. In research terms, self-reported holiness does not always correspond with observer ratings.

I still appreciate the charismatic spiritual tradition, but my more recent spiritual dwelling place has been within the contemplative Christian tradition. The psychological orientation and emotional tempo of contemplative spirituality is in many ways almost the opposite of charismatic spirituality. The contemplative tradition promotes stillness, reflection, and quiet listening prayer. Catholic spiritual writer Sebastian Moore argues that the core of spirituality involves desire and attention.[1] Contemplatives throughout the ages have commended the value of sustaining spiritual desire and attention while also tolerating the mysterious hiddenness of God during dark nights of the soul. These dark nights and the accompanying emotional pain can be part of a spiritual formation process of maturing toward deeper spiritual intimacy and union with the divine.

1. Sebastian Moore, *Let This Mind Be in You: The Quest for Identity through Oedipus to Christ* (Cambridge, England, and Hagerstown, MD: Harper & Row, 1985).

One of my first experiences with contemplative spirituality came several years ago when I joined some seminary colleagues in group spiritual direction for a couple of years. I remember the first morning we drove to our spiritual director's farmhouse and for two hours she led us through a rhythm of silent listening prayer followed by one person sharing verbally with the group, followed by more silence before anyone responded. Unlike the highly spontaneous and verbal Bible study groups I was accustomed to, this format called for holding one's thoughts before speaking. For me, the rhythms of silence simultaneously heightened the sense of space between us in the group and intensified the spiritual experience of emotional and relational intimacy. At the end of that first morning, I felt an incredible sense of inner calm and perceptual clarity.

Spiritual Arousal and Soothing

Spirituality includes the relationally dialectical process of arousal and soothing. I have described only two differing examples of the many spiritual traditions and experiences that can generate heightened neurobiological arousal and soothing.[2] Spirituality can be part of the psychological activation and intensification of arousal that motivates people toward action. And spirituality can also be part of the calming or soothing of anxiety and other emotions. In Christian theological language, the Holy Spirit both convicts and comforts.

Catholic spiritual writer Ronald Rolheiser defines spirituality in a symbolic fashion as the relational interplay of fire and water, as "what we do with the fire inside of us."[3] For Rolheiser, spirituality includes the arousing fire of passion, energy, or *erōs* and the soothing, cooling, integrative soulfulness that keeps us glued together. Constant arousal without soothing eventually overwhelms the capacity of the human system to integrate intensification. Perpetual attempts at soothing without activating arousal can result in stagnation and detachment from life. Some powerful spiritual experiences appear to involve simultaneous activation of both the arousal and the soothing functions of the brain.[4] Optimal human health and well-being require a wise balancing and integration

2. Andrew Newberg, Eugene d'Aquili, and Vince Rause (*Why God Won't Go Away: Brain Science and the Biology of Belief* [New York: Ballantine, 2001]) describe their theory of the neurobiological roles of the autonomic nervous system and the limbic system in spiritual and religious experience. The sympathetic nervous system regulates arousal, and the parasympathetic nervous system regulates soothing or quiescence.

3. Ronald Rolheiser, *The Holy Longing: The Search for a Christian Spirituality* (New York: Doubleday, 1999), 11.

4. Newberg, d'Aquili, and Rause, *Why God Won't Go Away*, 39.

of arousal and soothing, and scientific research can help describe the varied roles for health-conducive spirituality and well-being.

Defining Health and Well-Being

There appears to be a growing global concern for promoting health. Scientific advances in the past century have contributed to increased life span, and researchers have been investigating factors that can promote human health. But this raises a crucial question—what exactly is *health*?

In 1948 the World Health Organization defined health as a "state of complete physical, mental, and social well-being and not merely the absence of disease or infirmity."[5] Yet the medical model of health as merely the absence of illness has dominated Western cultures, at least until recent years.[6] Researchers and health professionals are challenging more and more a strictly medical model of health in two primary ways. First, there is growing recognition that definitions of health are culture-laden.[7] The language, metaphors, stories, and philosophical categories used to describe ideals of health will necessarily rely upon cultural artifacts. In some cultures illness can be a sign of a privileged spiritual calling to become a healer or shaman whereas in others the same symptoms can be interpreted as a cursed sign of sinfulness. Across many cultures, spirituality and health are considered closely connected. Second, many researchers and practitioners are becoming more interested in moving beyond a focus on pathology to understand salutary or optimal human health.[8] What are the health-promoting strengths or virtues that help some individuals, families, and communities to grow and even flourish through the stressors and traumas of life while others fall victim to compromised health and pathological functioning?

Positive Human Health

Carol Ryff and Burton Singer offer three wise principles for formulating models of positive human health. First, they have argued that

5. World Health Organization, "Constitution of the World Health Organization" (1948), in *Basic Documents* (Geneva: The Author), 28.

6. C. D. Ryff and B. Singer, "The Contours of Positive Human Health," *Psychological Inquiry* 9 (1998): 1–28.

7. Ibid., 5–7.

8. For background on the concept of salutary functioning, see A. Antonovsky, *Unraveling the Mystery of Health* (San Francisco: Jossey-Bass, 1987).

the task of defining models of positive human health is better suited for the field of philosophy than medicine. I would add theology to their nomination of philosophy. Models of positive health and optimal functioning rely upon philosophical conceptions of the "good life" and human flourishing. Positive health can also connote spiritual well-being or holiness and be related to ultimate concerns in many spiritual traditions. And so theology can inform ideals of health and the integration of health and holiness.

Virtue is a construct that is relevant to the topic of positive human health, for virtues have traditionally been understood as character qualities that promote healthy living and social well-being.[9] Virtues, such as compassion and gratitude, are human strengths that can serve to integrate the goals of personal health and community benefit. That is, virtues should generally be salutary or healthy for both individuals and their communities. Virtues are often closely related to spirituality and represent, for many people, sanctified or holy ways of living. Martin Seligman, principal leader in the emerging positive-psychology movement, argues that the authentic happiness of the good life is generated by developing strengths and virtues that promote gratifications for both self and others.[10]

Ryff and Singer also suggest a second principle, that positive human health is "at once about the mind and the body and their interconnections."[11] Understanding the interconnections between the mind and body is crucial for overcoming outdated dualistic perspectives and for transforming models of spirituality and health. Like health, human spirituality is embodied and influenced by both the mind and physiological processes. As LeRon suggested in chapter 2, this is consistent with an incarnational Christian theology.

Third, Ryff and Singer suggest that "positive human health is best construed as a multidimensional dynamic process rather than a discrete end state."[12] Human health is not static but a process that contains ways of engaging the unfolding tasks of living. It is easy to overlook the dynamic, ever-changing process of health, but a dynamic view of health can be more readily integrated with relational models of spiritual transformation. States of health and well-being emerge from the ongoing process of adaptation in life. Virtues are human strengths of character that promote personal and social health, but they are often developed

9. S. J. Sandage and P. C. Hill, "The Virtues of Positive Psychology: The Rapprochement and Challenges of an Affirmative Postmodern Perspective," *Journal for the Theory of Social Behaviour* 31 (2001): 241–60.

10. M. E. P. Seligman, *Authentic Happiness* (New York: Free Press, 2002).

11. Ryff and Singer, "Contours," 2.

12. Ibid.

through growth cycles of stress and suffering. Healthy individuals often take on certain types of stress, such as exercise or self-examination, that can promote future resilience and virtue. This requires a wise balancing of dwelling and seeking, relaxing and stretching.

Health and Well-Being

There is a fascinating historical background to the growing contemporary interest in positive health, well-being, and spirituality. Classic or premodern worldviews tended to integrate ethics and health around the concept of virtue.[13] A key shift of modernity was to deny a moral order to which human nature should conform. This served to radically divide the relationship between wholeness and holiness in the modern worldview, thereby separating ethics and spirituality from psychological and physical health. Neal Weiner describes the historical innovation whereby the modern "healthy" person "can be a bad one."[14] Modern scientists could investigate health, and philosophers and theologians could explore morality and ethics. The quest to somehow integrate health, happiness, and virtue has led to recent efforts to overcome this modern dualism. But tracing the development of modern notions of health as happiness and adjustment provides helpful context for transforming models of spirituality in psychology.

Health as Happiness

Contemporary psychologists and therapists have inherited from ancient philosophers questions about the nature of happiness and methods for achieving the good life. Historian of psychology Thomas Leahey describes differing views of happiness and well-being in ancient Greek culture that provide an interesting parallel to our contemporary context.[15] Aristotle's conception of happiness or well-being was *eudaimonia*, which implied the virtuous realization of one's true potential.[16] In contrast to the private pleasure of the individual, *eudaimonia* was oriented toward the telos of the good of society or the *polis*. Plato's system was different from Aristotle's, but both agreed that health and happiness should be connected to moral virtue in the public sphere.

13. N. O. Weiner, *The Harmony of the Soul: Mental Health and Moral Virtue Reconsidered* (Albany: State University of New York Press, 1993).
14. Ibid., 12.
15. T. H. Leahey, *A History of Psychology: Main Currents in Psychological Thought*, 5th ed. (Englewood Cliffs, NJ: Prentice Hall, 1999).
16. Cf. Alasdair MacIntyre, *After Virtue*, 2nd ed. (Notre Dame, IN: University of Notre Dame Press, 1984); Ryff and Singer, "Contours."

The Hellenistic and Roman periods, which followed the classical Greek age, were marked by rapid social and political turmoil. Philosophers were no longer consulted with grand metaphysical questions, and they turned to more modest goals. In a time of cultural instability, people wanted practical advice that would relieve anxiety and the pain of life. Hellenistic and Roman philosophers were given government support to develop schools of thought on achieving happiness, such as Epicureanism, Skepticism, Stoicism, and Cynicism. These philosophers became doctors of the soul, or what we would now call therapists. The Hellenistic and Roman concepts of health and happiness also shifted from virtuous *eudaimonia* to the more utilitarian and hedonistic notion of *ataraxia*. *Ataraxia* implied peace of mind or freedom from disturbance, and the connections to moral virtue and communal concern were divorced from popular construals of health and happiness.[17]

Some of the major modern Western psychotherapies have construed happiness and well-being in an individualistic and utilitarian manner that is reminiscent of morally neutral *ataraxia*. For example, Albert Ellis drew on Stoicism and Epicureanism in developing his rational emotive therapy. Carl Rogers's theory of personality and therapy was likely influenced by Skeptic philosophy. Both Ellis and Rogers transformed these ancient philosophies into more individualistic schools of thought. Modern psychotherapies have proven effective in treating many forms of individual suffering but have not been tested for an equal capacity for promoting human flourishing or communal well-being.[18]

Modern mental-health care, at least outpatient psychotherapy, could be viewed as arising from some analogous sociological influences as occurred in the Hellenistic and Roman periods. Modern industrial and technological revolutions have contributed to increasingly individualistic cultures in the West and have tended to fragment social support and a sense of community. As Phillip Cushman has argued, this has likely contributed to the widespread sense of emptiness that the psychotherapy and advertising industries have promised to fill.[19] Technological advances have increased the cultural tempo and mobility of society, further escalating levels of stress and dislocation for many. Over the past two decades, managed mental-health care providers have often promoted and even required brief models of therapy that focus on the pragmatic goals of symptom alleviation rather than growth or character development. This was part of a modern trend toward viewing health as adjustment.

17. Leahey, *History of Psychology*.

18. D. S. Browning and T. Cooper, *Religious Thought and the Modern Psychologies*, 2nd ed. (Minneapolis: Fortress, 2004); Seligman, *Authentic Happiness*.

19. P. Cushman, *Constructing the Self, Constructing America: A Cultural History of Psychotherapy* (Reading, MA: Addison-Wesley, 1995).

Health as Adjustment

After World War II, a primary mission of psychology in the United States was to foster adjustment or the homeostasis of society.[20] Psychological health came to be viewed as the ability to cope or adjust to the demands of society. The older religious character or virtue ethic was replaced by a personality ethic. In most virtue paradigms, soul health entails orienting the relationship of one's character to a transcendent moral and spiritual order. In the adjustment paradigm, health entails the functional ability to adjust one's personality to environmental demands. The standard health curriculum of the modern psychology of adjustment has tended to focus on language such as coping, self-esteem, stress management, boundaries, and communication. These are legitimate and helpful concepts and terms, ones I use frequently myself. But the functional language of health as adjustment has lacked conceptual and linguistic traction toward the goals of optimal health, meaningful spirituality, and communal virtue.

Hedonic versus Eudaemonic Health and Well-Being

The history and complexity of these various definitions and theoretical positions on health and well-being can be served by a heuristic model that summarizes two of the primary streams of thought. Psychologist Robert Lent has reviewed contemporary empirical research on well-being in relationship to the hedonic and eudaemonic philosophical traditions, thereby providing such a heuristic model.[21] I have adapted in several ways a summary table from Lent's article to relate the implications of these philosophies of well-being for corresponding views of health and spirituality (see table 4).

Table 4. Philosophical Views of Well-Being, Health, and Spirituality

Philosophical Views of Well-Being	Primary Goal of Health	Contemporary Research Construct	Primary Goal of Spirituality
Hedonic	Adjustment	Subjective Well-Being	Spiritual Well-Being
Eudaemonic	Virtue	Psychological Well-Being	Spiritual Maturity

According to Lent, both ancient and contemporary hedonic views of well-being emphasize happiness as life satisfaction, feeling good, and

20. Leahey, *History of Psychology*.

21. R. W. Lent, "Toward a Unifying Theoretical and Practical Perspective on Well-Being and Psychosocial Adjustment," *Journal of Counseling Psychology* 51, no. 4 (2004): 482–509. Also see R. M. Ryan and E. L. Deci, "On Happiness and Human Potentials: A Review of Research on Hedonic and Eudaemonic Well-Being," *Annual Review of Psychology* 52 (2001): 141–66.

not feeling bad. The hedonic view resonates with the ancient Greek philosophy that defined happiness as *ataraxia* and also with contemporary research on subjective well-being or feeling good.[22] In contrast, the eudaemonic view of well-being emphasizes growth, purpose, meaning, and actualizing one's potential. The ancient meaning of *eudaimonia*, or happiness, as the pursuit of virtue roughly parallels contemporary research on psychological well-being, strengths, and virtue. For example, Carol Ryff's theory of psychological well-being includes the maturity dimensions of self-acceptance, positive relationships, purpose in life, and personal growth among others. In Ryff's view, happiness and subjective well-being should be "the by-product of a life that is well-lived."[23] Ryff's view is more consistent with the eudaemonic quest to grow in maturity, virtue, and life purpose rather than with simply trying to feel better. Happiness and well-being become by-products of personal growth, often following stressful periods of self-imposed challenge as depicted in the crucible model described in chapter 1.

These contrasting views of subjective well-being versus psychological well-being, feeling good versus pursuing growth, also parallel debates in the field of psychotherapy. Theorists favoring cognitive-behavioral, solution-focused, and other brief, pragmatic models of therapy often emphasize symptom alleviation and helping clients feel better rapidly. In the field of couples therapy, John Gottman's approach focuses on practical skills that couples can utilize to rapidly change the emotional set point and health status of their relationship. These pragmatic models target hedonic, subjective well-being. Theorists promoting psychoanalytic, humanistic, and existential and other depth models of therapy often construe suffering as a potential pathway to the characterological development and personal growth necessary for sustaining health. Whereas Gottman openly disparages an emphasis on personal maturity, David Schnarch's crucible model of couples therapy discourages a skills focus and promotes a courageous quest toward maturity and realizing one's potential.[24] Growth models such as that of Schnarch target eudaemonic psychological maturity through crucibles of transformation. Psychological researchers are beginning to empirically map the differing dimensions of well-being and maturity.

22. E. Diener, S. Oishi, and R. E. Lucas, "Personality, Culture, and Subjective Well-Being: Emotional and Cognitive Evaluations of Life," *Annual Review of Psychology* 54 (2003): 403–25.

23. Ryff and Singer, "Contours," 5.

24. See J. M. Gottman, *The Marriage Clinic: A Scientifically Based Marital Therapy* (New York: W. W. Norton, 1999), 184–85; Schnarch, *Passionate Marriage*.

Well-Being and Maturity

Psychological well-being and maturity are different goals and only modestly correlated. Jack Bauer and Dan McAdams have argued that psychological models of personality development can be heuristically organized into two main categories: (a) those focused on the development of social-emotional well-being and (b) those focused on the development of social-cognitive maturity or complexity.[25] Secure attachment is a good example of a developmental predictor of social and emotional well-being, but it does not require developmental maturity or complexity of awareness. Intrinsic commitments to internalized values, such as that represented by intrinsic religiosity, also tend to be positively correlated with health and well-being indices. In contrast, ego development and the capacity for differentiation of self represent maturity constructs that emerge out of challenging growth periods that could be related to the themes of questing and seeking. In this way, maturity constructs are not always as highly correlated with well-being as some other intrinsic constructs because of the stressful processes maturity requires. Social-desirability influences on self-reported levels of well-being also tend to decline as people mature cognitively and emotionally. Healthy relational "dwelling" predicts high socioemotional well-being or happiness, sometimes at the risk of less mature authenticity and self-awareness. Maturity requires seeking, exploring, and tolerating transitions that lead to transformations. The relational dialectic of attachment and differentiation is central to the processes of human development that involve balancing well-being and growth toward maturity.

Can people be both happy *and* mature? Psychologist Laura King has framed this empirical question in relation to the ancient search for "the good life."[26] There has been very little empirical exploration of this provocative question to date. The limited available data suggest that people who report transformations that correlate with both well-being and maturity are exploring deeper or more complex understandings of relationships.[27] This again affirms the potential value of thematizing relationality.

25. J. J. Bauer and D. P. McAdams, "Growth Goals, Maturity, and Well-Being," *Developmental Psychology* 40 (2004): 114–27.
26. L. A. King, "The Hard Road to the Good Life: The Happy, Mature Person," *Journal of Humanistic Psychology* 41 (2001): 51–72.
27. Ibid.; J. J. Bauer, D. P. McAdams, and A. R. Sakaeda, "Interpreting the Good Life: Growth Memories in the Lives of Mature, Happy People," *Journal of Personality and Social Psychology* 88 (2005): 203–17.

An analogous set of questions can be asked about relationships between spiritual well-being and spiritual maturity. Most of the empirical research on spirituality has investigated spiritual well-being rather than spiritual maturity. But there are spiritual writers in most traditions who have described the difficult process leading to spiritual maturity. This liminal quest toward spiritual maturity can include ambiguous "dark nights of the soul" and stressful times of desert or wilderness. The hedonic view of subjective well-being corresponds with a primary spiritual goal of spiritual well-being, or feeling satisfied about one's spiritual life. The eudaemonic view of psychological well-being corresponds with a primary spiritual goal of spiritual maturity, although defining the contours of maturity is a highly value-laden or tradition-laden task. For example, the Aristotelian eudaemonic tradition generates views of well-being and virtue that are less individualistic than the hedonic traditions, but LeRon and I both read eudaemonic views as more individualistic than our ideal for Christian spirituality. Actualizing my personal potential can require stretching toward health and maturity, but it may not involve concern for the growth and well-being of my neighbors and the wider global community. Eudaemonic views could promote setting up "growth enclaves" where individuals try to actualize their potential well-being while excluding those who are different. A communitarian Christian ethic calls for wider systemic awareness of how the dynamics of personal, relational, and communal well-being interact in promoting or inhibiting social justice. As Gustavo Gutiérrez points out, Christian spirituality "is a community enterprise" that should also foster participating in justice-building relationships with those who are *other* to us.[28] It is encouraging that some therapists and social scientists are developing communitarian approaches to mental health that work toward personal, relational, and community well-being.[29]

Spiritual maturity can be consistent with high spiritual well-being, but some phases of the process toward maturity can also include reduced levels of well-being. Chapter 8 will explore the challenges of spiritual darkness, and chapter 9 will consider the dynamics of spiritual maturity. The remainder of this chapter will focus on spiritual well-being and health. This will set the stage for questions regarding the pathways toward spiritual maturity and the accompanying perils of spiritual darkness.

28. Gustavo Gutiérrez, *We Drink from Our Own Wells: The Spiritual Journey of a People*, 20th anniversary ed. (Maryknoll, NY: Orbis, 2003), 137.
29. E.g., W. J. Doherty, *Soul Searching: Why Psychotherapy Must Promote Moral Responsibility* (New York: Basic Books, 1995).

Spiritual Well-Being

What is spiritual well-being? Can it really be measured and studied? New approaches to research on spirituality, health, and well-being are rapidly emerging. To date, however, the Spiritual Well-Being Scale (SWBS), developed by psychologists Craig Ellison and Raymond Paloutzian, is one of the only measures of spiritual well-being used in multiple studies.[30] Ellison defines spiritual well-being within a Christian worldview as constituted by wholeness and transcendence arising from "a positive relationship with God that grounds a person in the knowledge and experience of his love."[31] The SWBS was developed for research with Christian samples and consists of twenty items—ten that assess religious well-being (satisfaction with one's relationship with God) and ten that assess existential well-being (life purpose and satisfaction). Items are to be endorsed along a six-point scale ranging from "strongly disagree" to "strongly agree."[32] For example, one of the SWBS religious well-being items offers this statement:

I believe that God loves me and cares about me.

One of the SWBS existential well-being items reads,

I believe there is some real purpose for my life.

Ellison suggests that spiritual well-being "is the result of the entire human system functioning in a balanced and harmonious way" although "it is especially interactive with transcendence."[33] He views health as formed through wholeness and transformed through the spiritual pursuit of transcendence. His emphasis on purpose, meaning, healthy relationships, and transcendence resonate with eudaemonic views of well-being.

Well-Being and Shalom

Theologically, Ellison grounds his view of well-being in the Hebrew concept of *shalom*, which is often translated "peace." In a broader sense, *shalom* connotes the "state of fulfillment that results from God's presence

30. R. F. Paloutzian and C. W. Ellison, "Loneliness, Spiritual Well-Being, and Quality of Life," in *Loneliness: A Sourcebook of Current Theory*, ed. L. A. Peplau and D. Perlman (New York: Wiley, 1982), 224–37.

31. C. W. Ellison, *From Stress to Well-Being* (Eugene, OR: Wipf & Stock, 1994), 173.

32. For psychometric limitations of the SWBS see W. Slater, T. W. Hall, and K. J. Edwards, "Measuring Religion and Spirituality: Where Are We and Where Are We Going?" *Journal of Psychology and Theology* 29 (2001): 4–21.

33. Ellison, *From Stress to Well-Being*, 176.

and covenantal relationship."[34] The Hebrew conception of personhood was unified or holistic, with the body, soul, and spirit as highly interactive rather than discrete dimensions. *Shalom* implies a sense of relational harmony, completeness, and wholeness of the integrated human system. Whereas Ellison focuses on individuals as human systems, the Hebrew concept of *shalom* was also strongly relational and communal. In Old Testament literature, spiritual well-being arising from *shalom* is highly relational or systemic in nature. *Shalom* is shaped by relational harmony and wholeness within and between persons as well as between persons and their environments. Ellison also argues that the pursuit of meaning and purpose is central to long-term well-being and the highest levels of *shalom*.

Studies using the SWBS have found positive correlations between spiritual well-being and various indices of physical and mental health. Individuals with higher levels of spiritual well-being have been found to possess lower levels of pain, depression, anxiety, loneliness, aggressiveness, dependence, and hopelessness about health problems. Spiritual well-being has also been positively correlated with self-esteem, internal locus of control, hope, and characteristics of self-actualization. These correlational studies cannot demonstrate causation, and so we cannot determine the causal direction of these relationships between spiritual well-being and health. It could be that health problems tend to reduce spiritual well-being in some people. But these results do support the construct validity of the SWBS with Christian populations.

Balancing Wholeness and Teleology

Quaker sociologist Parker Palmer is one of the many spiritual-formation writers who have also suggested that spiritual well-being is shaped by the quest for wholeness and integrity of personhood.[35] In Palmer's view, symptoms of restlessness, distress, or reduced well-being can reveal the need to search spiritually for a hidden wholeness and integration. In a similar fashion, Ellison describes the quest for spiritual maturity as requiring the motivation to tolerate the stress and suffering that are often part of a growth process. The New Testament word for maturity, *teleios*, is often translated "perfect" but in fact connotes undivided wholeness of the person or integrity rather than anxiety-driven perfectionism. These eudaemonic views of Ellison and Palmer suggest that long-term spiritual well-being typically involves both a systemic balancing and a teleological pursuit of spiritual maturity.

34. Ibid., 11.
35. Parker J. Palmer, *A Hidden Wholeness: The Journey toward an Undivided Life* (New York: Jossey-Bass, 2004).

Psychopathology can be defined in a manner that is theoretically consistent with this dual orientation toward relational balancing and growth. For example, James Maddock and Noel Larson define psychopathology as occurring when "the intrapsychic ecology is structured in a maladaptive way that does not fit well with the structure of the environment, resulting in distortions of meaning and behavior."[36] In their view, psychopathology represents a lack of personal wholeness in balanced fit within a relational ecology, resulting in distortions of meaning that impede healthy growth and development. Impediments to growth and maturity can, in turn, exacerbate individuals' lack of balanced fit within their relational ecologies. As an example, individuals with severe mental illness sometimes struggle with certain symptoms, such as hearing persecutory voices, that can make it challenging for them to form healthy relationships within spiritual communities. The more isolated they become, the more difficult it can be to pursue the meaningful growth that leads to and sustains well-being.

Relational or systemic theories can also focus our attention on the ecological dynamics that can positively and negatively influence spiritual well-being. Chapter 6 suggested that human development unfolds within relational contexts or cultures of embeddedness. Throughout the life span, this necessitates the balancing of attachment and differentiation, or relational connection and personal freedom.

Scientific Research on Religion, Spirituality, and Health

What can scientific research tell us about the empirical relationships between religion, spirituality, and health? A large body of research has explored the relationships between various measures of religion and spirituality in connection to physical, mental, and relational health. In summary, religion and spirituality show largely positive associations with health with a smaller number of negative effects. The vast majority of studies in this area are correlational, and the methodological rigor of some studies is quite limited. Again, this makes causation impossible to determine, and some authors have largely dismissed this body of work as irrelevant.[37] Others have been too quick to herald the scientific justification of spiritual and religious practice. I concur with the voices in the scientific community that view this body of research as suggestive of the largely salutary effects of spirituality and religion on health but with

36. J. W. Maddock and N. R. Larson, *Incestuous Families: An Ecological Approach to Understanding and Treatment* (New York: W. W. Norton, 1995), 81.

37. R. Sloan and E. Bagiella, "Claims about Religious Involvement and Health Outcomes," *Annals of Behavioral Medicine* 24 (2002): 14–21.

an ongoing need for methodological rigor and evaluation of potential negative effects.[38] The following section will briefly summarize some of the major empirical findings on religion and spirituality in relation to physical health and mental health. This brief overview will focus on areas where significant effects for spiritual and religious variables have been found, but it is important to note that many studies have failed to find significant effects for some indices of spirituality and religion. This is the case most frequently when simple categorical or demographic-type measures are used (e.g., religious denomination).

Physical Health

Two helpful review articles on spirituality, religion, and physical health were produced by members of the National Institute of Health Working Group on Research on Spirituality, Religion, and Health and published in *American Psychologist*.[39] These researchers evaluated the levels of supporting scientific evidence for various propositions on the basis of the quantity and quality of available studies. Studies in this area have tended to investigate the effects of religious practices or meditation and relaxation practices on health indices. Religious practices include church or religious-service attendance, religious commitment, and being the target of intercessory prayer. (Obviously, these are also spiritual practices for many people.) Meditation or relaxation practices in these studies include evaluations of Zen, yoga, mindfulness, and transcendental-meditation practices. Some studies of these meditation/relaxation practices did not include explicit religious or spiritual content in the intervention. A summary of some of their evaluations is offered in table 5, which does not include health areas where there was little or insufficient support.

Table 5. Levels of Scientific Evidence Supporting the Effects of Religious and Spiritual Practices on Dimensions of Biological and Health Functioning

Biological or Health Dimension	Religious Practices	Meditative Practices
Protects against Mortality	Persuasive	NA
Lower Blood Pressure	Reasonable	Reasonable
Better Immune Functioning	Reasonable	NA
Lower Cholesterol	NA	Reasonable

38. W. R. Miller and C. E. Thoresen, "Spirituality, Religion, and Health: An Emerging Research Field," *American Psychologist* 58 (2003): 24–35.

39. L. H. Powell, L. Shahabi, and C. E. Thoresen, "Religion and Spirituality: Linkages to Physical Health," *American Psychologist* 58 (2003): 36–52; T. E. Seeman, L. F. Dubin, and M. Seeman, "Religiosity/Spirituality and Health: A Critical Review of the Evidence for Biological Pathways," *American Psychologist* 58 (2003): 53–63.

Biological or Health Dimension	Religious Practices	Meditative Practices
Lower Stress Hormone Levels	NA	Reasonable
Better Health Outcomes for Patients	Some	Persuasive
Differential Brain Activity	NA	Reasonable

Adapted from Powell, Shahabi, and Thoresen, "Religion and Spirituality"; Seeman, Dubin, and Seeman, "Religiosity/Spirituality and Health." Ratings of the strength of scientific evidence in these reviews ranged from "persuasive" (highest) to "reasonable" (intermediate) to "some" (lowest) support in these areas where empirical studies were available. "NA" means that studies were not available for review.

In general, available studies have explored the relationships of various measures of religion and spirituality with mortality (death) and morbidity (illness).[40] The strongest level of evidence ("persuasive") exists for church or religious-service attendance protecting against death or mortality.[41] Those who regularly attend religious services tend to live longer than those who do not. In some studies, this effect has been particularly strong for women[42] and African Americans.[43] An intermediate level of evidence ("reasonable") exists for the effect of some religious practices on lower blood pressure and better immune functioning. Some evidence exists for the effect of intercessory prayer on health outcomes for clinical patients in three studies. This research is suggestive that spiritualities of dwelling that encourage relational and communal connections might be conducive to long-term health and survival.

The reviewers also suggest strong evidence for the effect of meditation/relaxation practices on various health outcomes for clinical patients in five studies. Research on the effect of meditation/relaxation practices on lower blood pressure, lower stress hormone levels, and lower cholesterol was rated at an intermediate level of evidence. Several studies have also demonstrated differential brain activity during meditation, indicating lower levels of physiological activation.[44] Meditation and relaxation practices may enhance health by increasing capacities for spiritual self-soothing.

40. R. J. Taylor, L. M. Chatters, and J. Levin, *Religion in the Lives of African Americans: Social, Psychological, and Health Perspectives* (Thousand Oaks, CA: Sage, 2004).

41. Also see M. E. McCullough, W. T. Hoyt, D. B. Larson, H. G. Koenig, and C. E. Thoresen, "Religious Involvement and Mortality: A Meta-analytic Review," *Health Psychology* 19 (2000): 211–22.

42. See Powell, Shahabi, and Thoresen, "Religion and Spirituality."

43. Taylor, Chatters, and Levin, *Religion in the Lives of African Americans*.

44. See Newberg, d'Aquili, and Rause, *Why God Won't Go Away*, 38–40.

Mental Health

Reviews of empirical research on religion and spirituality in relation to mental health have generally found positive correlations, although results have varied depending upon the measures used. For example, Timothy Smith and his colleagues conducted a meta-analysis of 147 different studies examining religiosity and depression.[45] Across the studies, they found a modest inverse relationship between religiosity and depressive symptoms; that is, greater religiosity was associated with fewer depressive symptoms. This effect tended to be stronger when the measure was of intrinsic religiosity (i.e., internalized religious commitment) or when the study included people coping with a recent life stressor (e.g., loss of a loved one).[46] These effects held up across age, gender, and three ethnic groups (African Americans, Euro-Americans, Northern Europeans). In contrast, negative religious coping (e.g., feeling punished by God) and an extrinsic religiosity (i.e., religion as a means to other ends) tended to be associated with higher levels of depression. The ways in which a person relates to the sacred seem to make a significant difference in associations with indices of mental health.

A similar pattern is seen in a smaller body of research on religiosity and anxiety.[47] Intrinsic religiosity tends to be negatively correlated with anxiety, particularly death anxiety. However, one study comparing Protestant and Catholic Christians found religious tradition to moderate this effect, with the intrinsic religiosity of Catholics associated with higher levels of anxiety and depression than was extrinsic religiosity.[48]

Several studies have also explored the relationships between religion, spirituality, and substance abuse. Intrinsic religiosity has been associated with lower use and abuse of substances.[49] This effect is particularly strong for adolescents with involvement in prosocial spiritual and religious communities serving as a protective factor with respect to tobacco and alcohol use. Some studies have found religious and spiritual involvement to positively predict recovery from substance abuse,

45. T. B. Smith, M. E. McCullough, and J. B. Poll, "Religiousness and Depression: Evidence for a Main Effect and the Moderating Influence of Stressful Life Events," *Psychological Bulletin* 129 (2003): 614–36.

46. Also see the review by T. G. Plante and N. K. Sharma, "Religious Faith and Mental Health Outcomes," in *Faith and Health: Psychological Perspectives*, ed. T. G. Plante and A. C. Sherman (New York: Guilford, 2001), 240–61.

47. Ibid.

48. Andrew P. Tix and Patricia A. Frazier, "Mediation and Moderation of the Relationship between Intrinsic Religiousness and Mental Health," *Personality and Social Psychology Bulletin* 31, no. 3 (2005): 295–306.

49. Plante and Sharma, "Religious Faith and Mental Health Outcomes."

and researchers have also found that levels of spirituality can increase for participants in secular recovery programs.

Studies of religion or spirituality and well-being have also generally found positive associations in samples of Euro-Americans and African Americans, particularly when measures target intrinsic or subjective religiosity.[50] In a longitudinal study of adults, Paul Wink and Michelle Dillon found that the personal importance of religiosity at midlife predicts well-being, community involvement, generativity, and relationship satisfaction decades later.[51] The effects of religiosity on later well-being tended to be stronger for people who experienced physical health problems, suggesting again that religion and spirituality may often prove to be particularly salutary when suffering intensifies.

At this point it is hard to determine the mechanisms that might mediate the effects of religion and spirituality on health and well-being, although numerous possibilities have been proposed.[52] For example, religious and spiritual communities often encourage certain health practices related to substance use, diet, and sexuality. Embeddedness within such communities might reduce the risk of adopting certain potential health-compromising behaviors. Spiritual and religious communities can also provide sources of social support. Social networks can contribute to the social-support and social-integration factors that have been related to better immune functioning.[53] Conversely, relational conflicts in religious communities can be associated with lower well-being.[54] Spiritual and religious practices might also facilitate certain cognitive and emotional states that are conducive to health and well-being (e.g., hope and self-esteem). Hope is one virtue that has been strongly correlated with well-being in empirical studies.[55] To turn this around, relationships between spiritual or religious factors and health that prove to be merely correlational (rather than causal) could also reflect the influence of certain personality traits (e.g., optimism) on attraction to spirituality and religion. Individuals with certain personality traits in certain social contexts might find it easier to participate

50. Taylor, Chatters, and Levin, *Religion in the Lives of African Americans*; Plante and Sharma, "Religious Faith and Mental Health Outcomes."

51. P. Wink and M. Dillon, "Religious Involvement and Health Outcomes in Late Adulthood: Findings from a Longitudinal Study of Women and Men," in *Faith and Health: Psychological Perspectives*, ed. T. G. Plante and A. C. Sherman (New York: Guilford, 2001), 75–106.

52. Taylor, Chatters, and Levin, *Religion in the Lives of African Americans*.

53. S. Cohen, "Social Relationships and Health," *American Psychologist* 59 (2004): 676–84.

54. Taylor, Chatters, and Levin, *Religion in the Lives of African Americans*.

55. N. Park, C. Peterson, and M. E. P. Seligman, "Strengths of Character and Well-Being," *Journal of Social and Clinical Psychology* 23 (2004): 603–19.

in the spiritual and religious communities and practices that carry the most robust health linkages. In this respect, it is worth considering that many of the biblical prophets of the Jewish and Christian traditions would probably not have scored high in health and well-being. Those who are marginalized from social networks for various reasons might find it much harder to access spiritual and religious resources that are conducive to health and well-being.

Wisdom and Health

Throughout history spiritual and religious traditions have offered teachings and practices intended to promote human health. Contemporary scientific research suggests that certain measures of spirituality and religiosity can be positively associated with health and well-being. Yet some studies also demonstrate the obvious point that spirituality and religion are not always associated with better health or well-being and by some measures can even be correlated with pathology. This means that the salutary integration of spirituality, religion, and health requires the virtue of wisdom.

Defining Wisdom

Wisdom is best understood as much more than abstract knowledge. The Hebrew word for "wisdom" (khokmah) implies a personal life dynamic that serves to integrate wholeness and holiness.[56] In biblical wisdom literature, wisdom provides discernment necessary for understanding the design of creation. According to Protestant theologian Cornelius Plantinga Jr., "the wise person knows creation . . . knows its boundaries and limits, understands its laws and rhythms, discerns its times and seasons, respects its great dynamics."[57] In the Jewish and Christian traditions, wisdom is rooted in a spiritual commitment to knowing God and walking in ways of integrity. The book of Proverbs teaches that wisdom generally leads to health and well-being whereas duplicity and foolishness typically result in distress.

Contemporary psychologists have developed scientific theories of wisdom. For example, Robert Sternberg's balance theory defines wisdom as tacit knowledge that serves to balance self-interests, the interests of others, and other interests in the various contexts in which one

56. C. H. Bullock, An Introduction to Old Testament Poetic Books (Chicago: Moody, 1988).

57. C. Plantinga Jr., Not the Way It's Supposed to Be: A Breviary of Sin (Grand Rapids: Eerdmans, 1995), 115.

lives toward the goal of a common good.[58] Sternberg's emphasis on the relational and contextual balancing function of wisdom resonates with both eudaemonic and biblical views by integrating personal and communal well-being.

Paul Baltes and Ursula Staudinger have generated the largest body of empirical research on wisdom. They define wisdom as "an expert knowledge system concerning the fundamental pragmatics of life."[59] By "fundamental pragmatics of life," they mean "knowledge and judgment about the essence of the human condition and the ways and means of planning, managing, and understanding a good life."[60] Baltes and Staudinger delineate multiple dimensions of wisdom, including (a) rich factual knowledge about life, (b) rich procedural knowledge about life, (c) contextual awareness of the human life span, (d) appreciation for human diversity, and (e) recognition and tolerance of ambiguity. Their developmental model focuses on the teleological or maturity functions of wisdom in orchestrating the integration of mind and virtue.

Deidre Kramer has described wisdom from an object relations perspective, as involving a mature integration of the conflicting parts of personal experience.[61] In her view, wisdom facilitates accurate representations of self and other, emotional intelligence, and healthy forms of interpersonal relating. Wisdom develops through a willingness to grapple with existential dilemmas and an openness to learning from challenging experiences.

Wisdom, Well-Being, and Spirituality

Biblical and psychological understandings concur in suggesting that wisdom is a developmental construct that should promote well-being, maturity, and the good life. Empirical evidence is emerging that wisdom is associated with well-being and spirituality. In a study of twenty-four virtues in a sample of more than five thousand adults, wisdom was positively correlated with subjective well-being.[62] The only virtues more

58. R. J. Sternberg, "A Balance Theory of Wisdom," *Review of General Psychology* 2 (1998): 347–65.

59. P. B. Baltes and U. M. Staudinger, "Wisdom: A Metaheuristic (Pragmatic) to Orchestrate Mind and Virtue toward Excellence," *American Psychologist* 55 (2000): 122–36, quote from p. 122.

60. Ibid., 124.

61. D. A. Kramer, "Conceptualizing Wisdom: The Primacy of Affect-Cognition Relations," in *Wisdom: Its Nature, Origin, and Development*, ed. R. J. Sternberg (Cambridge, CT: Cambridge University Press, 1990), 279–313; "Wisdom as a Classical Source of Human Strength: Conceptualization and Empirical Inquiry," *Journal of Social and Clinical Psychology* 19 (2000): 83–101.

62. Park et al., "Strengths of Character and Well-Being."

strongly associated with well-being were hope, zest, gratitude, curiosity, and love. Separate measures of wisdom and spirituality showed similar correlations with well-being.

In a longitudinal study of adults, Dillon and Wink investigated wisdom and well-being in relation to Wuthnow's contrast of spiritual seeking and religious dwelling. Their measure of wisdom was weighted toward introspective insight. They found that spiritual seeking in late middle adulthood (fifties to early sixties) predicts levels of both wisdom and well-being from personal growth in late adulthood (late sixties to late seventies). Curiously, they also found that religious dwelling in early adulthood (thirties) but not in late middle adulthood predicted wisdom in late adulthood. These data are suggestive that a sense of religious community in early adulthood might contribute to wisdom and relational well-being decades later but also that the midlife development of internalized spirituality can predict later wisdom. This suggests that a developmental journey that balances spiritualities of dwelling and seeking might optimize the achievement of wisdom and well-being.

Practical and Reflective Wisdom

The human development of wisdom is multidimensional. Biblical wisdom literature reflects this multidimensionality of wisdom and can be organized around two major schools of wisdom—practical wisdom and reflective wisdom.[63] Philosopher John Coe draws an insightful parallel between the discipline of psychology and the genre of wisdom literature of the Hebrew sages (e.g., Proverbs, Job, and Ecclesiastes), and he highlights some issues related to the practical and reflective schools of wisdom.[64] According to Coe, the Hebrew sage was like an ancient psychologist, searching to understand the natural laws of human behavior or "creation-wisdom." The book of Proverbs, for example, affirms a spiritual ordering structure that governs human nature. Proverbs teaches that the wise person should live in harmony with this spiritual and moral order to find happiness. The "practical wisdom" of Proverbs (also called "prudential wisdom") generally promotes effective skill in living and is optimistic about the outcome of such a life.[65] Practical-wisdom literature

63. Steven J. Sandage, "Power, Knowledge, and the Hermeneutics of Selfhood: Postmodern Wisdom for Christian Therapists," *Mars Hill Review* 12 (1999): 65–73; "The Ego-Humility Model of Forgiveness: Implications for Couple and Family Dynamics and Therapy," *Marriage and the Family: A Christian Journal* 2 (1999): 277–92.

64. J. H. Coe, "What Solomon Learned from Psychology: An Integrative Look at Ecclesiastes," paper presented at the annual meeting of the Christian Association of Psychological Studies, San Antonio, TX, April 1994.

65. B. W. Farley, *In Praise of Virtue: An Exploration of the Biblical Virtues in a Christian Context* (Grand Rapids: Eerdmans, 1995), 87–91.

promotes virtues such as diligence, civility, honesty, optimism, and self-control, which are proposed as contributors to a life of well-being.

Much of modern psychology has likewise been concerned with practical wisdom and skill in living. For example, cognitive-behavioral and other schools of psychology use the language of effective behavior, personal adjustment, healthy coping, and stress management to promote strategies of practical wisdom, mainly through facilitating human autonomy and self-control. The book of Proverbs does differ from most of contemporary psychology in saying that "the fear of the LORD is the beginning of wisdom" (Prov. 9:10a NIV). But the shared feature of practical wisdom, whether biblical or contemporary psychology, is the optimistic search for healthy life practices that, if implemented, generally lead to well-being and even flourishing.

The reflective-wisdom tradition focuses on the themes of mystery, tragic suffering, and the unpredictability of life.[66] Whereas practical-wisdom literature tends to focus optimistically on the prospects of making wise, healthy choices, reflective-wisdom literature (e.g., Job and Ecclesiastes) promotes an authentic look at life when even the righteous suffer. Job loses everything despite his righteousness, with no explanation from God, while his friends tell him to repent. Ecclesiastes provides a constraint on a purely naturalized psychology and probes the meaning of life given the reality that all good things come to an end. Many contemporary postmodernists echo the Hebrew sage in crying, "Meaningless! Meaningless! . . . Everything is meaningless!" (Eccles. 1:2 NIV). The simple confidence in an ordered universe that is apparent in Proverbs is lost in the painful questions of ultimate meaning that are raised in Job and Ecclesiastes. In a parallel fashion, the buoyant optimism of contemporary positive-psychology researchers is questioned by some postmodernists, who argue that authenticity about the dark side of life can be a meaningful pathway to deeper wisdom and wholeness.[67] Chapter 8 will explore some of these dark spiritual pathways and the *via negativa* in greater depth.

I have found it helpful to work toward integrating practical and reflective wisdom in both clinical practice and in my own spiritual formation. Practical wisdom encourages hopefulness about my chances of experiencing well-being when I make wise choices, practice good emotional boundaries, and commit to disciplines of self-control. At a spiritual level, practical wisdom arises from a positive trust that God wants to help me find good things in life. But at another level, I also know that there are

66. Ibid.; cf. C. R. Wells, "Hebrew Wisdom as a Quest for Wholeness and Holiness," *Journal of Psychology and Christianity* 15 (1996): 58–69.

67. B. S. Held, "The Negative Side of Positive Psychology," *Journal of Humanistic Psychology* 44 (2004): 9–46.

no guarantees that healthy choices or good boundaries will necessarily protect me from the pain and tragedy of life. Good choices do not always pay off, and loss finds its way to everyone's doorstep. Church attendance will not cure death. I need to also cultivate the reflective wisdom to find enough meaning in the midst of this suffering world that the anxiety of risk does not paralyze me or make my life choices too safe and inauthentic. Practical wisdom can facilitate the balance necessary for well-being, and reflective wisdom becomes crucial for courage during painful and purgative growth cycles.

Several integrative theorists in the field of psychology have recognized the dialectical value of both practical and reflective wisdom. Marsha Linehan's dialectical behavior therapy is aimed at helping clients achieve "wise mind" by integrating logical and emotional states of mind.[68] Wise mind is deeply intuitive and integrates all ways of knowing, which is tremendously challenging when people are accustomed to defenses that split states of mind.

There is also a developmental progression to biblical wisdom literature that makes sense psychologically. Proverbs was probably initially written as the moral and spiritual curriculum for young Hebrew boys. Children and those at earlier phases of faith development can benefit most from the hopeful optimism of practical wisdom, which emphasizes wise choices and the cultivation of virtue. Job and Ecclesiastes are probably best viewed as advanced wisdom reading, which becomes developmentally appropriate for adolescents and adults who have experienced or started to suspect unpredictability and tragedy in life. Jesus was precociously wise, and some young people become capable of complex wisdom at an early age. But deeper levels of reflective wisdom most commonly become a task during adult development, when the quest for more complete wholeness often intensifies.

The spiritual integration of practical and reflective wisdom is also fostered by narrative. Building upon hermeneutical theorists, Don Browning argues that wisdom "always has a narrative envelope."[69] Wisdom rests upon worldview images that are grounded in faith assumptions. Browning suggests that narratives and metaphors are vehicles for conveying the assumptions of wisdom. This is the reason that most spiritual traditions have used stories, parables, proverbs, paradoxes, poems, and ritual dramas to signify spiritual wisdom teachings. For those who have experienced profound tragedy and suffering, it becomes particularly

68. M. M. Linehan, *Cognitive-Behavioral Treatment of Borderline Personality Disorder* (New York: Guilford, 1993), 214.

69. D. S. Browning, *A Fundamental Practical Theology: Descriptive and Strategic Proposals* (Minneapolis: Fortress, 1991), 11.

crucial to find the reflective wisdom that narrates meaning and coherence in the "paradoxical context of disorder."[70]

Curiously, one theme unites the wisdom literature of Proverbs, Job, and Ecclesiastes. The Hebrew sages agree that "the fear of the Lord" is the beginning of wisdom (Job 28:28; Prov. 1:7; Eccles. 12:13–14). Spirituality is, in part, a relational process of arousing and soothing anxiety. The fear of the Lord can be an arousing intensification of existential anxiety and spiritual awakening that can repeatedly catalyze spiritual transformation and the development of wisdom.

Health-Conducive Spirituality

My former colleague Jane Burg offered one of the simplest but best definitions I have heard of healthy spirituality. She said, "Healthy spirituality is life-giving," which is a rather good informal criterion. Scientific research suggests that certain indices of spirituality and religion can be consistent with health, well-being, and the good life, whereas other life-draining approaches to the sacred are associated with pathology. I have suggested that wisdom is a multidimensional virtue that can foster the developmental integration of spirituality and health. But even wise spirituality cannot guarantee life-giving health. In fact, those who suffer various health challenges often demonstrate the most profound levels of spiritual maturity. And so a realistic goal is to describe the contours of a health-conducive spirituality. This is, in part, a theological task, one that different traditions will answer somewhat differently. LeRon's chapters articulate the theological contours of healthy spirituality. Based on psychological theory and research primarily developed in Western Christian contexts, I will outline several dimensions that I consider essential to health-conducive forms of spirituality that promote eudaemonic well-being. Spirituality is typically most health-conducive when (a) intentionally embodied, (b) developmentally generative, (c) relationally connected, (d) justice-enhancing, and (e) narratively coherent.

Intentionally Embodied

Human spirituality is embodied. Chapter 2 offered a theological critique of radically dualistic models of personhood that imply that spirituality somehow bypasses the body. Human spiritual experiences engage bodily functions. Neurological, respiratory, cardiac, and all the other physiological subsystems are active in spiritual experience. The

---

70. Wells, "Hebrew Wisdom," 60.

question is not whether spirituality is embodied but whether a person makes spirituality *intentionally* embodied.

I have suggested that spirituality emerges in relation to the dialectical process of anxiety arousal and soothing, and this is obviously an embodied process. Most spiritual traditions offer practices intended to sanctify the human body and can help regulate and balance bodily functioning. For example, prayerful and meditative practices are quite diverse, but many are aimed at focusing attention and producing a calming, soothing effect on the mind and body. Many traditions also sanctify eating and promote disciplines of fasting and good nutrition. In some traditions, arousal and activation are sanctified through lively worship music and dance. Sexuality and the desire for intimacy can be sacralized in most traditions, although sex is also frequently considered profane.

My clinical observation is that negative, shame-prone attitudes toward the body can often constrain spiritual well-being and health. My personal experience is that my own evangelical Christian tradition, which Richard Foster calls the word-centered tradition, is much stronger in verbal and social spirituality than embodied spirituality.[71] I spent many years suspicious of spiritual practices that involved disciplines of breathing, stretching, or repeating certain prayers. Health can certainly become an idol, but neglecting wise treatment of the body is hard to justify in most spiritual traditions. Moreover, Toinette Eugene and James Newton Poling have described the connections between theologies of disembodied spirituality and racism and sexism. They advocate the contextualization of an Afrocentric and African American ethic of black love and embodied spirituality.[72]

Developmentally Generative

As suggested in chapter 6, healthy spirituality should facilitate human development. Spirituality that is health-conducive will facilitate meaningful developmental transitions and rites of passage. Research consistently suggests that spirituality and religion are most health-conducive when they are internalized and engaged with intrinsic motivation. Extrinsically motivated or conformist spirituality seems to offer limited developmental or health benefit. This suggests that health-conducive spirituality is consistent with healthy selfhood and the developmental balancing of attachment and differentiation, as well as other developmental virtues. This emphasis on human development may seem like an excessively

71. R. J. Foster, *Streams of Living Water: Celebrating the Great Traditions of Christian Faith* (San Francisco: HarperSanFrancisco, 1998).

72. T. M. Eugene and J. N. Poling, *Balm for Gilead: Pastoral Care for African American Families Experiencing Abuse* (Nashville: Abingdon, 1998).

humanistic perspective to some, but the alternative seems to require an anthropology that divorces spirit from psyche and the developmental process.

Relationally Connected

Health-conducive spirituality should facilitate relational connection. The research summarized above associates spiritual and religious dwelling (i.e., positive connection to a sacred community) with health and well-being. From a relational perspective, healthy spirituality should tend to promote growth in relational maturity. It is unrealistic to think that spiritually healthy individuals will get along well with everyone. But a chronic, cross-situational pattern of relational dysfunction would be inconsistent with healthy spirituality.

Justice-Enhancing

The unit of analysis for health-conducive spirituality can be the individual, but most spiritual traditions offer a prophetic critique for extreme individualism. Chapter 4 demonstrated the theological significance of justice and altruistic love for Christian spirituality. If we shift the unit of analyses to more systemic levels, the connections between spirituality, health, and social justice become especially important. In a world teaming with poverty, malnutrition, ethnic hatred, disease, and oppression, spirituality will be health-conducive at the systemic level only if it is justice-enhancing. That is, healthy spirituality should move people toward compassionate alterity or a widening circle of concern for others. Ronald Rolheiser calls for a Christian spirituality of social justice that motivates the transformation of social systems and is "grounded in the equality of all human persons before God."[73] The empirical correlations between spiritual variables, social-justice concerns, and individual health have been largely ignored. I will return to the relationship between justice and spiritual maturity in chapter 9.

Narratively Coherent

Finally, spirituality will likely be most salutary when facilitating narrative meaning and coherence. Meaning and a sense of coherence about one's life are strong predictors of well-being. Spiritual and religious traditions can offer narrative horizons that inspire health-promoting virtues, such as hope and gratitude. Spiritual narratives also offer exemplars of faith and heroes of healthy development. Brain researchers Andrew

73. Rolheiser, *The Holy Longing*, 173.

Newberg and Eugene d'Aquili have suggested that two neurological mechanisms, the causal operator and the binary operator, explain the nearly universal human propensity to employ spiritual narratives for meaning-making.[74] The human brain utilizes stories or myths to make causal sense out of life and to reconcile binary opposites that are woven into the fabric of life (e.g., good and evil, life and death).

As mentioned in chapter 6, Dan McAdams and other narrative psychologists in the field of personality have described the storied nature of selfhood and the developmental pull toward viewing one's life as a narrative. Spirituality and religion offer powerful resources for narrating one's life story. Conversely, spiritual life narratives that lack meaning and coherence are not conducive to well-being.

Spiritual-Health Risks

Some ways of relating to the sacred are often associated with health and well-being whereas other approaches to spirituality and religion frequently show either little effect or deleterious health effects. It is easy to understand how negative spiritual experiences, such as feeling abandoned or punished by the divine, could be linked to anxiety and depression, and we will explore the dynamics of spiritual darkness in chapter 8. But can relational spirituality ever be too intensely *positive*? Are there any potential health risks of positive spirituality?

Spiritual Grandiosity

A common element of spiritual experiences is a sense of transcendence or transcending the bounds of selfhood. The intensification of spirituality is often experientially inflating. A person can feel a heightened sense of "specialness" in experiencing a unique spiritual insight, calling, or vision. The book of Genesis describes young Joseph's spiritual dream of his eventual rise, which elicited the envy and resentment of his older brothers. Many transforming spiritual encounters also involve a feeling of being deeply loved by God, which can inflate one's sense of importance.

Jungian analyst Robert Moore has argued that spiritual experiences often activate psychological grandiosity or narcissism.[75] Narcissism is defined by psychologists in various ways but commonly means self-involvement. Moderate levels of what Heinz Kohut called "healthy narcissism" are consistent with the confidence and self-esteem that is conducive

74. Newberg, d'Aquili, and Rause, *Why God Won't Go Away*.
75. R. L. Moore, *Facing the Dragon: Overcoming Personal and Spiritual Grandiosity*, ed. Max J. Havlick Jr. (Wilmette, IL: Chiron, 2003).

to mental health and wholeness. Leaders, in particular, typically need enough healthy narcissism to confidently articulate a vision, inspire others, and make decisions. Healthy narcissism and self-confidence can coexist with capacities for virtues such as empathy and humility. In fact, spiritual traditions that overvalorize self-negation risk promoting the false humility that eventually results in covert narcissism.

Grandiosity is the inflating function of narcissism. Most spiritual traditions offer wisdom warning about overinflation. Moore points out that spiritual experience interacts with a person's characterological or ego structures formed through psychological development. Intense, inflating experiences of relational spirituality that are not accompanied by psychological development and the maturing of ego functioning put a person at risk of narcissistic "overcooking." That is, a person can become spiritually inflated in ways that lead him or her to feel relationally superior to others. In the worst-case scenario, spiritual intensification that inflates grandiose narcissism without the containment of mature ego functioning can turn destructive. The spiritually grandiose can feel that the only way of maintaining favor with the sacred is to destroy the infidels.

Spiritual inflation or grandiosity can also become a health risk by inducing a sense of invulnerability. This can make it hard for persons to accept their humanness or "get their feet on the ground." A college student who had experienced a powerful spiritual transformation described this spiritual inflation, recounting that he had been aggressively telling Satan to "bring it on!" After a series of spiritual setbacks, he had decided to try to be less spiritually provocative and more humble.

Narcissistic grandiosity can also promote illusory spiritual health or overestimations of spiritual health and well-being. Todd Hall and Keith Edwards have researched illusory spiritual health and developed the Spiritual Assessment Inventory (SAI), an empirical measure of Christian spiritual maturity and spiritual pathology that includes a spiritual-grandiosity subscale.[76] The SAI is one of the few measures of spirituality that includes a validity scale to detect impression management. Not surprisingly, those who score higher in spiritual grandiosity also tend to score higher in spiritual impression management. This suggests that their self-reported level of spirituality probably exceeds reality. The spiritually grandiose are not necessarily consciously lying but feel an internal

76. T. W. Hall and K. J. Edwards, "The Spiritual Assessment Inventory: A Theistic Model and Measure for Assessing Spiritual Development," *Journal for the Scientific Study of Religion* 41 (2002): 341–57. Also see K. J. Edwards and T. W. Hall, "Illusory Spiritual Health: The Role of Defensiveness in Understanding and Assessing Spiritual Health," in *Spiritual Formation, Counseling, and Psychotherapy*, ed. T. W. Hall and Mark McMinn (Hauppauge, NY: Nova Science, 2003), 261–75.

pressure to present themselves in a spiritually virtuous manner that may lack authenticity. Although positive illusions about the self can be adaptive at times, illusory spiritual health that is chronically grandiose can prevent necessary spiritual growth and eventually contribute to emotional and relational problems.

Spiritual Compulsivity

In addition to spiritual grandiosity, an emphasis on spirituality and health also risks spiritual compulsivity and scrupulosity. Compulsivity is expressed in anxiety-driven behaviors motivated by rigid attempts to maintain control and order in life. By definition, compulsivity involves a lack of freedom and self-control. Eventually, compulsive behaviors become very hard to stop because one's whole system (mind, body, and spirit) becomes organized and stabilized by the compulsive rituals. Compulsivity always works against authentic relational intimacy. In fact, compulsive rituals offer a tempting alternative to the more challenging task of cultivating relational intimacy with God and others. Compulsive behaviors include substance problems commonly identified as problematic by health professionals (alcoholism or nicotine dependence), as well as other self-medicating behaviors that can result in dependency in some individuals (e.g., gambling, pornography use, shopping). Although probably rare, some spiritual behaviors (prayer, confession, Bible reading) can become compulsive when the internal motivation to avoid anxiety perpetually overrides the commitment to embrace formative relational growth toward maturity. Spiritual compulsivity might even be reinforced as a positive sign of devotion or commitment. The Spanish mystic St. John of the Cross describes a "secret pride" in some individuals that forms a combination of spiritual grandiosity and spiritual compulsivity:

> The devil often increases the fervour that they have and the desire to perform these and other works more frequently, so that their pride and presumption may grow greater. For the devil knows quite well that all these works and virtues which they perform are not only valueless to them, but even become vices in them . . . for they are anxious that all they do shall be esteemed and praised.[77]

One dimension of spiritual compulsivity can be excessive scrupulosity. By "scrupulosity," I mean an intensification of rigid spiritual boundaries and moral self-examination to the point of compulsivity. A legalistic perfectionism takes over the spiritual health of some people, causing

---

77. John of the Cross, *The Dark Night of the Soul*, trans. E. A. Peers (Garden City, NY: Image Books, 1959), 39–40.

spiritual practices and disciplines to lose their life-giving benefit. Anxiety and shame begin to motivate extreme caution and promote harsh ways of spiritually relating to self. Most spiritual traditions include subgroups that become excessively ascetic and legalistic, denigrating embodied pleasures that those traditions legitimate in moderation.

The purity codes that also emerge in the history of most spiritual traditions can foster "conscientiousness-based" virtues, such as diligence, loyalty, justice, and self-control.[78] These virtues can promote healthy practical wisdom but can also contribute to a scrupulous fixation on the dualistic opposition of clean and unclean. This can lead to unjust exclusion of "unclean" outsiders and the naive and stigmatizing view that people suffer only because of their own sin. The "warmth-based" virtues that many spiritual traditions also promote, such as compassion, forgiveness, gratitude, and love, represent a balancing set of virtues. Both individuals and larger spiritual traditions seem to differ in the balancing of conscientiousness-based and warmth-based virtues, and optimal spiritual well-being probably requires a dialectical, health-conducive balancing of these virtue dimensions. Forgiveness without justice fails to transform systems in ways that promote healthy long-term relational functioning and trust. Justice without forgiveness separates offenders from nonoffenders but lacks a valuable means of relational transformation and reintegration.

Conclusion

Scientific research suggests that certain forms of spiritual and religious dwelling and seeking tend to be associated with health and well-being whereas other forms show neutral or negative effects. A virtue-oriented or eudaemonic view of developmental well-being can be consistent with a relational model of Christian spiritual formation. Wisdom is a central developmental virtue necessary for navigating spiritual pathways conducive to health and for avoiding spiritual pathways that generate pathology.

Spiritual formation requires systemic balancing for well-being and, periodically, transformative growth cycles that move toward a telos of maturity. Although spiritual intensification can be conducive to growth and well-being, intensification without corresponding psychological development can result in spiritual and relational pathologies of grandiosity and compulsivity. St. John of the Cross and other contemplatives have

78. E. L. Worthington Jr., J. W. Berry, and L. Parrott III, "Unforgiveness, Forgiveness, Religion, and Health," in *Faith and Health: Psychological Perspectives*, ed. T. G. Plante and A. C. Sherman (New York: Guilford, 2001), 107–38.

described the transformative potential of "dark fire" (periods of spiritual aridity and purgation) that can move spiritual seekers beyond initial spiritual health toward greater spiritual maturity. Using the imagery of human attachment, he writes,

> When they believe that the sun of Divine favour is shining most brightly upon them, God turns all this light of theirs into darkness, and shuts against them the door and the source of the sweet spiritual water which they were tasting in God whensoever and for as long as they desired. . . . God now sees that they have grown a little, and are becoming strong enough to lay aside their swaddling clothes and be taken from the gentle breast; so He sets them down from His arms and teaches them to walk on their own feet.[79]

Chapter 8 will explore the spiritual and relational dynamics that form pathways of darkness.

79. John of the Cross, *Dark Night of the Soul*, 62–63.

8

SPIRITUALITY
AND DARKNESS

For the way to God lies through deep darkness in which all knowledge and
all created wisdom and all pleasure and prudence and all human hope and
human joy are defeated and annulled by the overwhelming purity of the
light and the presence of God.

Thomas Merton, *New Seeds of Contemplation*

I feel a mix of hope and anxiety every time I read the quote above.
Merton's description of the "light and presence of God" lures my hope,
and the part about "deep darkness" raises my anxiety. Like many contemplatives, Merton is saying that the way to God's relational presence
is not around but through deep darkness. I keep reading Merton because
his description resonates with my own spiritual journey. There can be
dark forests of transformation along the pathway to spiritual light.

Light and darkness are two of the most prominent themes across spiritual and religious traditions. The sacred is often depicted as providing light
that dispels the darkness. The Gospel of John says, "The light shines in the
darkness, and the darkness has not overcome it" (John 1:5 NIV mg). And
although spiritual light and darkness are often held in opposition, their

relationship is also construed in more complex ways. Darkness is a metaphor used for various types of spiritual struggles. Some forms of spiritual darkness are profoundly alienating or destructive whereas other forms of spiritual darkness are deeply transformative. Chapter 7 summarized research suggesting ways that spirituality and religion can be conducive to health and well-being. But spirituality and religion can also lead to an intensification of darkness and spiritual strain.[1] St. John of the Cross offers a challenging description of the intensification of spiritual darkness:

> But there will come a time when God will bid them grow deeper. He will remove the previous consolation from the soul in order to teach it virtue and prevent it from developing vice. . . . They will beg God to take away their imperfections, but they do this only because they want to find inner peace and not for God's sake. They do not realize that if God were to take away their imperfections from them, they would become prouder and more presumptuous still.[2]

Spirituality seems to lead some people out of darkness and into light, but many mystics and contemplatives describe recurring episodes of darkness that can provide transformative space along the pathway toward spiritual maturity. The psalmist praises the Lord, for "even in darkness light dawns for the upright, for the gracious and compassionate and righteous" person (Ps. 112:4 NIV). This chapter will consider some of the varieties of spiritual darkness from a psychological perspective. I will also conceptualize spiritual struggles through the lens of relational spirituality and relational processes of transformation.

Varieties of Spiritual Darkness

Spirituality and darkness are related in a variety of ways. Psychological theory and research can provide a useful complement to theology in understanding spiritual struggles with darkness. Ken Pargament and his colleagues define spiritual struggles as "efforts to conserve or transform spirituality that has been threatened or harmed."[3] In Pargament's model,

1. On spiritual and religious strain, see J. J. Exline, "Stumbling Blocks on the Religious Road: Fractured Relationships, Nagging Vices, and the Inner Struggle to Believe," *Psychological Inquiry* 13 (2002): 182–89.

2. John of the Cross, *The Dark Night of the Soul*, trans. E. A. Peers (Garden City, NY: Image Books, 1959), 41–42.

3. K. I. Pargament, N. A. Murray-Swank, G. M. Magyar, and G. G. Ano, "Spiritual Struggle: A Phenomenon of Interest to Psychology and Religion," in *Judeo-Christian Perspectives on Psychology: Human Nature, Motivation, and Change*, ed. W. R. Miller and H. D. Delaney (Washington, DC: American Psychological Association, 2005), 245–68.

spiritual struggles represent ways of attempting to cope with threats or injuries to one's relationship with the sacred. These coping strategies can include efforts to conserve or maintain one's present relationship with the sacred or transform that relationship in some significant way.

**Table 6. Potential Sources
of Spiritual Struggle and Darkness**

Sin

Evil

Social Oppression

Physical and Mental Health Problems

Psychopathology

Loss

Trauma

Failure

Relational Conflicts

Developmental Transitions

Table 6 provides a general taxonomy of potential sources of spiritual struggle and darkness. This taxonomy is composed of differing semantic domains of language related to suffering.[4] For example, sin and evil are primarily religious terms, loss and trauma are psychological constructs, illness has medical connotations, and language related to social oppression is rooted in sociological and political discourse. An integrative model of spirituality requires fluency in these differing linguistic domains because the multiple sources of spiritual darkness are interactive rather than discrete. For example, social oppression, such as racism, can generate experiences of terrifying trauma. A conflicted marriage can provide the context for deliberate sin, such as when a wife having an affair is murdered by her angry husband. A depressed adolescent who develops the cognitive ability to question her faith around the same time she loses her mother to cancer is at risk for darker forms of relational spirituality.

Dark spiritual struggles can physically, mentally, socially, and spiritually impair health and functioning. In the most recent edition of the *Diagnostic and Statistical Manual of Mental Disorders*, the task force acknowledged that spiritual and religious conflicts can lead to impairment in psychological functioning.[5] Psychologist William Hathaway has helped initiate an

4. A. Dueck, "Speaking the Languages of Sin and Pathology," *Christian Counseling Today* 10 (2002): 20–24.

5. R. P. Turner, D. Lukoff, R. T. Barnhouse, and F. G. Lu, "Religious or Spiritual Problem: A Culturally Sensitive Diagnostic Category in the DSM-IV," *Journal of Nervous and Mental Disease* 183 (1995): 435–44.

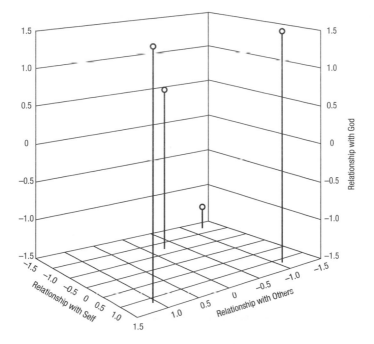

Figure 2. Model of Relational Spirituality

emerging effort to argue that mental disorders can also impair spiritual functioning, suggesting that spiritual impairment is vitally important to many people.[6] For example, adults who meet criteria for attention deficit/hyperactivity disorder (ADHD) often find spiritual disciplines such as contemplative prayer and meditation exceedingly difficult until their symptoms are effectively treated. As I suggested in chapter 7, various dimensions of human functioning (physical, mental, social, spiritual) are related.

A Model of Relational Spirituality

The next section will consider a typology of struggles of relational spirituality. But first I want to introduce a visual depiction of the heuristic model of relational spirituality being proposed. Any visual model of a construct as complex as spirituality will be a vast oversimplification.

Figure 2 depicts a model of three-dimensional space based on the interactive dimensions of (a) relationship with self, (b) relationship with

6. W. L. Hathaway, S. Y. Scott, and S. A. Garver, "Assessing Religious/Spiritual Functioning: A Neglected Domain in Clinical Practice?" *Professional Psychology: Research and Practice* 35 (2004): 97–104.

others, and (c) relationship with God. The specific label for the third dimension—relationship with God—best fits theistic spiritualities, although this dimension could also be broadened to refer to the sacred as discussed in chapter 6. The relational framework and research reviewed in chapters 6 and 7 suggest that these three dimensions are distinct but also highly interactive. The simple negative-to-positive values refer to a person's general internal working model of relating to self, others, and God, and this allows for locating hypothetical persons in three-dimensional space. The developmental and transformative processes that change these dimensions of relational spirituality reflect the liminal movement of spiritual seeking or questing, which I will explore further in this chapter.

Struggles of Relational Spirituality

My relational orientation leads me to adapt Pargament's coping model to explore spiritual struggles relationally. Exline suggested a typology of spiritual and religious struggles, including (a) interpersonal strains, (b) negative attitudes toward God, (c) problems associated with virtuous striving, and (d) inner struggles to believe.[7] I will use a relational model to cluster spiritual struggles into (a) relational struggles with others, (b) relational struggles with God and the sacred, and (c) relational struggles with oneself. The section "Spiritual Questing and Liminal Space" will consider Exline's third category, inner struggles to believe.

Relational Struggles with Others

Interpersonal conflicts in sacred contexts can be a disturbing source of spiritual darkness. There is limited empirical research in this area, but the available studies suggest that interpersonal tensions in religious contexts are not uncommon and can be particularly disappointing given the ideals of religious community.[8] Chapter 7 summarized research suggesting that the social-support function of spiritual and religious communities might be one of the strongest influences on health and well-being. A strong sense of spiritual dwelling in a sacred community can provide rootedness and a safe haven of connection. But relational conflicts and betrayals can neutralize these positive health benefits.

7. Exline, "Stumbling Blocks."
8. M. E. Nielsen, "An Assessment of Religious Conflicts and Their Resolutions," *Journal for the Scientific Study of Religion* 37 (1998): 181–90. R. J. Taylor, L. M. Chatters, and J. Levin, *Religion in the Lives of African Americans: Social, Psychological, and Health Perspectives* (Thousand Oaks, CA: Sage, 2004).

Case Example 1

Ed (age twenty-eight) experienced a dramatic Christian conversion at a church revival. He joined the church and formed a very strong attachment with the senior pastor, who discipled him weekly. Ed had never been close to an older male, as his father had been mostly absent from his life. After Ed had been at the church for two years, the pastor and the church trustees had a heated conflict that resulted in the pastor's resignation and a move to a church in another city. Ed was devastated and bitter at the trustees. He left the church and withdrew from spiritual community altogether.

Psychologically, Ed's conversion experience helped him regain an opportunity for relational connection and idealization he never really had with his father. James Jones draws on the self psychology of Heinz Kohut to offer a rich psychoanalytic theory of spirituality as a form of idealization.[9] Kohut argued that we have a developmental need to idealize our parents or other relational figures early in life. Calm, stable idealized figures can provide positive selfobject experiences that are internalized to develop a cohesive sense of self. The best-case scenario is that the de-idealization of parents and authority figures sets in gradually and keeps pace with the positive internalization of selfobject experiences. When de-idealization happens too traumatically or parents and leaders completely fail to carry idealized projections, narcissistic injuries and deficits in healthy selfhood can result. Jones suggests that the developmental desire to idealize can be transferred to the sacred with similar potential risks for de-idealization and disappointment.

Jones's theory of spiritual idealization offers a compelling fit with Ed's case. Ed had idealized his pastor, whose defeat at the hands of the trustees and subsequent absence reactivated his early narcissistic injuries. Whereas some people with a more secure relational history might have accepted the loss or simply moved on to another church, Ed fell into disappointed cynicism and self-protection. His shame manifested itself in his sense of "foolishness" for having opened himself relationally and spiritually, and he lost his connection with God along with his attachment to the church. The pastor might have helped partially mitigate Ed's spiritual impairment if he had been better attuned to Ed's pain or had processed some closure in his relationship with Ed. Perhaps the pastor's own losses and internal struggles with the church worked against his emotional availability for Ed.

Too often there seems to be a mistaken assumption in spiritual and religious communities that healthy community simply happens as a result of good intentions. More realistically, almost any experience of

9. J. W. Jones, *Terror and Transformation: The Ambiguity of Religion in Psychoanalytic Perspective* (New York: Brunner-Routledge, 2002).

community provides a context where interpersonal conflicts will eventually emerge. These conflicts can be formative opportunities for relational growth and healing, but this requires work and wise guidance.

"Pseudo-community" is the experience of group cohesion based on avoiding any significant differences within the group.[10] It can feel safe to focus on points of consensus where everyone in the group is "on the same page." The anxiety of difference usually arises at some point, and differences can be repressed or managed through extreme relational maneuvers of power and control.[11] Tolerating the anxiety of within-group differences can promote the differentiation of those within the community, which can allow opportunities for deeper knowing and intimacy. In some cases, decisions to leave a spiritual community may result, but important differences can be better understood and respected.

Case Example 2

Sharon (age twenty-six) was a Korean American adult adoptee who was part of a small group in a predominantly white evangelical Protestant church. She had joined the church at the end of college after a spiritual transformation that helped her find "secure love" in God. She had been part of this small group for two years but started to go through both a faith and an identity crisis. She had been adopted as an infant by a white family and grew up isolated from other Asians. She had always thought of culture as irrelevant to her identity, but over the past year she had been drawn toward trying to understand Korean culture and to reflect on her ethnic identity. Initially these issues felt "secular" and separate from her faith, but she began to see that this was because her spiritual community was mainly composed of white people who seemed unconcerned about issues of race and ethnicity. She tried sharing some of her process with her small group but felt shot down by the white male leader, who made comments such as "We are all really the same in Christ." Sharon was struggling spiritually and thought about simply leaving the group and the church to find a community more supportive of her spiritual quest. She felt alienated but also did not want to be a distraction to the group or question the leader. In a very courageous move in one group session, however, she took the risk of candidly voicing her dilemma. She relayed saying something like the following: "Here's where I am at. I have come to see I've been taught to deny my *Korean-ness* and that my ethnicity is not relevant to my relationship with God. But I don't believe that anymore. This really hurts because it is too much like the racism I experience in society, people saying skin color doesn't matter but then treating people differently based on race. I feel like

10. M. S. Peck, *The Different Drum: Community-Making and Peace* (New York: Touchstone, 1987), 86.

11. For power and control systems, see J. W. Maddock and N. R. Larson, *Incestuous Families: An Ecological Approach to Understanding and Treatment* (New York: W. W. Norton, 1995).

God is leading me to explore my roots and what it means to be Korean,
and this group does not feel like a supportive place to do that. Comments
like 'we are all the same' feel discounting to me."

According to Sharon, the group leader became silent and withdrawn,
but one woman in the group became very engaged. She said she too
had wanted to talk about sexism she had experienced in the church
but had felt scared to raise it. A third group member became tearful
and admitted he had missed the significance of these issues to Sharon
until that point. For Sharon, this provided what Daniel Stern refers to
as a "moment of meeting," a transforming relational encounter where
false selves are pulled back and people experience a more authentic
connection.[12] Stern describes moments of meeting as resulting from
relational intersubjectivity or shared states of mind where people are
relating subject to subject rather than subject to object.[13] Sharon did
leave the group and the church for a spiritual community that better fit
the next leg of her spiritual journey, but she continued to meet with the
two group members she "met" more deeply as a result of her truth telling.
Her initial attachment to that community or place of spiritual dwelling
eventually led to the need to differentiate and reorient her spirituality
and identity. Some were able to connect with her in her move toward
differentiation, and some were not.

Relational Struggles with God and the Sacred

Human relational conflicts have analogous versions in relational conflicts with God and the sacred. Research suggests that a secure attachment with the divine is generally associated with emotional well-being,
resilience, and healthy forms of coping with extreme stress. An insecure
attachment with God and the sacred is expressed in many experiences
of spiritual darkness. Spiritual writers throughout history have voiced
feelings of sacred confusion, disappointment, abandonment, betrayal,
and even persecution. The prophet Jeremiah complained, "O LORD, you
deceived me, and I was deceived; you overpowered me and prevailed"
(Jer. 20:7 NIV). These words follow shortly after a narrative of Jeremiah's
beating for speaking the word of God. When chaos and trauma are the

12. D. N. Stern, *The Present Moment in Psychotherapy and Everyday Life* (New York:
W. W. Norton, 2004).
13. On the relationship between intersubjectivity and forgiveness, see S. J. Sandage,
"Intersubjectivity and the Many Faces of Forgiveness: Commentary on Paper by Steven
Wangh," *Psychoanalytic Dialogues* 15 (2005): 17–32; F. LeRon Shults and Steven J. Sandage,
The Faces of Forgiveness: Searching for Wholeness and Salvation (Grand Rapids: Baker,
2003).

result of obedience, those who trust and serve God might be particularly at risk for episodes of spiritual darkness.

Trauma is an experience where the physical integrity of the self is threatened in ways that overwhelm coping resources and produce extreme fear and helplessness.[14] Trauma can arise in experiences of combat, rape, or other experiences of abuse and usually involves losses. These can include physical losses, relational losses, or psychological and spiritual losses. The famous World War II saying "There are no atheists in foxholes" is probably an overgeneralization and misses the diverse range of spiritual responses to trauma. When a person meets criteria for posttraumatic stress disorder, his or her spiritual orientation can become hardened, numb, or intensely angry, as was the case with Pete in chapter 6.[15] Questions about the meaning of life and the character of God may take on a new urgency, or these same questions might be anxiously avoided.

Couples therapist Susan Johnson describes "attachment injuries" that threaten safe bonding and emotional intimacy in close relationships. She defines attachment injuries as "wounds arising from abandonment by a present attachment figure in a situation of urgent need."[16] The experience of aloneness in the face of the "dragon" of trauma can be estranging and lead to relational walls. It seems that the category of spiritual-attachment injuries is yet to be explored psychologically. When people face trauma and do not feel sacred presence or support, the existential anxiety of aloneness can be overwhelming. Mark's Gospel even records Jesus crying out, "My God, my God, why have you forsaken me?" (Mark 15:33 NIV).

Losses can also darken spirituality, at least temporarily, for many people. The absence of a loved one, of a meaningful place or object, or of a phase of life can offer a taste of death or what James Loder called "the void." "The void" is a name for existential negation or nonbeing. Most people generally recover from losses after a period of grief, but experiences of the void can also provide a catalyst for human development and spiritual transformation.

Case Example

Asante (age thirty-one) and Prem (age thirty-four) were a Christian couple who experienced a miscarriage at the twentieth week of Asante's first pregnancy. After some difficulty getting pregnant, this came as a particularly

14. S. M. Johnson, *Emotionally Focused Couple Therapy with Trauma Survivors: Strengthening Attachment Bonds* (New York: Guilford, 2002).

15. J. P. Wilson and T. A. Moran, "Psychological Trauma: Posttraumatic Stress Disorder and Spirituality," *Journal of Psychology and Theology* 26 (1998): 168–78.

16. Johnson, *Emotionally Focused Couple Therapy*, 15.

painful loss. They had prayed daily together for the baby, with Prem frequently voicing a prayer close to Asante's stomach. The loss not only dashed their dream; both also felt shame for hoping with such vulnerable trust. Prem could not bring himself to pray, explaining, "What good does it do to talk with God when he obviously doesn't care what happens to us?"

Individual differences are profound in the variety of responses to dark struggles of relational spirituality. Some people seem spiritually impervious to darkness and the struggles described above. These include William James's category of the healthy-minded mentioned in chapter 6. For some, God is exonerated from blame no matter what happens in life, usually with an appeal to human freedom. For others, the authentic sufferers James called "sick souls," the pathway toward healing seems to require engaging God redemptively through "a deeper dose of religion." In the Jewish and Christian traditions, this can include spiritual lament. Lament is authentic spiritual complaint where God is engaged amidst the pain of life. For example, throughout the Psalms, God is asked, "How long?" How long will your anger last, God? How long will the suffering continue? These are not faithless questions but honest and courageous acts of worship. The protests of lament can express a hidden spiritual hope that refuses to give up on attachment to God.[17] The prophet Hosea voices God's own lament that the people of Israel "do not cry out to me from their hearts but wail upon their beds" (Hosea 7:14 NIV). Hosea is offering a prophetic contrast between a relational spirituality of authentic lament and one of passive self-pity.

Theologian James Cone describes the music of black spirituals and the blues as often combining lament and hope. Music and spirituality are deeply integrated in African American history. Songs that express despair and hopelessness often protest conditions of oppression and voice the deeper hope that God will ultimately liberate. For example, "Nobody Knows the Trouble I've Seen" ends with "Glory Hallelujah!" which voices a belief that "trouble is not the last word."[18]

Empirical research supports a diverse landscape for spiritual struggles with God and the sacred, depending on the nature and chronicity of the struggle. Pargament's research with medically ill elderly patients found that chronic spiritual strugglers showed reduced well-being and

17. Dan Allender, "The Hidden Hope in Lament," *Mars Hill Review* 1 (1994): 25–37. For an attachment interpretation of women's anger and protest as a potential expression of hope, see D. C. Jack, "The Anger of Hope and the Anger of Despair: How Anger Relates to Women's Depression," in *Situating Sadness: Women and Depression in Social Context*, ed. J. M. Stoppard and L. M. McMullen (New York: New York University Press, 2003), 62–87.

18. James H. Cone, *The Spirituals and the Blues: An Interpretation* (Maryknoll, NY: Orbis, 1991), 58.

228   Transforming Spirituality in Psychology

physical health and increased depression relative to other groups over a two-year period.[19] This suggests that spiritual turbulence may only diminish health and well-being when people become stuck in their struggles. Pargament's research on spiritual and religious coping has also found that feeling punished by God is generally related to lower levels of well-being, particularly among the elderly.

In our research with seminary students, my colleagues and I have found that spiritual disappointment and spiritual instability are two forms of relational spirituality that are negatively associated with spiritual and emotional well-being.[20] Those high in spiritual instability can feel both abandoned and punished by God. They can feel high levels of both shame and frustration with God. High levels of spiritual instability are also associated with higher levels of psychological symptoms of physical and emotional stress and lower levels of gratitude, forgiveness, and intrinsic religious commitment. In attachment terms, the spiritually unstable often feel negative about their relationship with both self and God. Empirically, spiritual disappointment is often less impairing than spiritual instability. The spiritually disappointed can also be struggling but are more likely to be seeking new spiritual understanding and resolving their attachment struggles with God. There is usually less extreme psychological splitting in authentic spiritual disappointment and more potential for the kinds of grieving or mourning that can foster spiritual formation during dark nights.

Relational Struggles with Self

Spirituality also involves struggles in relating to the self. Narcissism and shame are two core psychological orientations toward the self. Both are traits, and so individuals differ in their baseline levels of narcissism and shame. But they are also states of psychological functioning that can intensify for a person at a given moment in time.

Chapter 7 drew upon the helpful work of Robert Moore to suggest that spiritual experiences of transcendence can promote grandiose inflation. If such experiences are not balanced with psychological and emotional growth in virtues such as empathy and humility, this inflation can have

19. K. I. Pargament et al., "Spiritual Struggle: A Phenomenon of Interest to Psychology and Religion," in *Judeo-Christian Perspectives on Psychology*, ed. W. R. Miller and H. D. Delaney (Washington, DC: American Psychological Association, 2005), 245–68.

20. S. J. Sandage, I. Williamson, and M. Helder, "Spiritual and Psychological Health Among Seminarians: A Cluster Analysis" (presentation, annual convention of the American Psychological Association, Honolulu, HI, August 2004); T. W. Hall and K. J. Edwards, "The Spiritual Assessment Inventory: A Theistic Model and Measure for Assessing Spiritual Development," *Journal for the Scientific Study of Religion* 41 (2002): 341–57.

potentially negative relational consequences. There are several possible reasons this can lead to forms of spiritual darkness. First, spiritual inflation unaccompanied by psychological growth might make a person more susceptible to the threat of ego injuries when facing spiritual diversity. Research on narcissism suggests that high levels of narcissism promote aggressiveness due to inflated self-esteem that is very vulnerable to outside threats.[21] Spiritual intensification that is unbalanced with maturity of ego functioning can result in increased reactivity toward those who might question or simply not acknowledge the person's definition of the sacred. In the extreme, this can lead to intimidation, terrorism, or other forms of violence toward the other. Spirituality and religion can promote well-being by assisting in the development of healthy and cohesive self-identity, but spiritual grandiosity can potentially wrap a stranglehold around the alterity (or otherness) of identity.

Spiritual inflation might also lead to shaming narcissistic injuries as the person fails to realize his or her own idealistic standards. Spirituality can involve striving for virtue, which is a double-edged sword.[22] Virtues can promote well-being, but the impossibility of achieving perfect virtue also challenges spiritual grandiosity and perfectionism. The perceived discrepancy between one's ideal spiritual self and one's actual self can be a source of depressive deflation and shame. Various types of failure experiences can instigate episodes of spiritual darkness and shame and raise internal questions of self-worth. Most spiritual traditions offer wisdom teachings aimed at somehow resolving these tensions and shame-oriented failure experiences. In Christian spirituality, humility provides a helpful contrast with shame and entails recognizing the limits of one's humanness.

Case Example

Brad (age seventeen) related the following story of spiritual transformation. His church youth group encouraged all the members to fast for a day. Brad had never done this before but was excited about his growing faith and eager to engage new spiritual discipline. Unfamiliar with the digestive influence of fasting, he broke the fast the following morning with a large, rich meal at a restaurant with friends. He became sick to his stomach, went to the restroom, and had a profound spiritual experience sitting on the floor. He described feeling a wave of humiliation and embarrassment for being so indulgent after the fast and not anticipating the consequences. And then he remembered a Bible passage that speaks of God's love despite human righteousness

21. R. F. Baumeister, *Evil: Inside Human Violence and Cruelty* (New York: W. H. Freeman, 1997).
22. Exline, "Stumbling Blocks."

being like "filthy rags." At that moment sitting next to a toilet in a public restroom, Brad said he felt as if he were wrapped in a warm hug and felt deep "grace from God."

Spirituality can promote ideals that activate narcissistic striving. This is not always bad, but it can set the stage for challenging episodes of shame and failure. The arousal of purgation can promote the pursuit of spiritual disciplines, and a failure with these disciplines requires the soothing effect of spiritual grace. In Brad's case, he seems to have psychologically encountered what Stern calls an "evoked companion" in his experience of a warm embrace from God that soothed his shame.[23] Perhaps some earlier experience of relational attachment was unconsciously employed in the service of spiritual transformation. This psychological conceptualization does not deny metaphysical spiritual influences but rather recognizes the relational dimensions of spirituality that operate within human embodiment. Brad also reported his intention to break his next fast more carefully, which suggested he was humbly learning the wisdom of embodied spirituality in caring for himself. It is not hard to imagine a different spiritual outcome for someone whose shameful disappointment in self was not soothed in any way (cf. Pete's case from chapter 6).

Spirituality that does not involve self-care raises the psychological issue of masochism. If spirituality concerns ways of relating to the sacred, then this also potentially includes sanctified relation between God and self.[24] Masochism implies harmful ways of relating to the self through pain or humiliation. Psychoanalyst Emmanuel Ghent offers an illuminating contrast between pathological masochism and transformative surrender.[25] Ghent suggests that the deep desire for surrender comes from a longing for wholeness, recognition, and an authentic identity that transcends the false self. However, Ghent views masochism and unhealthy forms of submission as mutations of surrender or efforts at undoing relational isolation that go awry. In masochism, a person submits to relational domination, control, and enslavement. Masochism does not promote well-being or healthy self-identity but rather solidifies a shame-prone sense of self. This might serve the psychological function of reducing anxiety about the possibilities of genuine recognition and relational intimacy with passive resignation

23. D. N. Stern, *The Interpersonal World of the Infant: A View from Psychoanalysis and Developmental Psychology* (New York: Basic Books, 1985), 111–22.

24. On relational selfhood also see LeRon's appropriation of Kierkegaard in chapter 3.

25. E. Ghent, "Masochism, Submission, Surrender: Masochism as a Perversion of Surrender," *Contemporary Psychoanalysis* 26 (1990): 108–35.

to one's worthless state. In some cases, masochistic ways of self-relating might even serve the unconscious purpose of torturing the other with one's pain.[26]

Spiritual asceticism and martyrdom are obvious examples for consideration as masochistic. Spiritual disciplines can be purgative and focusing in ways that foster spiritual formation. The issue is whether the discipline serves to ultimately promote spiritual liberation, health, and relational love or whether the psychological goal is one of shame-prone narcissism and self-punishment. I am also not suggesting all martyrs are masochists. It seems to me that spiritually mature martyrs would make sacrifices with an authentic acknowledgment of preferring not to suffer, as was the case with Gospel accounts of Jesus. Ego-syntonic martyrdom involves a masochistic need to suffer and to be seen by others as a "suffering servant."[27] This narcissistic drive toward suffering reduces spiritual and relational freedom in that spirituality is viewed as only leading to pain and self-abnegation and never toward healthy celebration or embodied intimacy. In Christian spirituality, episodes of darkness can be formative and redemptive, but the goal should not be chronic spiritual darkness and suffering.

Perhaps the most ubiquitous category used to understand spiritual struggles in relating to self is that of sin. Sin is the classic moral category that many traditions employ to explain spiritual struggles. In the Catholic tradition, the seven deadly sins have been richly described as pathologies of the soul that diminish spiritual and relational well-being. Across traditions, many metaphors have been used to describe the dark entanglement of sin and diagnose the effect of sin on spirituality. Most narrowly, behavioral views of sin focus on cataloging a list of behaviors that are wrong and to be avoided. A behavioral approach offers clear prohibitions but misses the motivational and relational dynamics of sin. A focus on surface behaviors can also lead to labeling as profane (i.e., outside the sacred) behaviors, emotions, or practices that could be sanctified (e.g., dance, sexuality, music, and anger). From psychological- and spiritual-formation perspectives, it is more helpful to consider the motivational and relational dynamics of sin. In theological terms, idolatry is a spiritual construct that also captures the self-defeating, disempowering psychological dynamics of sin. Idolatry entails giving power over to something or someone beyond what that source can de-

26. N. McWilliams, *Psychoanalytic Diagnosis: Understanding Personality Structure in Clinical Process* (New York: Guilford, 1994).

27. For consideration of some of these complex issues in the life of Simone Weil, see S. J. Sandage, T. W. Wiens, and C. M. Dahl, "Humility and Attention: The Contemplative Psychology of Simone Weil," *Journal of Psychology and Christianity* 20 (2001): 360–69.

liver.[28] For example, looking to complete oneself or find personal worth in a romantic relationship can be disappointing at best and enslaving at worst because other-validation is such an unreliable source of self-esteem for adults.[29]

Numerous theologians and a few psychologists, usually white males, have explored pride or narcissism as a core dynamic of sin. From a psychoanalytic perspective, the narcissistic motivation of defending one's omnipotence can lead to the internal, and perhaps the external, destruction of the other. In its pathological forms, narcissism is self-defeating in demanding impossible levels of other-validation resulting in relational dependence or isolation. The spiritual language of sin as bondage, enslavement, or a snare reflects this psychological dynamic of sin.

Some spiritual writers and psychoanalysts have also described sin as a commitment to a false self that masks authentic identity (e.g., Thomas Merton and Donald Winnicott). In this view, the psychological effect of sin is to prioritize impression management and social face-saving over deeper self-acceptance and authentic relatedness. This could be described as a selling out on oneself because of the anxiety of social rejection. The sinful effect on spirituality is this: when looking good on the outside becomes more important than internal spiritual promptings there is a dangerous possibility of deadened responsiveness to the voice of God. Social hypervigilance is hard to integrate with integrity.

Theologian Miroslav Volf has also described exclusion of the other as a core dynamic of sin that perpetuates the evil of victim/perpetrator cycles of violence and prevents the formation of community. I have described the stranger anxiety that promotes defensive exclusion as a key dynamic in the challenges of interpersonal forgiveness.[30] Sin as exclusion of the other who seems strange invites a more systemic and relational view of sin. As Volf suggests, exclusion can become internalized in the self-identity of the excluded, which can encourage oppressive ways of relating to self. This understanding of sin is also more readily contextualized among populations beyond white males in which levels of narcissism are often more modest.

In his crucible model of couples therapy, David Schnarch suggests a definition of sin as a refusal to grow spiritually and relationally. He applies this view to "dark nights" in couples' relationships where it becomes tempting to remain stuck in a dysfunctional but familiar way of

28. W. Smith, "The Dynamic of Idolatry: The Work of Luke T. Johnson with Implications for Psychotherapy," *Journal of Psychology and Christianity* 15 (1996): 5–16.

29. David M. Schnarch, *Passionate Marriage: Keeping Love and Intimacy Alive in Committed Relationships* (New York: Henry Holt, 1997).

30. Shults and Sandage, *The Faces of Forgiveness*, esp. ch. 2; Sandage, "The Many Faces of Forgiveness."

relating rather than face the anxiety of growth. Anxiety is not sin, but anxiety comes with existential dilemmas of ultimate trust versus mistrust and readies us for temptation.[31] It is often possible to repress or self-medicate purgative anxiety, but if a growth cycle is needed to transform a relational system, there will eventually be symptoms reflecting a lack of spiritual vitality.

The language of sin is emotionally loaded. When used reductionistically, language about sin can promote deep shame and shallow repentance. By "shallow repentance" I mean defensive maneuvers aimed more at expedient anxiety reduction than reflective wisdom or relational growth. When conceptualized from an integrative perspective, the various languages of sin, trauma, loss, failure, evil, depression, and other struggles can all contribute to a multidimensional understanding of spiritual darkness. Dark nights of the soul are not always rooted in personal sin or moral compromise. In fact, our crucible model of spiritual transformation suggests that dark nights of spiritual questing can sometimes result from developmental transitions and having the personal courage and integrity to enter liminal space.

Spiritual Questing and Liminal Space

In Wuthnow's dialectic of spiritual dwelling and seeking, spiritual seekers look for the sacred outside the officially authorized places. Seekers engage in the authentic quest toward new spiritual insights, fresh spiritual adventures, and personal experiences of transformation. Spiritual seekers or questers are willing to face doubt and question their spiritual tradition in the interest of personal transformation and possibly even transforming that tradition.

Spiritual Questing

Questioning and questing can lead to or emerge from episodes of spiritual darkness. It can feel dislocating and disloyal to honestly engage spiritual and religious questions. The dissonance and confusion of being less certain about one's beliefs or relationship with the sacred can be scary. It is not unlike the anxiety an estranged couple can feel when they start admitting their real feelings about their relationship.

Social psychologist of religion C. Daniel Batson defined a quest orientation toward religion as involving a willingness to face existential dilemmas, to doubt one's faith, and to remain open to new understand-

31. T. Peters, *Sin: Radical Evil in Soul and Society* (Grand Rapids: Eerdmans, 1994).

ings about religion.[32] Research on Batson's version of the quest construct has suggested that high levels of questing are associated with greater cognitive complexity and lower impression management, but also higher levels of stress and spiritual turbulence. In Batson's view, questing results from cognitive dissonance and an ability to tolerate the anxiety of authentically engaging existential questions. Empirical validation is lacking for Batson's assertion that his quest measure captures religious maturity, but it appears to be a good measure of openness to religious and spiritual movement.

Developmental psychologist James Fowler constructed a stage model of faith development that attempts to explain intrapsychic changes in ways of orienting to ultimate concerns. Cognitive stage models, such as Fowler's, have received many valid critiques. The most helpful contribution of Fowler's model might be the attention to developmental changes in both cognitive and ego functioning that can affect faith and spirituality, particularly at the transitions into young adulthood and midlife. For some young adults, there is a quest to critically examine their faith and to become more personally reflective. In Fowler's stage of conjunctive faith, typically achieved at midlife (if at all), there is a deeper quest to integrate unconscious and paradoxical dimensions of spirituality and selfhood into one's conscious faith and meaning system.[33]

The developmental transitions of questing described by Batson and Fowler can force experiences of spiritual darkness that become transformative moments. Spiritual questing is the movement of spiritual formation, the *becoming* that can result in second-order transformations of *being*.[34] Questing is the epistemological search that potentially transforms developmental ontology, the willingness to not know in the hope of coming to know more deeply and intimately. In biblical terms, questing is asking, seeking, and knocking.

32. C. D. Batson, P. Schoenrade, and W. L. Ventix, *Religion and the Individual: A Social-Psychological Perspective* (New York: Oxford University Press, 1993).

33. J. W. Fowler, *Stages of Faith: The Psychology of Human Development and the Quest for Meaning* (New York: HarperCollins, 1981).

34. Robert Kegan, "There the Dance Is: Religious Dimensions of Developmental Theory," in *Toward Moral and Religious Maturity*, ed. J. W. Fowler and A. Vergote (Morristown, NJ: Silver Burdette, 1980); *In over Our Heads: The Mental Demands of Modern Life* (Cambridge: Harvard University Press, 1994). The debate in the empirical psychology of religion between the correspondence and compensation hypotheses often seems to miss the possibility of this ongoing dialectical process. The correspondence hypothesis suggests that God representations correspond to internal working models of relationships (e.g., secure-secure or insecure-insecure), whereas the compensation hypothesis suggests that God representations potentially compensate for insecure interpersonal attachment. The spiritual quest for compensatory relational transformation might eventually result in secure relational correspondence. On the dialectic of form and process, stability, and change, in transformation, see B. P. Keeney, *Aesthetics of Change* (New York: Guilford, 1983).

Liminality

Spiritual questing can lead to dark passageways into liminal space. Anthropologist Victor Turner described liminality as a period of transition in rites of passage. The Latin word *limen* means "threshold." Liminal space is "betwixt and between" relational statuses. Liminality involves a detaching from a prior social identity and a breaking down or humbling of personal and communal structures. Turner points out that liminality is "frequently likened to death, to being in the womb, to invisibility, to darkness."[35] The darkness of liminal space can feel like a transit into death as separation anxiety intensifies and attachments are transformed.

Religion scholar Belden Lane offers three insightful points about evangelical spiritual traditions, liminality, and the geography of the sacred.[36] First, the evangelical revivalist tradition of liminality reveals the unpredictable landscape of the sacred and God's itinerant freedom to transform people in any context (e.g., fields, barns, marketplaces). In fact, a strength of evangelical spirituality has been the creation of liminal space for seeking within the natural ecologies of those outside formal religious dwellings. Second, narratives of conversion or spiritual "turning" often highlight the transit dimension of liminality. Spiritual transformations often occur as people are displaced or en route somewhere. Lane observes, "Early Christians were not inappropriately characterized as people of the Way, a people involved in passage and movement."[37] Third, Lane suggests that evangelical liminality, at its best, promotes spiritual inclusion of the marginalized and displaced. Turner referred to this temporary leveling of social hierarchy as *communitas*, and revival traditions can offer "outreaches" of spiritual transformation that bridge demographic divides.

Liminal space provides opportunities for spiritual transformation through the humility of unknowing and the courage of authentic selfhood.[38] Liminal transitions purgatively strip off masks of false selfhood and re-form illuminative identity in deeper integrative wholeness. Psychoanalysts have described this liminal process as "adaptive regression."[39] Development does not always move in a linear fashion toward greater complexity. Regression involves a purgative dismantling of the false-self

---

35. V. W. Turner, *The Ritual Process: Structure and Anti-structure* (Ithaca, NY: Cornell University Press, 1969), 95.

36. B. C. Lane, *Landscapes of the Sacred: Geography and Narrative in American Spirituality*, expanded ed. (Baltimore: Johns Hopkins University Press, 2001).

37. Ibid., 184.

38. I. Alexander, F. MacKay, J. Meteyard, D. O'Hara, and C. Brown, "Liminal Space and Transitions in the Journey," *Conversations* 2 (2004): 18–23.

39. K. Fauteaux, "Self-Reparation in Religious Experience and Creativity," in *Soul on the Couch: Spirituality, Religion, and Morality in Contemporary Psychoanalysis*, ed. C. Spezzano and G. J. Gargiulo (Hillsdale, NJ: Analytic Press, 1997), 11–42.

structures in a return to more archaic states of self-other relating. Some psychoanalysts have been interested in the intrapsychic processes of creativity and religious experience that involve "regression in the service of ego."[40] Regression that is adaptive is similar to Ghent's notion of healthy surrender in fostering more authentic selfhood and integration of unconscious and conscious levels of processing.[41]

Entering the crucible of liminal space and tolerating the accompanying darkness can lead to revelations that are scary and painful. Yet the transforming process can promote a more secure attachment with God and the differentiation of self that allows for greater spiritual and relational intimacy.

The *via negativa*

In the Christian tradition, contemplative spiritual writers have described a transformative process that parallels these social-scientific models of spiritual seeking, questing, liminality, adaptive regression, and differentiation of self. The kataphatic, or affirmative, traditions of Christian spirituality have emphasized God as revealed and imaged. In contrast, the apophatic traditions of contemplative and desert spirituality have emphasized the *via negativa*, or negative way, of unknowing. As LeRon described theologically in chapter 3, apophatic spirituality centers on the mystery and hiddenness of God. This *via negativa* requires a willingness to enter into silence and the purgative void of spiritual emptiness. The apophatic approach helps deconstruct idolatrous images, as no image perfectly captures God completely. This spirituality is aniconic and affirms that God cannot be fully signified by an icon or contained within a sacred place.

The *via negativa* both promotes and necessitates humility and naked trust. Dark nights of the soul reveal secret spiritual pride and demandingness. When spirituality is completely pleasurable, it is easy to appear grateful and content. When God begins to feel absent, prayers do not seem to be answered, and spiritual idealism wears down, a person's spirituality can turn surprisingly dark. Feelings of spiritual entitlement, disappointment, and abandonment can come to the surface. At the same time, a longing for God's loving presence can intensify, and the relational basis of spiritual commitment can be reevaluated. Do I really want to have a relationship with a God who can feel impervious to my struggles?

40. Ibid.; quote is from E. Kris, *Psychoanalytic Exploration in Art* (New York: International Universities Press, 1952), 60.
41. T. W. Hall and S. L. Porter, "Referential Integration: An Emotional Information Processing Perspective on the Process of Integration," *Journal of Psychology and Theology* 32 (2004).

Is it worth the risk of trying to love a God who is so mysterious? Janet Hagberg and Robert Guelich use the apt metaphor of "hitting the wall" for this phase of faith development.[42]

The fourteenth-century English author of *The Cloud of Unknowing* proposes the image of a dark cloud of unknowing that surrounds God to describe the mystery of God's presence. The author recommends learning to be "at home in this darkness." St. John of the Cross also describes the ambiguous presence of God and encourages perseverance in desiring and loving God during the dark nights when spirituality does not feel reinforcing.

Some contemporary theorists have integrated contemplative spiritual formation and psychoanalytic theories of development.[43] James Jones explores the possibility of healthy spirituality and religion "beyond idealization," that is, after spiritual grandiosity has been deconstructed. He suggests that the negative way can be a normal and constructive, if difficult, part of spiritual formation:

> The *via negativa* begins from and returns to the ordinary routines of religious traditions: its beliefs, texts, rituals, and symbols. Gradually, after a time . . . these forms begin to lose their profundity. Not because of secularization or some intellectual critique of religion, for this process occurred to people long before the advent of modernity. Rather because the religious practitioner is coming to the limits of any finite form in the face of the ultimate. Thus the *via negativa* arises out of traditional religious practices taken to their limit. . . . Psychologically the *via negativa* involves the willingness to go beyond these forms—often driven beyond them by the trajectory of experience—into the void.[44]

Religious signifiers can lose their power to arouse and soothe. Psychologists would say this is due to either habituation or developmental growth. Contemplatives such as St. John of the Cross would say it is the intentional work of God to draw us toward deeper intimacy. Whichever explanation you prefer, there do seem to be points in a spiritual journey where the liminal void of transformation is the only pathway to spiritual and relational maturity. Some try to avoid liminal space, or "hitting the wall," by returning to grandiose certainty or spiritual productivity. Others embrace uncertainty but bypass the *via negativa* through chronic wandering and commitment avoidance, preferring the

---

42. J. O. Hagberg and R. A. Guelich, *The Critical Journey: Stages in the Life of Faith* (Salem, WI: Sheffield, 1989), 114–15.

43. R. A. Watson and M. W. Mangis, "The Contribution of the Desert Tradition to a Contemporary Understanding of Community and Spiritual Intersubjectivity," *Journal of Psychology and Christianity* 20 (2001): 309–23.

44. Jones, *Terror and Transformation*, 114.

lack of boundaries and containment offered by "liminoid space."[45] Both approaches entail avoidance of the relational containers necessary for spiritual transformation.

Dark Containers for Spiritual Transformation

I have suggested that spirituality, from a psychological perspective, involves ways of relating to the sacred that include the dialectical processes of arousal and soothing. Spiritual transformation requires the intensification or the heating up of anxious arousal, which re-forms a person's ways of relating to God, self, and others and is followed by spiritual soothing or cooling. The image of fire is used frequently in the Bible and throughout spiritual literature to describe the phenomenological experience of spiritual intensification and arousal. In Psalm 39 David says, "My heart grew hot within me, and as I meditated, the fire burned" (v. 3 NIV). St. John of the Cross speaks of the "Divine fire of love" that acts on the soul "in the same way as fire acts upon a log of wood in order to transform it into itself."[46]

This relational process requires contexts or containers that "hold" the process of spiritual transformation. The metaphor of a crucible captures this image of the need for a container that can hold the intense heat that fires human "jars of clay," which are "hard pressed from every side" for transformative shaping.[47] The relational nature of transforming containers is also central to our models. Chapter 6 mentioned Winnicott's notion of holding environments, the web of relational supports that strongly shape infant development but also impact selfhood throughout the life span. Robert Moore symbolically describes relational containers of transformation as an "archetypal mother" or "a womb."[48] And Kegan describes cultures of embeddedness that provide relational contexts or dwellings for development at each phase of the life span. Containers of transformation are formed by relationships with people and contexts.

It is striking how often containers of spiritual transformation are described as dark places. Comparative-religion scholar Mircea Eliade

45. On liminal versus liminoid space, see R. L. Moore, *The Archetype of Initiation: Sacred Space, Ritual Process, and Personal Transformation* (Philadelphia: Xlibris, 2001), especially pp. 37–56.

46. John of the Cross, *Dark Night of the Soul*, 127–28.

47. 2 Cor. 4:7–9. Also notice the preceding text on spiritual transformation into the image of Christ, which is described as relational intimacy, using the metaphor of "unveiled faces" (2 Cor. 3:12–18).

48. Moore, *Archetype of Initiation*, 64.

described rites of passage and symbols of spiritual transformation from around the world. Eliade suggested that many cultural and religious traditions viewed initiatory rituals and transformations as including a process of death and rebirth. The passage into death has been symbolized in rituals and narratives by means of various dark images, including the forest, the womb, the belly of a sea monster, night, a hut or cabin, a cave, or a tomb. "Passing from the profane world to the sacred world implies the experience of death."[49] Ritualizing sanctified symbols of death and rebirth narrates a transitional process of "starting over," a conversion to a new way of being. It also symbolizes the spiritual transcendence of death in its many faces, including failure, loss, and suffering.

Alan Jones relates the following story from desert writings: "In Scetis, a brother went to see Abba Moses and begged him for a word. And the old man said: go and sit in your cell, and your cell will teach you everything."[50] Jones goes on to explain that sitting in one's cell can feel like entering into a tomb and the death of self. Henri Nouwen described solitude as "the furnace of transformation."[51] This solitude can serve the transforming process of differentiation only if one cooperates with the discipline of containment.

Biblical narratives are replete with images and metaphors of dark containers of spiritual transformation. Table 7 lists several of the biblical containers of spiritual transformation. In these biblical narratives, an individual is spiritually transformed through intensification within a confined space, which typically includes some level of deprivation and a high level of stress. The intense stress of this containment is frequently a source of lament or spiritual protest in biblical literature. The poetic complaint of Lamentations 3:7 gives voice to this feeling by saying, "He has walled me in so I cannot escape; he has weighed me down with chains" (NIV). And Job complains of being "hedged in" by God: "Why is life given to a man whose way is hidden, whom God has hedged in? For sighing comes to me instead of food; my groans pour out like water. What I feared has come upon me; what I dreaded has happened to me. I have no peace, no quietness; I have no rest, but only turmoil" (Job 3:23–26 NIV).

49. Mircea Eliade, *Rites and Symbols of Initiation: The Mysteries of Birth and Rebirth*, trans. Willard R. Trask (Putnam, CT: Spring Publications, 1958), 9.

50. A. Jones, *Soul-Making: The Desert Way of Spirituality* (San Francisco: Harper-Collins, 1985); Y. Nomura, ed. and trans., *Desert Wisdom* (Garden City, NY: Doubleday, 1982), 14.

51. H. J. Nouwen, *The Way of the Heart: Desert Spirituality and Contemporary Ministry* (New York: HarperCollins, 1981), 25.

Table 7. Biblical "Containers" of Spiritual Transformation

Containers	Text
Prison or Dungeon	Gen. 39; Jer. 37; Acts 16
Cave	1 Kings 19
King's Palace	Esther
Cistern or Well	Jer. 38
Cooking Pot	Ezek. 11; 24
Fiery Furnace	Dan. 3
Lions' Den	Dan. 6
Belly of a Whale	Jonah
Desert	Luke 4
Garden of Gethsemane/Mount of Olives	Matt. 26/Luke 22

The boundaries of transformative space contain the trying process of intensification, which includes confrontation with spiritual temptations and existential dilemmas that test personal and spiritual integrity. Esther has to decide if she will embrace the integrity necessary to take a dangerous stand against injustice on behalf of her community. Daniel and his friends are faced with the temptation to sell out on their faith to avoid the fiery heat of persecution. When biblical characters do not sell out despite the anxiety-provoking trials, their spiritual integrity and maturity is strengthened. In the contemporary language of social science, the intensification has increased their differentiation of self.

In some biblical narratives, there is also a social or relational transformation that is generated in the system outside the confined space by a change in the protagonists. Nebuchadnezzar is transformed by his inability to destroy Daniel and his friends. Esther persuades King Xerxes to spare her Jewish people, bringing to ruin the wicked Haman. Jonah ends up preaching to the Ninevites, and all end up spiritually transformed.

Dark containers can produce fruitful, transforming effects when protagonists hold on to their attachment to God and to their integrity or, it is fair to say, the patterns of their relational attachments are transformed and held differently. Psalms 57 and 142 are prayer songs written by David while hiding in a cave, and much of the New Testament consists of prison letters. These biblical examples parallel much of the crucible model of spiritual transformation we have developed from Schnarch's model of therapy. Spiritual darkness can intensify or arouse the fires of anxiety, which test the integrity (or integration) of a person's characterological structures and internal commitments. When integrity falters during containment through selling out, the transformative potential is lost.

Jeremiah confronts the problem of idolatry with the metaphor of "broken cisterns that cannot hold water" (Jer. 2:13 NIV), meaning containers that cannot hold the transformative power of the Spirit and allow it to drain away. When spiritual transformation does happen, it is a process that stretches capacities for trust in ways that can strengthen both the security of attachment and the wholeness of differentiation. St. John of the Cross poetically describes the transformative result in this way:

> In darkness and secure, By the secret ladder,
>   disguised—oh happy chance!
> In darkness and concealment, My house being now at rest.[52]

Conclusion

There are numerous reasons for spiritual darkness. Simplistic or surface spiritualities that lack engagement with traditions of reflective wisdom can promote notions of sin and evil that actually inhibit spiritual formation and transformation. Spiritual darkness can lead to doubt and despair. But contemplative traditions of spirituality and relational models of psychotherapy agree that when warmly contained, darkness can provide liminal transformative space. And yet spiritual darkness is not always transformative. Chapter 9 will explore the contours of mature relational spirituality that has been refined by the fires.

52. John of the Cross, *Dark Night of the Soul*, 149.

9

SPIRITUALITY
AND MATURITY

"With what shall I come before the LORD,
   and bow myself before God on high?
Shall I come before him with burnt offerings,
   with calves a year old?
Will the LORD be pleased with thousands of rams,
   with ten thousands of rivers of oil?
Shall I give my firstborn for my transgression,
   the fruit of my body for the sin of my soul?"
He has told you, O mortal, what is good;
   and what does the LORD require of you
but to do justice, and to love kindness,
   and to walk humbly with your God?

Micah 6:6–8

This entire volume is essentially about the first question in the opening line of Micah 6:6—"With what shall I come before the LORD?" How should

I relate to God and the sacred? Which forms of relational spirituality foster the good life that enhances well-being for self and community? These are questions that lead to the task of defining the contours of spiritual maturity.

Many therapists and spiritual leaders share an interest in understanding and promoting maturity in people they care for. Social scientists study maturity by examining the character strengths and developmental pathways that lead to optimal human functioning. Theologians provide conceptual clarity for understanding moral and spiritual ideals of human nature. As suggested in chapter 7, the construct of virtue invites (or even requires) interdisciplinary work, as virtues represent the mature integration of wholeness and holiness. Across differing traditions, virtues are understood as qualities of character that can promote human flourishing and ultimate purpose in life. If the good life is defined as the integration of happiness and meaning, then capacities for maturity are often necessary to sustain meaning and recover happiness in a life that has turned darkly painful.[1]

Although a large amount of empirical literature is available on spirituality and health, relatively little social-scientific research to date explicitly focuses on spiritual maturity. Perhaps the reason is that as one tries to define the ideals of spiritual maturity, the project becomes even more value-laden and tradition-bound than when one defines spirituality more broadly. Some social scientists interested in spirituality have been trying to define spirituality generically in order to develop measures that can apply across spiritual and religious traditions. This often represents a well-intended goal of conducting research that has wide-ranging validity across diverse populations and with minimal offense to any subgroup. Theologians and philosophers who critique either the inclusiveness or the theoretical thinness of generic measures of spirituality sometimes miss the methodological challenges of conducting empirical research toward theory validation with differing samples.

Still, I am persuaded that searching for a generic spirituality completely devoid of contextual referents is unwise and that these contextual referents become particularly important in the area of spiritual maturity. Cultural and religious traditions provide referents that narrate and shape visions of spiritual maturity and virtue.[2] Some virtuous qualities of maturity seem to emerge within most of the major spiritual and religious traditions (e.g., wisdom, self-control, forgiveness), although even these virtues carry significant differences and nuances

---

1. L. A. King, "The Hard Road to the Good Life: The Happy, Mature Person," *Journal of Humanistic Psychology* 41 (2001): 51–72.

2. Alasdair MacIntyre, *After Virtue*, 2nd ed. (Notre Dame, IN: University of Notre Dame Press, 1984).

across traditions. The most dangerous move in defining spiritual maturity is to deny one's own set of influencing contexts and traditions. This chapter will outline the contours of a relational model of spiritual maturity that is shaped by my identity as a Christian and a psychologist working largely in the context of evangelical Protestant communities. At this point in my journey, I have participated at some level in most of the major "streams" of Christian spirituality as identified by Richard Foster (charismatic, word-centered, holiness, social-justice, contemplative, and incarnational), although my dominant experience has been in versions of the word-centered or evangelical stream.[3] I will start by exploring the ancient text above from Micah because it provides a rich summary of mature relational spirituality. Then I will review theoretical, biblical, and empirical work that is relevant to a relational model of spiritual maturity.

Micah's Revelation of Relational Spirituality

The prophet Micah was likely a village peasant whose spiritual message called for a social transformation and redistribution of power in an unjust system that exploited the poor. Micah 6 paints the dramatic image of a courtroom and covenant lawsuit, with Israel on trial and God voicing a lament: "O my people, what have I done to you?" (v. 3). Verse 4 recounts the exodus, the paradigmatic liberating event in the history of Jewish spirituality. Forgetting the exodus necessitates a spiritual awakening.

The underlying reasons for the fractured relationship between God and Israel are then revealed. In verses 6–7, the prophet unmasks some *mal*forming or immature ways of relating to the sacred before recounting the ways that are *good* and salutary for spiritual formation. Micah's systemic critique is that a spirituality of relational intimacy, one that benefits the whole community, cannot be bought through the posturing of social power to protect socioeconomic enclaves. Bidding for God's favor with outward ritual displays of calves, rams, and even rivers of oil reveals a lack of trust in the Giver of all gifts. Micah is reminding the community that God is beyond their social system, and so the exploitive ways of relating may work within the system but will not work with God.

The content of these ancient spiritual tactics exposed by Micah can sound foreign to my contemporary ears. Personally, I have no livestock

---

3. Richard J. Foster, *Streams of Living Water: Celebrating the Great Traditions of the Christian Faith* (New York: HarperSanFrancisco, 1998).

or oil to offer in an attempt to impress God. But if we view this text as uncovering ways of relating to God, I am challenged to consider external rituals I use in an attempt to earn or secure God's favor. In contemporary psychological terms, compulsive efforts at productive approval seeking offer one spiritually defeating parallel. If only I can offer enough, achieve enough, obtain enough, then maybe God will be impressed with my power. If the calves don't do it, perhaps I'll try the rams, or better yet rivers of oil. The anxiety that fuels spiritual idolatry is not satiated by external rituals, so the temptation is to try more of the same behavior. Verse 7 culminates with one of the extreme measures of relational spirituality, a masochistic gesture of self-atonement by offering a firstborn to pay for sin.

Spiritual formation includes a progressive revelation of our modus operandi in relating to the sacred. These modes of operating can include hiding out, seeking approval, pretending positivity, grandstanding, negative attention seeking, denying feelings, policing wrongdoers, solving mysteries, and many other relational strategies. Such strategies can represent personal strengths that become problematic if they are overutilized in rigid ways that prevent a necessary transformation. Spiritual transformations can accomplish a broadening of ways of relating to the sacred.

The broad message from Micah is that spiritual well-being is a hopeful possibility for Israel but only through a transformation toward mature relational spirituality. Micah 6:8 is an oft-quoted Bible verse. Having remembered the transforming exodus, Israel is now reminded of what is good. The Hebrew word for "good" (*tob*) connotes that which brings happiness, wellness, moral good, benefit, and value. In short, the good involves the virtues that integrate well-being and maturity. The good life is the relational *shalom* that was the telos of the exodus liberation. Micah 6:8 is a summary of mature Jewish spirituality rooted in trust of God and wholehearted living.[4]

Mature relational spirituality includes "doing justice," or, as argued by LeRon in chapter 4, *acting* justly. Justice includes action toward social transformation. Micah is not calling for talking about social justice but acting justly in covenantal agency with God.[5] Ironically, intensified spirituality can work so effectively in promoting well-being that there is some risk of narcissism developing and the needs of others being forgotten. Spirituality can become part of a personal success strategy that ignores social justice. Theologian Nicholas Wolterstorff calls it an

4. M. Bockmuehl, *The Epistle to the Philippians* (Peabody, MA: Hendrickson, 1998).

5. W. Brueggemann, S. Parks, and T. H. Groome, *To Act Justly, Love Tenderly, Walk Humbly: An Agenda for Ministers* (New York: Paulist, 1986).

attempt to "get the blessing without the ethic."[6] Micah makes it clear that spiritual maturity is evidenced by participation in the transformation of social power and economic resources toward *shalom*.

In addition to doing justice, mature relational spirituality "loves kindness." This passage suggests the integration of what contemporary psychologists are calling warmth-based and conscientiousness-based virtues.[7] Doing justice (conscientiousness-based) and lovingkindness (warmth-based) are a unique combination of relational virtues. The word for "kindness" (*khesed*) is sometimes translated "mercy" and can be closely related semantically and empirically with several warmth-based virtues of relational solidarity, including love, compassion, empathy, altruism, mercy, and forgiveness. Justice transforms social power, and kindness transforms social control. The person or community that can spiritually balance and integrate justice and kindness is certainly mature.

Finally, Micah says that the good life of spiritual maturity includes walking humbly with God. This implies a spirituality of relational communion and intimacy with God grounded in a posture of humility. Humility is a realistic way of relating to self that counters the pathological dialectic of pride and shame. The humble person who walks intimately with God feels no need to try narcissistic strategies for impressing God or shame-prone strategies of self-atonement. From a biblical perspective, humility means accepting one's limitations *and* one's responsibilities in light of a covenantal relationship with the God of the universe.

Spiritual Well-Being and Spiritual Maturity

This passage from Micah can invite questions about the relationship between spiritual well-being and maturity. Spiritual well-being and spiritual maturity are distinct endeavors. The same proposal has been offered about psychological well-being and maturity, which are only modestly correlated across numerous studies.[8] This means that if I have an index of a person's present spiritual or psychological well-being, it tells me nothing about their level of spiritual or psychological maturity. Well-being and maturity can be integrated. Indeed, psychologist Jack

6. N. Wolterstorff, "Justice as a Condition of Authentic Liturgy," *Theology Today* 48 (1991): 16.

7. E. L. Worthington Jr., J. W. Berry, and L. Parrott III, "Unforgiveness, Forgiveness, Religion, and Health," in *Faith and Health: Psychological Perspectives*, ed. T. G. Plante and A. C. Sherman (New York: Guilford, 2001).

8. King, "The Hard Road."

Bauer and his colleagues define the good life in a eudaemonic fashion as the integration of happiness and meaning in life.[9] But well-being and maturity are in fact different goals that correlate in somewhat differing ways with other psychosocial constructs.

There is only a small body of empirical research on spiritual maturity. Throughout these chapters, however, I have joined the company of other theorists in suggesting that we relate to God and our sense of the sacred through the same psychological and sociological processes that mediate our relationships with other people.[10] Psychological and spiritual dimensions of human development overlap and interact. This means that the psychological and spiritual dynamics of personhood are mutually influencing, that is, psychological factors can influence spiritual experience and spiritual dynamics can influence psychological experience.

Researchers have defined psychological maturity in differing ways, usually emphasizing some combination of ego development, cognitive complexity, secure attachment, and generativity or concern for others. Psychologist Laura King's approach to psychological maturity as ego development is an influential example.[11] King draws on Jane Loevinger's model of ego development, in which more mature stages include a differentiated and integrated view of the world and sense of self.[12] A person high in ego development would typically have a healthy self-identity, a capacity for goal-directed action, an ability to integrate multiple points of view, and robust capacities for relational connection and moral reflection.

An overview of some of these psychological definitions of maturity appears below, but first we will examine the four potential constellations of spiritual well-being and spiritual maturity. For the purpose of considering differing profiles of well-being and maturity, I will oversimplify the interaction of these constructs by using a hypothetical 2 x 2 matrix based on being above or below the median on spiritual well-being and spiritual maturity.

9. J. J. Bauer, D. P. McAdams, and A. R. Sakaeda, "Interpreting the Good Life: Growth Memories in the Lives of Mature, Happy People," *Journal of Personality and Social Psychology* 88 (2005): 203–17.

10. D. G. Benner, *Care of Souls: Revisioning Christian Nurture and Counsel* (Grand Rapids: Baker, 1998); T. W. Hall and B. F. Brokaw, "The Relationship of Spiritual Maturity to Level of Object Relations Development and God Image," *Pastoral Psychology* 43 (1995): 373–91.

11. King, "The Hard Road."

12. J. Loevinger, *Ego Development: Conceptions and Theories* (San Francisco: Jossey-Bass, 1976).

Low Well-Being/Low Maturity

This profile is not hard to imagine and can be influenced by varieties of spiritual darkness mentioned in chapter 8. These could include William James's category of "sick souls" who are sensitive to suffering internally and in the world. Those low in both spiritual well-being and spiritual maturity could include people going through a developmental process that has not yet resulted in the formation of enhanced spiritual maturity. Some individuals could argue that they have high psychological well-being or maturity that they do not define as spiritual, but general items about existential meaning or purpose included in most measures of spiritual well-being would probably prevent extremely low scores.[13]

For those who are concerned about low levels of spiritual well-being and maturity, one target of assessment would be the person's style of relating to the sacred. Some styles of relational spirituality that do not foster change would be neglect, avoidance, and passivity. Spiritual directors often encourage people to become relationally engaged with their spirituality to work against the entropic forces of passivity. Another relevant issue is that low levels of spiritual well-being could be related to emotional or mental-health problems. Curiously, one study found a secular form of psychotherapy for depression without any explicit spiritual intervention was effective in increasing spiritual well-being (though not as much as spiritually integrated interventions).[14]

High Well-Being/Low Maturity

Some people can feel very good about their spiritual well-being but not necessarily score high in measures of spiritual maturity. This could be due to developmental dynamics, such as a recent convert who is excited or even idealistic about a newfound spirituality that has not been challenged over time. High well-being and low maturity could also be due to strong defense mechanisms that promote grandiosity and the illusory spiritual health described in chapter 7. Healthy-minded spirituality could operate with high levels of denial about darkness in both self and the surrounding world, and this could inhibit the anxious dissonance and

13. David Wulff has criticized this as a limitation of the Spiritual Well-Being Scale. See D. M. Wulff, "A Field in Crisis: Is It Time for the Psychology of Religion to Start Over?" in *One Hundred Years of Psychology of Religion: Issues and Trends in a Century Long Quest*, ed. P. H. M. P. Roelofsma and J. M. T. Corveleyn (Amsterdam: VU University Press, 2003), 11–22.

14. R. S. Hawkins, S. Y. Tan, and A. A. Turk, "Secular versus Christian Inpatient Cognitive-Behavioral Therapy Programs: Impact on Depression and Spiritual Well-Being," *Journal of Psychology and Theology* 27 (1999): 309–18.

self-confrontation that can promote movement toward deeper relational maturity. This is one reason there is a perennial need for prophets, such as Micah, who can penetrate thick defenses and arouse spiritual awakenings about needed transformation.

Low Well-Being/High Maturity

A different scenario is the person who is moving toward greater spiritual maturity but is presently experiencing a reduced level of spiritual well-being or a "dark night of the soul." Chapter 8 considered the varieties of spiritual darkness and suffering that can, in some cases, provide a context for movement toward greater spiritual maturity. Spiritual maturity is not an immediate achievement following an initial conversion or spiritual transformation. The developmental journey of life is complicated by personal and social change, and so the need for multiple episodes of transformation is realistic.

The intensification model of spiritual transformation introduced in chapter 1 draws on David Schnarch's crucible model of transformation in the relational systems of couples. Periodically in life, couples can reach a point of homeostatic stagnation or gridlock that is familiar but not life-giving. At this point, anxiety can intensify to what Schnarch calls "critical mass," which destabilizes the equilibrium of the relational system. LeRon and I likened this spiritually to the intensified arousal of the purgative way. In Schnarch's crucible model of marriage, if one or both partners embrace the process of differentiation, the system could be transformed either toward enhanced connection and intimacy or toward dissolution of the relationship.

Sociologically, one of the common limitations with the contemporary word-centered stream of Christian spirituality that dominates white evangelicalism is the lack of a spiritual-formation paradigm that facilitates spiritual transformations subsequent to an initial transformation at conversion. Too often spiritual transformation is implicitly considered a onetime event accomplished at conversion. Few people would probably endorse this view explicitly, but I have worked with many Christians who are shocked or terrified to discover a need for second-order changes since they were already "saved." Spiritual communities that lack a clear and compelling vision of spiritual maturity and an appreciation for the ongoing process of spiritual formation and transformation that move toward maturity can exacerbate this problem.

This might be one reason that some Christians struggle with intense anxiety about "losing their salvation" when they are grappling with post-conversion spiritual darkness. This anxiety might prove constructive if it promoted further transformation and sanctification, but the connection to ultimate salvation can often make this a situation where ontological (being), epistemological (knowing), and ethical (doing) anxieties converge in ways that are difficult to contain. Questions of eternal security have obvious parallels to attachment, and it is helpful to view this as one among many issues that can be part of the ongoing process of spiritual formation and transformation.

Alternatives to the view of conversion as onetime transformation include charismatic and Pentecostal models of sanctification (e.g., baptism of the Holy Spirit) that suggest subsequent transformations with highly specific criteria. Part 1 has provided a critique of these views theologically, but there are also psychological problems. When such specific behavioral criteria for transformation are required (e.g., speaking in tongues), individual differences in the outward expression of spiritual transformation can be obscured. More important, the emphasis on outward public criteria that can be socially validated might impede the deep internal processing or implicit knowing that facilitates differentiation and transformation. Some people seem to become distracted from internal spiritual experience and vigilant to ways they might conform to the expectations of their social context. This effort to fit in might promote the social well-being gains that can be found in spiritual communities, but this is also the very reason that differentiated movement toward spiritual maturity can involve temporary reductions in well-being. Those who pursue differentiation and transformation usually meet with some level of relational resistance. This awareness of relational resistance can be helpful in making sense out of Jesus' seemingly harsh teaching about the value of letting "the dead bury their own dead" and even hating family members (Matt. 8:22; 10:34–39). The processes of differentiation of self and spiritual transformation can require a loosening of the present form of attachments so that internal working models of relationships can be transformed.

The modest statistical correlation between well-being and maturity does not tell the whole story, but on average, it suggests that reinforcement for progress in spiritual maturity needs to come largely from intrinsic motivation and integrity. Gains in spiritual maturity often fail to provide the immediate gratification or dramatically increased well-being that are more common with initial conversions. For many people, an initial conversion or transformation can powerfully increase a sense of peace and well-being. The slower and harder work of maturity may also yield gains in well-being, but the effects can often be more subtle and come with tolerating greater complexity and ambiguity. This also suggests that, for many people, spiritual maturity may not become a goal until their level of intensification reaches critical mass and the anxiety of a growth cycle becomes preferable to maintaining an unsatisfactory status quo.

High Well-Being/High Maturity

High levels of spiritual well-being and spiritual maturity would represent the spiritual good life. This is an area of integration that has not been well researched empirically. A few saints seem to develop an exceptional integration of spiritual well-being and maturity, but moderate levels of such integration are probably more common. Empirical studies of psychological well-being and maturity are, however, beginning to accumulate.

King has found that mature individuals who score high in ego development tend to demonstrate accommodative coping strategies in dealing with difficult life experiences as opposed to purely assimilative strategies. When stressors or dissonant events hit, it is easiest to try avoiding significant change by assimilating the experience into existing frameworks. This was the approach of Job's friends who tried to make sense out of his tragic suffering within their "just world" theology. Assimilation is an essentially conserving or conservative strategy of coping.[15] Accommodation entails the harder work of transformation because it includes making changes in one's framework in order to develop deeper meaning. King describes accommodation as an active strategy of exploration that can catalyze paradigm shifts and leads to greater resilience for tolerating future stress.[16]

The desire for rediscovering happiness or well-being after a period of struggle might also drive movement toward psychological maturity. On the basis of her research, King suggests the possibility that "the happy, mature person matures to be happy."[17] Jack Bauer and Dan McAdams asked adults to tell stories about transitions in their careers and religion.[18] They found that individuals with high levels of both well-being and maturity tended to articulate "integrative and communal themes," meaning that they tended to be capable of thinking in complex ways about relationships. Relational well-being tends to be strongly associated with overall well-being, yet relationships can also be a significant source

15. K. I. Pargament, *The Psychology of Religion and Coping: Theory, Research, and Practice* (New York: Guilford, 1997), 108–9.

16. King's view of accommodation is quite similar to the model of transformation in James E. Loder, *The Transforming Moment* (Colorado Springs: Helmers & Howard, 1989).

17. King, "The Hard Road," 67.

18. J. J. Bauer and D. P. McAdams, "Personal Growth in Adults' Stories of Life Transitions," *Journal of Personality* 72 (2004): 573–602.

of distress. Maturing in relational understanding can be a wise way of increasing the possibilities of maintaining high levels of well-being.

As mentioned in chapter 7, psychologists Todd Hall and Keith Edwards have developed the Spiritual Assessment Inventory (SAI), a well-validated measure of Christian spiritual maturity based on object relations theory and contemplative spirituality.[19] The SAI includes two subscales that assess spiritual maturity: (a) Awareness (of God's presence) and (b) Realistic Acceptance. Realistic Acceptance is a construct that connotes mature capacities for object constancy and secure attachment. It includes an ability to tolerate ambiguity and disappointment in connection with God while maintaining a commitment to the relationship.

In our research with Bethel Seminary students, Awareness and Realistic Acceptance are both associated with spiritual well-being, although the effect for Awareness is much stronger.[20] This raises the question whether awareness of God's presence might be better understood as primarily related to spiritual well-being rather than spiritual maturity. The contemplative and relational model of Christian spirituality I have been advocating would value the capacity to consistently experience the presence of God. Yet I have also followed many contemplative writers in suggesting that the perceived absence of God can be formative toward spiritual maturity. High levels of self-reported awareness of God's presence can also be part of an illusory spiritual-health profile, suggesting that Awareness is a complicated index of maturity but more clearly related to well-being.

Our research has also found Realistic Acceptance to be more strongly associated with both trait forgiveness and differentiation of self than is Awareness. This further supports the construct validity of Realistic Acceptance as a measure of spiritual maturity. It suggests that those who can tolerate relational disappointments and conflicts with God tend also to have a differentiated, nonreactive, and complex sense of self. In addition, they tend to report high levels of forgivingness toward others. One might expect the stronger correlation would be between Awareness and trait forgiveness in that those who report high levels of awareness of God could also be at risk for idealism about their capacities for forgivingness. The fact that we did not find this indicates that reported capacities for interpersonal forgiveness might be helpful in differentiating those high

19. T. W. Hall and K. J. Edwards, "The Spiritual Assessment Inventory: A Theistic Model and Measure for Assessing Spiritual Development," *Journal for the Scientific Study of Religion* 41 (2002): 341–57.

20. S. J. Sandage, I. Williamson, and M. Helder, "Relational Spirituality, Gratitude, and Forgiveness among Seminarians: A Structural Relations Model" (presentation, annual convention of the American Psychological Association, Honolulu, HI, August 2004).

in spiritual maturity from those who are high in spiritual well-being alone. It is also possible that those extremely high in awareness of God might be at risk for spiritual grandiosity that could promote valuing wrath as much as forgiveness.

Psychological Models of Developmental Maturity

Empirical research on well-being and maturity has tended to focus on forms of psychological functioning, but we have also been considering ways these forms change and mature over time. Human development emerges from the dialectic of form and process, being and becoming.[21] Several psychological theorists have proposed stage models of human development in domains related to spiritual maturity. Table 8 provides a comparison of five models that are relevant to our model of relational spirituality.[22] All of these theorists build upon the constructive-developmental tradition of Jean Piaget and Lawrence Kohlberg, but each theorist also articulates a model that extends this tradition beyond a cognitive focus to include the emotional and relational dynamics of self and other. As mentioned previously, Jane Loevinger's model describes stages of ego development. Robert Kegan's model of orders of consciousness examines the developmental transformation of subject-object configurations. James Fowler's model of stages of faith development describes forms of relating to the ultimate. Heinz Streib's model of the development of religious styles builds upon Fowler but with more attention to relational psychoanalytic and hermeneutical perspectives. Elizabeth Liebert does not construct her own model but offers a helpful synthesis of the models of Loevinger and Kegan. Since my interest here is in adult developmental maturity, I will focus on the middle to upper stages of these models. I will not engage Loevinger's "integrated" and Fowler's "universalizing faith" stages, since their research failed to generate substantive samples at these stages.

21. B. P. Keeney, *Aesthetics of Change* (New York: Guilford, 1983).

22. E. Liebert, *Changing Life Patterns: Adult Development in Spiritual Direction*, expanded ed. (St. Louis: Chalice, 2000); Loevinger, *Ego Development*; Robert Kegan, *The Evolving Self: Problem and Process in Human Development* (Cambridge: Harvard University Press, 1982); *In over Our Heads: The Mental Demands of Modern Life* (Cambridge: Harvard University Press, 1994); J. W. Fowler, *Stages of Faith: The Psychology of Human Development and the Quest for Meaning* (New York: HarperSanFrancisco, 1981); H. Streib, "Faith Development Theory Revisited: The Religious Styles Perspective," *International Journal for the Psychology of Religion* 11 (2001): 143–58; *Hermeneutics of Metaphor, Symbol, and Narrative in Faith Development Theory* (Frankfurt, Germany: Lang, 1991). J. W. Fowler (*Faith Development and Pastoral Care* [Philadelphia: Fortress, 1987]) relates his model to Kegan's.

Table 8. Comparison of Psychological Models of Developmental Maturity

Elizabeth Liebert Life Patterns	Jane Loevinger Ego Development Stages	Robert Kegan Orders of Consciousness	James Fowler Faith Development Stages	Heinz Streib Religious Styles
Impulsive	Impulsive	Impulsive	Intuitive-Protective Faith	Subjective Style
Self-Protective	Self-Protective	Imperial	Mythic-Literal Faith	Instrumental-Reciprocal Style
Conformist	Conformist	Interpersonal	Synthetic-Conventional Faith	Mutual Style
Self-Aware	Self-Aware			
Conscientious	Conscientious	Institutional	Individuative-Reflective Faith	Individuative-Systemic Style
Individualistic	Individualistic			
Interindividual	Autonomous	Interindividual	Conjunctive Faith	Dialogical Style
Integrated	Integrated		Universalizing Faith	

Constructive-developmental stage models were popular in the 1970s and 1980s but also drew substantial criticism for numerous reasons. These reasons included a cognitive bias, the implausibility of invariant stage sequences, and culture-bound philosophical assumptions about ideals of human functioning. In the latter part of the twentieth century, postpositivistic social scientists became increasingly adept at uncovering in developmental models normative assumptions and implicit values about human functioning. There is a difficult tension in social-scientific theories between the descriptive and the prescriptive. Stage models attempt to describe differences in human development but also inevitably prescribe, at least implicitly, better or more mature levels of functioning. As suggested earlier, there is no way to completely avoid this tension if one attempts to describe qualities of developmental maturity. The wisest approach is to admit one's traditions, cultural contexts, and orienting values in doing so.

Cultural and religious conservatives sometimes criticize these same developmental models as too individualistic, particularly with respect to valuing self-reflexivity at the postformal levels. On the one hand, I agree that these models can valorize individualistic values and self-reflexivity in ways that do not fit the cultural contexts of certain populations and regions of the world. Loevinger and Liebert even use the term "individualistic" for one higher-stage transition, and Fowler and Streib use "individuative" in a higher-stage label. At the same time, the social and technological advances of the modernization that affects much of the world increasingly call for adults to develop an adaptive level of self-reflexivity, particularly in the West. These culturally shaped models offer insights about movement toward the developmental capacities to integrate self-reflexivity with a spirituality that also values alterity (otherness). Overcoming widespread ethnic and religious conflict seems to require such development. Using Liebert's categories, I offer here a description of three general developmental patterns—conformist, conscientious, and interindividual.

Conformist Pattern

The strengths of the conformist level of development can include a strong commitment to community, relational loyalty, tradition, and authority figures. At this level, "we are our relationships."[23] In Kegan's model, we are embedded in interpersonal relationships and mutuality. Spiritual formation at this level is "formed with" others in a manner that is reinforced by other-validation.[24] God might be imaged as a friend or partner or deeply revered as the Sovereign One.[25] There is usually a strong concern about relativism and obeying one's tradition at this phase. The growing capacity for taking a social perspective can create concern for others, a concern typically constrained by an equal concern for one's own social standing.

A limitation of conformist levels of development is the lack of self-awareness. Individuals are too embedded in group identification to be able to objectify the self and appreciate individual differences. The advantages of community and group solidarity can also turn into the disadvantages of conformity to unhealthy group dynamics. Spiritually, this can include obliviousness to social injustice and exclusion. Submission to spiritual and religious leaders can lead to valuable and empowering mentoring relationships, or it can result in dependency that inhibits growth and spiritual launching. Conformist spirituality is likely to promote obedience and relational commitment, but greater self-awareness can lead to significant gains in relational intimacy and multicultural competence.

Conscientious Pattern

The conscientious stage, as Loevinger calls it, includes increased self-awareness. People develop the capacity to self-reflect or objectify the self and think about value commitments. External authority is increasingly internalized. This growing psychological-mindedness can be fostered

23. Liebert, *Changing Life Patterns*.
24. Fowler, *Faith Development and Pastoral Care*.
25. Streib, "Faith Development Theory Revisited," 152.

by leaving home, higher education, or other developmental experiences. There is movement beyond the rules focus of the conformist stage toward greater awareness of motivations and relational dynamics. There is a stronger capacity for "conscience" and a richer inner spiritual life. Individual differences often become prominent through a growing awareness of personality traits and other forms of human diversity.

Fowler and Streib describe the spiritual or religious dimensions of these developmental advances as providing the ability to reflect on one's beliefs or practices. In technologically advanced societies, this developmental need for self-reflexivity emerges in ways that shape a confrontation of spirituality and modernity.[26] This confrontation can result in both the achievement of a "reasoned" faith and the loss of some symbolic elements of faith. Kegan points out that these phases of development also lead to an "institutional self" that is epistemologically embedded in a particular system. For example, a college student might learn a particular exegetical method, personality theory, or some other system of knowing the world. This can lead to new insights and discoveries as the person develops confidence about tools for knowing beyond reliance upon authority figures. But it can also result in overconfidence about one's system of knowing and a limited appreciation for other systems. Anxiety can arise when relating to people with differing epistemologies or theoretical systems. The conscientious pattern continues to be haunted by relativism as the self clings to a particular system that is thought to provide freedom.

Interindividual Pattern

The "interindividual" pattern is originally Kegan's term, and he suggests that the mental demands of a multicultural, postmodern social context increasingly call for intersystemic awareness. The interindividual level includes a greater appreciation for paradox and dialectical thinking, which also facilitates tolerating ambiguity. A person becomes more aware of being embedded in multiple interacting social systems and also having multiple dimensions of the self. Loevinger refers to the "autonomous stage" of ego development as the pattern that not only enables a person to act with mature autonomy but allows others greater autonomy. This means that there is less need for anxious control over others and there is a willingness to affirm the freedom and responsibility of others.

Fowler refers to this pattern as "conjunctive faith," and Streib calls it the "dialogical religious style." There is typically an increased capac-

26. A. Giddons, *Modernity and Self-Identity: Self and Society in the Late Modern Age* (Stanford, CA: Stanford University Press, 1991).

ity for the kinds of contextual thinking that can prompt concern about systemic evil and social injustice. Spirituality often involves a greater concern for cultivating diverse relationships and reducing exclusion at the same time that it mitigates against grandiose efforts at rescuing others. There may be a commitment to embracing other streams of one's spiritual tradition, which can parallel the developmental pull toward integrating the self. Spiritual and theological themes that previously seemed contradictory can be held in tension (e.g., self-denial and self-care, the immanence and transcendence of God). There may be periods of spiritual "unknowing" and dis-integration as previous images of God are challenged and uncertainty is tolerated. The interindividual pattern can contribute to enhanced spiritual capacities for wisdom, justice, and intimacy. But this pattern can also lead to dislocation, loneliness, and even marginalization, depending upon a person's social networks.

Biblical Perspectives on Spiritual Maturity

Psychological models of development describe changing forms of spirituality, and biblical authors shape a set of ideals of spiritual maturity. Beyond Micah's rich summary, the Old and New Testaments are replete with texts that describe the contours of spiritual maturity in the Judeo-Christian tradition. Part 1 has provided constructive engagement with biblical and theological perspectives on Christian spirituality. This section will highlight a few central themes that characterize biblical perspectives on maturity. These developmental qualities of spiritual maturity differentiate spiritual "infants" from spiritual adults.[27]

Wholeness

As mentioned in chapter 7, the primary New Testament word for maturity, *teleios*, is often translated "perfect" but in fact means wholeness or completeness rather than the possible connotation of moral perfection.[28] Aristotle used *teleios* in a eudaemonic fashion to mean actualizing one's potential or fulfilling one's purpose. In New Testament usage, maturity implies the wholeness of an undivided heart. The apostle Paul describes the goal of his ministry as that of presenting everyone whole and complete (mature) in Christ.[29] Consistent with Micah 6, spiritual maturity in the New Testament includes embodied virtue and undivided integrity.

27. Eph. 4:14 NIV; Heb. 5:13. On giving up "childish" ways, see 1 Cor. 13:11.
28. G. Delling, "τέλειος," in *Theological Dictionary of the New Testament*, ed. G. Friedrich, trans. and ed. G. W. Bromley, 10 vols. (Grand Rapids: Eerdmans, 1964–1976), 8:67–87.
29. Col. 1:28; see also Eph. 4:13–14.

The biblical meaning of mature wholeness is not intended to encourage compulsive perfectionism or the presumption of grandiose achievement but is a goal to motivate the journey of spiritual formation.[30]

Endurance

Biblical perspectives on spiritual maturity also affirm the need for endurance through suffering. James 1:2–8 parallels Jewish wisdom teachings by suggesting that maturity and completeness result from perseverance or endurance during trials.[31] Paul makes the similar point that "suffering produces endurance, and endurance produces character, and character produces hope" (Rom. 5:3–4). In Luke's version of the parable of the sower, the seeds that fell on thorns do not mature as they choke from worries and pleasures, whereas the seeds that fell on good soil "bear fruit with patient endurance" (Luke 8:14–15). The virtue of endurance (*hypomonē*) that leads to maturity includes "the growing capacity to experience disappointment and challenge with grace, courage, and resolve."[32] This biblical emphasis on endurance is not unlike the psychoanalytic notion of working through painful emotional conflicts toward character growth. James 4:7–10 goes on to describe several purgative spiritual disciplines (submission, resisting the devil, confession, and mourning) that promote transformation into mature humility.

James also associates spiritual maturity with wisdom, which is a gift from God to those who ask (James 1:5). James contrasts wisdom with the unwise, immature person who relates to God through doubt and "is like a wave of the sea, driven and tossed by the wind," and is "double-minded and unstable in every way" (1:6–7). James could be interpreted as suggesting that spiritual doubt is always unproductive and immature. Yet the particular type of doubt James is warning against is doubt about whether one really wants to receive God's gifts and move toward maturity. Therapists call this ambivalence. James is saying it is foolish to ask God for wisdom if one is ambivalent about growing in wisdom. Jesus dealt with this dynamic while relating to the man with a disability at the pool of Bethesda, when he asked him the seemingly insensitive question "Do you want to get well?" (John 5:6 NIV). His question cut right to any potential ambivalence.

30. See Bockmuehl, *Epistle to the Philippians*, on Phil. 3:15.
31. P. J. Hartin, "Call to Be Perfect through Suffering (James 1,2–4): The Concept of Perfection in the Epistle of James and the Sermon on the Mount," *Biblica* 77 (1996): 477–92.
32. W. F. Brosend II, *James and Jude* (Cambridge: Cambridge University Press, 2004), 38.

James's view of spiritual maturity through endurance and wisdom resonates with what contemporary psychologists of religion call a secure attachment with God. Those with a secure attachment with God generally trust God's benevolent intentions and feel confident of God's consistent presence and availability. A secure attachment with God is associated with the types of spiritual commitment and resilient coping with stress that fit with the biblical definition of endurance. In contrast, those with an insecure attachment with God tend to doubt God's love or consistency or both.

Chapter 8 mentioned our research findings that spiritual instability tends to be associated with lower levels of spiritual and emotional well-being and maturity whereas spiritual disappointment is less spiritually destructive and typically characterized by more modest or neutral association with these measures.[33] Extreme forms of spiritual instability characterize people with traits of borderline personality disorder (BPD), a personality style that involves significant problems with emotional regulation. Individuals who meet diagnostic criteria for BPD or have traits of this disorder often come from invalidating relational environments where abuse and scapegoating are common. These environments can contribute to mistrustful internal working models of relationships and ambivalence about both personal success and relational intimacy. Whatever relational connection individuals with a BPD profile received growing up usually came with suffering as a victim of scapegoating or abuse. Independence or success was often discouraged or punished in these relational environments, creating severe doubt about the value of positive growth and the value of oneself. James can be read as offering ancient wisdom that penetrates the internal dilemma of spiritual instability and of those with borderline traits—why ask God for wisdom (i.e., growth or well-being) if my internal relational model says that authority figures punish me for growth? These doubts work against tolerating the challenges that build spiritual endurance and inhibit the formation of wisdom and maturity. In contrast, authentic engagement with God about spiritual disappointments and doubts can be part of developing spiritual endurance and maturity.

Secure Love and Intimacy with God

Another central feature of spiritual maturity in the Bible is secure love and intimacy. LeRon considered the theological significance of spiritual intimacy in chapter 3. This includes the mature integration of

---

33. S. J. Sandage, I. Williamson, and M. Helder, "Relational Spirituality"; Hall and Edwards, "The Spiritual Assessment Inventory."

the two great commandments of loving God and loving others, with love holding together all the Christian virtues.[34] John makes love central to Christian identity and spirituality, saying, "Whoever does not love does not know God, because God is love" (1 John 4:8 NIV), and affirming that loving, sacrificial action demonstrates spiritual integrity (1 John 3:16–20). In his Gospel, John records Jesus' prayer that all who believe the Gospel may know the same love he experienced from the Father, that such intimate love "may be in them" (John 17:26). Paul also provides a future image of complete spiritual intimacy and union with the promise of seeing God face-to-face, knowing fully, and being fully known (1 Cor. 13:10–12). Union with God is the pinnacle of mature spiritual intimacy in contemplative and mystical traditions.

Wisdom

Biblical perspectives on spiritual maturity also emphasize wisdom. Chapter 7 described the integration of practical and reflective wisdom. Practical wisdom includes embodied healthy practices and moral boundaries that promote well-being and character development. Reflective wisdom is a task that is unique to adult development and includes finding meaning and relating to God in the midst of suffering and loss. Paul connects growing in love with the wisdom of determining "what is best" (Phil. 1:10). This phrase is similar to a wisdom-related description of the mature who have "trained themselves to distinguish good from evil (Heb. 5:14 NIV)."[35] The mature are contrasted with dependent infants who still need "milk" rather than "solid food" (Heb. 5:12–13).

New Testament scholar Robert Jewett interprets maturity (expressed in the word *teleios*) as a primary theme of the book of Hebrews and argues that the author is countering gnostic teaching on spiritual perfection and the manipulation of spiritual powers.[36] Jewett suggests that Hebrews describes a spirituality of pilgrimage that acknowledges the alien horizon of an uncertain world while also offering a vision of a relational spirituality grounded in dialogue with God as covenant partner. Christians can "take hold of the hope" of this relational spirituality with God as "an anchor for the soul, firm and secure" (Heb. 6:18–19 NIV). The book of Hebrews suggests that wisdom and mature spirituality come from a secure relational attachment with God rather than through cultic practices that attempt to manipulate angelic and demonic powers.

34. G. Delling, "τέλειος."
35. Bockmuehl, *Epistle to the Philippians*, 67.
36. R. Jewett, *Letter to Pilgrims: A Commentary on the Epistle to the Hebrews* (New York: Pilgrim, 1981).

Fruitfulness

A final theme of biblical spiritual maturity can be summarized as fruitfulness. The New Testament describes each member of the body of Christ as spiritually gifted with something to contribute. Ephesians 4:14–16 is one of many biblical texts suggesting that growing in spiritual maturity entails every part of the body contributing work toward building the community. Contemporary psychologists in the developmental tradition of Erik Erikson call this generativity, the commitment to contribute to the well-being of others, particularly the next generation. James says that religion "pure and undefiled" includes the generosity of caring for orphans and widows (James 1:27). Jesus says to "go and bear fruit—fruit that will last" (John 15:16 NIV), but even branches that are fruitful get the pruning of purgation in order to increase fruitfulness (John 15:2). Hebrews 5:12–14 relates spiritual maturity to the capacity for teaching others instead of continuing to need teaching on the "basic elements" of faith. Stewarding one's gifts and resources toward a generative contribution requires the wisdom and compassion of maturity.

The Psychology of Spiritual Maturity and Virtue

Table 9 presents a heuristic summary of core psychological constructs that are consistent with adult spiritual maturity and particularly relevant to spiritual leadership. These psychological constructs have been organized on the basis of our model of relational spirituality and the primary dimensions of relating to self, God, and others, although these dimensions are interactive. The table also lists the virtues that correspond to these psychological constructs on the basis of empirical or theoretical literature. These psychological constructs and related virtues have been discussed in chapters 6–8. As mentioned earlier, empirical research on Christian spiritual maturity is, ironically, in its infancy. The constructs and virtues summarized in this table offer a set of capacities for spiritual maturity that could be assessed in both applied and research settings, although empirical research is quite limited in some areas (e.g., humility). Development of better, theoretically-grounded measures are needed in this area.

Table 9. Psychological Dimensions of Spiritual Maturity and Related Virtues

Relational Dimensions	Psychological Constructs	Related Virtues
Relating to Self	Differentiation of Self	Integrity
	Secure Attachment	Hope
	Narrative Identity	Wisdom

Relational Dimensions	Psychological Constructs	Related Virtues
Relating to God	Intrinsic Religiosity/Spirituality	Commitment
	Spiritual Openness	Humility
	Realistic Acceptance	Gratitude
	Embodied Spiritual Practices	Self-Control
Relating to Others	Generativity	Generosity
	Empathy	Compassion
	Multicultural Competence	Justice
	Healthy Sexuality and Intimacy	Courage

Dialectical Wisdom and Relational Spirituality

Mature adult development requires the ability to integrate differing dimensions of personhood and life experience. Virtue pairings such as hope and humility or forgiveness and justice can seem contradictory. Several theorists have promoted dialectical or postformal models of human development that account for the systemic balancing of various oppositional poles of human experience.[37] LeRon emphasized dialectical identity, agency, and presence in his chapters. Chapter 6 introduced some dialectical themes or constructs of human development, especially attachment and differentiation. David Bakan described the human dialectic of agency and communion, two themes emphasized throughout this book.[38] This section will offer an overview of how a dialectical perspective can promote mature wisdom for understanding the dynamics of spiritual transformation. I will then extend my earlier consideration of dialectical constructs that are central to our model relational spirituality and transformation.

Dialectical Wisdom

Dialectical models emphasize systemic relatedness and wholeness and attempt to understand the complexity of a system in light of the whole.[39] Such perspectives are particularly helpful for attending to the relationship between form and process, structure and change.[40] Dialectical models

37. M. Basseches, *Dialectical Thinking and Adult Development* (Norwood, NJ: Ablex, 1984); Kegan, *Evolving Self*; Loder, *The Transforming Moment*.
38. D. Bakan, *The Duality of Human Existence: Isolation and Communion in Western Man* (Boston: Beacon, 1966).
39. M. M. Linehan, *Cognitive-Behavioral Treatment of Borderline Personality Disorder* (New York: Guilford, 1993).
40. J. W. Maddock and N. R. Larson, *Incestuous Families: An Ecological Approach to Understanding and Treatment* (New York: W. W. Norton, 1995). Also see Keeney, *Aesthetics of Change*.

suggest that relationships constitute opposing tensions or conflicts and that these tensions actually help generate change. This emphasis on tension and conflict can complement eudaemonic or teleological models of becoming by serving to identify transformative sources of intensification (or heat) as well as sources of resistance to change. Dialectical theories also suggest that wisdom entails transcending polarities and appreciating paradoxical truths. For example, Jesus taught that the one who wanted to be spiritually great should become a servant (Matt. 20:26) and that trying to save one's life would result in losing it (Matt. 10:39).

Transformations emerge relationally out of systemic rebalancing that re-forms a new system. Spiritual transformations often represent a "return from exile" for previously excluded parts of a person or larger system that are once again included and embraced. These can be marginalized parts of a person's self that have been exiled, or they can be marginalized members of society. This is one reason that evangelical Christian revival movements have such a prominent role in the history of spiritual transformation.[41] A strength of the evangelical tradition, along with some other movements of spiritual transformation and revitalization, has been the history of generating episodes of *communitas* that temporarily suspend structured social hierarchies in favor of inclusively reintegrating marginalized groups.[42]

Dialectical perspectives invite looking at the function of relational tensions between subsystems within a person or larger relational system (e.g., marriage, family, community, nation). Dysfunctional patterns are important but must be viewed in dialectical relation to the seeming functionality of these patterns. The cognitive and emotional capacity to view problems dialectically can often generate change by opening new frames of understanding.

Groups and individuals characterized by extreme fundamentalistic styles of cognition can be described as engaging in the psychological defense of splitting, which reduces complexity by viewing either the self or the other as completely bad.[43] This can promote group solidarity through tight boundary maintenance and the perception of within-group homogeneity. Fundamentalistic systems usually rely upon relatively strong or rigid mechanisms of relational power and control in an effort to conserve meanings and prevent social transformation within the group.

41. B. C. Lane, *Landscapes of the Sacred: Geography and Narrative in American Spirituality*, expanded ed. (Baltimore: Johns Hopkins University Press, 2001).

42. V. W. Turner, *The Ritual Process: Structure and Anti-structure* (Ithaca, NY: Cornell University Press, 1969); also see Anthony Wallace's classic work on revitalization movements, A. F. C. Wallace, *Culture and Personality* (New York: Random House, 1970).

43. R. L. Moore, *Facing the Dragon: Overcoming Personal and Spiritual Grandiosity*, ed. Max J. Havlick Jr. (Wilmette, IL: Chiron, 2003).

This allows fundamentalistic systems to maintain a balance that those outside the system have trouble understanding.[44] Instead of denigrating fundamentalism in a symmetrical relationship of hostility, dialectical perspectives could invite nonfundamentalists to a sociological awareness of the larger systemic tensions between various forms of fundamentalism and the forces of modern secularization. The most vital goal globally for Christians in the coming decades might be the cultivation of forms of relational spirituality that can resist polarization and transform the hostile and paranoid process of mutual projection.

Dialectical Constructs

Table 10 presents two sets of dialectical constructs that serve to heuristically illuminate the tensions and processes of relational spirituality and transformation. These diverse constructs are drawn from a range of disciplines. They have been organized into two general sets on the basis of Robert Wuthnow's categories of "spiritual dwelling" and "spiritual seeking." Relational spirituality is about the risk of trust (dwelling) and the quest for wholeness (seeking). Admittedly, there is a risk of expansive oversimplification in even using this table as a heuristic. Still, there is a surprising level of theoretical, and in some cases empirical, correlation within the sets across a wide range of disciplinary matrices.

Table 10. Dialectical Constructs of Relational Spirituality

Spiritual Dwelling	Spiritual Seeking
Attachment	Differentiation
Socioemotional Well-Being	Social-Cognitive Maturity
Liturgy	Justice
Priestly	Prophetic
Intrinsic Religiosity	Quest Religiosity
Practical Wisdom	Reflective Wisdom
Hermeneutical Confidence	Hermeneutical Humility
Tenderness	Passion
Love	Integrity

Spiritual dwelling can offer a sense of tradition, rootedness, community, belongingness, and social identity. In the best cases, this provides depth, location, and relational support to a person's spirituality. In the

44. R. W. Hood Jr., P. C. Hill, and W. P. Williamson, *The Psychology of Religious Fundamentalism* (New York: Guilford, 2005).

worst cases, the systems that offer opportunities for spiritual dwelling are oppressively enmeshing or neglectfully disengaged.

Spiritual seeking is an orientation toward journey, questing, pilgrimage, and finding the sacred anywhere. Whereas communities of dwelling hold and incubate spiritual transformation, seeking is the liminal movement within the process of transformation. Thus, episodes of seeking are necessary for transformation, but seeking can also result in lonely isolation and liminoid wandering.

The dynamics of spiritual dwelling parallel the developmental issues of attachment. Secure attachment includes trust in a safe haven of connection. The secure-base function of attachment promotes exploration. In the language of Christian spirituality, a secure attachment to a spiritual community for dwelling can facilitate worship and mission, communion and agency.

The dynamics of spiritual seeking parallel the developmental issues of differentiation. Differentiation requires a willingness to go into solitude to face loneliness and anxiety in the interest of one's integrity.[45] High levels of differentiation include an ability to connect intimately with others but without the seeker being dependent on other-validation. Optimal spiritual maturity is characterized by a secure style of spiritual and interpersonal attachment and high levels of differentiation of self.

Psychological research on human development suggests that well-being and maturity map onto attachment and differentiation somewhat differently. Secure relational attachment tends to correlate strongly with measures of socioemotional well-being, whereas traits of ego development and differentiation correlate strongly with sociocognitive maturity.[46] Although this body of work has not been applied directly to spiritual variables, it is suggestive of the hypothesis that, comparatively speaking, spiritual dwelling can be more conducive to well-being, and spiritual seeking more generative of maturity. This would further support the dialectical value of both spiritual orientations.

Theologian Nicholas Wolterstorff suggests the Christian spiritual dialectic of liturgy and justice. Liturgy is clearly related to a spirituality of dwelling, attachment, and worship. I would broaden the category of "liturgy" to include spiritual practices of prayer and meditation that facilitate intimacy and union with God. It is noteworthy that one study found that petitionary prayer was associated with an anxious-ambivalent attachment style whereas a secure attachment style was associated with

45. David M. Schnarch, *Constructing the Sexual Crucible: An Integration of Sexual and Marital Therapy* (New York: W. W. Norton, 1991); *Passionate Marriage: Keeping Love and Intimacy Alive in Committed Relationships* (New York: Henry Holt, 1997).

46. Bauer, McAdams, and Sakaeda, "Interpreting the Good Life."

meditative and conversational prayer.[47] This data provides support for LeRon's theological proposals about transforming prayer in chapter 3.

The archetypal spiritual dweller is the liturgical priest who narrates healing and reconciliation.[48] But priestly systems can become stagnant or even corrupt, and liturgies can need transformation. Priestly types who avoid differentiation may end up defending the unjust status quo in a system.

Commenting on Micah 6, Wolterstorff heralds the spiritual theme of justice as a balance to liturgy. I would also broaden the category of "justice" to include multicultural competence. Multicultural competence is consistent with valuing social justice but also includes well-developed capacities to relate to diverse *others*.

The archetypal spiritual seeker is the prophet of justice who courageously unmasks façades and offers a generative vision of a new, transformed community. Prophetic types who perpetually avoid healthy attachment to a community or tradition can become withdrawn critics who lob in complaints from a safe emotional distance. Or they can be grandiose rescuers that lack self- and cultural awareness. Optimal spiritual maturity, however, is fostered by practices of liturgy, ritual, or healing and by justice, vision, and transformation. The spiritually mature can relate to God in intimacy and to others with cultural sensitivity.

In the psychology of religion, the construct of intrinsic religiosity resonates with spiritual dwelling, whereas quest religiosity resonates with spiritual seeking. Intrinsic religiosity represents an internalized relational commitment and often generates the health-conducive connections that are associated with social-emotional well-being. Mature spiritual commitment does not include defensive avoidance of doubt or of spiritual diversity. Quest religiosity represents openness to exploring change along with authenticity about doubt. The complexity of questing is often quite stressful but can also promote social-cognitive maturity. Mature questing is driven by active, genuine spiritual seeking rather than chronic commitment avoidance. Optimal spiritual maturity includes intrinsic motivation and commitment together with a willingness to quest toward authenticity, diverse community, and new understandings of the sacred.

The ancient and contemporary dialectic of practical and reflective wisdom can be suggestive of spiritual maturity. Practical wisdom parallels

47. K. R. Byrd and A. Boe, "The Correspondence Between Attachment Dimensions and Prayer in College Students," *International Journal for the Psychology of Religion* 11 (2001): 9–24.

48. On the contrast of priestly and prophetic modes of religiosity, see D. G. Bromley, "Remembering the Future: A Sociological Narrative of Crisis Episodes, Collective Action, Culture Workers, and Countermovements," *Sociology of Religion* 58 (1997): 105–40.

spiritual dwelling with an emphasis on spiritual discipline and relational commitment, two dimensions that generally promote well-being. Reflective wisdom parallels spiritual seeking with an emphasis on authentically facing suffering and doubt, which can cultivate deeper meaning. Reflective wisdom promotes questing beyond the health-promoting benefits of practical wisdom by allowing or even promoting spiritual struggle and lament. Yet reflective wisdom culminates in the capacity for gratitude and spiritual "reorientation," which Walter Brueggemann locates in certain psalms that resymbolize and redescribe life following an episode of disorientation.[49] Relational psychoanalysts describe maturity as including an integration of object relations, that is, an integration of "good" and "bad" representations of both self and other, which reduces defensive splitting. A spiritually reflective wisdom moves toward this intrapsychic goal with a growing capacity to accept oneself, others, and God in spite of disappointments. At the same time, practical wisdom continues to provide a useful dimension of spiritual maturity by encouraging embodied disciplines of spiritual practice, self-soothing, and the development of virtue.

Spiritual maturity also entails transformation in ways of knowing. From a psychological perspective, spiritual maturity builds upon the dialectic of hermeneutical confidence and hermeneutical humility.[50] Hermeneutical confidence parallels the theme of spiritual dwelling through attachment and commitment to a communal tradition. Spiritual maturity should include self-awareness about one's spiritual identity, interpretive tradition, and social location. This is different from a more immature spiritual grandiosity that fails to recognize that one has a perspective or interpretive vantage point. This requires hermeneutical humility, which thematically parallels spiritual seeking and differentiation. Humility is a virtue that promotes a willingness to be self-critical, consider the perspectives of others, and remain open to new discoveries.

In terms of relational intimacy and sexuality, spiritual maturity could serve to integrate capacities for both tenderness and passion. Psychologists Stephen Goldbart and David Wallin develop this dialectic in connection to intimate love:

> Passion is kin to desire, tenderness to affection. In passion we feel transported, in tenderness we are present. When we love with tenderness we are more aware of our partner; when we love with passion we are at least as

49. W. Brueggemann, *The Psalms and the Life of Faith*, ed. Patrick D. Miller (Minneapolis: Fortress, 1995).

50. M. W. Mangis, "An Alien Horizon: The Psychoanalytic Contribution to a Christian Hermeneutic of Humility and Confidence," *Christian Scholar's Review* 28 (1999): 411–31.

aware of ourselves. The culmination of passion is ecstasy and/or orgasm, while tenderness may evoke tears, then security or contentment.[51]

The description of tenderness as affection, security, and commitment resonates with dwelling. The emphasis on passion as transport, self-awareness, and ecstasy parallels spiritual seeking. Schnarch insightfully points out that one of the psychological and spiritual advantages of monogamy for developing sexual potential is that a relational attachment with one person over time can provide a crucible-like container of passionate transformation.[52] This idea can also apply to relational spirituality, as the Christian tradition is interpreted by most evangelicals as calling for the boundaries of spiritual monogamy. The spiritual philandering of jumping from god to god can be a means of avoiding the intensification necessary for transformation and the integration of passion and tenderness.[53]

Perhaps these two dialectical sets of constructs can be summarized as pointing toward the virtues of love and integrity. Love is the quintessential warmth-based virtue, and integrity is arguably the core of conscientiousness-based virtues. Mature expressions of spiritual dwelling are centered in love for God, love for self, and love for neighbor. Love provides a pivotal axis for continued growth toward greater maturity, since few things are harder in life than mature love. The quest toward greater spiritual intimacy can challenge my anxiety about relational closeness, about loving and being loved. Mature expressions of spiritual seeking are also grounded in the virtue of integrity, which includes honesty about the difference between genuine questions and commitment avoidance. Integrity requires openness to prophetic truth and commitment to social justice. Integrity also means actively admitting to myself when I am not really committed to God or spiritual growth without hiding behind shame. The relational core of spiritual maturity includes being "quick to listen, slow to speak" (James 1:19) but then "speaking the truth in love" (Eph. 4:15).

The Spiritual Maturity of Differentiated Attachment

Throughout chapters 6–8 I have argued for a relational model of spirituality that views attachment and differentiation, dwelling and seeking,

51. S. Goldbart and D. Wallin, *Mapping the Terrain of the Heart: Passion, Tenderness, and the Capacity to Love* (Northvale, NJ: Jason Aronson, 1996), xvi.

52. Schnarch, *Passionate Marriage*, 311–13.

53. However, grounded openness and humility toward other spiritual traditions is different than spiritual philandering.

as forming a dialectical relation that can be generative for the process of formation and transformation. Spirituality involves arousing and soothing, and the virtues of love and integrity provide characterological support for the internal and relational crucible of transformation. Most spiritual traditions agree that attachments must be transformed to move toward spiritual maturity. Spiritual maturity in the Christian tradition can be described as a relational spirituality of *differentiated attachment*. This entails a solid sense of dialectical identity and intentionality about intimate connection with God and sacredness in life. Yet differentiated attachment also promotes humble ways of relating to others without the excessive stranger anxiety that prompts rigid power and control. Theories of attachment and differentiation both suggest that maturity includes a willingness to explore, resilience in the midst of suffering, and a healthy sense of boundaries. These are all qualities of relational spiritual maturity.

I conclude with brief consideration of a narrative episode of spiritual transformation in the life of one of the most transformative spiritual leaders of the last century—Martin Luther King Jr. I can think of no other Christian leader in the past hundred years who was more generative of social transformation and the relational spirituality described in Micah 6:8. In his excellent theological and comparative biography of Malcolm X and Martin Luther King Jr., James Cone describes King's transformative "vision in the kitchen."[54] It came shortly after one of the boycotts, during which King experienced many death threats each day. One evening he received another threat, and this time it really got to him as he thought about his wife and baby daughter. King recounted that he went into the kitchen, "thinking coffee would give me a little relief." Cone explains that in the midst of this agonizing dark night, King "searched for a place where he could stand."[55] King then later explained,

> Rationality left me . . . something said to me, you can't call on daddy now; he's in Atlanta, a hundred seventy-five miles away. . . . You've got to call on that something, on that person that your daddy used to tell you about, that power that can make a way out of no way. And I discovered then that religion had to become real to me and I had to know God for myself. And I bowed down over that cup of coffee. I never will forget it. Oh yes, I prayed a prayer. And I prayed out loud that night. I said, "Lord, I'm down here trying to do what's right. I think I'm right. I think the cause that we represent is right. But Lord, I must confess that I'm faltering, I'm losing my courage, and I can't let the people see me like this because if they see

54. James H. Cone, *Martin and Malcolm and America: A Dream or a Nightmare* (Maryknoll, NY: Orbis, 1991), 124–25.
55. Ibid., 124.

me weak and losing courage they will begin to get weak. . . . Almost out of nowhere I heard a voice, "Martin Luther, stand up for righteousness. Stand up for justice. Stand up for truth. And lo, I will be with you, even until the end of the world."[56]

After this experience, King said he was "ready to face anything." King's experience involved the intensification of threat and arousal, partly due to an existential awareness of his relational commitments. He found himself located in liminal space and in a crucible symbolized by the "container" of the kitchen. He allowed a spiritual self-confrontation that moved toward differentiation of self and a deeper commitment to an internalized spirituality. This seemed to provide a source of self-soothing of anxiety along with an intensified feeling of attachment with God. He became centered—his feet beneath him, so to speak—as he was ready to "stand up for justice" and "face anything." This is a profound description of differentiated attachment formed and transformed in the spiritual and relational crucible of one of the pivotal events in the history of the United States.

Conclusion

A relational model of Christian spiritual maturity can serve to integrate doing justice, lovingkindness, and walking humbly with God. This requires a differentiated form of spiritual attachment to God, self, and others. Differentiated attachment can promote intimacy with God and others and at the same time represent a relational orientation of justice. Part 3 will consider some clinical case studies that further illustrate the dynamics of our relational model of spiritual transformation.

---

56. Quoted ibid., 124–25. Also see Martin Luther King Jr., *Strength to Love* (Philadelphia: Fortress, 1981), 113–14.

Modeling Spiritual Transformation

F. LeRon Shults
and Steven J. Sandage

10

TRANSFORMING
SPIRITUALITY
IN CONTEXT

Part 3 will engage three clinical case studies that provide examples of spiritual transformation. This will allow us to explore the dynamics of spirituality and transformation in some differing social and relational contexts. These clinical case examples are based on clients who worked with Steve in therapy; names and identifying details have been changed to protect anonymity. Significant change is common in therapy, but client experiences of spiritual transformation during therapy are probably less common.[1] These cases offer stories from the "lived world" in which spiritual transformation seemed to occur. Although all three cases

---

1. To date, empirical research focused explicitly on spiritual transformation in psychotherapy is a lacuna of the field. For empirical evidence that mental health treatment can impact spirituality see R. S. Hawkins, S-Y. Tan, and A. A. Turk, "Secular Versus Christian Inpatient Cognitive-Behavioral Therapy Programs: Impact on Depression and Spiritual Well-Being," *Journal of Psychology and Theology* 27 (1999): 309–18; T. C. Tisdale et al., "Impact of Treatment on God Image and Personal Adjustment, and Correlations of God

concern people seeking change within the context of therapy, the cases also illustrate a variety of challenges and possibilities that occur in the process of transformation.

We suggest that you pay close attention to your personal reactions as you read the stories. With whom do you sympathize? With whom do you not sympathize? What seems surprising or implausible to you? Does anything remind you of your own spiritual journey? What might you interpret differently? In this way, the case stories may also contribute to your own hermeneutical self-awareness and facilitate new ways of interpreting spiritual experience.

Juan: Transforming Spirituality in Prison

Juan (age forty-three) was a Latino inmate in a federal prison, serving a fifteen-year mandatory minimum sentence for cocaine distribution. In his second year in prison, he was diagnosed as HIV-positive. Juan was now in his seventh year in prison, and his T-cell count had been falling, bringing him close to meeting criteria for AIDS. He pursued individual psychotherapy to complement his spiritual and health practices and to have a private place to process his anxiety and life concerns.

Juan's parents had immigrated to the United States from Mexico when he was seven. His family eventually settled in Houston. He had grown up Catholic and recounted positive memories of his grandmother praying with him and his siblings. He said she had great reverence for God, the Catholic Church, and priests and nuns. "God was very holy, very important to her," Juan explained.

Juan's urban neighborhood as he was growing up was tough—short on jobs and educational opportunities and teeming with drugs and violent crime. He developed an early interest in science and hoped to become an electrician. At age nineteen, he enrolled in a technical school to become an electrician and worked as a mechanic to help pay for tuition. But his father died of a sudden heart attack that year, and he dropped out to help support his mother and younger siblings. Juan came to realize that something in him also died at that point. He lost his hope for an honest life and trade when they buried his father. He described his dad as a tough, stoic man who had risked it all to lead his family toward a better life in America. The loss of his father left a huge gap in Juan's life as he searched for a way to make life work.

Image to Personal Adjustment and Object Relations Development," *Journal of Psychology and Theology* 25 (1997): 227–39.

He found men in his neighborhood who provided some of the only available mentoring and economic opportunity—unfortunately, in the drug trade. Juan was arrested a couple of times in his twenties, and he said he made brief attempts to "do the right things." But the money was seductive and other jobs were hard to get as an "ex-con." He eventually joined a very tight-knit, highly structured gang that strongly valued loyalty, "a bit like a drug-dealing military," Juan explained. The lifestyle of selling drugs, however, led to the risky behaviors that exposed him to HIV.

Juan said that his federal arrest and long sentence were devastating but nothing compared with the day the prison doctor told him he was HIV-positive. At first he became depressed. Then he started remembering his grandmother praying and the stories of miracles he heard as a child. With the help of medical professionals, he also came to realize he could take steps to care for his health. If he did not care for his body and follow the medical regimens, which included up to twenty pills a day, he might die much sooner. And so he started praying that God would help him be strong and wise. This was totally new for Juan, as he had not been comfortable asking God for anything. And it was hard for him to feel worthy of God's help as he sat in prison. But one day he felt an inner warmth as he prayed and remembered his grandmother saying, "God loves all his children." That day was a turning point in Juan, making his spirituality part of his self-care. He began praying a simple Jesus prayer while exercising, while working, while studying, while taking his medications, while attending religious services—pretty much throughout his days in prison.

But Juan experienced increased stress that led to his seeking psychotherapy. He had developed several red, precancerous blotches on his skin. It was well known to many inmates that such blotches were symptoms of AIDS, and an inmate who was known to have AIDS was at risk of being killed by other inmates simply out of an irrational fear of transmission. Juan had to work hard to try to hide his body from other inmates, which was quite a challenge in this setting.

In one session we were talking about the stress of hiding his symptoms from everyone else. Juan had also chosen not to tell his family about his illness, and he had reflected about this in great depth. He was aware that if he died, his family might be angry that he had not told them, but he was particularly concerned about two sisters whom he knew would agonize about their limited ability to help him if he did tell them. I (Steve) asked Juan if it felt lonely to struggle with all of this. His voice softened and he smiled at me and said, "Oh yes. Yes it is very lonely. But you see, loneliness has become my best friend. And in my loneliness I have come to know Jesus much better. He was lonely too and a sufferer who others stigmatized. He is my comfort in my loneliness."

Case Interpretation

One irony in this case is that while Juan described loneliness as his "best friend" and his meeting place with Jesus, he willingly shared his loneliness with me as his therapist. During the six months I worked with him before his transfer to another prison, I experienced him as capable of an unusually deep level of emotional intimacy and personal connection. This was particularly surprising for me in a prison, a "total institution," which tends to promote a culture of objectification and relational avoidance rather than intimacy. And Juan showed other signs of spiritual formation.[2] He developed an interest in social-justice issues, particularly poverty in urban areas. He read voraciously about urban politics, and his study informed his prayers. He also described times of feeling overcome by emotion when he saw some tragedy on the news, so that he needed to leave the TV room quickly because he was starting to cry. While this may have represented Juan's personal identification with victims, praying to "the God of the brokenhearted" in such situations offered him a sense of purpose even behind the walls of prison.

Juan was challenging himself toward spiritual formation in a relational context that was extremely stressful and not designed to promote positive change. In some periods of North American history, there have been prisons organized toward the goal of the spiritual and moral transformation of inmates. The name "penitentiary" was initially drawn from the concept of spiritual "penance" as part of a correctional philosophy of creating a relational context of transformation. Many Quakers were influential in advocating for prisons that could facilitate transformation, which they considered a spiritual issue of social justice. With some notable exceptions, however, most contemporary North American prisons are oriented toward a correctional philosophy of punishment or social control rather than transformation or rehabilitation.

But Juan had experienced an intensification and spiritual transformation in the "non-facilitating environment" of this prison.[3] He had allowed the intense existential negations of incarceration and HIV to move him toward transformative despair and changes in his identity and spiritu-

2. The concept of total institutions originated with sociologist Erving Goffman, *Asylums: Essays on the Social Situation of Mental Patients and Other Inmates* (Garden City, NY: Anchor, 1961).

3. D. W. Winnicott, *The Maturational Processes and the Facilitating Environment: Studies in the Theory of Emotional Development* (NY: International Universities Press, 1965).

ality. His long prison sentence had confronted his ability to continue to use his familiar coping strategies for securing his life. Incarceration with the label "drug dealer" had offered him a potential social identity of "not wise," "not just," and "not free."

The turning point in Juan's redemptive story, however, came with his HIV diagnosis. Philosophically, we might say that this anxious purgation further negated his sense of freedom and beauty. The unjust social stigma of HIV can convey a kind of personal ugliness that assaults a sense of self-dignity and beauty. Although the stigmatizing of HIV may be lessening, it still provides a contemporary parallel to leprosy in the ancient biblical context. In Juan's case, his health required that he experience a transformation in how he related to himself and to his body. Previously Juan had a lifelong history of not wisely caring for himself and his body. He had lived with a common male grandiosity that operated on an implicit assumption that he was physically invincible and did not need to concern himself with self-care. Once diagnosed with HIV, Juan awakened to the realization that if he did not experience a transformation in how he cared for himself and his body, he would likely die. And ironically, he also realized that in his prison context, if he did not take care of himself, no one would.

Juan began to intentionally embrace the practical wisdom of developing good habits of exercise, rest, nutrition, and spiritual discipline. He understood that his health status could be affected by his choices in stress management, and he demonstrated growing agency by purging unhealthy influences from his life. He mentioned that his "body is God's temple," a biblical reference that showed he was sacralizing his health practices. Yet Juan's was not a simplistic, positive-minded religion that avoided facing difficult realities. His growing reflective wisdom was evident in his authenticity about his suffering, his ability to tolerate ambiguity about his health and future, and his appreciation for spiritual paradoxes.

Juan cultivated his spiritual formation in prison by attending Christian worship services and Bible studies, often stretching himself to relationally engage the chaplains and religious volunteers out of respect and appreciation. My assessment would be that for most of Juan's life, he seemed to show an avoidant attachment style of keeping emotional distance from others and refusing help. It was not easy for him to trust others, and it felt easier to expect little in relationships as a way of avoiding disappointment. His avoidant attachment style seemed to correspond to his relational spirituality for most of his life. He had some degree of respect or fear of God, but he related to God dismissively through distancing and low expectation. If he did not trust God with the practical realities of his life, he could not be disappointed.

Juan's avoidant attachment style is one dimension that was undergoing spiritual transformation. He responded to the existential predicaments of his incarceration and HIV diagnosis through the relational spirituality of risking trust in God. His grandmother provided a spiritual-attachment figure that Juan drew upon psychologically in his transformation. His memories and internal representations of his grandmother's spirituality and her words of security that "God loves all his children" became a source of hope to enable him to explore a new way of relating to God. Initially it felt awkward to Juan to pray and petition God for help. In a parallel fashion, he resisted asking for help from anyone—chaplains, medical professionals, fellow inmates, or psychology staff. He began to realize that allowing God and others into his life did not have to be a shaming experience of weakness. Instead of feeling weak and helpless, Juan began to integrate an internal sense of vulnerability and strength in relating to both God and others. He accepted responsibility for his life and health but also began to open up to the challenges of relational intimacy with God and others. His prayer grew increasingly meditative as he learned the practice of breathing deeply, calming himself, and resting in God's presence.

Juan's case also illustrates interesting spiritual dynamics related to the balancing of seeking and dwelling, solitude and community. On the surface, he looks like a lonely seeker who was spiritually transformed mainly outside the dwelling space of an officially sanctioned religious community. And from a clinical perspective, his pull toward lonely solitude could be questioned as potentially too ego-syntonic for his own good. But Juan was also beginning to stretch himself relationally toward greater capacities for intimacy and social concern. Even if some of his emotional reactions to the suffering of others were motivated by identification, he was starting to relate to a wider set of spiritual concerns.

Interdisciplinary Explorations

The way in which spirituality is related to the whole of one's life, all of the relations within which the dynamic movement of the human spirit is embedded, is clearly illustrated in Juan's longing for transformation. As we observed in chapter 2, Kierkegaard defined the human spirit as a relation that relates itself to itself as it relates itself to an other. This relating of the relation is a coming-to-be in the dialectic of remembering the past and anticipating the future of one's embodied and social (spatial) relations. Juan's relating to his remembered past is often painful, and its effects on his body impact the way he tends to himself in the present. As he orients himself toward a healed and whole future, his motivation toward spiritual transformation includes an affirmation of his body as "God's temple." Tending to his embodiment and his illness is an essential part of his relational spirituality. Juan's current context—the space and time of prison life—inescapably mediates his longing for redemption. He is literally unable to escape from this context, but his story illustrates how divine grace may break into the most difficult of relations and begin to transform them.

Prayer was a particularly important aspect of Juan's ongoing spiritual life in prison. He indicated that he found strength by repeating a "Jesus prayer" throughout the day. Such prayers typically take the form of a short petition, such as, "Lord Jesus Christ, have mercy on me." As we observed in chapter 3, prayer both forms and is formed by the believer's experience of knowing and being known by God. Juan's desire to become wise was made explicit during therapy, and his growing interest in studying suggests that a longing for truth is driving his spirituality. Calling out for help in prayer on a constant basis shapes Juan's sense of identity, helping him to acknowledge his dependence on divine wisdom.

Throughout his life, he had been identified in negative ways—as a gang member, then a convict. His grandmother's insistence that "God loves all his children" became for Juan a catalyst for learning to receive a new, transformed identity as he accepted God's gracious identification of him as "child." If he continues to experience the invitation of the Spirit to intimacy with God and neighbor, Juan may find additional strength in more contemplative forms of prayer. As his life becomes a transforming prayer, his intimacy with the One who knows him so deeply will manifest itself in the way he identifies with others.

Juan also exhibited a longing for justice and freedom. His incarceration perhaps made each of these desires poignant in a way that many of us will never understand. His new sense of identity in relation to God had led him to reflect on his own agency. Acknowledging that he had behaved in unjust ways, his intentionality was broadened to a concern not simply for himself but for the structures of society that crush the agency of the poor, especially in urban areas. We can imagine that the idea of freedom had a special meaning to Juan, but it seems that even within the walls of prison, he was coming to find a new sense of being-free in relation to the divine presence. His avoidant attachment style had made it difficult for him to really "be there" with and for others. Intimacy was a problem well before imprisonment, which brings its own worries about getting too close to the other. Juan was beginning to experience a different kind of liberation, for where the Spirit of the Lord is, there is true freedom (2 Cor. 3:17).

Juan had suffered and was continuing to suffer. How is this related to his spirituality? Was he sharing in the suffering of Jesus Christ? Here we are on dangerous ground, for the church has too easily condoned social injustice or attempted to quiet victims by telling the oppressed not to complain when they suffer. In Juan's case, part of his suffering was indeed a direct result of his behavior. Suffering with Christ does not mean, however, passively accepting disease or allowing urban poverty to continue. Christian believers "suffer"—respond to experiences beyond their control—by entrusting "themselves to a faithful Creator, while continuing to do good" (1 Pet. 4:19). Suffering is redemptive only when it shares in Jesus' way of laying down his life for others in the service of manifesting divine love. Christ experienced the world on the basis of his reception of the love of the Father, which opened him up to radical solidarity with those whose lives were crushed. Christian suffering *consoles* (2 Cor. 1:4) the other by bearing the other's burdens and inviting the other into peaceful fellowship.

Those whose spirits have been broken may not have the strength to console others, but as they enter into a *koinōnia* of consolation (2 Cor. 1:7), they are called toward a redeemed agency that will empower them to console others. This process of transformation takes time and space, and it ultimately depends on sharing in the "glory" of Jesus Christ. Juan's anxiety about his agency will be healed as he finds his own metaphysical weight upheld in the presence of God, placing his hope for redeemed being in the arrival of the reign of divine peace, not on his own power to hold on to life. As he learns to receive his own being "in the Spirit," in the presence (face) of the shining divine countenance, his way of presenting himself to others will be conformed to the image of Christ. Most of the faces that confront Juan are hostile, and it will be difficult in his environment to mediate the presence of the God of hope. But even in this place (and time) of intense discomfort, he may continue to experience transformation as he struggles with the results of his past intentionality and moves forward toward a future of intimacy with God and neighbor.

Juan's spirituality may also be understood in relation to the modeling of Christian faith, love, and hope. The intensification of the faithful bindings of trustworthy community will be difficult in prison, but the goal would be for him to find his own identity upheld by the faithful identification of others, especially his therapist and fellow spiritual travelers in his Bible study. As we have seen, human love has to do with using our power to secure the objects of our desire. Juan has experienced the frustration and limits of this power, and the inability of drugs and other behaviors or commodities to bring the good life he desires. The intensity of his failure opens him up to the possibility of calling out for intimacy with the One who is the absolute Good, in a way that the rich young rulers of the world might miss. The intensification of faith and love is inseparable from the intensification of hope. The transformation of Juan's longing to belong-to, and be longed-for, in harmonious fellowship—for the joy of peaceful mutual presence—will take shape precisely as his identity and agency are redeemed in community.

At this point, we are tempted to say to the Juans in our world, "Goodbye and good luck in your spiritual journey." But the whole point of our relational modeling of spirituality is that we are in this together. It is important to ask not simply, "What should Juan do to become more spiritually mature," but also, "What should we, the Christian community, do to provide the space and time within which Juan can experience the intensification of the relation to the Spirit for which he longs?" and, "How can we learn from people like Juan, who have experienced spiritual transformation even in the darkest of contexts?" Our spirituality is diminished as we break off our relations to the lives of those who need us to bind ourselves to them in trustworthy communion.

Transforming spirituality can occur for both Juan and us as we visit those who are in prison (Matt. 25:31–46), as well as others in excluded contexts, facing them in ways that manifest the wisdom of God. Juan's ministry and hospitality, as well as ours, can only be transforming as we allow the Spirit to conform us to Jesus' way of acting and being, taking the form of a servant and making room among us for those who have been excluded. Juan's spirit was crushed and abandoned in community, as he was forced to move to a new country and tried to survive by joining a gang. It is only through finding his sense of belonging in a redemptive community that his spirit will experience deeply salutary transformation. This will not be fostered by idealistic or patronizing forms of outreach, but requires relational formation toward spiritual maturity. Reflecting on the dynamics of transforming spirituality should lead us to ask how *we* can become wise, just, and free as we welcome others into life in the Spirit.

Renae and Sid: Transforming Spirituality in Marriage

Renae (thirty-five) and Sid (thirty-seven) were a Euro-American couple who had been married for ten years when they pursued couples therapy. They had two boys, ages five and seven. Renae was an actor and drama instructor and had been working part-time with a small theater company. Sid was an associate pastor of administration with a growing evangelical church that he helped plant five years earlier. A year before starting couples therapy, Renae had an affair with a male coworker at the theater company. She eventually felt very ashamed, started individual therapy, and told Sid she had been attracted to the coworker and had gone out for coffee with him a couple of times. Sid was initially quite angry but then dropped it and didn't ask more questions, since Renae was remorseful. They told no one. Now, a year later, Renae had two deep concerns. First, she was wracked by guilt for not telling Sid the full truth about the affair. Second, she was realizing more clearly that she was very dissatisfied with her marriage and wanted change.

When Renae told Sid that she and the coworker kissed on several occasions, he became enraged and insisted she quit her job in order not to have contact with the coworker. She reluctantly complied, but the loss of her job and creative outlet propelled her toward a shame-laden depressive episode. And Sid was so hurt and angry that he vented his disgust toward Renae most evenings after trying to mask his struggles at the church all day. He said that he would "divorce her in a heartbeat" if it were not for the kids and his ministry career.

During the initial session of couples therapy, Sid sat tensely with his arms and legs crossed, leaning away from Renae on the couch. Renae made little eye contact and sat leaning forward with her elbows on her legs, as if to apply pressure to a nervous stomach. Sid explained that he was angry at Renae since he would "never do anything like that," but wanted to "trust her unconditionally again" and "to get back in synch . . . knowing she is looking out for my interests and me for hers."

Renae said, "I can't stand that I ruined Sid's life. I can't stand him being angry with me. I need to know what I can do about this." She wanted him to forgive her, and she said that she would not be able to forgive herself until this happened. But she was also frustrated that Sid checked her cell phone and e-mail almost daily and gave her frequent "inquisitions" about any men she had contact with.

Other issues began to come to the surface. Sid knew that Renae had been pre-occupied for years, probably their whole marriage, with memories of the fellow actor she dated before meeting Sid. She described it as an intense relationship, as dramatic as the plays they were in together. She eventually found out that he was cheating on her, which was deeply wounding and disorienting. At that point she started attending a Bible study with some friends and made a commitment to Christ.

Renae and Sid met through mutual Christian friends. To Renae, Sid seemed warm, caring, and extremely wise about the Christian faith. She felt she could count on him. She tried to forget about her earlier romance and appreciate Sid's dependability, but in recent years she found herself wondering how her old boyfriend was doing and whether he ever thought of her. She asked God to take away her thoughts of him, but they continued to linger.

Sid was initially attracted to Renae's passion for her newfound faith and her lively sense of humor. She was relatively "unchurched," and Sid found her to be "a breath of fresh air." They married relatively quickly, struggled financially while Sid went to seminary, and then turned their attention to raising children and starting the church.

Sid had his own preoccupation—ministry. Initially he found it a great rush right after seminary, but the multiple demands and interpersonal challenges had started to wear on him. He found it hard to focus at home, especially if he and Renae had conflict. He had been mentored by the senior pastor, who was an inspiring preacher and teacher. Sid had been drawn to this man's strong emphasis on discipleship and his vision of Christian community. At the same time, he was frustrated that his mentor was beginning to seem distant and relationally inaccessible. Sid had approached him about his marital problems, and the pastor seemed uncomfortable and asked Sid if he and Renae were having devotions together regularly.

Case Interpretation

Renae and Sid were each facing a major dilemma in their marital life together. They could each try to maintain the equilibrium of the status quo in their relationship and regain a sense of stability. Or they could each accept the challenge of more fully entering the intensification and growth cycle of what David Schnarch calls the crucible of marital trans-formation.[4] They both longed for a deeper level of intimacy but were also scared of the process it would take to pursue authentic intimacy. It was a dilemma they each needed to face, and each needed to make their own decision one way or the other. The only other option was divorce, and neither wanted to go down that path.

Sid felt stuck, victimized by his conflicting love for Renae and hate for the pain he felt she had caused him. He wanted to be able to trust her again and have a better marriage, and he certainly did not want the embarrassment and spiritual consequences he anticipated if they divorced. Renae also experienced a painful conflict between her desire to have a better relationship with Sid and her unwillingness to continue to accept their previous ways of relating. These are the types of integrity dilemmas that can catalyze transformation.[5]

Both were initially stuck because they believed it was generally up to the partner to change their marriage. For example, Sid wanted to trust Renae again, but he experienced this as dependent solely on her actions.

---

4. D. M. Schnarch, *Constructing the Sexual Crucible: An Integration of Sexual and Marital Therapy* (New York: W. W. Norton, 1991); *Passionate Marriage; Resurrecting Sex: Resolving Sexual Problems and Rejuvenating Your Relationship* (New York: HarperCollins, 2002).
5. Schnarch, *Passionate Marriage*.

Renae wanted to be closer with Sid again, but she felt this could only happen when he stopped being angry with her. This kind of dependence on one's partner to initiate positive change ("I need you to make my marriage better") usually feels frustrating because it involves giving one's power and agency over to another person. The frustration is symptomatic of the reality that most adults find it hard to respect themselves when they are that dependent on another adult. As Schnarch's crucible approach suggests, the alternative—constructively pursuing what I can change about myself in marriage without any guarantee my partner will do likewise—is anxiety-provoking and usually involves painful self-confrontation. The cliché "stuck between a rock and a hard place" aptly fits this dilemma. Spiritual transformation and differentiation can happen when people are willing to sit in the fire (intensification) of this type of dilemma instead of passing the anxiety of the dilemma to others to solve for them.

In cases following affairs, I (Steve) generally first try to communicate to partners in Sid's position that I understand they have their reasons for their mistrust of their partner. It is hard for people in Sid's position to trust and form an attachment with people who cannot empathize with their mistrust. It is usually helpful if they can begin to be aware that their mistrust is an understandable defense against further vulnerability and pain. But I eventually ask, as I did with Sid, "What do you think you need to do to become the kind of husband she won't want to cheat on?" After a pause, I add, "Knowing there is no guarantee you can control what she does."[6] This can sound like blaming the victim, but in fact this question invited Sid to move out of a chronic victim stance toward greater agency and differentiation. His choices were fairly simple. He could continue the control strategy of "patrolling" her communications or take the more proactive risk of trying to attract her with his best self.

Initially Sid indicated he did not know what it would take to become this kind of husband. But to his credit, he started to take the question seriously and acknowledged that he had been insecure for years, feeling he "didn't have what it takes to sustain her love." This had led him to focus more on ministry at church, hoping to draw significance there to compensate for the lack of validation he felt with Renae. Eventually Sid admitted that his approach to most relationships involved attempting to be a highly conscientious "nice guy" who helped people feel safe. This was, in part, how he initially attracted Renae after she was burned by a "bad guy." Sid related to God in the same way, attempting to please God

6. I am grateful to Dr. James W. Maddock for suggesting this specific type of intervention, as well as the overall clinical approach illustrated in this case. See J. W. Maddock and N. R. Larson, *Incestuous Families: An Ecological Approach to Understanding and Treatment* (New York: W. W. Norton, 1995).

and have a positive attitude. But this meant that Sid kept major parts of himself out of his relationships with others and with God. He hid the passionate, spontaneous, and erotic parts of himself, and this resulted in those closest to Sid sometimes feeling bored in the safe dependability he provided.

Renae's initial challenges in therapy concerned the related goals of (a) understanding why she had the affair and (b) determining who would be responsible for her sense of selfhood and "forgiven-ness." These were related issues because she would not feel the emotional and spiritual freedom necessary to reflect wisely on her attraction to other men if she continued to be focused on shame-prone penance with Sid. She rather quickly came to the conclusion that God had forgiven her and that she would need to allow Sid to sort out his own forgiveness without beating herself up every time his anger and hurt resurfaced. She felt that she had done her best to sincerely apologize for the ways she had hurt him but that it was up to him to decide if his life was "ruined." Accepting the proposition that she could literally ruin or save his life was rather messianic and spiritually grandiose anyway. It often feels scary to accept this much power over another adult's well-being, and for both psychological and theological reasons we should avoid taking on such a role.

I asked Renae (with Sid present) why she had given up her job at the theater company. She said she did so because Sid had insisted. She did not think it was actually a problem for her to work there. I then asked if her decision was more out of penance or out of blackmail. Sid objected to the term "blackmail," but I assured him I was not suggesting he was necessarily trying to blackmail her. I was just trying to understand how Renae experienced her decision, given that she did not feel it was necessary. When Renae finally answered, she said, "Some of both but mostly blackmail." She began to see that she had "sold out" on her self, to use another one of Schnarch's terms, in order to lower the intense anxiety and conflict they were experiencing after she told Sid about the affair. Rather than go through the intense darkness of the crucible, she and Sid had tried to reduce it as quickly as possible.

The problems with this were threefold. First, Renae did not experience wise agency or a sense of her own integrity in making her decision to give up her job but did it as a victim of Sid's wrath. Sid's intense anxiety caused her to fold in on herself, which was a pattern throughout their relationship. She was managing Sid's anxiety more than responding to her own spiritual discernment. Eventually she missed her work and felt simply punished and deprived, a painfully familiar feeling in her life story. Second, the automatic decision to give up her job worked from the assumption that Sid could not compete with other men Renae might find attractive. By giving in, Renae reinforced Sid's insecurity. Third, the decision left unaddressed Renae's reasons for being attracted to other men. By focusing exclusively on trying to shut out or control the influences of other men, Sid and Renae were failing to cultivate their own capacities for intimacy.

Renae eventually took responsibility for understanding her own attraction to other men, including her old boyfriend and the man from the theater. At first, exploring this terrain often seems spiritually unwise to clients. Renae and Sid both wanted to simply forget about these other guys. The problem with this strategy is that it assumes that the attraction is "out there" somewhere in the environment rather than inside the person and that it will go away with repression. I suggest to clients that they at least try not taking the attraction so "literally" in that it has to be mostly about that specific person. Instead I invited Renae to think about what it was that she was attracted to in relating to these other guys and how this differed from what she experienced with Sid. Once she got over her initial hesitations, she said that in both cases the guys were passionate, spontaneous, a little dangerous, and deeply interested in the arts. She felt validated by both men, at least until her old boyfriend cheated on her. "I felt alive with them," she explained. In a certain sense, Renae had been seeking types of vitality and intimacy she had not found a way to integrate within the commitments of her relational dwelling.

Renae then began to struggle with the question of whether she could bring some of this passionate, alive danger into her marriage in a healthy way. This was an intensifying question for both Renae and Sid. Renae laughed at first and said, "No way. Sid would never go for that." Sid's face reddened with what looked like defensive anger as he blurted, "How do you know?" Then Renae explained that marriage is not supposed to be like that. "Do you mean passionate and alive?" I asked. We all three laughed, although the tension remained thick in the room. "Well, maybe it's that a Christian marriage isn't supposed to be like that," Renae clarified with a smile.

Renae eventually began to confront the internal relational split of her passionate "bad self" and her spiritual "good self." She could relate to her husband and her faith only out of part of herself, a part that was dependent, hardworking, and compliant. This inevitably led to boredom and detachment. She experienced her passionate, sexual self as "bad" and dangerous, and so she unconsciously kept this part in hiding as long as she could. The fact that she still thought about her old boyfriend was evidence that this part of herself was still alive. Her challenge became one of bringing her whole self into her marriage, which required a spiritual transformation in how she related to both God and her husband. She worked at being less dependent on male validation, which meant less "performing" for audience approval. This provided the spiritual and emotional freedom to pursue intimacy with less shame and hiding. Over time she began to experience a more integrated identity with an enhanced ability to relate to herself beyond her social roles as a wife and mother.

Sid began to confront himself about his lack of passionate relating in his marriage, in his relationships with others, and in his relationship with God. This intensified his awareness of some painful family-of-origin dynamics. His father, a traveling salesman, had been absent a great deal and emotionally distant when he was at home. Sid had longed to connect with his father but this had never happened. By contrast, Sid felt too close to his mother. Since he was the oldest son, his mother had often referred to him as "the man of the house" when his dad was gone. Sid's shame and confusion about his relationship with his mother had taken the form of disgust and contempt at what he called her "manipulative ploys" with him even in adulthood. He felt safest with women when he was in an emotionally detached duty role or when they were in the one-down position of needing help. The pull of intimacy in marriage had repeatedly activated Sid's shame, and he had typically responded through control moves by limiting Renae's influence on him. Ministry had previously been a perfect fit for this control strategy because there was always ministry work to do, and it had been hard for Renae to believe she was entitled to connect with Sid when he was supposedly doing spiritual work.

Once Sid and Renae began to tolerate the intense anxiety and purgation of self-confrontation, they started to come into new, illuminating insights. They developed the ability to tolerate the anxiety of seeing difficult things about themselves and the other. They also experienced a deeper appreciation of spiritual grace as they realized God's love could penetrate the shame they felt about themselves. They began to laugh at the absurdity of trying to hide parts of themselves from God, a marital spirituality strategy epitomized in the Garden of Eden. And they also each took responsibility for trying to grow in their ability to be emotionally present and attached with the other and with God. Their relational spirituality became more embodied, and this translated into their valuing their own sexuality enough to grow in that area. Their marital union was spiritually transformed.

Interdisciplinary Explorations

Transformations that occur within marriage—or other long-term intense relationships—offer particularly good illustrations of the tensions involved in the struggle to be "united" with others and the ultimate Other.

The fear and fascination that characterizes the longing for intimacy is intensified in relationships that are intentionally maintained and oriented toward deeper "union." The apostle Paul makes his claim that "anyone united to the Lord becomes one spirit with him" (1 Cor. 6:17) in the context of a broader discussion of the importance of embodied fidelity; he metaphorically links spiritual union to the significance of sexual union in which a man and woman "become one flesh" (Gen. 2:24). The metaphor obviously (and appropriately) breaks down—we must acknowledge the infinite qualitative difference between the union of two finite creaturely persons and the union of finite persons with the truly infinite Spirit. However, because Christian communities affirm that the gracious gift of union with the trinitarian God is mediated through our relations with one another, the healing and nourishment of particular human unions takes on a redemptive significance.

It is often in intense long-term relationships like marriage that the differences in the way we experience the longing for transformation come to the fore. As LeRon observed in chapter 2, the narrative structure of every person's desire for God is unique, but we can make a general distinction among three modes of spiritual longing—based on our tendency to focus on the pursuit of truth, goodness, or beauty—as we seek transformation. In the current case study, Renae illustrates the inclination toward beauty. She is excited by the aesthetic and feels happiest engaged in the arts. Sid, on the other hand, seems to have a predilection for privileging the search for truth. This is partly due to the emphasis on propositional knowledge of God that has shaped his evangelical background. These desires are not mutually exclusive; on the contrary, they are intertwined along with the longing for goodness. Recognizing that the significant others in our lives tend to prefer one strand of this braided passion for God may help us understand and tolerate the knots in our relationships. Moreover, it may also help us learn to appreciate the value and importance of the other's way of seeking and to thematize our own need to find balance in all of our noetic, moral, and aesthetic desiring.

Over time Renae and Sid became more capable of handling the tension of the relational unity of a lively marriage. Their fear of and longing for the intimacy of knowing and being known was graciously transformed as they endured the crucible of intensification. This intensification of faith (mutual trust) was not isolated from the intensification of love and hope in their marriage. Each of them struggled with objects of desire that they believed would ultimately bring them the good life (sexual passion or respected ministry). They used the finite power of their agency to secure these goods, or to control their desires, but this only led to further anxiety. It was only as they thematized the way in which others were mediating their agency that they came to be able to tolerate their impotence long enough to explore the possibility of a transformation of their agency toward healthy differentiation. This process can also be described as an intensification of hope. Based on their shared remembered past, Renae and Sid were anxious about their future. Therapeutic intervention helped them recognize that they had been trying to use their own metaphysical weight to control their desires and each other. Only as they were opened up to acknowledge their interdependency—and ultimate dependence on God—were they able to find new hope for the well-being of their relationship.

Tim: Transforming Spirituality in Families

Tim (age thirteen) grunted and slumped past my greeting as he entered my office for the first time. He plopped into a chair followed by his mom, Cindy (age thirty-six), and his younger brothers, Shawn (age ten) and Micah (age eighteen months), who filled up the small couch. "Tim needs to talk to somebody," explained Cindy in an exasperated tone. Tim rolled his eyes without looking my way. Cindy continued, "He seems down, and he's mad at me all the time. He won't forgive me and I'm tired of it. I've got a therapist for Shawn and one for me, and Tim needs one, too." With Shawn and Micah now tearing into some toys on the floor, Cindy proceeded to tell the difficult story of her family's previous four years following her divorce from Ray (age forty), the father of Tim and Shawn.

Around the time of the divorce, Cindy started drinking and using cocaine with a new boyfriend who was selling drugs. She went through two months of inpatient drug treatment while the boys stayed with their grandparents. She quickly relapsed, but this time she was arrested for her association with her boyfriend. After seven months in jail, she tried to start over, but her difficulty finding a job as an ex-convict eventually led to another drug relapse and another round of inpatient treatment. The boys shuttled between living part-time with their grandparents and part-time with their father. When Cindy was released from her second round of treatment, she and the boys spent two months at a transitional group home, which may have been the worst situation of all. Around that time, a brief relationship led to Cindy's pregnancy, but Micah's father chose to have no part in their lives.

At present, Cindy was working at her recovery, rebuilding her Christian faith, and holding down a decent office job while trying to be a single parent of three boys. Tim and Shawn were living with their father during the week and staying with Cindy on weekends, although Tim often said he would prefer to stay with his dad all week. Ray did not take the boys to church and considered himself a religious "skeptic." Cindy wanted to take the boys to her evangelical, charismatic church and youth program, which Shawn enjoyed. Shawn especially liked the sports activities and contemporary music at the youth group. In contrast, Tim complained about the church. "He says the youth group is boring and the music is stupid. He even says he thinks God is a joke. And yesterday he said he's not sure he believes in God at all!" Cindy said as she choked back tears of panic.

At this point I (Steve) invited Cindy to take Shawn and Micah to the waiting room so that I could talk with Tim, who sat silently throughout Cindy's story. As the door shut behind his mom and brothers, he turned to me and said, "I thought I read somewhere that psychology is really just voodoo medicine." This highly intelligent young man had an impressive range of talents and interests, including painting, songwriting, professional wrestling, documentary film, and piano. He liked to talk about political figures and social issues. Whereas his brother Shawn tended to get into trouble at school, Tim was a model of responsibility. He was getting good grades, was popular with his teachers, and was extremely conscientious. From a family systems framework, Tim was a parentified child who carried more than his share of family responsibility. It was not uncommon for him to be asked to watch his younger brothers without adult supervision. He was the "nonproblem" child who counterbalanced Shawn's acting out. If he had not been voicing religious dissent, Cindy seemingly would have had no basis for a complaint about Tim. Perhaps his spiritual "symptoms" were the only way he would end up in a therapist's office.

Despite his charge of "voodoo medicine," Tim agreed to give individual therapy a try. Initially his trust of another authority figure was understandably low. He usually started sessions looking sullen and bored and offered almost nothing in response to questions about himself or his family experience. He was most engaged when we talked about politics, music, or art. As I often do, I invited him to bring some of his sketches, paintings, and music to sessions. His art and his music were dark and peppered with angry questions and protest, a stark contrast to his over-controlled, unaffected presentation. It seemed to me he was searching for meaning in life through artistic darkness, which was probably quite a stretch for youth leaders at his more positive-minded church.

Gradually Tim began to share some of his practical struggles in life. What should he do when his parents argued with each other through him? How should he deal with his boredom after school in a new neighborhood where he had no friends? What could he do when his dad drank too much and overslept for work? And how could he deal with the difficult memories of his mom's absence and the chaotic group home experience?

Eventually Tim shared more probing theological and moral questions. For example, during one session Tim posed this question: "Why did God even create Adam and Eve if he knew they would just sin anyway?" Tim had thought harder about the problem of evil than most adults I have met. The sacred needed to be questioned, in Tim's mind, as God's motives were unclear to him. Tim's life had stripped back protective illusions about the benevolent predictability of authority figures. It seemed that, for Tim, any relational pathway toward the recovery of the sacred would need to include authentically facing the darkness that had ravaged his life.

Tim was also quite interested in talking about whether he would ever try drugs in the future. This is not uncommon when children see their parents use drugs. For Tim, however, it was not an immediate issue of peer pressure but rather a focal issue for beginning to think about the meaning of life. He was quite intrigued with exploring possible reasons for not using drugs and with discovering ways to find an alternative source of pleasure and meaning, but he clearly resisted authority figures telling him he could not experiment with drugs. It seemed almost as if he could not buy a future script that did not include trying drugs, but it also seemed that he wanted to consider a story line that would allow him to avoid the addictive snares that had plagued his parents.

A final note from this case helps summarize my interpretation of Tim's spiritual transformation. After the first couple of months of therapy, Tim indicated he "did not mind coming" because therapy was "a decent source of intellectual stimulation." He especially seemed to like it when I offered him a question to reflect upon before the next session. On one occasion I used a question I have raised with several artistic thinkers like Tim—"What is the difference between a prophet and a cynic?" Tim spent hours online researching the question and solicited input from several adults. His conclusion was that both prophets and cynics see problems in the world, but only prophets find a hopeful vision for a better world.

Case Interpretation

Tim and his family were struggling to cope with a formidable set of stressors and developmental challenges. Tim was a very bright, caring, and conscientious adolescent whose depressive symptoms and spiritual resistance reflected his difficulty continuing in the role of family caretaker or "nonproblem child." His developmental transition into adolescence served to intensify his symptoms and spiritual resistance and shaped the context of his relational spirituality.

Tim's parents both cared for him and made commitments to try to be helpful to him. Yet they were each struggling with their own developmental challenges, and they each had a different type of anxiety about allowing Tim to differentiate into his own person. These relational dynamics made intervention from therapists outside their family system a valuable resource for catalyzing change.

Cindy struggled with intense anxiety about Tim's spiritual resistance and questioning of the Christian tradition, which she personalized as a shaming result of her addictive problems. She wanted Tim to forgive her and, ironically, found it hard to forgive him for not forgiving her. She also found it difficult to deal with the intensity of dialogue with Tim about his spiritual and theological questions without reacting and trying to shut him down with strong control moves. On the one hand, this gave Tim too much power over her on many occasions. That is, his questioning knocked her off balance. At the same time, Cindy's difficulty managing her own anxiety about Tim prevented the more securely attached and empowering move of taking his questions seriously and exploring together the implications of these questions. Cindy tended to be intense with Tim in unhelpful ways that involved handing her anxiety back to him.

In contrast to Cindy, Ray was less intensely engaged in conflict with Tim. His parenting philosophy seemed to be one of giving Tim large amounts of responsibility and freedom and then minimizing problems when they came up. Whereas Cindy found it anxiety-provoking to step back from issues with Tim, Ray found it anxiety-provoking to move into facing intense issues with Tim. He openly suggested that therapy was a waste of time and that it was better to simply forget their past problems and move on. This style of parenting offered Tim a certain amount of breathing room, but it failed to provide the kinds of emotional attunement, relational presence, and wise guidance that Tim needed. Ray seemed to implicitly communicate that he would not join Tim in the intensity of his questioning and suffering. This may have been one reason that Tim was so focused on male political celebrities, who can represent archetypal "King" figures that symbolize benevolent, authoritative guidance.[7]

Fortunately, several factors converged in promoting positive changes in Tim. First, Cindy developed greater resilience in handling Tim's emotional distancing, mistrust, and underlying anger. She started to accept the notion that forgiveness is a process and that it was unrealistic to expect (or

7. R. L. Moore, *The King Within: Accessing the King in the Male Psyche* (New York: W. Morrow, 1992).

demand) that Tim forgive her immediately. Through her own therapy and spiritual growth, she came to feel less "held hostage" by Tim's process, which allowed him the freedom to be a thirteen-year old rather than a God-like selfobject who determined whether his mother felt forgiven. Cindy was developing a healthier, more differentiated self that also allowed Tim to be different from her.[8] This was expressed in her lower reactivity to his spiritual resistance and questioning, and she became capable of talking openly and less defensively with him about these issues.

Cindy and Ray also made commendable changes in Tim's relational community. They quit arguing back and forth through Tim and also stopped overburdening him with too much supervision of his brothers. With less responsibility as a coparent and family therapist, Tim was freer to deal with his own developmental tasks.

Tim also experienced important developmental changes. He went out for and made the basketball team. His nomadlike travels the previous few years had worked against consistent involvement with a sports team and the structure and discipline that this can provide. He also found that he was good at basketball and liked "mixing it up" under the boards with the other guys. More important, basketball provided a means of building a sense of belongingness with his peers to complement his more solitary hobbies of art and music, which had tended to keep him in his bedroom. At one point his mom pulled him out of a pregame practice to attend a therapy session with me, but we quickly decided that basketball was probably as therapeutic at that point as our sessions. Missing a game because he was seeing his therapist would not have helped Tim's sense of belongingness.

Another positive development for Tim came a couple of months later when he walked into a session and announced, "I just found out something new. I guess I'm cute!" Girls were starting to take notice of him at school, which provided a powerful illumination of personal beauty. In the relational world of most thirteen-year-olds, few things generate hope like being recognized by peers as attractive. And to Tim's credit, he received this social gift as a new insight about himself instead of anxiously scrambling to try to manage the impressions of others.

Tim worked on numerous issues in therapy, including the traumatic impact of his family chaos. He eventually displayed a surprising ability to understand that his anger toward his mom was about the dilemma of whether to trust her again, almost a perfect parallel to his mistrust of a God who would allow so much chaos and suffering. Talking about his feelings regarding these dilemmas with someone who would not lecture him seemed to help.

8. On selfobjects, see H. Kohut, *The Restoration of the Self* (New York: International Universities Press, 1977).

Tim eventually experienced a spiritual transformation during the latter part of his eighteen months in therapy with me. This was rather surprising to me, given that we only had a couple of discussions about spirituality much earlier in therapy, and these were focused on his questioning and resistance to his mom's influence. He simply announced during one session that he was attending his mom's new church and the youth group and enjoying them a great deal. And he said, "I feel like I can believe in God again." The new church did not sound to me much different from the old one that Tim had described as boring and stupid. But Tim was different. His depressive symptoms and relational withdrawal had been transformed. This case highlights how sometimes positive psychological and relational changes seem to precipitate spiritual changes without much or even any explicit spiritual intervention in therapy. From the perspective of relational spirituality, this can happen because of the potential connections between internal models of relationships with self, others, and the sacred described in part 2.

Interdisciplinary Explorations

As with so many adolescents, who have not yet learned to repress or hide their desires, Tim's anxious longing for truth, goodness, and beauty kept spilling out in ways that made his parents (and others) nervous. He enjoyed intellectual stimulation and wondered whether it is true that God exists. He was conscientious about doing what is right, and he questioned the prevalence of evil in the world. He found pleasure in his music and art, but both of these aesthetic expressions also manifested a fascination with darkness.

The relations within which his life is embedded and the plotline that had forced his parentification all shaped his spirituality. The transformation of Tim's spirituality impacted the relations that structure his whole life, not merely his explicit questioning of God and his resistance to going to a particular church. We should not ignore his embodied and psychological and social context as we try to understand and facilitate Tim's transformation, but we should also think theologically about the ultimate desires that are guiding his search.

This case also provides an illustration of a person intensely struggling with intentionality. Others have not tended to him well, and he finds himself required to attend to others in ways that stretch his capacity. His openness in therapy suggests a longing for intimacy but also a deep fear. Toward the end of therapy, Tim indicated that he could believe in God again. How can we describe this intensification of faith? Notice that he did not simply receive new data, nor was he given more warrant for the assertion that God exists. His sense of being bound in faithfulness had begun to be healed, and theologically we may identify this as the grace of God. But this grace was mediated through new experiences of faithful relationships in therapy and his parent's learning to tend to him with fidelity. Tim is bright and wants to secure the truth. He enjoys studying and struggling with tough questions. Through a therapeutic process that allowed him to question, he developed a new way of responding to the tension in his understanding of God. The possibility of trusting God, even in adversity, became real for him.

Tim is also longing for the Good. This is evident in his fascination with the problem of evil, which emerged out of his own experience of injustice and lack of a good life. Ironically, because of his willingness to thematize the difficult questions of spirituality, he may have accelerated his journey through spiritual intensity. But at this stage of development, if he is encouraged to ask such questions and if they are validated non-anxiously, he may feel the relational connection and conceptual space to keep exploring. We can think of this in terms of his dialectical agency. He tried to use his own power to secure the good life for his siblings and even his parents, but he was feeling despair over the reality that he was not sufficiently powerful. He resisted depending on the power of another because others had failed him so often. Even the idea of trying drugs suggests that his agency, his decision about which objects of desire to pursue, was being mediated through his experience of his parents' agency. His transformation involved being exposed to agents who provided other possibilities, other potential story lines, for him to explore.

Expecting Tim simply to accept his suffering could be abusive at this stage in the development of his agency. The telos of transformation is for him to develop a dialectical agency that is mediated by the consoling presence of the Spirit of Christ, but Tim first needs to have redemptive interpersonal space and time to develop a healthy agency, which he can then learn to lay down for the service of others. As the Christian community serves him by caring for his spiritual needs, Tim may be drawn into a life of transforming ministry. He had been made to serve others, especially his brothers, but as he discovers healthy relational supports he might come to see this as in a small way transforming his world—as a meaningful part of his spirituality. The intensification of love has to do with power and desire for goods, as we have seen. Tim and his family feel powerless. The God he has had described to him does not seem to be a power that loves him. Still, eventually he can find his own agency transformed as he comes to experience loving and being loved in a way that calls him into a share in the divine life. This cannot be rushed; transforming spirituality takes space and time. His learning to love will also shape his learning to be faithful and trustworthy and his coming into an experience of hope that secures his being.

Tim's overall longing to belong in peaceful community and patterns of harmony also permeates his story. The uncertainty of his experience of space and time, the lack of a secure and hospitable place in which to grow up, has led Tim to thematize his metaphysical weightiness. His parents have depended on him to provide ontological space for his siblings, and although he has performed well, this parentification has worn him down and feelings of anxiety have emerged in the form of questions about the ultimate guarantor of order in the cosmos. Although the idea of glory is sure to seem foreign to him, the language of weight and presence might not. He knows what it means to feel both crushed and abandoned. We may describe to him and become for him the place where he is welcomed into a community that cares for him and calls him to become just and free.

Like all of us, Tim longs to belong-to and be longed-for in peaceful community. In order for his intentionality to be healed, he had to be tended to in a way that provided space and time for intimacy. His own spiritual transformation was mediated as his parents learned to let him have his appropriate role in the family and as he found groups in which he could belong (basketball, the youth group). He also found that he was being longed-for by members of the opposite gender. These therapeutic relations gave him the space and time to explore deeper questions of belonging. His response to the question about cynics and prophets is also telling, since prophets can be those who find hope and give hope to others.

Our interest is in figuring out not merely what steps he as an individual should take but how we as the body of Christ can welcome him into life in the Spirit of Christ, a life that really transforms. For those who are called to dwell with Tim and who hope to guide him in his spiritual seeking, it is important to remember that the divine Spirit is the ultimate origin, condition, and goal of his spiritual longing. Only as he comes into relation to God, who is love, will he find this longing fulfilled, but we may love him in concrete ways that mediate divine love. Living in the Spirit will mean that we—together with Tim and his family—come to be in relations that really do mediate the good life. This does not mean obtaining everything we want but rather learning to want in a way that shares in God's redemption of the world.

All of us are called to tend to one another in faith, love, and hope as we live "in" the Spirit, inviting one another to share in divine grace as we seek (and dwell in) wisdom, justice, and freedom in the delightful terror that is the crucible of spiritual transformation.

INDEX

F. LeRon Shults (Ph.D., Princeton University; Ph.D., Walden University) is professor of theology at Agder University in Kristiansand, Norway, and the author of several books, including *Reforming the Doctrine of God* and *Reforming Theological Anthropology*.

Steven J. Sandage (Ph.D., Virginia Commonwealth University) is a licensed psychologist, associate professor of marriage and family therapy at Bethel Theological Seminary, and coauthor of *To Forgive Is Human*. Shults and Sandage are the coauthors of *The Faces of Forgiveness*, winner of the Narramore Award from the Christian Association for Psychological Studies.